Women's lives

What are the patterns dominating women's lives today? What are the issues which confront women in their relationships, their work, and their families? From adolescence and adult partnerships, through motherhood, to growing old, *Women's Lives* explores themes which are central to women's experience, focusing on areas such as growing up, women on their own, sexuality, bringing up children, and family relationships.

Sue Llewelyn and Kate Osborne argue that a multi-faceted approach is needed to understand a woman's life, taking in not only her personal psychology but also the social context in which she lives. Tha authors are both clinical psychologists with an interest in psychotherapy, and they draw on their own direct experience of working with women in distress, as well as on feminist writing, novels, and autobiographies, to illustrate their arguments. Each chapter presents a detailed case history, highlighting an important aspect of women's lives, and demonstrates the increased understanding to be gained from a combined approach using social psychology, feminist ideas, and psycho-dynamic insights.

Designed for a wide readership, including psychologists, doctors, social workers, counsellors, and nurses, *Women's Lives* will also be of great value to people on women's studies courses and to those seeking a greater understanding of themselves or others.

The Authors

Sue Llewelyn and Kate Osborne have both worked with Britain's National Health Service for over ten years. They have also taught psychology, Sue Llewelyn at the University of Nottingham, Kate Osborne at the University of Wales, Cardiff. Sue Llewelyn is currently Principal Clinical Psychologist, East Dorset Health Authority, and Kate Osborne is a writer on women's psychology. Both are married and have young children.

Women's lives

Sue Llewelyn
and
Kate Osborne

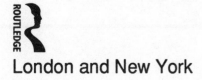

London and New York

First published 1990
by Routledge
11 New Fetter Lane, London EC4P 4EE

Simultaneously published in the USA and Canada
by Routledge
a division of Routledge, Chapman and Hall, Inc.
29 West 35th Street, New York, NY 10001

© 1990 Sue Llewelyn and Kate Osborne

Typeset by LaserScript Limited, Mitcham, Surrey
Printed and bound in Great Britain by
Mackays of Chatham PLC, Chatham, Kent

British Library Cataloguing in Publication Data
Llewelyn, Susan P.
  Women's lives.
  1. Women. Psychology
  I. Title II. Osborne, Kate
  155.6'33

Library of Congress Cataloging in Publication Data
Llewelyn, Susan P.
  Women's lives / Sue Llewelyn and Kate Osborne.
  p.   cm.
  Includes bibliographical references.
  1. Women--England--Psychology--Case studies. 2. Developmental
  psychology--England--Case studies. 3. Life cycle, Human--Psychological
  aspects--Case studies.   I. Osborne, Kate, 1948- . II. Title.
  HQ1206.L57   1990
  155.6'33--dc20

ISBN 0-415-01701-7
ISBN 0-415-01702-5 pbk

Contents

Acknowledgements

First of all, we would like to thank all of the women who have talked to us about their lives. Without them this book would not have been possible. We sincerely hope that we have adequately represented their experiences, and that through retelling their stories, other women may benefit.

Next, of the many individuals who have been particularly supportive and helpful in the writing of this book, we would like to thank the following people, for providing sensitive and encouraging supervision, perceptive criticism, or for commenting on earlier drafts of the book: Marjorie Calow, Angela Douglas, Luise Eichenbaum, Guy Fielding, Sue Gregory, Jeremy Hazell, Jim Kelmen, Mary Ann Kernan, Janet Sayers, Eddy Street, and Maryon Tysoe. We are also grateful for the support and encouragement of many of our other friends in Britain and in France who have helped in numerous ways. The remaining faults are our own.

In addition, we would like to thank Mary Fielding and Antonia Whitaker for their help in typing parts of the manuscript, and Lyn Courtney for assisting with library searches.

Finally, we would like to give our thanks to Noel and Guy for their love and encouragement, and to our children, Klervi, Ronan, Morgan, and Josephine, for helping us to know at a more personal level what mothering means.

Chapter one

Women's dilemmas
Psychodynamic, social, and feminist perspectives

Ann's story

Ann, a woman in her mid-thirties, told us about herself after she had spent a considerable amount of time in psychotherapy. We wanted her to talk to us about why she had decided it was necessary for her to enter therapy, and what she felt she had gained from the experience. We felt that her story would serve as an excellent introduction to our discussion of the issues which confront many women today, in their relationships, their work, and their families. The following account is a summary description of her experiences, as she told them to us.

'I seemed to reach a crisis point in my late twenties', Ann recalled:

I had a fascinating job in social work, employed by a charity which cared for handicapped children. This mostly involved visiting families who were interested in adopting a handicapped child, which often meant working long hours since the majority of visits took place in the evenings. Lots of people seemed to be dependent on me and thought I was strong and reliable, but I was aware of intense feelings of depression and a lack of confidence which lay behind this facade. As a single woman with a steady job, I was relatively well-off financially and had my life apparently well organised, but underneath I often felt in utter chaos. I spent my working life helping couples to consider the strengths and limitations of their relationships, yet felt a complete failure at making a relationship for myself which would last.

Ann then explained that since early adulthood, she had been having relationships with men who were ultimately unable to commit themselves to her. This had led her to feel inadequate in her work, and undermined her confidence both in her own abilities and in her interactions with others. She also longed to have children, but wanted to do this with another person, rather than on her own.

Ann described how her first real experience of an intimate relationship occurred at college, when she had fallen in love with a fellow student named Mike. He had apparently returned her feelings, but once they started living together, he seemed to become fearful of any further intense emotional involvement with her. Whenever she tried to get emotionally close to him he would suddenly 'disappear', either by burying himself in his books in the library or going home to visit his mother. Although Mike continually needed support and encouragement in his work, he was critical of Ann's achievements and disparaging about her intended career. Painfully, Ann had finally decided to break off the relationship with Mike, and after the initial loneliness found that it was a relief not to be constantly criticised and undermined by him. She also discovered new strengths in herself, which other people soon appreciated. For a couple of years she threw herself into her new job, although she also felt somewhat dissatisfied that she didn't meet any men who really interested her. Nevertheless, she was aware that, for the moment, there were plenty of other aspects of her life to resolve, especially coping with the demands of her work.

'Then one day', Ann said, 'I met Bill at a conference, and knew from the moment I saw him that he was going to be very important in my life. What I didn't know at first was that Bill was married with two children whom he adored.' When she discovered this, Ann was determined not to see Bill again, but he continued to contact her, and eventually her desire for him outweighed her guilty conscience, and they began to meet in secret:

> At first I was intensely happy, as he seemed to be all that I had ever wanted in a man. But slowly the strains and limitations of such a relationship began to tell on me. I always wanted more time with him than he could spare, but hardly dared to ask him for more, because I was only too aware of the needs of his family. Also I was fearful that I would lose him altogether if I pressed him to spend much more time with me. I gradually learnt to cope with lonely weekends and long school holidays when Bill would be away with his family, and the sadness of never being able to spend the night with him and to wake up in his arms. But I was also aware that my work was suffering, as I was becoming increasingly depressed. I found it hard to go to sleep at night and woke regularly in the early hours of the morning. I had difficulties in concentrating and was often behind in my report writing. Slowly I realised I would have to end the relationship since Bill could never provide me with the companionship and commitment that I desperately wanted.

But after deciding to leave Bill, to her despair Ann found that her subsequent relationships with men showed remarkable similarities. The men she was attracted to were either married with families of their own, or divorced but not ready to form another stable relationship. Ann gradually realised that a pattern was developing whereby she seemed to be repeatedly the third person in relationships, never having an equal share in her partners' lives, and always holding back because of her guilt. Feeling that her own personal history was somehow contributing to this unsatisfactory pattern, it was at this point that she decided to enter psychotherapy.

Ann explained that as the therapy progressed, she was able to think more clearly about her early experience of relationships in her own family. In describing her childhood, Ann allowed herself to admit the importance of having been thrown into a 'third-person' situation with her own parents. During her childhood, her mother had contracted a serious and incurable disease, and when Ann was a young teenager, had moved into a hospital on a fairly permanent basis. Ann had then tried to replace her mother in the family by being a partner for her father in the running of the house, and a 'mother' for her younger sister, who then became very dependent upon her. Ann said she felt a mixture of love, anger, and guilt towards her father:

> I felt responsible for him, yet angry that I had to grow up so quickly without experiencing all the normal adolescent fun. I also felt that I had to try to keep a stiff upper lip and not show him how sad I was, because if I cracked up he would too.

Ann claimed that she was almost completely unable to express or escape from her emotional confusion at this time. But during the course of her psychotherapy sessions, Ann found support and encouragement to express the grief that she had not previously been able to show. She could then examine her current relationships, and the distress she caused to herself and to the men she chose to love. In doing so, she began to suspect that she was in some senses repeating an earlier established pattern. With this knowledge, Ann said that she began to notice other aspects of the nature of her relationships:

> The men I fell in love with were always older than me, usually married men who had children, despite my making several efforts to have relationships with younger, unattached men. I always found these younger men to be unsatisfactory, since I was irritated by the apparent naïvity of men of my own age, and found them shallow and uninteresting.

As Ann explained, the men she loved, by contrast, were always fathers themselves, and she loved them most when they were being fatherly to their children, even if this meant that in doing so, they were withholding love from her:

> I wasn't sure at the time what they saw in me, but looking back I suppose it was that I seemed to be strong and in a way maternal, which allowed them to relinquish some of their responsibilities and depend upon me.

Ann was also aware that the passage of time had also produced a social factor, in that increasingly often, the men she met were older and already married with children, while the unmarried men became younger in comparison. Her guilt was intensified by her developing commitment to feminism, since she now felt increasingly that her relationships betrayed other women, the wives of the men she loved.

'On top of all of this', Ann said:

I was becoming increasingly fed up with my job. I felt that I was often making second-best arrangements for children whose emotional and social problems were so complex. I also came to see that it was no accident that I had chosen to become a social worker, as this job allowed me to be responsible for others as I had been all my life. It also gave me contact with children, which I loved, and to a certain extent replaced the lack of children of my own. But I wanted a family life for me, too.

With her therapist's support, Ann decided that she would give up her job for a while and take a course in art history. This was an interest that she had always had, but had never felt able to 'indulge' before. Becoming a student again put Ann in contact with some of the feelings she had fleetingly experienced when much younger, which the first time around had been constrained by the need she had felt to be the 'little mother', following her own mother's illness. In becoming a student, Ann was freed from her past work responsibilities, and could live without also feeling that she had to be a responsible 'parent' to everyone.

Some time after this change of situation, she met and was attracted to a man some years younger than herself. In freeing herself from her previous way of interacting with others, she described how she allowed herself to appreciate the qualities of someone who was able to convince her that he, too, could be caring and mature, without being literally a father. Slowly, Ann had found a new way of loving which did not require her to repeat the same old pattern. Not only had she struggled to understand what was happening to her in the present, but she had also experienced the support of her therapist in recounting the pain of her premature adulthood. Finally, by putting herself in a novel social situation, she was freer to explore new ways of approaching people, which allowed her to appreciate the strengths in another person which she may previously have ignored.

Julia's story

Julia is another woman whom we have met, and whose story illustrates some of the dilemmas being faced by women today. Julia's difficulties also concerned her close personal relationships, which as in Ann's case, probably had their origins at least in part in events way back in her personal history. Unfortunately, however, we were not able to uncover some of the issues which lay beneath her dilemmas in any depth.

Julia telephoned one day in a state of panic, saying that she really felt in need of some help, and asking for an urgent appointment. When she arrived, she explained that she had recently found out that her husband was having an affair with someone else, and that she just could not cope with it. She also expressed her puzzlement about it all: it wasn't, she said, as if she and her husband Peter had a bad relationship. In fact, Julia had thought that things between them had been improving of late. As far as she could see, their sexual relationship was a good one, and they always seemed to enjoy each other's company. Further, the pressures on them both had lightened considerably over the past few years, since their two young sons had settled happily in school and Julia had been able to start back at work as a part-time secretary. Hence Peter's disclosure that he had been seeing Carol for the past few months had come as a very unpleasant shock.

This is how she described her current feelings:

Since he's told me, I know exactly when he's going out to see her. It sounds a cliché, but he rings and says he has to stay late at the office. I try to distract myself by taking the children out or watching television, but I know what's going on. I can picture them together in bed, and it makes me feel physically sick. I can't sit still: once I just left the boys and took the car and drove around the streets: I'm not sure what I was looking for but I suppose it was for some sign of them. Then I have the most dreadful fantasies. I imagine Peter involved in a gory accident, usually a train crash, with blood streaming down his face, which is smashed into little pieces. I'm really shocked to find how much better I feel after having one of these fantasies. Other times I go to bed, and try to sleep. Sometimes I sleep for a while, and then I wake up in a panic, missing Peter's body next to mine. My heart pounds, and I want to scream to get rid of the pain inside me. I even have to bite the pillow to stop myself from waking the kids.

Some nights he never comes home, but rings to say that he's called in to have a drink with a friend, and has had too much to be able to drive. I really want to murder him, but I also desperately want him to finish with Carol. I've begged him to stop seeing her, but he said that he somehow needs to see her, he just can't live without her. He's told me that I shouldn't worry, as he really does love me and the kids too. I feel particularly angry with her, as I resent the fact that she always has the best of him, like he has the best of her. I mean that when Peter and I go to bed, it's after a long day, so we're both tired, whereas they can go to bed anytime. She doesn't have another boyfriend, so can spend all of her time dolling herself up for him. One of my friends has told me that I should feel sorry for her, as she lives alone and is really very lonely. But I can't feel anything but hatred for her, although I suppose she may be OK. I know she is attractive, but she can't be a very nice person.

But I don't feel a nice person either. In fact, worst of all is how I feel about myself. Peter knows me better than anyone else, and he's rejecting me in favour of someone else. I keep asking, 'Why isn't my body as good as hers?' I feel so dull and dowdy, and utterly destroyed as a person. I feel more miserable than at any other time in my whole life. I'm really at Peter's mercy, and there's not much point in doing anything. It hurts me somewhere deep in the pit of my stomach, and I feel sick most of the time. I watch myself going about my daily routines and think, 'There goes the frumpish little housewife, approaching middle age, whose husband is sleeping with a mistress.' I hate myself and I hate him. My friends tell me

I shouldn't feel jealous, and I should pull myself together. Peter also says I'm being immature, and should be able to cope without being jealous. I suppose I do feel pretty helpless. In fact I've told Peter that he should make up his mind about what should happen to us, as I can't decide. I've never been able to decide things like this for myself; even when we got married it was really Peter's decision, not mine. I sort of went along with it all. I have thought about leaving him, but I suppose I feel it would be wrong of me to deprive him of the boys, or equally, to deprive the boys of their dad. Being a father is very important to Peter, and I don't see how I have the right to do that. Also, I don't know where I would go if I left, and I can't possibly earn enough to keep myself and the boys. I only earn a pittance, and there's very little chance of me getting a better job around here. I feel really trapped, and disgusted with myself for being so pathetic about the whole business.

Having told her story, Julia said she felt considerably better, and did not think she needed any further help. Nevertheless, she still looked very anxious, as if expecting condemnation for her violent fantasies, and her feelings of jealousy. She clearly felt that she was in the wrong, as well as being wronged. In addition, she apparently didn't know why it had all happened, or what to do about it.

Perhaps it was because she was not condemned or told that her feelings of rage were wrong that Julia gained some relief from the single session she had. But it seemed sadly unlikely that this would be the end of the troubles between Julia and Peter, particularly as Julia felt so desperately out of control of what was happening in her life. She could have used this crisis in her life as an opportunity to learn more about herself and her relationships. It was a chance to discover why she felt so lacking in personal resources, and to find out how she could develop a greater sense of self-esteem. But many women feel guilty about taking up a therapist's time and are uncomfortable about the unusual experience of being listened to themselves. There are also very real constraints on a woman like Julia entering psychotherapy in terms of time and finances, given her position as a housewife with two small children, and only the salary of a part-time secretarial job to support them. Unfortunately, we were never able to discover what finally happened to Julia: whether she simply lapsed into greater dependence on Peter irrespective of the emotional cost to herself, or whether she was able to start to make choices about her life, and take more control over her own destiny.

Women's lives and dilemmas

'Why can't a woman be more like a man?' So laments many a bewildered husband, lover, or father, following Professor Higgins from *My Fair Lady*. Not only in everyday life, but also in scientific accounts and professional contexts, women are judged according to expectations and standards based on how men are assumed to behave. Professor Higgins' song goes on to list the often-heard complaints about women, that women are irrational, over-react emotionally, and cannot make up their minds. Indeed, women are so often accused of prevaricating and of being unable to make decisions, that many women even believe it about themselves.

Yet, as we intend to show in this book, for women to resolve the dilemmas that they face throughout their lives often entails seeking out complex and apparently no-win solutions in a society where women are still second-class citizens with limited access to economic, educational, and professional equality with men. Women often have to struggle with hidden agendas which augment the difficulties of decision-making, the classic case being that of motherhood. Women who do not have children are not considered to be 'real' women, yet mothers who stay at home to care for their children lose their independent adult status and lack both professional identity and financial security. Conversely, women who combine paid employment with motherhood are provided with no automatic rights to child-care facilities in order to ease their double workload, and are often blamed for any emotional or developmental difficulties which their children may experience.

Throughout this book, we have provided opportunity for women to speak for themselves. The first two women we have described, Ann and Julia, are two of the many women who have talked to us about their lives, and whose experiences form the basis of this book. As with all the other women whom we describe, we have changed a number of identifying details so that their anonymity is preserved. But the stories themselves reflect as closely as possible some of the dilemmas facing women today, with which we have become familiar.

As we have seen, Ann and Julia made different uses of the possibility of learning more about themselves within the framework of a therapeutic encounter. Ann wanted an extended time to help resolve the depression and hopelessness she often felt about a life that seemed to hold no prospect of either a satisfying long-term relationship or the children she very much wanted. Julia, on the other hand, simply needed someone to listen to her panic about the crisis in her marriage, but basically did not want to dig any deeper to find out why it might have happened. Each of these women had a different commitment to making changes in their lives and each made their own choice about how to resolve their current dilemmas.

The stories of Ann and Julia, like those of other women which we will tell later in the book, clearly demonstrate a number of points. First, they show how women's behaviour and feelings do not happen randomly, but instead result from a complex interplay of forces, both past and present, internal and external, which are often difficult to shift or control. But besides demonstrating how patterns repeat themselves, and how over-determined some of our behaviours are, Ann's story in particular illustrates a second point, which is the way in which there may be great resistance put in our way if we want to change the way we are. For instance, other people benefited from Ann's 'mothering', as she was caring and concerned about her clients, friends, and colleagues. The men with whom she had affairs also rewarded her for her nurturance. Hence she had little clear encouragement from others to change the way she acted, even though at times she also made herself, and them, unhappy. Third, Ann's story shows how constrained we can be by social situations. Ann found herself surrounded by couples and only infrequently met unattached men with whom she might have been able to form less complicated relationships. Once again she felt trapped in her pattern of living. Julia, likewise, felt even more obviously trapped by her feelings for her husband and her children, as well as by her position of economic dependence.

Ann's story also demonstrates a fourth point: how some encouragement or help is often needed from outside if any change is to be made in what is frequently a very painful set of circumstances. Given the experience of repeating patterns, it is often only with the help of others that we can find a way to change things. It was chiefly through the support of her therapist that Ann was able to break the pattern which seemed to be controlling her life, and find some caring for herself which was not dependent on her skills as a parent, or her need for a parent herself. It would have been very hard for her to do this on her own, because of the complex nature of her relationships, past and present, of which she was only dimly aware. Her therapist was able to help her to understand some of the pressures upon her, and to support her in making some choices and decisions about controlling her own future. Sadly, Julia seemed to be unable to take control of her life herself, and was waiting for her husband to make choices for her: maybe a therapist could have unearthed with her the origins of her feelings of helplessness, and encouraged her to begin to take the difficult steps of making decisions of her own. Yet having unburdened herself, Julia claimed to have found the strength to sit out her current crisis. Perhaps the knowledge that there was someone she could turn to gave her the courage she needed.

The issues raised by these stories also clearly demonstrate the interaction of psychodynamic and social aspects of women's lives. The repetitive nature of Ann's involvement with older married men, for example, generated feelings of safety and recaptured experiences of both maternal and paternal love, but the price she paid was always to have this love in very limited supply. Her triangular relationships allowed her only a restricted portion of her lovers' time and energy, which were shared out among other family members. Yet as a single woman in her thirties, she felt she had access to few viable alternatives.

Last, the stories of Julia and Ann illustrate well how women often have to struggle very painfully in their adult relationships both to free themselves from parental and social influences, yet also to recreate the longed-for features of intimacy which they may have experienced in their early years. No matter how painful they may be, intimate relationships are central to most women's lives, and in the making and the breaking generate much meaning and joy, as well as distress. These are intensely personal experiences, so that any attempt to understand the texture of women's lives almost inevitably involves an examination of individual struggles as well as general social infuences.

In this book, we will tell the stories of women who have reached critical points in their lives, in which they feel confused or stuck, and who have sought help because they are aware of the need for some rethinking of their current way of living and relating to others. During these stories, it will become clear how in women's relationships with others there is always this complex interaction of patterns that develop during childhood, pressures which come from others to perpetuate these patterns, and social structures which encourage conformity to particular ways of living. For to an amazingly high degree, women (and indeed men) often find themselves being attracted to the same sort of person, or battling with the same kind of issue, so that the same situations keep on cropping up time and time again with different people. Yet these other people and surrounding social structures, such as the institution of marriage often seem to prevent change from taking place, and because it is often convenient for others if things stay as they are, there seems to be no other possible way of behaving. This isn't surprising, as in our interactions with other people we are both seeking to meet our own needs and also responding to the demands of the other person. Further, social change is by necessity difficult, and is usually strongly resisted by those who benefit most from present arrangements, as well as by many of those who benefit least. These are some of the reasons why change is so difficult, and why people sometimes need the support of an outsider who is not so involved, such as a professional therapist, in order to be able to break away from repeating their previous histories.

Issues to be covered in this book

Over the different chapters of this book we consider some of the dilemmas that women face at different stages of their lives: in employment and unemployment; in forming partnerships and in being alone; through motherhood and the menopause. Some of these issues have always faced women, while others are relatively novel. Many changes have taken place over the last few decades in the way that women, at least in more affluent parts of the west, expect to live their lives. The constraints and limitations on personal development felt by our mothers and grandmothers have been modified, so that increasing numbers of women now expect to participate in a wider world of employment and social life outside the confines of home and family. Yet the 'choices' open to women are not always freely or easily made. Whilst women in western society may no longer have to slave over pans of boiling linen on wash day, nor to bear yearly preg-nancies and experience the deaths of many of their children in infancy, it is still assumed that they, as women, are ultimately responsible for their family's health and wellbeing. In addition, increasing numbers of women have a double work-load, performing the domestic tasks of household management and care of children whilst also working outside the home. Women's employment, however, is still considered to be secondary to the 'main' job of home-maker, and is subse-quently undervalued and underpaid.

Our motivation to write this book stemmed from a desire to share with others the information we have collected from a wide variety of sources concerning women's psychology throughout the life span. As psychologists, working at different times both as teachers and as psychotherapists, we have found that both we and other women can be helped in making sense of our experiences, not only by being able to talk through what is happening, but also in hearing from others how they live their lives, the different options they create, and what factors influence the choices they make. Such a sharing has also formed the basis of consciousness-raising and self-help groups, which have done much to alleviate the physical and emotional isolation of women. For as Jo Freeman (1975) has argued, women have often been denied access to discourse with each other, and have even been encouraged to think that talking to each other 'does not count', or has no importance. But by creating women's spaces, in the absence of the equivalent of the local pub or football club, many women are positively re-evaluating and revaluing what they hear and talk about with each other. This book represents *our* attempt to create such a space. In writing it we have found that frequently we have had to work hard to understand our own and other women's lives in a world that often appears to be confusing, oppressive, and, increasingly, violent. We have observed repetitions in our own feelings and actions, as did Julia and Ann, and have struggled to create ways of living and working that are based upon mature reflection, rather than upon patterns of interacting with others, which are derived from responses acquired early in our lives.

Theoretical influences in this book

Since we are both trained in and influenced by a psychodynamic framework, we are particularly interested in the way that women's adult lives can be understood through exploring the nature of early psychological development. We believe that the psychological context in which women are born and gain their early emotional experiences has a major influence upon every adjustment which each woman makes to subsequent life events, and shapes the organisation of her adult identity. This theme will recur throughout all the chapters of this book, even when we are pointing to some of the wider, more socially constructed influences on women's lives.

More specifically, in this book we will make particular use of feminist psycho-dynamic thinking, such as that stemming from the work of Luise Eichenbaum and Susie Orbach (1982), which has provided us with new understandings into the way in which, as mothers and daughters, women are often caught up in a spiral of emotional conflicts which resonate throughout their lives. Eichenbaum and Orbach's rethinking of object-relations theories of psychological development focuses on how, as young children, women's emotional environments are defined by the women who care for them, whether this be their biological mother or her substitute. They have also pointed out how, as second-class citizens doing 'women's work' for low or non-existent wages, women in caring roles are both powerful figures in children's emotional lives, and at the same time are powerless in society's terms, performing the complex tasks of child care under difficult conditions of isolation, stress, and, frequently, poverty. Finally, Eichenbaum and Orbach have pointed to the close identification which often exists between mothers and daughters, and can lead to girls growing up feeling both responsible for and failed by, their mothers. This, they suggest, often makes intimacy within, and separation from, later adult relationships particularly problematic. All of these are points which we have found very helpful in developing our understanding of women's psychology.

Another major influence in writing this book has been the contribution of conventional social, developmental, and clinical psychology. As psychologists, we are also aware of the value of well-conducted psychological research, and where possible we have tried to integrate relevant findings into our thinking. Inevitably we have been selective, but have tried to draw upon work which sheds most light on the current position of women in a society which still defines the male as the 'norm' and women as being essentially a 'minority' group (see Sue Wilkinson, 1985). We have therefore been particularly interested in academic work on sex differences, and research which has examined the influence of sex and socially defined gender on people's personal experiences.

This has also necessitated an examination of men's lives, for two main reasons. First, many of the social and psychological factors which can be detected as influencing women's lives mean that in growing up, women often feel unsure of who they are, lacking a sense of autonomy. This itself is often considered to be innately 'feminine', but in fact illustrates the psychological effects of women's low status in current society, as compared with that of men. An understanding of how men respond to women, and to their more privileged position in society has therefore been necessary in order to examine the dynamic between men and women. Second, despite men's relative uninvolvement in child care, and the emotional and physical void this generates, women's relationships with their fathers can also be psychologically powerful, particularly in the way that men's presence (or more often absence) affects the women who care for children. Psychoanalytic writers within the Freudian tradition, such as Juliet Mitchell (1974), for example, have expressly described the considerable influence of this aspect of masculinity on women's psychology. For these two reasons we have drawn from work on men's psychology to interpret some of women's experiences.

Personal and political issues

In writing this book, we have also often found that novels and autobiographies have been as important to us as academic psychology in understanding women's lives. Although such sources are often seen as subjective and anecdotal, and therefore as being of less worth than so-called objective sources, we have nevertheless found the insights that they have often given us into human experiences and dilemmas have been invaluable. Despite the frequent criticism that too much introspective focusing on personal problems is a distraction from wider social and political issues (see, for example, arguments by Sheila Rowbotham, 1979; Juliet Mitchell and Ann Oakley, 1976), we have nevertheless found that some of the issues addressed in novels, although often seeming to concern only one or two fictional characters, in fact raise far more profound issues. In a similar vein Doris Lessing, in her preface to her novel *The Golden Note-Book*, has attempted to answer those who have criticised her for focusing on individual women's problems. She says:

At last I understand that the way over, or through this dilemma, the unease at writing about 'petty personal problems' was to recognise that nothing is personal, in the sense that it is uniquely one's own. Writing about oneself, one is writing about others, since your problems, pains, pleasures, emotions . . . can't be yours alone. The way to deal with the problem of 'subjectivity' that shocking business of being preoccupied with the tiny individual who is at the same time caught up in such an explosion of terrible and marvellous possibilities, is to see him (*sic*) as a microcosm and in this way to break through the personal, the subjective, making the personal general, as indeed life always does, transforming a private experience – or so you think of it when still a child, '*I* am falling in love', *I* am feeling this or that emotion, or thinking that or the other thought – into something much larger: growing up is after all only the understanding that one's unique and incredible experience is what everyone shares.

(Lessing, 1973:13–14, emphasis in original)

Although we would not agree that everyone, to this extent, shares the same experiences, since individual histories do cause people to react differently, and social positions do impose different life events, there is sufficient commonality for women to be helped through uncovering the similarities in their lives, and to tolerate, celebrate, and support each other in their differences. Novels and autobiographies are often excellent vehicles for doing just that.

As well as influencing our interpretation of women's psychology, a feminist analysis has also influenced our perception of this issue. We agree with Liz Stanley and Sue Wise (1983) that 'personal experiences can be used as an important resource, both in order to understand as individuals how and why we think, feel and act as we do, and how we can go about creating change'. They argue that through describing and analysing personal experiences, and the context in which they take place, we can counter the victimisation and self-blame experienced by many women, providing a framework in which to understand the reactions of anger, hopelessness, or depression that women frequently feel.

Despite the incapacitating nature of personal unhappiness, we are often challenged in our work to justify our emphasis on personal issues, when the world poses so many more global problems of intolerance, starvation, sickness, and inhumanity. But we do not see individual change as precluding wider action;

rather we think that, as feminism has always stressed, 'the personal is the political', in the sense that women's individual, personal experiences are affected by the political position of women; and conversely, that social and political change can only come about through the actions of women re-establishing their personal power within their own lives. We firmly believe that both types of action are important, but in different ways. Various examples bear witness to this, ranging from the peace camps of Greenham women in the UK demanding the removal of missiles, to women's health groups in many countries, critical of male-defined medicine and claiming a more women-centred approach, for instance over childbirth practices. Both these types of action involve women personally as well as politically. We also think that there are many possible arenas for action: for example, conventional psychiatric treatment of women, based largely on psychotropic medication, has been challenged by both the women's therapy movement and by individual women working in state services. This has generated many new ideas about women's emotional health, and has provided both an alternative structure of women-centred therapy and counselling outside state services, as well as training for mental health professionals working within established health and welfare services. Numerous individual women have therefore benefited from the attempt to bring about change in both social and personal spheres.

Commenting on these trends, Janet Sayers has argued that a psychodynamic understanding of women's lives can help women to:

become more fully conscious of the contradictions of their social lot so that they might thereby deal with these contradictions more effectively and thus have some hope of realizing their needs and desires . . . to become makers of their own history, drawing in the process on the imaginative and creative possibilities, rather than on the nightmarish stranglehold of the phantoms of the past.

(Sayers, 1986:179–80)

We would fully concur with this view. But, as Sayers also points out, a psychodynamic understanding alone is not sufficient to alter people's lives, since changes in individual consciousness cannot alone bring about the societal changes necessary for an improvement in women's social and economic position. She recognises, as we do, that this depends on 'social as well as individual change, and on collective as well as individual struggle' (Sayers, 1986:181). But in order to act effectively with and for each other, we must first free ourselves from the burden of our own emotional past. Collective action is particularly difficult to achieve if the personalities of those who want to bring about change with others are unable to surmount the complex dynamics that such inter-relationships often generate. In understanding more about ourselves, we can become freer to form work and social relationships unhindered by infantile defensive reactions. Hence individual psychological change is often needed before effective social or political change can take place.

Biological and social influences on women's lives

Another issue which reccurs throughout this book is the relationship between biology and culture, or social reality, in women's lives. Many of the dilemmas faced by women during their lives do relate clearly to biological events: menstruation, pregnancy, parturition, lactation, the menopause, ageing, and death. These are experiences which can be either responded to passively, or integrated more actively into a woman's evolving sense of who she is. Other experiences are more socially defined: friendships, intimate relationships, employment, caring for children and other dependants. These all necessitate women's involvement in complex sets of relationships, which are often conflictual. But like the biological changes, these social experiences can be better negotiated once there is an understanding of how past experiences affect current emotional needs, and hence interactions with others. Yet often these social aspects of women's lives are described as being determined by biology. However, like Janet Sayers (1982), we reject simple biological determinism as an explanation of women's psychology. Instead we are aware of the transactions between women's biological and social selves. This is nowhere clearer than in the way that women's bodies often express emotional and social dilemmas, as seen when a woman diets, abuses, purges, and over-exercises her body when life becomes too difficult, as examined, for example, by Marilyn Lawrence and colleagues (1987).

Rather than being governed by biology, we see women's lives as being punctuated by transition points such as pregnancy or the menopause, which, although often biologically marked events, depend for their meaning on the social, political, and economic aspects of women's lives, as well as on each woman's personal psychology. As the Jungian writer Bani Shorter (1987) has argued, when these transition points are successfully negotiated, the way is opened to a wider and fuller life. However, if a woman becomes 'stuck', these events can result in internal chaos, and leave emotional scars which may be difficult to heal. Hence we see this emphasis on the negotiation of such transitions between different socially significant, yet biologically marked, events to be the most helpful way of understanding the relationship between biology and culture in women's psychology.

Scope and limitations of this book

We hope that the information and ideas we present here will not only help women themselves to understand their lives better, and what they might do to change them, but also be of help to those in a position of offering professional advice and counsel to women, such as lawyers, social workers, doctors, psychologists, or counsellors. We would also like this book to be a resource for those who work on a self-help basis, offering specific support services such as post-natal groups, rape crisis centres, or women's refuges. Furthermore, we hope that we will stimulate more research about women, for as Liz Stanley and Sue Wise (1983) point out, good research often comes from collecting one-person case studies. Like novels (which is why we have made reference to some in order to illustrate particular experiences), such descriptions of individual lives often shed more light on women's psychology than official theorising and research ever does.

However, we also acknowledge that we are inevitably limited by our own language and experiences. In particular, our case studies reflect the women who have worked with us in psychotherapy, all of whom so far have been white and many of whom are middle-class. This illustrates clearly the way in which psychotherapy is still a privileged option. Working-class women, black women, and women of other ethnic minorities in personal crises are more likely to be prescribed medication to reduce symptoms of emotional distress and to be treated as inpatients in psychiatric services, than to receive outpatient psychotherapy (see also Eric Bromley, 1984). They are less likely to have access to information about alternatives, or the time and money to get to them. We regret this situation, and are working in different ways to change it, both inside and outside the state system.

In criticising what she sees as a middle-class emphasis on traditional family forms in the literature on mother–daughter relationships, Lynne Segal (1987) has argued that researchers have often failed to discuss how class and race impinge upon family life. We are certainly aware that in struggling to bring up children with inadequate housing or without a regular income, personal relations (including the children's emotional development) may seem like a luxury; hence Segal's criticisms could also be said to apply to us. But despite the different, even more severe, pressures on them, when working-class and ethnic minority women do have the opportunity to describe their personal crises (for example, Pearlie McNeill, Marie McShea, and Pratibha Parmar, 1986) we find that the underlying psychodynamics of women's lives remain essentially comparable. We therefore believe that the issues raised in this book *do* relate to women from a variety of backgrounds, even if the pressures from the social contexts in which they live may differ very considerably.

Structure of this book

This book is structured on a developmental basis, presenting a roughly chronological picture of some of the issues which often concern women at different points of their lives. Hence we follow the unfolding pattern of women's lives, with one chapter devoted to each of the major developmental stages of a woman's life, from adolescence to old age, with additional chapters concerning women in employment, and women on their own. Each chapter opens with the story of a woman drawn from our experiences of those who have come to one of us wanting help with some aspect of their current lives. This is then followed by a discussion, from a theoretical viewpoint, of some of the issues raised by each woman's story, together with other issues which often occur in other women's lives at that point.

Each chapter then ends with a discussion of some of the therapeutic implications of what has preceded. Only a small proportion of what is included in each chapter relies solely on the experience of women in trouble and who are seeking therapeutic help, as the majority of the issues raised are common to most women, whether or not they classify themselves as being in need of therapy.

Of course, we cannot deal in a book as short as this one with all of the issues which occur during women's lives, and we have therefore had to be highly selective. In particular, we are aware that we have not dealt other than super-ficially with the later stages of a woman's life. But in addition, there are bound to be an enormous number of other issues which are of major concern to some women, for example, caring for a handicapped child, experiencing religious beliefs and conflicts, having a major physical illness, relating to homosexual men, being disabled, or being involved in crime and the penal system (to name but a few), which we have barely touched upon. All of these issues may have concerned some of the women who have consulted us over the years, but have not been discussed in depth in this book, simply because each of these topics could constitute a book in itself.

The structure of the book is as follows: Chapter 2 concerns adolescence, and some of the questions often faced by girls as they grow into women in a society which sends very mixed messages about what being a woman should entail. Chapters 3 and 4 concern the establishment and maintenance of relationships with others, and in particular, how pressures from both within and without are experienced and resolved through the relationships which are made. Chapter 5 concerns women in the workplace, and shows how there can never be a clear-cut distinction between women's roles at work and their roles at home. Chapters 6 and 7 concern fertility, pregnancy, and motherhood, and look at the ways in which the needs of mothers and children are often so conflicted. Chapter 8 exam-ines the experiences of women living on their own, outside of a conventional 'couple' relationship, and raises some of the satisfactions and problems asso-ciated with this way of life. Chapter 9 then looks at women in their later years of life, and how their responsibility for others, especially for elderly people, influences the choices and options which are open to them at this stage. The book is completed by Chapter 10, in which there is a restatement of the theoretical viewpoint which has been developed throughout the book.

One distinguishing feature of this book, which has probably already become apparent, is that when citing the research and theories of other writers, we have always used the first name of the authors as well as the surname. We have done this because so much of women's work is invisible, hidden by the relative anonymity of initials. It is often assumed that most literary and academic work is carried out by men: yet it will become clear that this is a complete misrepresent-ation of reality. Most of the authors we have cited are in fact women, and we have done this not because they are women, but because they have done much of the best work in this field. To have used only the surname, which is the usual academic convention, would simply have perpetuated the invisibility of women's contribution.

In describing contemporary women's experiences – as daughters, lovers, mothers, or workers, we have attempted to outline the major psychological parameters which structure women's lives. Whichever ways forward women see for themselves: in personal or spiritual growth, through political action, in creative or productive work, or through personal relationships with others, an understanding of the extent to which personal histories affect current feelings and actions can provide a richer knowledge base from which women's future lives can take shape. This book attempts to encourage such an understanding. As a consequence, we hope that women may be able to gain more soundly based control over their own lives and futures.

References

Bromley, E. (1984) 'Social class issues in psychotherapy', in D. Pilgrim (ed.) *Psychology and Psychotherapy: current trends and issues*, London: Routledge & Kegan Paul.

Eichenbaum, L. and Orbach, S. (1982) *Outside In ... Inside Out. Women's Psychology: a feminist psychoanalytic approach*, Harmondsworth: Penguin.

Freeman, J. (1975) *The Politics of Women's Liberation*, New York: David McKay.

Lawrence, M. (ed.) (1987) *Fed Up and Hungry: Women, oppression and food*, London: The Women's Press.

Lessing, D. (1973) *The Golden Note-Book*, 2nd edn. London: Granada.

McNeill, P., McShea, M., and Parmar, P. (eds) (1986) *Through the Break: women in personal crisis*, London: Sheba.

Mitchell, J. (1974) *Psychoanalysis and Feminism*, Harmondsworth: Penguin.

Mitchell, J. and Oakley, A. (eds) (1976) *The Rights and Wrongs of Women*, Harmondsworth: Penguin.

Rowbotham, S. (1979) 'The women's movement and organising for socialism', in S. Rowbotham, L. Segal, and H. Wainwright (eds) *Beyond the Fragments*, London: Islington Community Press.

Sayers, J. (1982) *Biological Politics: feminist and anti-feminist perspectives*, London: Tavistock.

Sayers, J. (1986) *Sexual Contradictions: psychology, psychoanalysis and feminism*, London: Tavistock.

Segal, L. (1987) *Is the Future Female? Troubled thoughts on contemporary feminism*, London: Virago.

Shorter, B. (1987) *An Image Darkly Forming: women and initiation*, London: Routledge & Kegan Paul.

Stanley, L. and Wise, S. (1983) *Breaking Out: feminist consciousness and feminist research*, London: Routledge & Kegan Paul.

Wilkinson, S. (1985) *Feminist Social Psychology*, Milton Keynes: Open University Press.

Chapter two

Growing-up woman

Lucy's story

I first heard about Lucy through a note from one of my male colleagues, a psychiatrist. He asked if I would see a very intelligent but disturbed young girl, aged 16, whom he had assessed the previous week at the request of her family doctor, and whom he suspected was suffering from the early stages of schizophrenia. Lucy had apparently told my colleague that everybody disliked her, and that she hated her own mother and father. She had also been discovered cutting her arms with a knife, apparently with the intention of mutilating herself. My colleague gained the impression that her speech was rather disordered and illogical. In addition, she had then refused to tell my colleague anything else, although she did agree to the idea of seeing a woman therapist, rather than take a course of one of the major tranquillisers, normally used for patients with schizophrenic symptoms, which had been prescribed for her.

The following week, Lucy was brought to see me by her mother. Lucy was a slim, gracefully built 16-year-old with wavy red hair, who was wearing a casual T-shirt and jeans. Apart from a very few quick glances in my direction, she refused to meet my eyes. Lucy's mother by contrast was very formally dressed, and appeared extremely eager to talk. She told me that in recent months, there had been endless arguments at home, and that Lucy had been repeatedly bursting into tears for no apparent reason. She had also been behaving in a rather unpredictable way at school, and had recently rushed out of an important exam in tears, although her academic abilities were not in doubt. In addition, she was showing considerable reluctance to make decisions about her future, except to say that she wanted to go into nursing rather than into the family business, which is what had been planned for her after leaving school. She would not talk to either of her parents, and did not appear to mix with friends at school, although she had previously been very popular, and had been elected school hockey captain. Instead, Lucy's mother said, Lucy had recently developed a rather 'worrying' relationship with an older girl, who worked as a nursery nurse in a nearby nursery school.

When Lucy and I sat down to talk with each other on our own, Lucy watched me very carefully for a few minutes before she began to speak. I had a very clear sense that she was testing me out. Was I to be trusted? Was I there to categorise her or to try to understand? She obviously thought it would be worth taking a risk, and her thoughts began to tumble out in a confused rush of emotion and anxiety.

She started by telling me about her mother:

> My mother wants to be the perfect mother. But I'm not allowed to show any emotion at home. And I need lots of reassurance about myself. But she doesn't see me as a person. She makes me feel outrageous, because I don't say the right things. I don't believe in lying, yet everywhere I look I see people telling lies. When I was 12, I looked around and I realised I didn't belong. I looked at people in shops and in town, and I wasn't part of it. I look in the mirror and I don't even recognise me. I can't believe that others have a mind like mine, I'm an alien, the thoughts I have, they are incredible. But deep down I don't believe in me either. People at school see me and they say, 'Look, there's Lucy, the hockey captain!' but they don't see *me*, the real me. I have to behave like I'm supposed to behave like. And at home, it is worse, I make myself agree with Mum, I put on an act. What I am at the moment is a lie, and I don't believe in telling lies.

She lapsed into silence, as if her own logic had driven her into a corner. It did not surprise me that anyone who was not listening carefully to what she was saying might assume that her thoughts were disordered. She went on slowly:

> I won't let people see the real me. It's not to be played with. I hide away. But I've gone too far and I can't come back again. Anyway, I can't see how I could mean anything to anyone. No-one who knew me could possibly like me. I feel I couldn't care less about anything, although really I care so much.

Again she looked away, and refused to look at me for the rest of the session.

Sensing that she had become scared of how much she had already told me about herself, but not yet having a firm sense of the underlying conflicts, I told Lucy a bit about how I work and how much I wanted to try to understand her. But I also told her that I would leave it up to her as to whether she wanted to try to let me get to know her. Then I spent the rest of the session finding out more about the practical details of Lucy's life. She was studying for her GCSE exams at school, and was expected to do very well, although her spells of crying meant that she was missing quite a few classes. Her main interests outside school were sport and reading. She did not want to go into the family business as her parents intended, but aimed instead to become a nurse for the mentally handicapped. She said she had plenty of friends, but that she didn't go out with them as 'it all seems so trivial'. She added, however, that her friends were on the whole very nice about her present state, and didn't ask much. The only one who really understood was her friend Grace, who worked at a nearby nursery school, and who, she said, 'treats me as a person'. Lucy's parents evidently disapproved of Grace, partly because of her apparent influence over Lucy, and also because of her job.

The next time I saw Lucy was after she had spent the weekend with her friend Grace's family. She said that she felt that perhaps I might be able to understand, and that she was desperate for someone to talk to. Although the weekend had gone well, she had been crying a lot since coming back home, and feeling even more intensely that she didn't know who she was, and that she was just having to play a role with everyone. She said she could not bear to be in the same room as her father, and felt intense anger towards her mother. Her school work was suffering as she kept bursting into tears in classes and having to leave in disarray.

During subsequent weeks Lucy told me about her recurrent impulses to injure herself, by scratching her arms with a razor blade: although it hurt, she somehow felt at peace after she had done it. When she did cut her arms, she felt as if she had achieved something positive in giving herself the attention she wanted, as well as the punishment she deserved. She also told me that she had been dieting very strictly, and felt that at least by not eating she could have some control over something in her life. She was also aware of how much this distressed her mother, but regarded this as her mother's problem.

After a few more sessions together, Lucy began to talk about herself as having two sides which could be identified as the child Lucy and the adult Lucy. The child Lucy was apparently unkind and unreasonable and wanted to inflict pain on herself and others, and also caused all the crying. The adult Lucy didn't want other people to see the child Lucy, because adults don't cry and run abruptly out of rooms in tears. But the adult Lucy also felt that the child was a part of herself, which she did not want to give up. Lucy then recalled with bitterness a recent visit to her family doctor for some minor physical complaint, and while there having been subjected to some close questioning about her psychological state. She had found herself telling the doctor more than she intended, and was then outraged when he responded by telling her to try and grow up and stop behaving like a child. She felt deeply misunderstood, and resentful, especially as she suspected that the doctor had been encouraged to try and intervene by her own mother, which reinforced her sense of anger at her mother's apparently underhand methods of acting.

My main intention during these weeks was to provide a time for Lucy in which she could express all of her discordant feelings and emotions, without insisting that she should be logical or adult. I was also concerned to provide for her a relationship in which she could feel understood, and where she could share her fears. I didn't remark on her decision to diet, although I did keep a watchful eye on her weight. One week, Lucy came in looking very cheerful, having had a good week with fewer crying spells. But as she told me about this, she began to feel dejected:

> I'm being dishonest. All the different parts of me keep coming and going.
> I despise myself when I think I'm all right, and that all the bits of me fit
> together. Actually, I'm really nothing, I feel really empty.

She then told me that she felt as if people were experimenting with her, and had almost succeeded in destroying her: she knew that these ideas might be crazy but she didn't really have any real self left with which to evaluate the sense of the ideas. She felt that her sense of self was on the verge of disintegration.

As Lucy spoke I became aware yet again that she was not looking at me, and I asked if she was frightened. She told me that she was frightened that I might 'take her over', and that I could be part of the plot. Yet she also knew this was crazy, and that after the session was over, she would have to 'plod on', despite all of her bad feelings. She said she wanted to build a wall around herself, and not let anyone in, so no-one, including myself, would see how bad she was. But she also agreed with my suggestion that 'acting crazy' would be a way of avoiding her growing awareness that relationships with others were, after all, not always totally bad.

Many weeks passed and when Lucy and I met she told me more about her frustrations with her mother, who appeared only to want a superficially peaceful relationship with Lucy, and about her father, who appeared only to be interested in Lucy's school achievements and how much she was eating. In addition, she told me how isolated and different she felt at school, since all her friends seemed interested only in boys and clothes. Her mother was also telling her how important it was for her to go into the family business as that was the best way of making money. Only Grace was supporting her in her decision to go into mental handicap nursing, and her parents kept putting obstacles in the way of the two girls meeting. It became apparent to me that the relationship between Lucy and Grace was causing Lucy to feel intensely guilty, but also very happy. Gradually, Lucy let me know that the two girls were involved in an erotic relationship, and that this confused her very much indeed. She didn't think of herself as a lesbian, but felt very drawn towards Grace. Yet nobody talked about it: her parents just muttered darkly about Grace's influence, and couldn't share in the happiness of the friendship. Lucy sensed that her feelings about Grace were simultaneously 'good' and 'bad', and didn't understand how she should feel and act.

One week Lucy told me that she had become aware of how artificial everything was, and how if she so chose, she could murder someone. She could see no good reason for morality, or justice, it was simply that most people didn't go around murdering each other, because they were frightened of the opinions of other people. As far as she could see, it was primarily a case of social convention. Not to admit this appeared to Lucy to be profoundly dishonest, although she also supposed she must be insane to think in this way. She then became rather scared of her own impulses, and wondered how anyone could ever trust her. We talked for a long time about her need for love and comfort, and yet how she felt guilty for finding it with Grace. Lucy was terribly anxious about being, as she thought, 'abnormal', yet she despised normality.

It was around this time that Lucy's school exams were taking place, and we both agreed that we would focus on talking about ways of her coping with the exams, rather than facing more difficult issues for the time being. She managed to complete all of her exams, although she was very annoyed by all her friends and teachers who thought that the exams were important. She also felt out of control of her emotions: 'It is like being in a lift in an empty apartment building. It keeps going up and down between the floors, but I don't know where or when it is going to stop.' Despite her impulses to run out of the exam room in tears, she managed to sit all of the papers, reporting rather proudly to me that her triumph was different from other people's because, after all, 'I sat a different sort of exam'.

After the exams Lucy and I explored in more depth her growing sense of despair at the way in which other people conducted their relationships. She said she felt a real sense of disgust at the way in which people exploited each other, especially in personal relationships. She looked at the way in which her parents related to each other, and saw what she thought was dishonesty and mutual deceit. In comparison, her friendship with Grace seemed pure and honest, yet she knew that everyone else would think it was dirty. But she gradually seemed more accepting of the contradiction, and appeared to be less intolerant of her own needs and feelings. This growing acceptance did not extend to her mother: one day Lucy had come home from school and found her mother crying 'because she was afraid I didn't love her any more', yet she could feel no concern for her mother, whom she labelled as dishonest. Lucy said that, unlike her mother, she wanted to 'see everything, no matter how much it might hurt me'.

During the next few weeks we did not meet as Lucy had a summer job working as a nanny with a family in the nearby town. When she returned she was subdued and angry; the husband had simultaneously treated her like a child and had behaved in a sexually provocative way towards her. This she took as further proof of the decadence of the human race, and her estrangement from others. It also confirmed her belief that all men were disgusting, and only interested in sex. But she also felt more in command of her emotions, and was not spending so much time shut up in her room crying. In addition, she had started eating normally again, and did not feel any concern that she had returned to her usual weight.

Lucy and I continued to meet for many months, and during this time discussed at length her decision to try to become a nurse working with mentally handicapped people. Her parents were very disappointed with her decision, as they felt she could have had an interesting career in the family business, as prospects were good and a suitable opening could easily be found for her. They also felt that she had been very disobedient and disrespectful to them, and had caused them both a lot of pain. Numerous family arguments developed, but Lucy felt more able to say what she felt openly, rather than having to refuse food or run out of the room in tears. She remained adamant about her decision. She could see nothing but competition and greed in the business future which her parents had mapped out for her. Instead, she said she wanted to help people who were helpless and often ashamed of themselves, because they weren't 'normal'. She wanted to use her own experiences to help others to grow, and to help others accept themselves as they are.

I kept in touch with Lucy during her first few months in nursing. She wrote that she really loved her work, and how she had made friends with a number of people at work. She was also very sad about the gradual cooling of her relationship with Grace, and guilty about the fact that although Grace kept writing very loving letters, she no longer felt so warmly about her friend. She knew she owed a lot to Grace, but she had found new friends, and didn't need to rely on Grace so much. She felt that they had grown apart, but that she still owed a lot to her friend. She was also pleased that she had been able to be honest with Grace about her changed feelings, although she still felt a little guilty about leaving her behind.

When she came back to town Lucy sometimes called in to see me. She impressed me with her gentleness and perceptiveness, although we both knew that there were times when she still felt very shaky in her sense of herself. But over the following year or so she continued to grow in confidence. In one letter she wrote:

> I went to visit a hospital recently for patients suffering from mental illness, and wanted to tell you how it made me realise how I've got through all of the darkness. I went to the hospital with a friend, and when we were leaving I realised she was crying. She kept saying how wasted the patients' lives were and how unnecessary it was. We sat and talked for ages after this. It was nice to be able to say that I had put it all behind me. I've not forgotten it all, but as each day passes I become more aware that I'm so much more settled, and have found people who I enjoy being with, something I used to think was impossible. I've also discovered how very much I want to nurse the handicapped: so many other people just do it as a job. But I'm also much more able to accept that, too.

It isn't easy to pinpoint a reason for Lucy's reconnection with herself and her refusal to cut herself off permanently from others. Partly it was because there were enough people around (myself and her friend Grace) at crucial moments to reassure her that she was not crazy, and to help her to express her feelings and fears. But primarily it was because of her own courage to remain true to what she felt, and not to make herself into the image that other people wanted. I don't know what the rest of life will offer Lucy, but she had passed perhaps the most serious and insidious of all tests: the development into adulthood as her own woman.

The psychological development of girls in their adolescent years

The stage of transition from childhood to adulthood is, in our culture, accorded a special status, and is assumed by most observers and 'experts' to be a time of conflict and turmoil. During adolescence, individuals of both sexes are understood to be undergoing a process of establishing their own personal and separate identity beyond the confines of the family; yet at the same time, for many adolescents, dependence on the family or educational institutions is still required or desired for many years to come. This potentially conflictual situation is assumed to underlie the rebelliousness and disturbance seen in many adolescents, especially boys, as they come into conflict with parents, authority, and the law.

Yet although the years of adolescence may cause difficulties for boys, particularly in terms of their tussles with authority, a wealth of evidence now exists which suggests that the experience of adolescence is actually more problematic for *girls*, at least on a psychological level (see, for example, Judith Bardwick, 1971; Morris Rosenberg, 1987). It is during the years of adolescence that young women start to display the markedly higher proportion of mental health problems, compared with young men, which will exist for the rest of their lives (see, for example, Monica Briscoe, 1982; Susan Penfold and Gillian Walker, 1984; Jenny Williams, 1984). The incidence of depression, anorexia, bulimia, phobic problems, depersonalisation, and attempted suicide are all higher in girls, while conduct disorders such as delinquency, excessive alcohol consumption, and truancy are higher in boys (see Jarad Kashani and colleagues, 1987). This chapter examines how and why this might be so by looking at some of the psychological and social issues which colour the years of adolescence as experienced by young women, and which particularly restrict the choices and opportunities open to them at this stage of their lives.

We shall open our examination of the vicissitudes of adolescence as experienced by young women by looking at the process of identity development in adolescence, to discover if this can help us to understand why and in what way this stage may be particularly difficult for girls. We shall then consider the issue of separation from the family, especially the mother, which is a crucial step to be taken by all adolescents, and which is often incompletely achieved by girls. Next, we shall look at a number of psychological issues in development, which may cause difficulties for some young women, although not for others, such as the experience of emotional turmoil, the development of sexuality, and the distressing experience of self-doubt. In all of the examples examined it will be seen that a clear perception of the nature of the social world, structured as it is by patriarchal values, is vital, if the girl's particular difficulties are to be adequately understood. Last, we shall consider the implications of this form of analysis for those who work therapeutically with adolescents. As we have pointed out in Chapter 1, in order to understand fully the adolescent's experience, it is necessary to consider both the pressures which exist outside the adolescent herself in her immediate culture, and also the pressures and feelings that exist within herself, and which are often located in the personal world of her family relationships and emotions. We shall therefore draw upon both social and psychodynamic perspectives in our analysis.

Identity development in adolescence

One of the key tasks facing every adolescent in modern advanced cultures is said to be the establishment of an independent, autonomous identity. Most of the widely available psychological theories which seek to explain adolescents' experiences of this process (for example, Jean Piaget, 1932; Erik Erikson, 1950;

Jane Loevinger, 1976; Lawrence Kohlberg, 1966; Daniel Levinson, 1979) do so using a stage theory; that is, they postulate that all individuals progress through a roughly similar set of stages, or steps, until maturity, or independent identity is attained. Each stage must be successfully resolved before the next stage can be attempted. For example, Erikson suggests that a person progresses from initial narcissism, through identification with the close family, to socialisation, to the eventual establishment of autonomy and intimacy. At each point, a number of dilemmas must be resolved, for example, between over-identification with a parent on the one hand, and role-confusion on the other (for further details, see Carol Franz and Kathleen White, 1985).

The basic tenet of theories such as Erikson's is that this process occurs in a similar way for boys and girls, given what Erikson called an 'average expectable environment' (see James Marcia, 1987:164). Indeed, most developmental theories work from a traditionalist stance; that is, they seek to establish how girls and boys learn to mould themselves into the requirements and traditions of their society, without questioning the meaning and content of the adolescents' experiences, or the restrictions of that society upon them. Taking this one step further, many conventional theorists of adolescence have conceptualised the development of the male as paradigmatic, so that 'normal' development is assumed to follow the path of the male.

What many of these theorists have then discovered is that girls 'fail' to attain the same level of maturity as boys, because they often progress in a different way through the developmental stages. This is then taken as evidence of female inferiority, while the developmental attainments of the girl, such as her ability to respond to the emotions of others, are not recognised. One clear example can be seen in the theory of moral development proposed by Lawrence Kohlberg (1969), which has been very effectively criticised by Carol Gilligan (1982). Kohlberg suggested that the moral decisions frequently made by girls demonstrated their moral poverty, in comparison with boys, because their decisions when faced with moral dilemmas are often based upon concern for other people, rather than upon abstract principles of right and wrong. As abstract theories are supposed by Kohlberg to be of greater moral value than concern with preserving human relationships or dignity, he concluded that the moral powers of the girl are inferior, or at least, less well developed than those of boys. Carol Gilligan, on the other hand, has pointed out that this presupposes that abstract notions, such as the importance of following rules, are of greater moral worth than looking after people: surely a moot point. We will discuss Carol Gilligan's arguments in greater detail later.

Besides neglecting those aspects of development which are often of more salience to girls than to boys, the problem with many of the conventional theories is that they also fail to address the nature of the task being faced by members of the two sexes, who do *not* live in the same 'average expectable environment'. What they miss out is the pressures on girls in particular *not* to achieve an autonomous identity, when this conflicts with the achievement of appropriate 'female' identity, demanding as it usually does the capacity to relate to others with empathy and nurturance, as well as to be passive and compliant. Attainment of sex-appropriate identification *is* seen as important by such theorists, but it is not usually seen as being simultaneously a hazardous threat to autonomous identity. The dilemmas which this presents to girls is then not usually recognised. Instead, girls are simply seen as less 'mature' than boys.

Yet for many girls, the experience of adolescence may well be the most crucial test that they will ever have to face during their lifetimes of their ability to withstand threats to their independent personhood, and simultaneously to develop their capacity for relationships with others. For it is during adolescence that they have to start to learn to 'do both', that is, to be independent and separate, yet also to be connected to others and nurturant. Of course the stronger of the two competing pressures is normally to conform to sex-appropriate behaviour, that is, to be nurturant, rather than to develop too much autonomy. Hence, it is during adolescence that the young girl child risks being transformed from an eager, physically active, and direct participant in life into a self-critical actress, who learns not to display too much intelligence for fear of appearing off-putting to boys; who is careful not to become engaged in physically demanding sports and activities like football or car racing for fear of being thought 'masculine'; and who must always watch her figure and clothes for fear of not being attractive enough to others. In many respects, adolescence is a tragedy for girls, when the demands of approaching womanhood begin to iron out the enthusiasms and adventurousness of childhood, in favour of conformity to the traditions and demands of femininity.

Further evidence for the nature of the difficulties being faced by young women when trying to establish their own identity as autonomous selves can be seen in the data noted previously concerning the prevalence of different types of disorder common in adolescent girls. The girl is less likely to be troubled by her relationship with some immediately evident external symbol of authority such as school or the police, than by her relationship with her own self and her body and the achievement of social and personal integration. Because the threats to her identity are often more insidious and difficult to face and challenge than more easily identified external manifestations of authority, the girl's very personal struggle can sometimes pass virtually unnoticed. An additional reason for this is that the underlying theme in the disorders experienced predominantly by girls during adolescence is the self-attacking nature of the behaviour: the girl in some funda- mental sense is involved in a process of continuous self-comparison and self- criticism in which she almost inevitably finds herself to be at fault, or inferior to others, and deserving only of self-punishment. When these attacks become serious enough, of course, they are noticed; Lucy, for example, used both strenuous dieting and self-mutilation to express her distress and self-hatred, and was then considered to be 'a problem'. Inevitably, the chief victim of her actions was herself.

It is not only the conventional developmental theorists who have been unhelpful to our understanding of the process of female development. A number of psychodynamic theorists have also worked from the premiss that female development is based on their innate inferiority. As children, girls are much more likely to admit openly that they wish they were boys than vice versa (see, for example, Alisa Burns and Ross Homel, 1986), although during adolescence, girls tend to be less clear about this, despite being in many ways even more painfully aware of the benefits in our society of being male, and the extent to which their options and privileges are limited, compared with those of boys. Notions such as penis envy have been used by orthodox psychoanalysts to explain the resentment felt covertly or overtly by many girls about being female, but these notions are now widely rejected as being over-simplistic (see, for example, the discussion of biological essentialism by Janet Sayers, 1982). However, the envy of girls for the privileges of boys is often quite evident, so that the concept of penis envy has been retained in a modified form by writers such as Juliet Mitchell (1974) to represent the girl's awareness of her second-class status in society, rather than her desire for a specific physical organ as such. Other writers such as Vivien Bar (1987), influenced by the theories of the French psychoanalyst Jacques Lacan, have pointed out that the very structure of language and the social interactions which language describes is predicated on the male organ as the signifier of the law of the father, and the woman as the 'other' who is subject to that law. Hence, according to these theorists, the attainment of female identity is bound up with an awareness of a lack, requiring the presence of another for psychological existence. Not surprisingly therefore, the issue of independent identity formation is a difficult one for girls.

More recently a number of theories of women's psychological development, such as those of Nancy Chodorow (1978); Carol Franz and Kathleen White (1985), and Sandra Bem (1974) have proved much more informative about the process of identity development in girls. Chodorow in particular has pointed to the importance in development of the qualities of affiliation and acceptance, which make up female identity in many cultures, and which have been neglected by most conventional theorists. Meanwhile Franz and White have attempted to extend the theories of Erikson to include the achievement of intimacy and interpersonal attachment as an essential aspect of psychological development for both boys and girls. Bem has suggested that truly mature individuals are psychologically 'androgynous'; that is, they possess both male and female qualities and can behave in the way that a situation demands, rather than the individual's strict sex-role. Hence (for example) a mature individual would be able both to care for young babies with nurturance and gentleness, and to chair large meetings with authority and decisiveness.

The merit of these theories is that they give equal value to qualities that are often undervalued in a largely male-run society, and see the process of identity development as consisting of the attainment of a balance between competing aspects of the self. They also recognise the complexity of the dual nature of the task facing girls in adolescence. As we shall see throughout this book, it is essential for women to have the ability to be themselves, and take control over their own lives, as well as to nurture others, if psychological health is to be maintained. Yet this is an attainment which is often discouraged at the very early stages of adolescence.

Separation

The other crucial issue facing all adolescents, and which is closely linked with identity formation, is separation. Separating from parents, particularly from the mother, who for most children has been the primary care-giver, is of course dependent on having a sense of self which is strong enough to withstand the demands of independent existence. Yet not only do many adolescent girls become aware of their own 'deficiences' compared with others, particularly boys, but they are also often lacking in confidence in their capacity to take on the burdens of future life as separate, autonomous adults. The result is of course the self-doubt and lack of confidence so evident in the majority of adolescent girls, and the depression and life-threatening behaviour present in all too many. As already noted, this awareness of her own inability to meet the demands required of adults also springs from the nature of the task: the adolescent has simul-taneously to try to become a woman, which means being acceptable to and dependent upon others, and at the same time to try to become independent, which means being herself irrespective of the views of others. Yet the sense of self is developed through relationships with others, and if for women in particular these relationships involve sensitivity to the needs of and approval from other people, then the stage of adolescence in which relationships with others become more complex and diverse will be particularly tricky for a girl. There will be a difficult balance to achieve between the various audiences, both internal and external, which she is trying to please, and a considerable need to control her own impulses in order to conform. In addition, the social restrictions on the opportunities that are open to her, for example, at school, further limit her capacity for inde-pendence and hence for full self-development.

However, perhaps even more central to the problem of separation is the nature of a girl's relationship with her mother. Luise Eichenbaum and Susie Orbach (1985) have pointed out how the process of separation is often especially difficult for girls: they argue, following Nancy Chodorow (1978), that mothers of girls identify much more closely with their daughters than with their sons, and, being highly conscious of the abundant dangers facing independent women in a poten-tially violent society, are much more careful to protect their daughters and thus to discourage independence. In addition, they suggest that the emotional burden carried by most adult women (which we will discuss in more detail in subsequent chapters) is sometimes off-loaded on to their daughters; hence girl children, conscious of the emotional neediness of their mothers, may attempt to mother their own mothers. On many levels, therefore, attainment of a separate identity is fraught with problems for girls, being discouraged both overtly and covertly.

The girl's identification with her own mother may also lead to a high level of conflict within the family, when she does at last attempt separation. Aware of the close nature of the bond between them, and the emotional neediness of her mother, the girl may well feel intense conflict when separating from her mother, and thus fail to convince her mother of her capacity to cope with the separation. Being conscious of her mother's anxiety about her growing independence, the girl may then curb her desire for separation, although she may also feel curiously angry and resentful about this. The result can be extremely hurtful family arguments, as was seen between Lucy and her mother, as the daughter feels that in some way she is bound by a tie far stronger than she or her mother can explain rationally. Hence rebellion against this tie is often fraught and highly 'irrational' in nature. Alternatively the anger may be denied, and expressed instead through a variety of self-destructive actions and depression.

It is relevant to note here that this conflicted desire for separation, combined with the girl's growing sense of discomfort about being 'a poor fit', is often centred on her body: the majority of girls are unhappy with their bodies in some way, seeing themselves as too fat, too small, too tall, or as simply ugly in comparison with the image which they believe to be acceptable to others. Luise Eichenbaum and Susie Orbach (1985) consider that this is connected with anxieties about boundaries between the self and the world, and that lack of confidence about the stability of these boundaries often lies beneath excessive concern with shape and size. This is a very widespread problem: research on body image (for example, by Elizabeth Davies and Adrian Furnham, 1986) shows that the level of dissatisfaction with the body increases progressively during adolescence, and is centred on those body parts which are most intimately connected with femininity, that is, breasts, upper thighs, and hips. Furthermore, just under half of all 14 to 18-year-olds think that they are overweight, despite the fact that only a minority do indeed have a weight problem in any medical sense. This preoccupation with and attention to body appearance is inevitably linked to the development of anorexia and bulimia, which we shall discuss later in this chapter.

It is particularly in adolescence that a girl's preoccupation with her physical appearance becomes enmeshed with her developing sense of self. In her novel *Jerusalem the Golden*, Margaret Drabble describes vividly the subtle conflicts over autonomy which occur when a young girl struggles to shape an identity which is different from that imposed by her parents. Clara, a girl from a dull and oppressive family living in the industrial north of England, senses that she was made for a more stimulating and adventurous life, despite her felt disadvantages, and this is expressed clearly through her developing body:

She had never expected to be beautiful because nobody had ever suggested that she might be so. Some mothers assume beauty in their daughters, and continue to believe it to be there, in defiance, often enough, of the facts, but Mrs. Maughan was not one of these mothers. She assumed plainness, and she found it. She was so devoted to the principle that beauty is a frivolity and a sign of sin that she would have been ashamed to have it in the house . . . Clara as a child had fully supported her mother's attitude, for she was in no way a pretty child; she was sullen, dirty and her features were too big for her face. As she grew older, however, her face grew as well as her hips and bosom, but her way of looking as though she was about to burst out of her clothes became an asset rather than a disadvantage. She had not expected to be such a kind of girl; she had watched this kind of girl for years . . . but she had never expected to become one. She had expected to be one of the others.

(Drabble, 1967:49)

Psychological problems in development

We shall now turn to an examination of some of the most frequently occurring problems which are often perceived by the families and friends of adolescents, and indeed by the adolescent girl herself, as evidence of the difficult nature of adolescence. Central to this examination must be an awareness of the fact that, upon entering the teenage years, the girl is no longer afforded the tolerance which she may previously have experienced in being just herself, but now has to begin to assume the responsibilities and rights of adulthood. But the adolescent has not simply to become an adult; she has to become an adult *woman*, and that means learning how to be what society thinks a woman should be. As expressed by Diane Mitsch Bush (1987), in adolescence 'parents, peers and teachers are all said to begin to require behaviours consistent with preparation for the traditional wife/mother role' (p. 208). Obviously the precise meaning of this varies from culture to culture, but it usually involves learning to be attractive to men; to accept without protest her 'biological destiny' of marriage and motherhood; to take on a supportive but less prominent role than that of her husband or brothers; and yet to maintain some control over her own life by some means or another, which may involve subterfuge, repression of her own feelings and thoughts, manipulation, flattery, or guile, all techniques used by members of subservient groups to maintain some degree of influence on those in a position of greater power than themselves (see Jean Baker Miller, 1976).

Learning to relate to others: emotional turmoil

During the years of adolescence, relationships with peers gradually become more important than those with family, leading in many cases to parental distress and anxiety, as well as uncertainty for the adolescent herself. The development of the adolescent's own very private emotions may be jealously guarded, like her personal diary, especially when parents presume that they are entitled to know what the girl is feeling and doing. Parental supervision of friendships which existed during the years of infancy becomes more circumspect, but simultaneously more careful, given the potential risks of involvement with the 'wrong' sort of friend. The adolescent therefore has to integrate within herself the influences of at least two different communities: her parents and her peers, which may add to her sense of confusion, and inability to answer the adolescent's question 'Who am I?' These concerns are especially marked for young women from ethnic minorities, who often experience a wide and painful gulf between the culture of their families to which they are expected to conform, and that represented by the aspirations and expectations of other girls in their country of residence.

As we have already pointed out, it is during the period of adolescence that the individual begins to separate herself from her family and to define her own uniqueness, hence establishing a personal sense of identity beyond the confines of her family. The sense of self which has been forming since infancy through relationships with others is further refined through the growing complexity of emotions which she now experiences, complicated by the onset of puberty. The result for at least some adolescents can be an overwhelming sense of confusion and fragility. The emotional turmoil which was experienced by Lucy, and which she described as like being in a lift in an apartment building, shooting apparently out of control from one floor to another, is a good description of the adolescent's confusion, and results from the individual's attempt to discover her own sense of self in the light of her increasing emotional responsiveness, and the growing complexity of her relationships. This confusion can become painful, especially when the adolescent girl feels fundamentally unsupported by significant others, particularly her parents.

In the early and middle stages of adolescence, the girl's personal relationships are often conducted with a good deal of passion, but also with a degree of anxiety, as she becomes aware that the 'proper' focus for her emotions is to find a stable (male) partner for herself. Yet it is usual during adolescence for friendships with other *girls* to deepen first, as the adolescent girl uncovers her potential for love, jealousy, and hatred. Boys of her age are not normally as interested in relationships and feelings as she is, as they are usually more instrumentally and achievement oriented than her (Rae Carlson, 1972; Christine Griffen, 1985). Since girls are usually much more person-centred and aware of other people than boys, not surprisingly, most girls at this stage therefore find relationships with other girls to be much more satisfying than those with boys. Sometimes these relationships with other girls may become eroticised, either in practice through mutual caressing and kissing, or they may remain sublimated, and simply be conducted with an intensity and passion which is normally assumed only to exist between adult lovers. If a close girl friend becomes involved with someone else, either a girl or a boy, this can be experienced as cruel betrayal, especially if there is some sense of guilt at the intensity of the original relationship.

As noted, it is particularly during the early and middle stages of adolescence that relationships with other girls are experienced as considerably more rewarding than those with boys, but as Sue Lees (1986) has shown through her research with teenagers, boys are none the less seen by most girls as the appropriate focus of erotic activity, and are also seen as having more power and prestige in the wider world than girls. Much effort has therefore to be devoted to 'finding a boyfriend', and to pleasing him without at the same time losing completely the support, respect, and friendship of other girls. Not surprisingly, this constellation of experiences (warm, satisfying friendships with other girls which have to be abandoned in favour of relationships with the emotionally impoverished but more powerful male) do not contribute much to the girl's sense of self-esteem, and may add to feelings of confusion about the adult world. The girl is usually pushed towards exclusive heterosexuality, and the possibility of maintaining intimacy with her female friends and developing bisexuality is not generally approved of. In addition, the girl's recognition of the fact that emotion and feelings are of lesser consequence in the outside world than are the skills and mastery of physical and intellectual tasks, further diminishes her sense of competence, and lessens her confidence in her ability to cope as an adult outside the sphere of her family.

Some of these dilemmas are beautifully portrayed in *The Diviners*, a novel by the Canadian writer Margaret Laurence (1975). In the novel, Laurence describes how two friends, Morag and Ella, commiserate over not being able to attract boys, yet refuse to 'act dumb'. Morag says:

'I want to be able to talk to boys the way they want to be talked to. Only I can't get the trick of it.'
'Boys like that are schmucks' Ella says furiously. 'But yeh, I know what you mean.'
'You too?'
'Yeh. I went out with this guy a coupla weeks ago, and I thought "Now this is it. Here is your opportunity, oh Ella Bella". So what did Ella the schlemiel do? Did she tell him how masterful and handsome he was? Not she. Oh no. She began talking in her winsome way about Marx's theory of polarity. Why? Why? I'll never see *him* again.'
'Well, then, why?' Morag is laughing, but not in mockery.
'I don't know,' Ella says gloomily. 'It just seemed phoney, somehow, all that whole mutual flattery bit. And why should I pretend to be brainless? I'm not brainless.'

(Laurence, 1975:181–2)

Despite such negative experiences, during adolescence the girl may also be able to start to develop her own interests and opinions in ways which are very satisfying to her, especially if she is encouraged to value herself and her own capacity for emotional responsiveness. She may at this stage have a very rewarding and rich emotional life, possibly being expressed through art or religion, as well as through her deepening friendships with others. If she can maintain these values and interests, they may sustain her through many of the difficulties that she will doubtless encounter later in her life.

The growth of sexuality

In addition to confusions over personal relationships, the adolescent girl's sense of emotional upheaval may well be combined with anxieties about sexuality following the onset of puberty. Whether the prospect of active sexuality is welcomed or feared will depend to a considerable degree on the nature of the girl's existing beliefs about the meaning of sexuality, which in turn will depend on her pre-existing experiences of sexuality, and what she has been told about sex both overtly and through example by her parents. In this sense 'the sins of the father may be handed on to the third and fourth generations': the girl's mother, who herself may have had to learn about sexuality in a context in which sex for women was considered more of a duty than a pleasure, may have difficulties in conveying to her daughter that sexuality is a positive and enjoyable aspect of life. Lucy's images of sexuality (p. 22) were by and large negative ('men are only interested in sex'). These were very probably connected with her perception of what sex meant for the woman she knew best, that is, her mother. It seems quite possible that Lucy's mother had been unable to convey to Lucy many positive feelings about sexuality, and consequently communicated on an unspoken level that men were disgusting animals, and that sex was something to be resisted or endured. This had not surprisingly led Lucy to feel acutely anxious about the prospect.

However, a number of other explanations are also possible for an adolescent's anxieties about the idea of active sexuality. The development of an independent erotic life is both an exciting and a frightening prospect. Family therapists (for example, Lily Pincus and Christopher Dare, 1978) as well as a number of psychodynamic theorists such as Vilja Hagglund (1981) have pointed out that another of the 'tasks' of adolescence is to reorientate sexuality from within the family towards eligible partners outside the family, a process which may initially seem more anxiety-provoking than pleasurable. This is especially the case if problems with separation have meant that the girl does not feel particularly confident in her ability to relate easily to people outside her immediate family circle.

Of course, the process of developing a satisfying adult sexuality is made infinitely more difficult if there has been any history of actual incest. Recent research concerning the incidence of child sexual abuse, reviewed by Karen Alter-Reid and her colleagues (1986), suggests that this is far more common than was previously assumed, such that approximately 38 per cent of women report that they were sexually abused during their early lives. A high proportion of this abuse is likely to have been perpetrated by male relatives, and although it is not always the case that the child victim suffers from severe psychological conse-quences, most victims do experience anxieties, dread, dislike, or avoidance of sexual activity in later life. It is likely to be in adolescence that the girl first has to face this issue. The gradual acceptance by at least some psychoanalysts (for example Alice Miller, 1984) that their adult women patients were not making up stories or wishful fantasies when they told of childhood rape by fathers or uncles, has at last allowed psychodynamic therapists to explore the considerable problems which stand in the way of women enjoying their sexuality, a question which we shall look at again in Chapter 4. But it seems likely that many victims of child sexual abuse never discuss their experiences with anyone else, and carry the burdens of their guilt and pain alone through their adolescence into their adult sexual lives.

The active involvement in and enjoyment of sexuality by all adolescents is not seen by most parents and educators as a positive good: to a considerable degree sex is still seen as something to be guarded against for as long as possible. As might be predicted, this depends on the sex of the adolescent. Many texts on psychological development in adolescence describe girls who are sexually active as promiscuous, while boys are seen as exploring, and experimenting with their sexuality. Further, in the UK Una Padel and Prue Stevenson (1988) have pointed out that 80 per cent of girls between the ages of 10 and 16 who are held in care have committed no crime, but are there because they are considered to be in 'moral danger', or simply 'in need of care'. The comparable figure for boys is 14 per cent. This attitude towards the roles of the sexes in sexual behaviour seems to be mirrored in the relationships between the boys and girls themselves: Sue Lees (1986) has reported from her interviews with adolescents that girls also appear to accept the view that those who have intercourse are 'slags' or 'whores', while boys are simply proving their masculinity. In addition, the burden for contraception usually remains with girls, who frequently do not use adequate precautions such as the Pill, or fail to insist on the use of the condom (the safest and least disruptive form of contraception from the point of view of the woman) for fear of displeasing the boy. Unwanted teenage pregnancy is of course one of the tragic results of this self-neglect, with its accompanying health, economic, psychological, and social complications. The consequences for the young mother's future options and development are, of course, enormous. We will discuss this issue further in Chapter 6.

Anorexia and bulimia

As the adolescent girl becomes more and more aware of some of the difficult issues which are likely to face her as a woman in the adult world, a number of responses are possible. One is the attempt to resolve the whole question by a total refusal of adult womanhood. Seeing what the world of adult women has to offer, and not liking what she sees (obedience to social convention, acceptance of second-class citizenship as a woman, submission to unwanted or problematic sexual attention) some girls may choose the path of anorexia as a way of apparently resolving this problem (see, for example, Sheila Macleod, 1981; Marilyn Lawrence, 1987). Anorexia nervosa is experienced predominantly by women (Hilde Bruch, 1974; Anthony Crisp, 1980) and involves a process of voluntary starvation sometimes to the point of death. The onset of emaciation involves cessation of menstruation, and a reduction of obvious secondary sexual characteristics, such as breast growth and body curves. Although there may be a multiplicity of other reasons for the onset of anorexia, such as the attempt to resolve family conflicts (see Salvador Minuchin, 1974), undoubtedly a major cause is the benefit that the girl perceives from holding on to her status as a child, albeit at the possible cost of her life. The illusion of a permanently sexless childhood can be maintained, without any of the unpleasant consequences of womanhood. In addition, the difficult issue of separation from mother can also be shelved, even if the refusal to eat is apparently causing the girl's mother great distress.

Bulimia, the 'binge-purge' syndrome, is also much more common in women than in men. Ruth Striegel-Moore, Lisa Silberstein, and Judith Rodin (1986) point out that in current society, there is a close link between thinness and femininity, yet at the same time there is increasing availability and pressure to consume tasty and fattening foods. Adolescence is a point at which girls are particularly worried about their acceptability to others, and when they become highly critical of their physical appearance. Striegel-Moore and her colleagues suggest that many women who abuse themselves in this way appear to be stereotypically 'feminine', that is, to be 'dependent, unassertive, eager to please, and concerned with social approval' (p.249). Hence any deviation from what is perceived to be the norm may cause anxiety and depression. Vomiting food may appear to solve the problem at least in the short-term. However, there are also likely to be psychodynamic reasons for bulimia: possibly the consumption of enormous quantities of food in binges may help the young woman to deal with confusions and emotions which seem too overwhelming for her, and the subsequent vomiting allows her to deny responsibility for her actions.

Rejection of the adult world

Another characteristic feature of adolescence is the growing awareness of the failure of adults to resolve the problems of the world, and the reaction of immense disgust at the world of social convention, dishonesty, and the corruption of others. Lacking the sophistication of adults in methods of political protest, and not having developed the tolerance (or apathy) acquired by experience, the adolescent may attempt to tackle what she sees as immorality head-on. She is then seen as naïve and idealist, and is frequently not taken very seriously. This can then lead the adolescent to feelings of intense anger, combined with self-doubt as others tell her that she is too young to understand such things. In addition, she may be aware of how much she needs and wants the love and approval of others, and fears their disapproval if she persists with her criticism. Wanting to be true to her ideals, to know everything and yet not to tell lies, the adolescent can only see adulthood as a failure, although at the same time she may feel disgust with herself and her own impulses towards warmth and comfort from others, since, as far as she can see, this is what has led to the moral failure of others. In particular, girls may, like Lucy, see their mothers as 'existential failures', who have compromised themselves to a life of wasted social convention. Yet they do not see what other options are open to them, in a world which has only restricted opportunities for girls. Failing to find an acceptable role-model in her mother, the girl may despair of ever being able to find for herself a way of life that she can positively respect. Hence she may instead bury those parts of herself which are aware of these conflicts, and then experience unaccountable feelings of both depression and anger, much of which may be self-directed.

Moral or idealistic outrage may in some cases be expressed quite straight-forwardly through intergenerational conflict, resulting in endless arguments with parents or other authorities. But if the girl does not feel able to face conflict directly with her parents, the dilemmas may be fought out within the girl herself. Some girls, such as those who are suffering from anorexia nervosa, may deprive themselves of comfort, love, or food for the sake of maintaining their sense of moral integrity; while others (like Lucy) experience simultaneous feelings of longing for others, disgust at their own impulses, and anger at the apparent weaknesses of others. In some cases suicidal attempts or self-mutilation may be the result.

Self-doubt and low self-esteem

As the sense of identity is forming, the adolescent may also experience great feelings of self-consciousness, in which she is convinced that others will be as aware of her thoughts as she is herself, and will condemn her for them. This is known as egocentric thought (see Jean Piaget, 1948), and may help to explain why so many adolescents are acutely fearful of the judgement of others, and find it so difficult to know what they really want. The girl may assume that others can read her mind, and may even be trying to take control of her. The result of this can be twofold: first the girl may begin to doubt her own personal identity, a process known as depersonalisation; and second, she may also start to hold very negative attitudes towards herself. A number of studies (for example, Morris Rosenberg, 1979; Roberta Simmons, 1987) have shown that girls are more vulnerable than boys to both depersonalisation experiences and low self-esteem, possibly because of their higher level of concern over the adequacy of their bodies, and the need to gain social approval. Low self-esteem often persists into adulthood, especially if the girl is not given enough encouragement and value for what she is.

At this point the adolescent is in considerable danger of extremely unhelpful advice from others, as her distress or anger may be formulated by others as symptomatic of an underlying mental illness or delinquency; or else it may be dismissed as the rantings of a child. In Lucy's case, both these reactions occurred: the psychiatrist saw her very eloquently expressed distress as a possible indicator of schizophrenia, while her family doctor saw her as a child who should try to grow up. Because the adolescent is not at all sure of herself and the veracity of her observations, she is particularly vulnerable to the reactions of others, and is quite likely to accept the 'wisdom' of others concerning her experiences. This may in turn complicate matters, as she tries to formulate her experiences in terms which are not her own. The result can be confusion and anxiety, as the adolescent does not know whether to trust her own judgements or whether to concur that she is indeed in the wrong.

Perhaps the judgement which the adolescent girl is most likely to dread is that she is not 'normal', a fear which will of course be supported if she is referred for medical or psychiatric help. But it is not only members of the helping professions who can threaten her sense of security: it is often her family and peers who can seem most insistent on her conforming to certain ways of behaving. The views of others loom particularly large in the eyes of adolescents who have not yet established a secure sense of self: the adolescent will repeatedly check on the presumed judgements of others, and constantly compare herself with what she assumes to be 'normal'. David Smail (1984) describes very vividly the consequences for the individual of trying to bury the truth of their own subjectivity in the language and standards of others:

Much of our waking life is spent in a desperate struggle to persuade others that we are not what we fear ourselves to be, or what they may discover us to be if they see through our pretences. Most people, most of the time, have a profound and unhappy awareness of the contrast between what they *are* and what they *ought* to be.... Behind many 'symptoms' of anxiety lies an injury to the person's self-esteem, a despairing inarticulate awareness that he or she has not lived up to the standards of adequacy which we are all complicit in setting.

(Smail, 1984:4–5)

School and parental pressures

A further source of pressure and self-doubt for the adolescent girl is the fact that for the majority, adolescence combines the time of maximum academic stress with the time of maximum personal and social growth. In a sense adolescence is the first encounter the developing woman will have with the demands of 'Superwoman', in that she starts to experience the pressures to be competent in both work and personal spheres. Being able to look good in school as well as having done the homework is simply too much for many girls who are faced with a choice. All too often they choose the former, with wide-reaching consequences for future life opportunities. It has become evident, for example, that co-education, despite appearing to offer girls a more natural life in school than single-sex education, has, in fact, deleterious effects on exam results, especially in maths, science and computing (Jennifer Shaw, 1980; Valerie Walkerdine, 1985). But whichever choice is made, girls are likely to experience a considerable degree of anxiety about their choices, which do not seem to be quite so acute for boys. Parents may also put pressure on their daughters to make certain career choices without paying close attention to their feelings; for example, Lucy's parents were not supportive of her wish to enter the career of nursing mentally and physically handicapped people. It is possible that Lucy was choosing this option because of unexpressed and unexplored fears of the adult world, and as a way of resolving her own need for nurturance, but neither her parents nor her teachers had really taken the time to discuss Lucy's preferences with her, nor to find out the reasons for her choice. Hence she may have become locked in to a certain choice, without ever really being able to explore the options in depth.

It is still surprisingly common that, as in Lucy's case, adolescent girls are discouraged both overtly and covertly from academic or professional ambitions, and are pressured against their wills into leaving school for a career which does not have good long-term prospects. Educational institutions at all levels ease girls into subjects which do not have high status (such as domestic science), and as Marlaine Lockheed (1985) has shown, effectively restrict the access of girls to computing and scientific facilities. Furthermore, many girls have a considerable amount of domestic responsibility at the same time as academic pressure; as we will show in Chapter 5, women and girls do far more housework than men or boys. Even if she is not asked to take on extra domestic responsibilities, the adolescent girl will also be aware of the need to develop her social and physical attractiveness, as well as her caring skills: all of which takes time and energy, and distracts her from academic achievement.

Implications for therapy

It is understandably difficult for those working with adolescents, who *do* change their views on what they think and what they want, *not* to assume that their views are of comparatively little account. This is especially true of girls who are likely to be less assertive then boys in insisting on their right to make their own decisions (Ann Dickson, 1982). In particular, girls' wishes to be acceptable to others, and to respond empathically to the needs of others, may mean that they do not have many opportunities to assert their own control over their life choices. These psychological hesitations, combined with the many existing legal, social, domestic, and traditionalist restrictions on the patterns of life open to women, mean that adolescence is a crucial time for choice-making, in a context which does not offer many choices to girls for both practical and psychological reasons.

There are, therefore, a number of implications for both individual therapists working with young women, and for the wider network of those who have responsibility for adolescents, to ensure that the adolescent girl is limited as little as possible by the society into which she has been born. We shall now consider a number of these implications.

Individual therapy

The first point to be considered by therapists working with adolescent girls is that they should be especially careful not to impose their own views on to the adolescent, but should instead try to encourage her to express her own needs and wishes. The adolescent girl may need considerable support in order to do so, as she is likely to be very sensitive to the judgements of others, even if she overtly denies this, and behaves in a very grown-up or defiant way. One of the major issues is likely to centre on autonomy and dependence, as the adolescent tries out her ideas and feelings, and simultaneously seeks protection and guidance from the therapist. It is almost inevitable that she will judge any therapist to have enormous power, and at least initially, to belong to the world of teachers and parents. Hence trust is a central issue, as the adolescent will probably be wary of either betrayal or any attempt to control her without her consent.

If trust *is* established between the two, the therapist can then, first through careful listening and then through analysis of the relationship which develops between them, gain insight into the nature of the girl's relationships with parents and other authority figures, and in particular, the extent to which she has managed to develop an autonomous sense of self. During therapy, the adolescent girl may at some stage start to act in a very childish way, as if to elicit parenting from her therapist. But in addition, she may crave or even demand respect and attention for her developing adult self. The therapist should attempt to maintain a special kind of relationship with the girl – one in which her needs to be both independent and nurtured are respected simultaneously.

Involvement of the wider network: the family

Since many of the conflicts and difficulties experienced by adolescents occur within the family, it may be helpful to offer family therapy for at least some adolescents. Very frequently the adolescent herself has become the medium through which some family pathology is expressed, and the conflicts which she is experiencing may be relieved when, for example, her parents deal with some issue between themselves. A very clear example of this is anorexia nervosa, which, according to Salvador Minuchin (1974), often demonstrates a pathological family structure, in which the anorexic child may have been acting as a substitute parent, or in which boundaries are so diffused between family members that the child expresses the distress felt by someone else. Alternatively, it could be the anorexic symptoms which hold the family together. Virgina Satir (1967) also suggests that lack of open family communication can cause disturbance in family members. She suggests that it is frequently adolescents who have less ability to defend or express themselves verbally who communicate the family distress through symptoms or disturbed behaviour.

Therapy in these circumstances involves the whole family. The task of the therapist is often to take the onus of the family problem off the adolescent, and to relocate it where it belongs, quite possibly between the parents. Although this form of therapy may appear to ignore the particular feelings of the adolescent herself, it is at least a very considerable improvement over other forms of treatment, for example, those for anorexia, which may involve forced feeding and strict behavioural regimes to control food intake. In some other circumstances, the difficulties experienced by the adolescent can only be resolved by removing her from home. The obvious example here is sexual abuse within the family, and where for some reason it is impossible to remove the offending relative. It is essential to help the adolescent to talk about her experiences, and to provide her with encouragement and support while she unburdens herself. As Karen Alter-Reid and her colleagues (1986) point out, if disclosure of sexual abuse is met with denial or disbelief, the girl is far more likely to suffer depression and self-blame. Some victims of abuse will regress to earlier stages of behaving, or start acting seductively towards their therapists or care-givers. This has to be responded to with support and respect, as it may be the only way in which the girl knows how to gain attention and love.

Involvement of the wider social network: schools, employers, and the media

Awareness of the difficulties faced by almost all adolescent girls in a male-oriented society is crucial for all those who have responsibilities for the development of young women. Numerous obstacles exist in the way of an adolescent girl developing into a mature and autonomous woman who is also able to have satisfying and mutually dependent relationships with others, yet too many agencies simply add to these obstacles by providing structures which push girls further away from the goal of autonomy and the ability to relate in an adult way towards others. It is essential, for example, that teachers become more aware of their sex-typed behaviour in schools (see Valerie Walkerdine, 1986, for a discussion of this issue); that girls are given more positions of authority in schools; that employers seek to eradicate sexually biased careers material; that the media place less emphasis on the attainment of thinness and beauty as a measure of the value of women; and that more social and sporting facilities are opened to women, in order to encourage them to develop their skills and abilities in a wide variety of areas. These are simply some examples of the changes which are needed if young women are to be allowed to develop themselves to anything like their full potentials. Yet they are vital if the full development of girls is not to be tragically stunted almost before it starts.

In the remaining chapters of this book, we trace the stages of women's development beyond adolescence, through the establishment of adult relationships, sexuality, and motherhood, into the mature years. Many of the issues initially raised in adolescence will recur, as questions of dependence and autonomy form the crucial arena in which psychodynamic and social influences are resolved, throughout the rest of the young woman's life.

References

Alter-Reid, K., Gibbs, M., Lachenmeyer, J., Sigal, S., and Massoth, N. (1986) 'Sexual abuse of children: a review of the empirical findings', *Clinical Psychology Review* 6: 249–66.

Bar, V. (1987) 'Change in Women', in S. Ernst and M. Maguire (eds), *Living with the Sphinx: papers from the Women's Therapy Centre*, London: The Women's Press.

Bardwick, J. (1971) *Psychology of Women*, New York: Harper & Row.

Bem, S. (1974) 'Measurement of psychological androgyny', *Journal of Consulting and Clinical Psychology* 42: 155–62.

Briscoe, M. (1982) 'Sex differences in psychological well-being', *Psychological Medicine*, Monograph Supplement I.

Bruch, H. (1974) *Eating Disorders*, New York: Basic Books.

Burns, A. and Homel, R. (1986) 'Sex role satisfaction among Australian children: some sex, age and cultural group comparisons', *Psychology of Women Quarterly* 10: 285–96.

Bush, D.M. (1987) 'Changing definitions of self for young women: the implications for rates of violence', in T. Honess and K. Yardley (eds) *Self and Identity: Perspectives across the lifespan*, London: Routledge & Kegan Paul.

Carlson, R. (1972) 'Understanding women: implications for personality theory and research, *Journal of Social Issues* 28: 17–32.

Chodorow, N. (1978) *The Reproduction of Mothering*, Berkeley: University of California Press.

Crisp, A.H. (1980) *Anorexia Nervosa: let me be*, London: Academic Press.

Davies, E. and Furnham, A. (1986) 'Body satisfaction in adolescent girls', *British Journal of Medical Psychology* 59: 279–88.

Dickson, A. (1982) *A Woman in Your Own Right*, London: Quartet Books.

Drabble, M. (1967) *Jerusalem the Golden*, Harmondsworth: Penguin.

Eichenbaum, L. and Orbach, S. (1985) *Understanding Women*, Harmondsworth: Penguin.

Erikson, E. (1950) *Childhood and Society*, New York: Norton.

Franz, C. and White, K. (1985) 'Individualism and attachment in personality development', *Journal of Personality* 53: 224–56.

Gilligan, C. (1982) *In a Different Voice: psychological theory and women's development*, Cambridge, MA: Harvard University Press.

Griffen, C. (1985) *Typical girls? Young Women from School to Job Market*, London: Routledge & Kegan Paul.

Hagglund, V. (1981) 'Feminine sexuality and its development', *Scandinavian Psychoanalytic Review* 4: 127–50.

Kashani, J.H., Beck, N.C., Hoeper, E.W., Fallahi, C., Corcoran, C.M., McAllister, J., Rosenberg, T.K., and Reid, J.C. (1987) 'Psychiatric disorders in a community sample of adolescents', *American Journal of Psychiatry* 144: 584–9.

Kohlberg, L. (1966) 'Stage and sequence: the cognitive-developmental approach to socialization', in D. Goslin (ed.), *The Handbook of Socialization Theory and Research*, Chicago: Rand McNally.

Kohlberg, L. (1969) 'Continuities and discontinuities in childhood and adult moral development', *Human Development*, 12: 93–120.

Laurence, M. (1975) *The Diviners*, Toronto: Bantam-Seal.

Lawrence, M. (ed.) (1987) *Fed Up and Hungry*, London: The Women's Press.

Lees, S. (1986) *Losing Out: sexuality and adolescent girls*, London: Hutchinson.

Levinson, D. (1979) *Seasons of a Man's Life*, New York: Random House Inc.

Lockheed, M. (1985) 'Women, girls and computers: a first look at the evidence', *Sex Roles* 13: 115–22.

Loevinger, J. (1976) *Ego Development*, San Francisco: Jossey Bass.

Macleod, S. (1981) *The Art of Starvation*, London: Virago.

Marcia, J. (1987) 'The identity status approach to the study of ego identity development', in T. Honess and K. Yardley (eds) *Self and Identity: perspectives across the lifespan*, London: Routledge & Kegan Paul.

Miller, A. (1984) *Thou Shalt Not Be Aware*, London: Pluto Press.

Miller, J. B. (1976) *Towards a New Psychology of Women*, Harmondsworth: Penguin.

Minuchin, S. (1974) *Families and Family Therapy*, London: Tavistock.

Mitchell, J. (1974) *Psychoanalysis and Feminism*, Harmondsworth: Penguin.

Padel, U. and Stevenson, P. (1988) *Insiders: women's experiences of prison*, London: Virago.

Penfold, P.S. and Walker, G.A. (1984) *Women and the Psychiatric Paradox*, Milton Keynes: Open University Press.

Piaget, J. (1932) *The Moral Judgement of the Child*, New York: The Free Press.

Piaget, J. (1948) *Language and Thought of the Child*, London: Routledge & Kegan Paul.

Pincus, L. and Dare, C. (1978) *Secrets in the Family*, London: Faber & Faber.

Rosenberg, M. (1979) *Conceiving the Self*, New York: Basic Books.

Rosenberg, M. (1987) 'Depersonalisation: the loss of personal identity', in T. Honess and K. Yardley (eds) *Self and Identity: Perspectives across the lifespan*, London: Routledge & Kegan Paul.

Satir, V. (1967) *Conjoint Family Therapy: a guide to theory and technique*, Palo Alto: Science and Behavior Books.

Sayers, J. (1982) *Biological Politics: feminist and anti-feminist perspectives*, London: Tavistock.

Shaw, J. (1980) 'Education and the individual: schooling for girls or mixed schooling – a mixed blessing?', in R. Deem (ed.) *Schooling for Women's Work*, London: Routledge & Kegan Paul.

Simmons, R. (1987) 'Self-esteem in adolescence', in T. Honess and K. Yardley (eds) *Self and Identity: perspectives across the lifespan*, London: Routledge & Kegan Paul.

Smail, D. (1984) *Illusion and Reality: the meaning of anxiety*, London: Dent.

Striegel-Moore, R.H., Silberstein, L.R., and Rodin, J. (1986) 'Towards an understanding of risk factors for bulimia', *American Psychologist* 41: 246–61.

Walkerdine, V. (1985) 'Science and the female mind: the burden of proof', *Psychological Critique*, 1: 1–20.

Walkerdine, V. (1986) 'Post-structuralist theory and everyday social practices: the family and the school', in S. Wilkinson (ed.) *Feminist Social Psychology*, Milton Keynes: Open University Press.

Williams, J. (1984) 'Women and mental illness', in J. Nicholson and H. Beloff (eds) *Psychology Survey*, 5, Leicester: British Psychological Society.

Chapter three

Making and breaking relationships

Laura's story

I first met Laura shortly after she had registered at college for her second year of studies. When she first came in to see me, I noticed that she was looking rather red-eyed and strained. She asked if she could have a few words, and told me that she had decided to abandon her present course of studies, and leave college at the end of term. In addition, she wondered if I knew how she could find out about possible job openings in social work or some related field, which might suit her better than her present course in English, despite the fact that she was obtaining good exam results. I asked Laura to sit down and explain why she suddenly felt this way:

> There doesn't seem to be much point going on with my studies. Every morning I get up and haul myself up to the library, where I sit and stare at a blank piece of paper. Sometimes it is such an effort that it almost feels as if I had lead running in my veins. I'm just not interested in English any more. Well, no, that's not quite true, I am interested in some of it, but it all seems such a drag and so useless. And there isn't much hope of a job afterwards anyway, so I might as well make a move now. Besides, I don't think I'm much good at it, and I may as well try to do something which is of some immediate use to someone else.

I asked her to explain what else was going on in her life at the moment. For example, had there been any personal changes recently? 'Not really. I suppose I should mention that my boyfriend Andy and I split up about five weeks ago. But I've got over that now, and anyway that shouldn't get in the way of my work.'

This news didn't really surprise me, given the emotional distress that Laura was evidently feeling, even if not admitting to herself. I asked her to say a little more about the split between her and Andy:

> It all happened so suddenly, because we were happy together, in fact lots of people said we were an ideal couple. I suppose I feel cross with myself for being so pathetic now. I don't know what to do, or how to feel any more. I met Andy about eighteen months ago, and we fell in love right away. We

met at a party, and it all seemed to be so perfect. We've been living together for over a year, and had been thinking about getting married at some point in the future. We've been sharing a flat near the city centre. Then apparently, a few months ago Andy met someone else, and, although of course it was a mutual decision, he sort of decided to leave. Well, I suppose it was really his decision, he wanted a new sort of relationship.

Laura then told me that Andy had broken the news to her quite suddenly, and within a day or so, had gathered up all of his belongings and moved in with his new girlfriend. A few of their friends had rallied round, and offered support to Laura, by inviting her to go out to the pub with them, and to share mealtimes. Yet every night, they went home in pairs, while she went back to an empty flat alone. Her heart ached, and she cried until her eyes were so red and sore that other people began to comment. She couldn't understand why the split had happened, and wanted to keep talking about it. Her friends were understanding for a while, but told her that she really should have got over it within a few weeks. Andy came to see how she was from time to time, and although she was glad to see him, she found it frustrating that he wouldn't really explain why he had left, apart from saying that he thought they had 'grown apart'. He also added that he felt that she had become too dependent on him. Apparently it was at this point that she had decided the best way of handling her feelings was to cover them up, and hope they would go away, although the thoughts and feelings would keep on intruding. Laura also added that she had not felt able to confide any of this in her parents, or to seek comfort from them, as they had never really approved of her living with Andy in the first place. 'They'd just say, "I told you so".'

I felt it would be important for Laura to discover for herself why the split had happened, so that she could learn to accept it and allow the possibility of other interests and relationships to develop in the future, especially as it appeared that her present attempts to cope with her grief through alternating periods of denial and rumination were actually hampering the process of growth and acceptance. I asked her to tell me more about her feelings about the relationship:

I suppose Andy was my first really serious boyfriend. He seemed so much fun and we had so much to talk about. I'm a very romantic sort of person. When I'm in a relationship I feel sort of complete. He was so wonderful, although I suppose if I'm honest I have to admit there were times when things weren't so great, and sex wasn't always all that good for me, though I thought it was for him. And sometimes I got the feeling that he didn't really love me, as me, but that it was convenient for him to have me around. But I thought I was doing what he wanted me to do, because he said he liked it if I was at home when he came back in the evenings. Then he said I was too dependent. Of course I was hurt when he first left, but I'm more or less over it now. There's more to life than a relationship with a man. And I *was* far too dependent on him. Anyhow, I always wanted to get myself established in a career, and here is my opportunity. . . not that I'm doing too well at it, am I?

In fact it seemed to me that Laura was still feeling very hurt by the loss of the relationship with Andy, and she was not being honest with herself when she said she had got over the break-up. She was also very confused by her feelings about Andy: she sensed that the relationship hadn't been quite as good recently as it had been in the past, which then seemed to her to mean that it *all* counted for nothing. At the same time she missed Andy a good deal. Her uneasiness about the quality of their relationship also seemed to be worrying her considerably, as did her confusion about whether she had or had not been too dependent on Andy.

Andy says that I was too dependent. He was probably right, which makes me feel even worse about myself and my ability to make judgements. I mean, my judgement was obviously at fault in that I had assumed that we were destined to stay together, and that he was happy with me. I always felt a little insecure, and kept asking him if he really loved me, although I assumed he did because he always liked to keep me to himself. I suppose in a different way, he was quite demanding, because he didn't really like it if I had too many other friends. But really I suppose it was my own fault, I was too clingy, I was too dependent and too demanding on him.

Laura and I talked for a long time that day, and agreed to meet regularly to talk things over in more depth. Over the next few weeks, Laura started to see that she was mourning the loss not only of her closest friend, but also of the future that she had anticipated as Andy's wife. In addition, she had lost a major way of structuring her practical and social life, since as her friend and companion, he had been intimately involved in how she acted on a daily basis, as well as being a part of her plans for the future. She slowly started to accept that her feelings of grief were natural, and to be accepted, not denied. But she then began to feel that without this central feature of her world, *nothing* seemed to have any structure or meaning, and that she herself was worthless:

I feel as if I've lost two things: Andy and most of myself. I feel so totally useless, so weak, so nothing. I don't mean that all women are nothing without a man, I mean that for *me*, I just don't feel right. Maybe what I really need is a new boyfriend.

My next aim was to help Laura to see that the loss of Andy probably resonated with other, older, long-forgotten losses. Facing this might help her to accept her present feelings, instead of despising herself for apparently being 'weak', or catapulting herself into another relationship. Such an awareness might then allow her to rebuild her sense of self-understanding and self-love on a more secure foundation. In an attempt to help Laura to understand what was happening to her, I therefore encouraged her to look again at the nature of her relationship with Andy, to see whether her feelings about it were similar to any which she had ever experienced before, with other people:

> Well, yes, I suppose so. With my father, and my mother too. I remember when I was little, I was always trying to please my parents, somehow I never seemed to be what they wanted me to be, I was always in the way and wanted too much attention. They were both incredibly busy people, which I don't resent at all, but I got the feeling that they were most pleased when I was keeping myself busy too. I have a very clear memory of staying with my aunt when I was about 8, and my parents had gone away for two weeks' holiday by themselves. I missed them terribly, and yet I knew I must never let on how desperate I felt. So I used to cry myself to sleep, but no-one ever knew. When they got home they gave me presents for being such a good girl, and being so grown-up. But I wasn't, I only pretended to be. Then I remember becoming obsessed with the question of whether my parents loved each other more than they loved me; they didn't seem to need me around, I felt almost as if I were an 'extra' in their busy lives. When I *did* want them, like to come to school or to play with me, I always felt I was being a nuisance, too demanding. I think I realised about then that friends were incredibly important to me. I used to have one special girlfriend, but when she went off with another girl, I felt awful inside. Do you know, it was rather like I feel now over Andy. When I was little I could never tell my parents if I was in trouble, I just felt so ashamed that I couldn't possibly tell them how I really felt. Like now: I couldn't face admitting to them about Andy and me splitting up.

Laura seemed quite surprised by the similarity of these childhood feelings with what was happening to her now. I tried to help Laura to accept that her shame, unhappiness, and confusion about suddenly being 'unnecessary' and unwanted was part of a bigger dread about being unacceptable in herself. The one person who had always seemed to want her and to need her no longer did so, and her other friends only wanted her up to a point. There appeared to be no-one around any longer who missed her presence; in a sense she therefore felt as if she herself was worth nothing. This realisation made Laura feel desperately unhappy, but also helped her to realise that Andy's departure wasn't the whole story. This in turn allowed her to start to look directly at herself, rather than herself-through-Andy's-eyes.

Laura came to see me frequently for a number of months, during which time she talked often about her feelings of worthlessness, which were heightened now that she was not 'in a relationship'. She gradually came to see how her attempts to deny the pain of Andy's loss, although understandable, had actually hampered her facing up to her sense of personal vulnerability. She also realised that now was not the time either to change careers, or to leap into another relationship. Despite the emotional pain, she looked hard at her self, and how little she valued that self unless given the approving mirror of the all-important 'relationship'.

This allowed her to reassess her early experiences of being loved and how her immense need to be reassured about that love led her simultaneously to deny her need for love and to demand it. The way in which she valued herself changed gradually: she began to see that she was herself at the centre of her world, not merely herself as seen through the eyes of another. Over the weeks, she seemed to become much calmer and less frenetic in her relationships with other friends, and was eventually able to visit her parents and tell them about the break-up with Andy without feeling too defensive. To her astonishment, they were very supportive and sympathetic, without the dreaded 'We told you so!' Eventually Laura told me that she no longer felt the need to come and discuss things with me any more, as she was feeling much more secure in herself. She also told me that she had made some new friends of her own, and had definitely decided to remain at college in order to complete her studies.

Making and breaking intimate relationships

In the second half of this chapter we will discuss how women feel and act when both establishing and ending emotionally significant relationships. Here, as elsewhere in this book, it will become clear that there are two major types of influence which constrain women's experiences: those that are exerted from within, often with origins in the past, and those that exist outside, in the 'real' social and cultural world. It is vital to consider both these sources of influence, since, as we saw in Chapters 1 and 2, either form of analysis on its own is inadequate.

Before we turn to the main subject matter of this chapter, however, it must be noted that we are concentrating here primarily on *intimate* relationships, as other sorts of relationships will be covered in other chapters. In addition, the topic of sexuality will be discussed separately, in Chapter 4. We also want to point out that although many of the examples discussed here are significant relationships between women and men, this does not mean that these are the only or even the main sources of emotional closeness or warmth that are available for women; in fact the support women give to and obtain from each other forms an important part of their emotional lives. Further, we do not want to suggest that the establishment of intimate couple relationships are desirable for all women at all times. It may be what someone wants or needs at a given point in her life, but this in no way means that it is right for all women all times, or that having an intimate relationship is 'necessary' for everyone. Our examples should not therefore be understood in any way prescriptively. Indeed, we will see later, in Chapter 8, that many women can gain strength and a strong sense of themselves outside a couple relationship, particularly perhaps following a disengagement from a previously complicated intimacy with another person.

Influences on the development of intimate relationships

We have described the case of Laura because it allowed us to introduce a number of important issues in women's relationships, not because we want to provide an answer or solution to Laura's particular life dilemmas. There are no painless ways of making or breaking relationships, beyond facing up to the fact that all women have to make choices about how to conduct their relationships, in a world where many choices are severely limited or already prescribed. Not knowing this, and not knowing about the limitations which exist both in the social world and in the inner world of each individual's self, can make a woman even more vulnerable, and even less able to control what happens to her in her life and future relationships. Self-knowledge does not guarantee happiness or solutions to problems, but it may allow each woman to know more about who she is, what to do about becoming who she wants to become, and achieving what she wants to do. Likewise, for therapists to understand the cultural constraints on women's relationships will not guarantee effective therapeutic interventions, but may at least provide them with a reasonable framework from which to attempt to be of constructive assistance to women in distress.

Developing such understanding and self-knowledge depends on an awareness of the nature of the many influences which operate upon each woman's experiences of her own personal relationships. In this chapter we shall therefore examine each of the two major types of influence: first the psychological and psychodynamic; and second the social and cultural. We shall then look in detail at one issue which causes a great deal of unhappiness to many women in relationships: the issue of jealousy. We shall conclude the chapter, as elsewhere in this book, by looking at some of the implications of what we have written for those who work therapeutically with women in distress.

Psychological and psychodynamic influences

First we shall look at some of the ways in which psychological and psychodynamic issues influence the ways that women construct and develop intimate relationships with others. The psychology of child development and the psychology of interpersonal interaction are relevant here, so we shall draw upon them both in developing the first part of our analysis. We shall then turn to an analysis of repeating patterns and collusion in relationships, in order to try to understand some of the problems which many women seem to experience in their intimate relationships.

The contribution of child development

Perhaps the most important point to make when attempting to understand the intimate relationships of adults from a psychological viewpoint is that as adults, we do not suddenly 'have' relationships which are unconnected to all our previous experiences with other people. Instead, the nature and depth of our relationships *develop* through and out of the relationships which we have had in the past with our families and childhood companions. Simultaneously, our emotional and personal development is profoundly affected by the nature of those interpersonal relationships. One of the most useful psychological explanations of this process is that emerging from within the object-relations perspective on psychodynamic theory, especially as described by one of the principal object-relations theorists, Harry Guntrip (1971). Other writers who have proved helpful in this field include Donald Winnicott (1957) and Heinz Kohut (1971).

Object-relations theorists consider that early childhood experiences hold the key to an understanding of later emotional development, and have described how the total dependence of babies on their care-givers slowly changes during infancy into a situation of partial dependence. This development, suggests Harry Guntrip (1971), is crucial for the later emotional wellbeing of the adult. Given secure enough conditions, small children may begin to feel confident in making tentative and initially brief explorations away from familiar people. The success of these separations depends to a large extent on the ability of the child to hold on to a 'memory' of safe, familiar people in their absence (see also Chapter 7). This process, known as 'internalisation', is then a central feature of successful emotional development. Slowly the child's ability to hold on to a memory of a familiar person matures, and children can cope with progressively longer separations. However, for those children who have not successfully attached themselves to a familiar person or people, two reactions may take place: either a protracted and augmented protest, which renders them desperately unhappy about separations long after their age-mates can cope successfully with them; or alternatively, a compliant toleration of separation where they appear not even to react when their habitual care-giver returns.

Guntrip suggests that such reactions, when maintained later in adulthood, may well underlie difficulties in intimate relationships. For example, there is on the one hand the over-dependence of those who cling desperately on to others and who fear being alone, preferring any company rather than being by themselves; and on the other hand, there is the withdrawn false independence of people who find it difficult to form relationships of any sort and who dare not risk too much emotional intimacy. Such people fear the loss of their autonomy in becoming involved with others, and remain fundamentally isolated. Harry Guntrip, following Ronald Fairbairn (1952) suggested that the optimal state for adults is one of 'mature dependence' in which the person can risk intimacy and closeness without fearing either that he or she will disintegrate if other people go away, or be suffocated by others.

However, Luise Eichenbaum and Susie Orbach (1983) have pointed out that the early experiences of girls often makes it very difficult for them to achieve the goal of 'mature dependence'. There is plenty of evidence to suggest that most women's upbringing stresses their sensitivity and responsiveness to the needs of others, often to the neglect of their own needs (see, for example, Rae Carlson, 1972; Judith Hall, 1978; as well as the discussion in Chapter 2 of this book).

Having been taught since babyhood that their main responsibility is to be responsive to the needs of others, many women feel profoundly uneasy when considering what they want themselves. As a consequence, when a woman *does* try to express what she wants, she will often do so with many apologies and much complicated circumlocution. Paradoxically, this is then understood as evidence of her demandingness, and inability to know what she really wants. This constellation of her reactions, together with the reality of her economic dependence on others, often means that it is relatively difficult for a woman to achieve mature, adult autonomy, or unconflicted dependence within her adult intimate relationships.

The contribution of studies of interpersonal interaction

A number of studies of the psychology of interpersonal interaction have recently suggested that relationships of all levels of intimacy have a major impact on constructing each individual's personal identity (see, for example, Sarah Hampson, 1988). Interpersonal relationships thus both create, and are created by, each individual. The significance of this deceptively simple statement for women's intimate relationships can perhaps be seen most clearly when comparing women's and men's experience of their relationships. Some writers have suggested that the two sexes inhabit different 'psychological worlds' which are based on the expectations and understandings that others have of them, as well as on each person's own individual experience (see, for example, Carol Gilligan, 1982; Nancy Chodorow, 1978; Alexandra Kaplan, 1986). One key differentiating factor between these two 'worlds' seems to be that for women, the location of a sense of self, as well as the main source of self-esteem, lies in relationships with others; whereas for men, self-esteem and selfhood lie in the achievement of control or mastery. As a consequence, interpersonal relationships are often more central in women's lives than in men's: women give more to them but also gain more from them.

In addition, evidence exists that the modes of relating which tend to be used by women and men differ: while women tend to relate to others through empathy and identification, men are more likely to use analytic or theoretical ways of relating, or making sense of things. A clear example of the distinction can be seen in the ways that individuals converse with each other: women tend to find it much easier than men to develop emotional intimacy, while men's relationships are far more likely to be based on shared interests and ideas (see Brian Little, 1972; Michael Argyle and Monika Henderson, 1985). Women are also more likely to sustain contact with those with whom they are close, whereas men are more likely to respond in an immediate way and not engage in many relationship-maintenance activities, such as letter-writing, making personal telephone calls, remembering special anniversaries, and so on (see, for example, Robert Bell, 1981).

Furthermore, as we pointed out in Chapter 2, Carol Gilligan (1982) has also suggested that the process of moral reasoning is different for men and women:

while men may make moral judgements on the basis of rules and principles, women are more likely to hold personal standards and axioms which are based on relational concepts. This difference can have considerable implications for people's intimate relationships. Gilligan's research suggests that when faced with a moral or interpersonal dilemma, women are more concerned with the preservation of personal relationships and the happiness of individuals than with moral abstractions, while men are more likely to be concerned with the rights and wrongs of the matter. Consequently, when trying to end a relationship, for example, a woman is much more likely than a man would be to be careful to preserve the other's self-esteem, while a man is more likely to insist on deciding who did or did not behave 'badly' according to some externally recognised moral code. It seems unlikely that these differences result primarily, if at all, from any predetermined, biologically fixed destiny, despite the suggestions of some traditional (and usually male) writers that this is the case. It seems more likely that such differences have resulted very largely from the different social and psychological contexts within which men and women live their lives.

Repeating patterns in relationships

In relationships with others, there is always a complex interplay amongst the patterns that develop during the process of growing up, the pressures exerted by others to perpetuate these patterns, and (as we shall argue shortly) the operation of social and cultural influences. But although these are powerful forces, none of them on their own successfully accounts for the nature of partner selection. Psychodynamic dimensions also play an important part in the development of relationships, and contribute a great deal to an explanation of how two people are attracted to each other in such a way that at least in some cases, they decide to make a long-term commitment to each other, with the intention of sharing affection, sexual intimacy, and support of an emotional and practical nature for the rest of their lives.

Modern forms of partner choice, although still influenced strongly by social class, educational background, and geographical factors, appear nowadays to be freer than in the past. A psychodynamic analysis suggests, however, that despite the apparent lack of constraints on partner choice, there are powerful emotional factors of which women and men may frequently be not fully aware, which also govern their attraction to others. Although it may be obvious to friends that a person always 'falls in love' with tall, thin, anxious men, or competent, generous women, this may not be so apparent to the individual involved. Indeed, to an amazingly high degree, people often find themselves being attracted to the same sort of partner, so that the same situations keep on cropping up time and time again with different partners. Of course, the problem is that the same sort of issues also seem to recur to cause the break-up of the relationship: paradoxically, the aspects of a person which are initially most attractive often also carry the seeds of the relationship's eventual dissolution or destruction. An example here is of a woman who is initially attracted to a man by his warmth and generosity towards others, including herself, but who then finds herself being infuriated by his apparent inability to stop giving (their) things away to other people. But then those attractive aspects are often what appeals to her most in the next person with whom she starts a relationship, which in turn may be destructive for exactly the same reasons.

At times it almost seems as if people are attracted by what they find most problematic. Of course, this is only true in a very limited sense, since very few people actively choose to be unhappy. Yet people often seem to find themselves repeatedly making the same 'mistakes' in relationships. The reason for this is quite simply that individuals are always seeking through their interpersonal relationships to meet their underlying emotional needs. Partners in a reasonably happy couple relationship have usually found some way of meshing their individual needs, so that most of their early emotional conflicts concerning intimacy and dependency are more or less resolved within the partnership. Partners in an unhappy relationship, however, are usually failing to meet each other's needs in some fundamental way. In fact, one of the best ways of trying to comprehend the dynamics involved between members of a couple is to look for similarities or complementarities in the types of emotional distress that they suffered as children, and thus to understand what kinds of 'needs' they have in present relationships.

Collusion in relationships

As we pointed out on p.49 when discussing the process of child development, early emotional experiences give rise to defensive reactions which are formed as a protection from the difficulties and anxieties that are encountered in daily life. These then often lead, in adulthood, to feelings of attraction towards other people who complement these reactions in some way. Thus, for example, one of the partners might habitually adopt a childlike stance when in a threatening situation, which the other partner reacts to by acting in a nurturing and motherly manner. Both partners collude with each other in playing out their respective roles, in that neither are aware of the habitual nature of their patterns of responding, or that they stem from similar childhood conflicts. For couples who can accommodate to each other fairly successfully, there may be a regular shifting in the balance of who acts in what way, so that overall no one person is in control all of the time, and the giving and taking is shared more or less equally. For others, however, the resulting relationship can be unsatisfactory for both. The person adopting, for example, the regressive 'child-like' position may well eventually feel stifled and dependent, while his or her partner, who takes the role of 'parent' all the time, may start to feel drained and exploited. These patterns can spiral until a crisis develops which may force the couple to change roles, or break out of the pattern in some other way. Less fortunately, and seeing no way to change, they may entrench themselves in their habitual ways of responding to each other, resulting in more pain for both.

There are many different patterns that such collusion can take: one common form has been called the 'master–slave' collusion (see Jurg Willi, 1984), in which one partner dominates the other, who willingly complies. Another example is the 'jealousy–infidelity' collusion, in which a shared fear of and yet fascination with sexual involvement with others leads to the development of a cycle in which one partner's excessive jealousy leads the other partner to feel trapped and hence pushed into infidelity. Eric Berne (1961) has also outlined some of the 'games' that couples can play, which despite being immensely destructive, can also have pay-offs for both partners in terms of mutual gratification and control. What all of these patterns, or collusions have in common is that they point to the powerful underlying reasons for mutual attraction between people, which often operate at a level below conscious awareness. The story of Ann in Chapter 1 is another good example of the operation of such underlying forces, which repeatedly and unhappily determined her choice of sexual partner.

Limitations of the conventional psychodynamic approach

A psychodynamic explanation can therefore help us to understand more about why women often tend to be attracted towards similar sorts of people. It helps to explain why, for example, a woman who leaves one violent relationship may find herself to her distress involved in another one, repeating the same pattern. However, conventional psychodynamic approaches tend to assume that women and men are equally able to have developed certain ways of responding, and that the choice of roles is based almost entirely on individual history. But this is evidently not the case. It is much more likely that women will provide the nurturant, passive, and dependent aspects of the relationship, thus playing what is conventionally known as the 'feminine' role. As a consequence, the opportunities for women to develop and experience other aspects of themselves in relationships are often severely limited.

Nancy Chodorow (1978) and Dorothy Dinnerstein (1978) have further argued that child-rearing practices can largely account for this situation. They believe that since it is women who provide the major part of children's early experiences, in that it is women who are the child's primary care-givers, society is constantly recycling a form of psychological development which perpetuates the inequality of access to feminine, caring roles in relationships. Girl children, with whom their mothers (or female care-givers) identify more closely, are brought up to show womanly responses (that is to be caring and sensitive to the needs of others); whilst boy children, who are 'different from' their mothers (or female care-givers), are less likely to be encouraged to be caring and sensitive to the needs of others. Chodorow and Dinnerstein both argue that as long as women are predominantly involved in caring for young children, as mothers, nursery nurses, nannies, infant-school teachers, and so on, sex differences in emotional responsiveness will continue. For these writers, change must come through the greater involvement of men in the tasks of motherhood. We will discuss the implications of these arguments on the nature of childrearing in more detail in Chapter 7.

Developments of the psychodynamic approach

Another recent and very helpful advance in thinking about women's psychological experiences in relationships has been put forward by Alexandra Kaplan (1986) and her colleagues. They draw upon findings from studies of both child development and interpersonal interaction, and suggest, in comparison with other, male-oriented theories which often emphasise separation and individuation, that it is *connection* with others which provides for women 'a primary context for action and growth, not a detraction from one's self-enhancement.... What is important is women's sense of taking an active role in the *process* of facilitating and enhancing connectedness with others' (Kaplan, 1986:235). Further, Kaplan suggests that psychological development is based on:

> mutual understanding and reciprocity of affect. It is the flow of empathic communication and mutual attentiveness from one to the other that not only permits the child to feel cared for, but also begins to develop in the child a sense of herself as actively participating in facilitating connection, and as one who derives strength and competence from these relational capacities.
>
> (Kaplan, 1986:239)

Hence the capacity to relate, and relationships themselves, are central to the definition and sense that a woman has of herself, rather than being merely stages in a process of self-actualisation.

Yet Kaplan (1986) also argues that since this capacity for relating is not highly valued culturally, women are restricted to 'less than the full use of their own resources' (p.235), and often fail to value themselves. In addition, as she places so much worth on relationships with others, a woman is particularly vulnerable to loss when relationships fail or end. The origins of this vulnerability may also lie in the past: Kaplan suggests that depression is extremely common in women who have experienced an unresolved sense of disconnection from their parent(s) in the past, together with an inability to reach mutuality and understanding with others in the present. The inability to relate satisfactorily to others then creates a deep sense of anger and inner destructiveness, and a loss of any sense of self-worth, which further deepens the woman's feelings of depression. The experiences described by Laura earlier in this chapter seem remarkably consistent with this view.

Social and cultural influences on relationships

We shall now turn to an examination of the second major type of influence on women's relationships: the social and cultural. An intimate relationship obviously does not develop in isolation, but is affected by the views and reactions of all those who know the individuals in the relationship; hence the formation and termination of an intimate relationship is a social as well as a personal event. This is the case not only because of the changes that forming or ending the relationship may entail for parents, children, and friends, but also because the individuals concerned have to establish new forms of identity for themselves, as members of a 'couple', or as 'single' people. This isn't simply a case of social pressure (although this clearly exists, as, for example, in the case of young couples who feel they should get married for their parents' sake, or indeed of parents who feel they must stay together 'for the sake of the children'), but in most instances is also a case of working out a new sense of social and personal identity for each individual concerned.

Being in a couple and being single

The need to work out a new sense of the self applies particularly to women who enter or end a 'formal' relationship, such as marriage, but it also applies to anyone who makes public a change in an intimate relationship. For example, the woman who 'declares' herself as part of a couple then has to learn new ways of behaving, and relating to others outside the couple, which may involve modifying her existing relationships with others outside the couple, or developing a whole new set of relationships. The reactions of others tend to reinforce the 'coupledom', for example by always inviting the partners together, or by suddenly ceasing to share intimate confidences. Furthermore, once a 'couple' relationship is started, people around usually develop expectations that it will continue, and if the relationship subsequently breaks down, some explanation is usually demanded. As another example, the woman whose relationship has terminated will usually have a sense of having violated social expectations, and may feel intensely uncomfortable with others, experiencing a sense of shame and guilt at having somehow 'let other people down'. This could be seen clearly in Laura's case: after splitting up with Andy, Laura did not know how to relate to others, especially as she was conscious in some way of having become a 'problem' to other people.

This sense of being a problem to others clearly reflects and is magnified by the assumption, made by a world which is organised around couples, that single people are single by default or accident, never by choice. As pointed out by Alison Light (1985), single women in particular are 'still the special focus of all kinds of fears and fantasies', and are frequently seen as 'odd'. George Gissing's novel *The Odd Women* (1982) describes very clearly how hard it was in the past for women to carve out a legitimate role for themselves when so many myths about them existed, and although things are changing now, so that being a single woman is becoming more acceptable, much social organisation is still based on the couple or family unit. We will discuss the choice to remain alone in more detail in Chapter 8, but for now we simply want to point out that for some women, the state of being single can often mean feeling ostracised and different. Besides having an effect on single women themselves, this will clearly also exert pressures on women in relationships to maintain those relationships, even in the face of awareness that all is not well, and that life as a single woman could in fact be preferable. Obviously the view of single women as being worthy of pity or condemnation is a view which will discourage women from risking a challenge to their existing relationships, and will also mean that making a choice to become single is much more difficult.

In addition to this social pressure to be part of a couple, there are also considerable institutional and traditional pressures to ensure that women remain in a dependent and interconnected position in relation to men. Jean Baker Miller (1976) describes how women are constantly defined in terms of their relationship to men, as, for example in their surnames, legal status, and financial position, and are also continuously warned against the dangers inherent in trying to be independent. She also suggests that in a manner which is typical of all 'dominant' classes, men retain the right to protect and control 'their' women, and thereby maintain their dominance and power. Being members of the 'subordinate' group, women do have some power, but it is restricted to areas which are not valued much by the dominant group, such as the ability to care for others, express emotions, or raise children. As a consequence, women have less overt power in their relationships, and have instead to strive to retain some form of covert control over their own lives often by using devious and informal strategies and bargains. These manoeuvres, not surprisingly, frequently lead to feelings of dissatisfaction, exploitation, and frustration in both partners.

Economic and social issues in relationships

In any society, a variety of expectations and social traditions concerning the way that people should interact means that intimate relationships have cultural as well as personal significance. In addition, these expectations and traditions govern much of the conduct of both partners in the relationship. The nature of these traditions and expectations will vary from one social group to another, although some common factors seem to exist across most cultures. For example, there is usually some expectation of reciprocity in intimate relationships, so that each partner will support and help the other, and that the two will share at least some of their real or symbolic commodities. Exactly how this is done varies between cultures, and over time, but a common view of women's place in intimate relationships is that she should 'trade' sexual favours for economic security. This is demonstrated by the emphasis placed by many cultures on her (but not his) virginity before, and sexual exclusivity after marriage, and his (but not her) financial support of the household. Nevertheless, this cultural emphasis actually conceals the fact that the woman's economic contribution is also a crucial part of the bargain. This is seen most clearly in the dowry system, but it is also evident in the fact that after marriage, most women will be expected to work without pay for their new husbands and families.

It is essential to realise that this traditional view does not just apply to 'primitive' cultures. In fact the pattern of contemporary marital partnerships (in which women and men at least theoretically share emotional and sexual feelings as well as forming the basis for an economic family unit) is in reality a relatively new one. Although historians of the family (for example, Alan Macfarlane, 1986;

John Gillis, 1986) continue to debate the precise nature of family forms which have existed in the past in western society, there does seem to be evidence that mutual love and affection has rarely been the main basis for determining partner choice over the past few centuries. For example, for the upper and emergent middle classes in the nineteenth century, the amassing and presentation of wealth played a major part in deciding upon what were, in effect, arranged marriages. Social-class factors modify this conclusion somewhat, in that children of poor families were possibly less constrained than those in propertied classes, but it is unlikely that economic considerations were unimportant in any social group.

It might have been assumed that changing social and economic structures, such as the limitation of the private ownership of property, and more legal rights for women, would, by freeing women from being 'sold' into loveless marriages like mere goods and chattels, have led to a greater likelihood of happiness in marriage. While this has indeed happened for some couples, it has not guaranteed happiness for everybody, for a number of reasons, including the tendency noted earlier that people in choosing their adult partners often repeat patterns laid down in their childhoods. But another reason for unhappy marital choice may be cultural in nature, with the result that many relationships in our culture are no more likely to bring happiness than those resulting from the older, arranged-marriage system.

This cultural reason is the operation of what can be labelled as 'the myth of romantic love'. By calling romantic love a 'myth' we are not saying that it does not exist, but rather that it exists at a very powerfully unconscious level both in individuals and in society as a whole, and has an enormous influence over people's behaviour in relationships. A myth can be described as an encapsulation of a set of beliefs and meanings which are important to the society, and which is handed on from generation to generation. The story of boy meeting girl, falling in love, overcoming some natural or supernatural obstacle which impedes the development of the relationship, leading eventually to a happy-ever-after ending, lies at the root of much of our poetry, folklore, fiction, and drama, and as such exists as one of the most powerful cultural beliefs in our society (see also Dennis de Rougement, 1956; Robert Johnson, 1984).

It is probably the case that romance is seen by most people in western cultures as the most desirable basis for the formation of an intimate relationship. Yet the myth of romantic love in fact dictates that *romance* rather than love or mutual concern, is the basis on which relationships should be built. In the typical romantic match, the couple meet when they are both young and beautiful, have to face a certain amount of opposition to their relationship from parents (maybe because of differences in background or religion) but appear to others and to each other to be an 'ideal' couple. The two see in each other all that is good, noble, or ideal and believe that happiness for life ever after will be ensured if only they can secure the affections of the other. Any slight 'defect' in the other is overlooked, parental opposition or practical difficulties are overcome, and the future seems rosy and bright.

However, after a short experience of being together, both members of the couple start to notice slight shortcomings in the other, which may at least initially simply mean that they no longer assume that the other is totally perfect. The longed-for rosy future has not quite materialised, and the ordinary problems of life, such as money worries, housing probems, or job insecurities, have not in fact disappeared. Thus it is ruefully discovered that romance does not conquer all. In addition, the other is no longer 'forbidden fruit' so there is no sense of novelty or excitement to disguise any lack of real concern for the other person as a real person. All of this then leads to resentment of the other for not living up to the myth. But such is the power of the myth that individuals rarely take time to look at themselves or each other, and ask why this has happened. Instead, each of them withdraws into a state of resentment, disappointment, and frustration in which the other is blamed for the failure. Before very long, one or both members of the couple may become involved, unknown to the other, in a series of clandestine and rather desperate love affairs with other people, which seem much more satisfactory, at least in the short term, and bolster up the romantic myth that someone somewhere is the perfect answer to all one's romantic yearnings and desire.

For women especially, the romantic story poses a problem. For a start, most of the active figures in such stories are men, and the main role allocated to women is to be beautiful, passive, and virginal. Most women, who are not beautiful or passive, and who cease very quickly to be virgins, therefore fail as romantic heroines. But more importantly, the vision of the relationship portrayed is just a fairy-tale one: there are no complete human beings in myths, although there is plenty of raw human emotion. In romance, the essence of the emotion is that the pair 'fall in love', rather than loving or knowing each other. Essentially, such 'falling in love' involves not really seeing the other as the other truly is, but instead seeing a romanticised version of the other, with no room for blemishes or faults. When one is 'in love', the world seems to be a better place, and the other is seen as the personification of all that is best or most admirable. In fact, in the view of the lover, the beloved is more an ideal than a human being.

As we have noted, such a projection of idealism is sooner or later likely to result in disillusionment, and resentment towards the other, who is often blamed for having cheated or misled the lover. This is especially true for women, in that the fairy-tale image of youth, beauty, gentleness, and virginity is unlikely to be sustainable for any length of time in the real, domestic world of crying babies, unpaid bills, and wrinkles. Any relationship which is built upon such a myth is destined for disappointment, as the real person underneath is gradually discovered.

Evidence for both the pervasiveness and the shortcomings of this myth can be seen in the divorce statistics, which show that in the UK for example, the divorce rate has increased six-fold in the last twenty years. Nevertheless, individuals still cling on to the belief that it will work next time: 30 per cent of marriages include at least one divorced partner, most usually the man (see Jackie Burgoyne, 1987).

Although the romantic myth is as deceptive for men as it is for women, the consequences of the myth for women are usually more serious, simply because it is usually harder, both socially and psychologically, for women to escape unscathed from unsatisfactory relationships. Especially if they have children, divorced or separated women are likely to be economically deprived and socially disadvantaged, and usually pay heavier financial penalties for the breakdown of a long-term relationship than men do. (We will discuss these points further in Chapter 8.) But in addition, since men have traditionally been taught to idealise women as pure, good, beautiful, and selfless, any deviation from this image of perfection on the part of an individual woman tends to be seen as a result of her personal weakness, as well as being a betrayal of his ideals. His accusations may therefore lead her to doubt her own worth and attractiveness, as well as causing her in some fundamental way to feel responsible for the failure of the relationship. Typically, like Laura, the woman trapped inside the romantic myth feels resentful and misunderstood, yet also guilty, and profoundly unentitled to any rights to consider her own needs in the relationship. She is then seen (and sees herself) as demanding and selfish, and as having 'let herself go', while he withdraws in a state of resentment, often to find someone younger who will conform at least for a while to his vision of what a woman 'should' be like.

The problem of jealousy

Having looked at some of the major influences on women's experiences in relationships, we will now turn to an examination of one issue which occurs repeatedly in most intimate relationships: jealousy. Jealousy is a powerful emotion because it simultaneously has implications for individuals at psychological, psychodynamic, social, and cultural levels. As was seen in the case of Laura in the first part of this chapter, and of Julia in Chapter 1, the relationships that we have with other people often make up the major components of our personal selves; hence a threat to a central relationship constitutes a serious threat to the self, and to self-esteem. In addition, the possibility of losing a partner is an extremely powerful threat because such a loss often resonates with earlier losses, usually those experienced during the formative stages of childhood. Further, because of the constellation of behaviours, social significances, and meanings that are developed between the couple, intimate relationships are particularly powerful confirmers or disconfirmers of our social identities, so that the individual's experience of the world is inevitably modified by the actions of his or her partner. When that partner disappears, or threatens to disappear, it is more than a relationship which is at risk: it is a major part of the person's social world.

Jealousy has been described as the response to a threat of being replaced by a rival. According to Jeff Greenberg and Tom Pyszczynski (1985) it is seen differently by different people: some see it as a sign of love while others see it as a sign of insecurity and fear of loss. Although it is an experience common to men and women, Jessie Bernard (1977) has suggested that it is felt and described differently by the two sexes. She reports studies of jealousy which suggest that women are more likely to feel anxious and personally threatened than men when they feel jealous, while men are more likely to feel sexually insecure. This she explains by pointing to the importance women place on personal relationships. It may well be because interpersonal relationships are so very central to women that the threat of loss of an exclusive intimate relationship is more damaging to a woman's stable sense of self than to a man's; while a man, who may feel a need to assert his masculinity through sexual control, may feel more threatened on a sexual level by the possibility of desertion.

On a personal, psychodynamic level, women's jealousy is rarely experienced simply as a fear of being displaced by someone else; it also tends to involve self-hatred and a feeling of being worthless and weak. This seems highly likely to relate to very early feelings of dependency and panic when threatened by loss. As we saw in Laura's story, an important aspect of Laura's unhappiness after the break-up of her relationship with Andy was her inability to accept her feelings of resentment and jealousy towards Andy and his new lover, and her sense of guilt and self-blame over her dependency on him. Similar feelings were reported by Julia (see Chapter 1).

In addition, there are of course numerous social consequences to threatened or actual loss of a partner. For a woman in particular it can bring economic ruin and damage to her social reputation. The social stigma attached to having been jilted, rather than doing the jilting, probably reflects this, as it is more than 'mere' emotional pain which is suffered when a partner goes off with someone else, but also injury to a person's sense of pride and prestige in the eyes of others. Yet most cultures actually encourage men, overtly or covertly, to be sexually adventurous, while women who are not 'faithful' to their husbands are treated very differently and with much less acceptance (see, for example, the work of Margaret Mead, 1931). This distinction is reflected both legally and culturally, and parallels beliefs held in different cultures about property and ownership. Kingsley Davis (1936) points out how sexual jealousy is a response to sexual rule-breaking, and how the emotion of jealousy therefore depends upon the way in which a particular culture determines the distribution of sexual 'property' amongst its members. This is in itself determined by how each culture views the legitimacy of the claims of different groups within that culture to own and control property of all types; which is in turn often dependent on race, sex, class, and colour.

Jealousy and intimacy

It is perhaps relevant to note at this point that possibly one of the most powerful impacts of the Women's Movement in the sixties and seventies was its attempt to help women to become more positive about themselves and their independence from men. Other life goals than merely finding a partner were accentuated, and women felt that within relationships they should not be dependent, clingy, neurotic, and needy in the way that they assumed women had been in the past.

However, as a consequence, many women, like Laura, came to regard some of their emotional feelings of possessiveness towards their sexual partner with suspicion and distaste. To their own surprise, they found themselves unable to overcome feelings of possessiveness and jealousy, and consequently added feelings of guilt to the distress. Yet such emotions are rarely under conscious control. Many jealous feelings stem from early childhood experiences of threat and panic at the apparent loss of love and attention from the mother, in favour of somebody else, either another child, or worse, because of an even more hopelessly and unbeatable rival, the father. This extremely anxiety-provoking experience is reinvoked when a loved one threatens to become intimate with someone else. Similar emotions of panic and desolation are awakened, and the deserted adult feels as powerless and desperate as the betrayed child.

As we will discuss in more detail in Chapter 4, intimate sexual relationships are especially powerful in their capacity to enhance or diminish views of the self. For most women, being sexually intimate isn't simply a question of establishing her social status and identity on the one hand, or of gaining physical and emotional pleasure on the other, but is also an opening of her self to another person through the sharing of vulnerability and caring. Sexual love is an opportunity to express tenderness rather than defensiveness, and to give as well as to receive. The boundaries between the self and the other don't have to be so carefully protected against the risk of invasion or damage; instead, the experience of intimacy is one of 'being merged' with the other. Feelings of oneness, only (if ever) previously experienced in babyhood with her mother, are reawakened, giving the woman an overwhelming sense of peace and security. Paradoxically, this also strengthens the sense of self. However, this interpersonal experience of at least temporarily and partially letting go of defensiveness and separateness is also frightening, since the self is exposed to the other without guard. By being open to the other, the individual has allowed the possibility of rejection of the weak or non-coping parts of the self.

Having exposed themselves in this way, lovers can either share a connection which is based on a mutual understanding of need and vulnerability, or they can in one way or another withdraw from each other. This withdrawal can take the form of damaging or hurting, such as when one lover takes advantage of the other or when one person accuses the other of inadequacy; or it may take the form of abandoning the other. Again, this resonates with excruciatingly painful childhood experiences, when the child is made to feel inadequate or when mother's love is apparently given to someone else.

We aren't intending to come up with a solution to the 'problem' of jealousy. Rather, our aim is to point out some of the dynamics which underlie it. Only at that point is informed action possible, whether this is to leave a relationship, stay with it as it is, or try to change it. A similar point is made by David Smail (1984) when he says that it is only when people stop deceiving themselves that they can act in their own lives with anything like confidence or freedom. This doesn't mean, however, that life without self-deception is painless; indeed it may be that self-knowledge will actually make people face up to things they don't very much like in themselves. But instead of struggling in the dark with forces which are beyond their understanding, such self-knowledge, albeit painful, allows people the freedom of knowing where they are, and hence, the freedom to act.

Implications for therapy

Because intimate relationships are so central to women's sense of who they are, and to their happiness, it is not surprising that dissatisfactions with personal relationships are very frequently the motivating factor for seeing a therapist. Feelings of loss, severe disappointment, inadequacy, and self-blame in relationships lie at the root of much depression, which, as has been very well established, is twice as common in women as in men (see, for example, Monica Briscoe, 1982; Jenny Williams, 1984; Rachel Jenkins, 1985). However, sensitivity to the complex interplay of social and psychological influences on women's relationships is unfortunately limited amongst many professional groups. Conventional psychiatric treatment on the whole considers these feelings to be essentially medical problems, to be cured with drugs, or in severe cases, by hospitalisation or electric shock therapy. One major consequence of this medical approach has been to emphasise the helplessness and physiological inadequacy of women, who then have to rely for help on the interventions of doctors and their pharmaceutical prescriptions. Psychotherapy is only available to a very small number of women, and furthermore, some of the therapies offered may in fact be counterproductive, as many conventional therapists still stress the need for women to adapt themselves into the patterns normally accepted by a predominantly patriarchal society (see, for example, Phyllis Chessler, 1974; Marcia Kaplan, 1983; and the report of the American Task Force on 'Sex-bias and Sex-role stereotyping in psychotherapy', reported in Jacqueline Voss and Linda Gannon, 1978).

However, some therapists are well aware of the issues described in the earlier sections of this chapter, and are therefore more likely to be of help to women with relationship difficulties. In particular, some women psychotherapists have developed therapeutic approaches which take into account not only the social reality in which women live, and in which they have limited access to power and control, but also the personal psychodynamic development of each individual within her family, past and present. In a therapy relationship with a therapist who is aware of these questions, a woman can develop an understanding of the meaning of the conflicts which underlie her unhappiness, and through analysis of both the transference and the nature of the real therapy relationship, can develop more confidence to accept herself and to take more control of her own life. (These issues have also been discussed elsewhere by ourselves, see Sue Llewelyn and Kate Osborne, 1983.)

Issues in the therapy relationship

It is important for therapists working with women to be aware from the very start that many women come to psychotherapy feeling highly ambivalent about therapy. They know that they are unhappy, and yet they may also feel profoundly unworthy of the therapist's time and attention, feeling that others are much more deserving of the therapist's help than they are. This issue is often the first to be faced in the therapy relationship, as it frequently mirrors the feelings of inadequacy and unentitlement which the woman has in her other relationships. Alexandra Kaplan (1979) points out that the act of seeking help, especially for independent, career women, can threaten the woman's precarious sense of herself as competent, and hence the therapy will at least initially consist of alternating attempts to regain control of the therapy, and demands for the therapist to be more caring. Luise Eichenbaum and Susie Orbach (1983) also report that many women will attempt to terminate therapy before the therapeutic work is actually completed, which again reflects anxiety about being greedy, and taking too much. Related to this is the fear of harming the therapist by overwhelming her or him with neediness, which also reflects the woman's conflicts about the acceptability of her emotional self. One additional issue, which also arises frequently, is the fear that some women may have of losing their own boundaries and becoming merged with the therapist. All these issues, clearly shown in the transference relationship with the therapist, must be examined and resolved.

In addition, there is also a real personal relationship with the therapist, which has to be understood and used. The therapist can quite straightforwardly provide encouragement and support as the woman faces previously warded-off and painful feelings, and then tries out the consequences of her newly discovered and clarified emotions. If she is herself a woman, the therapist can act as a model who has also had to face similar issues in a patriarchal society, and to come to terms with her own needs for dependence and autonomy. Both these exeriences offer a sense of solidarity and support.

Recognition of the woman's own needs and goals

It is also essential for therapists working with women who have relationship problems to be aware of the psychological and social constraints and limitations which exist on them outside the therapy situation. This has at least two consequences. First, the therapist must be sensitive to the tendency of the woman to behave in a sex-appropriate way which may not in fact be helpful to her, although it may suit the culture in which she lives. In particular, the woman may seek to deny the legitimacy of her own needs in relationships, seeing her own task to be the emotional support of others. From a behavioural viewpoint, Jeanne Parr Lemkau and Carol Landau (1986) call women's conflicts over the legitimacy of their own needs the 'selfless syndrome', and suggest that therapy can include tasks such as the woman monitoring the time that she spends per day on activities for other people, compared with activities for herself. They also suggest cognitive restructuring and reframing techniques which allow women to question the logic of some of their prior assumptions about the 'right' way for women to behave in relationships. Some therapists (for example, Sheila Ernst and Lucy Goodison, 1981) have also suggested self-help therapy groups, including techniques such as fantasy work, role-play, and assertion training to help women to become confident in taking more control of their own needs in significant relationships.

The second consequence of which therapists should be aware is the importance of *not* imposing yet another set of demands upon the woman, this time from the therapist, to become someone who is more like the therapist's ideal. In her later work, Alexandra Kaplan (1986) points out that there is a considerable risk for women in therapy that self-expression through relationships will be mistaken for immature dependency, and that therapists may persuade women to be less selfless and to pursue goals of greater autonomy, irrespective of the woman's own personal wishes: in a sense imposing a male-oriented model of psychological development on to the woman. Yet this may not actually suit all women, whose personal development may depend more on their ability to develop themselves through relationships than on externally defined achievement. Another risk for women in therapy with therapists who are aware of some of the issues raised in this book and yet who fail to acknowledge the importance of individual emotional needs is the imposition of a model of the 'well-adjusted woman' as a replication of the therapist herself. Such a model may be simply inappropriate or impossible for many women in their own social contexts (see also the discussion by Joy Anne Kenworthy, 1979). These issues are particularly important when considering therapy with women who choose a different sexual identity or life style from that of the therapist (see Angela Douglas, 1987).

Issues in couple therapy

Difficulties in relationships are sometimes best approached not in individual therapy but with both partners. Yet here, too, conventional therapy can sometimes be profoundly unhelpful to women. Orthodox therapists tend to have very clear ideas about the appropriate ways for men and women to behave, which are often encouraged in couple therapy. One of us recently presented some of the ideas discussed in this book to a British conference of marital and sexual therapists, and received an extremely hostile reception from at least some of the therapists, who declared that men were men and women were women, and '*Vive la difference*'! Such therapists often consider that the best solution to relationship problems, usually brought initially by the woman, is adjustment to the socially accepted norms in which men hold the position of ultimate authority, and women are most appropriately kept busy servicing men and children. Hence the woman should learn to mould herself to meet the man's needs, and not be too demanding or 'selfish' about her own. Similar views about the distribution of authority between men and women are held by some family therapists, who will endeavour to support flagging male authority if the woman is considered to be too dominant, too possessive, or too 'anything unfemale' (see the discussions by Rachel Hare-Mustin, 1978; Molly Layton, 1984).

Of course, therapy which concerns relationships almost always means a change in the woman's feelings and actions towards others who are important to her. Hence a woman's therapy is likely to have consequences for her partner, both positive and negative. It is therefore often considered important to invite the partner, man or woman, into the therapy situation at some stage. In the isolation of individual therapy, the therapist may be totally unaware of significant issues between a couple which are only apparent when both partners are present. Luise Eichenbaum and Susie Orbach (1983) suggest that a key issue is dependency, which is frequently labelled as the woman's problem and reacted to with anger by her partner, which in turn is met by the woman's fear and resentment. This process, they suggest, may in fact divert attention from the man's own neediness and vulnerability. They comment: 'The man's defensive anger entwines with the woman's fear of anger and her feelings of unentitlement' (p.189) with the result that both are unhappy and disappointed with their relationship. Therapy with couples has therefore to be directed at uncovering the hidden needs of both partners, and seeing how unresolved childhood feelings are clouding the present relationship. The aim is to help each member of the couple to acknowlege their own needs, and hence to be able to develop their own autonomy as well as the capacity to express their desire for nurturance and care from each other.

One of the most important issues in most intimate relationships is, of course, sexuality. Because it is central to many women's lives, and has major implications for women's personal relationships, as well as for their ability to live independent and fulfilled lives, the following chapter is devoted entirely to the topic of sexuality.

References

Argyle, M. and Henderson, M. (1985) *The Anatomy of Relationships*, London: Heinemann.

Bell, R.R. (1981) 'Friendships of women and of men', *Psychology of Women Quarterly* 5: 402–17.

Bernard, J. (1977) 'Jealousy and marriage', in G. Clanton and L. Smith (eds) *Jealousy*, Englewood Cliffs, New Jersey: Prentice Hall.

Berne, E. (1961) *Games People Play*, Harmondsworth: Penguin.

Briscoe, M. (1982) 'Sex differences in psychological well-being', *Psychological Medicine*, Monograph Supplement 1.

Burgoyne, J. (1987) 'Marital happiness', *New Society*, pp. 13–14. 10 April.

Carlson, R. (1972) 'Understanding women: implications for personality theory and research', *Journal of Social Issues* 28: 17–22.

Chessler, P. (1974) *Women and Madness*, New York: Avon.

Chodorow, N. (1978) *The Reproduction of Mothering*, Berkeley: University of California Press.

Davis, K. (1936) 'Jealousy and sexual property', *Social Forces* 14: 395–405.

de Rougement, D. (1956) *Love in the Western World*, New York: Pantheon Books.

Dinnerstein, D. (1978) *The Rocking of the Cradle*, New York: Souvenir Press.

Douglas, A. (1987) 'Feminist psychotherapy and lesbianism: implications for theory and practice', paper presented at the Feminist Psychotherapy Conference, Leeds, UK, April.

Eichenbaum, L. and Orbach, S. (1983) *What do women want?* London: Fontana.

Ernst, S. and Goodison, L. (1981) *In Our Own Hands*, London: The Women's Press.

Fairbairn, W.D.R. (1952) *Psychoanalytic Studies of the Personality*, London: Routledge & Kegan Paul.

Gilligan, C. (1982) *In a Different Voice: psychological theory and women's development*, Cambridge, MA.: Harvard University Press.

Gillis, J.R. (1986) *For better, for worse: British marriages, 1600 to the present*, Oxford: Oxford University Press.

Gissing, G. (1982) *The Odd Women*, London: Virago.

Greenberg, J. and Pyszczynski, T. (1985) 'Responses to romantic jealousy and responses to jealousy in others', *Journal of Personality* 53: 468–79.

Guntrip, H. (1971) *Psychoanalytic Theory, Therapy and the Self*, New York and London: Basic Books.

Hall, J. (1978) 'Gender effects in decoding nonverbal cues', *Psychological Bulletin* 85: 845–7.

Hampson, S. (1988) *The Construction of Personality*, 2nd edn. London: Routledge.

Hare-Mustin, R. (1978) 'A feminist approach to family therapy', *Family Processes* 17: 181–94.

Jenkins, R. (1985) 'Sex differences in minor psychiatric morbidity', *Psychological Medicine*, Monograph Supplement 7.

Johnson, R.A. (1984) *The Psychology of Romantic Love*, London: Routledge & Kegan Paul.

Kaplan, A.G. (1979) 'Towards an analysis of sex-role related issues in the therapeutic relationship', *Psychiatry* 42:112–20.

Kaplan, A.G. (1986) 'The "self in relation": implications for depression in women', *Psychotherapy* 23: 234–42.

Kaplan, M. (1983) 'A women's view of DSM-III', *American Psychologist* 38: 786–92.

Kenworthy J.A (1979) 'Androgyny in psychotherapy: but will it sell in Peoria?' *Psychology of Women Quarterly* 3: 231–40.

Kohut, H. (1971) *The Analysis of the Self*, New York: International Universities Press.

Layton, M. (1984) 'Tipping the therapeutic balance: masculine, feminine or neuter?' *Family Therapy Networker*, May/June, 81–27.

Lemkau, J.P. and Landau, C. (1986) 'The selfless syndrome: assessment and treatment considerations', *Psychotherapy* 23: 227–33.

Light, A. (1985). 'No man's land', *The Guardian*, 30 October.

Little, B.R. (1972) 'Psychological man as scientist, humanist and specialist', *Journal of Experimental Research in Personality* 6: 95–118.

Llewelyn, S. and Osborne, K. (1983) 'Women as clients and as therapists', in D. Pilgrim (ed.) *Psychology and Psychotherapy: Current Trends and Issues*, London: Routledge & Kegan Paul.

Macfarlane, A. (1986) *Marriage and Love in England 1300–1840*, London: Blackwell.

Mead, M. (1931) 'Jealousy: primitive and civilised', in S.D. Schmalhausen and V.F. Calverton (eds) *Woman's Coming of Age*, Liveright Publishing Corporation.

Miller, J.B. (1976) *Toward a New Psychology of Women*, Harmondsworth: Penguin.

Smail, D. (1984) *Illusion and Reality: the meaning of anxiety*, London: Dent.

Voss, J. and Gannon, L. (1978) 'Sexism in the theory and practice of clinical psychology', *Professional Psychology* 9: 623–33.

Willi, J. (1984) *Couples in Collusion*, Claremont, CA.: Hunter House.

Williams, J. (1984) 'Women and mental illness', in J. Nicholson and H. Beloff (eds) *Psychology Survey* 5, Leicester: British Psychological Society.

Winnicott, D. (1957) *The Child and the Family*, London: Tavistock.

Chapter four

The special intimacy of sexuality

Edith's story

Edith came to see me at the suggestion of the women working at a rape crisis centre. She had been in telephone contact with them for several weeks after having phoned one night in distress. Her boyfriend had apparently arrived home drunk, had physically attacked her and had tried to force her to have intercourse. She had managed to run out of the house and spent the night with a friend, who had persuaded Edith to phone the crisis help-line because she was frightened about going back home again. When she eventually went back a few days later, she had found that her boyfriend had moved out, taking with him many of her possessions. Edith had then become rather depressed, hence her visit to me.

In the early sessions with me, Edith remained very quiet and sad. Gradually she told me a little bit about herself. She was 25 years old, had no academic or vocational qualifications, and had done a variety of different jobs since leaving school, mostly in the catering trade. She was currently working in a hospital canteen, which she preferred to her previous jobs in pubs and restaurants because it was more secure, the pay was better, and she liked the company of the other women. The main drawback was her boss, who was very demanding and often made her work after hours without any overtime pay.

At first Edith didn't want to talk about her boyfriend and the events that led up to her contacting me. 'I'm an idiot,' was all that she would say:

He sponged off me for months, he never had a proper job, and left me to pay for the rent and all the food. When I got my pay packet he'd want his share, and it would be all spent on one night's booze. But I just let him get away with it: it was my fault really.

Gradually, however, her anger at his treatment of her replaced her self-blame, and after a while she was able to express quite vehemently her feelings about his behaviour towards her. But when I asked her if this kind of thing had happened before, she grew sad again. 'They're all the same,' she concluded. 'Every single man I've ever known has walked right over me. They'd be all sweet and nice to start with, then as soon as I gave in to them a bit they'd take me for granted.'

When Edith started to talk about her previous relationships, it emerged that she had a history of involvement with men who had treated her very badly indeed. She had often been forced into sexual practices that were abhorrent to her, and she was frequently physically assaulted. Yet it was always the men who walked out on her, rather than the other way around, and she despaired of ever having a warm and loving relationship.

By the time she had told me all of this, we had got to know each other quite well. Edith had been coming regularly to see me on a weekly basis, having originally said it would not be worthwhile, but having subsequently decided to continue. However, one week she missed a session without any warning, and phoned the next day to say that she had been too upset to keep the appointment. When she next came she looked dreadful. She had obviously been crying a lot, and her face was pale, with bloodshot eyes. I asked her what had been happening.

It was my Dad's birthday,' she said.

Mum always insisted that I go back to visit them, even though I hate going home and can't really afford the fare. But I couldn't let them down. While I was there, I kept thinking about what it was like when I was little.

When I asked her what she meant, she started to weep profusely and then slowly began to tell me about her parents:

Dad's a big bully. He's always bossed Mum around, and he was very strict with us girls. We weren't allowed to have any friends to play with or go out anywhere. When I was about 10 my eldest sister, who must have been about 16 at the time, left home. She and my Dad had had a furious row. I didn't know what it was about, but she just packed a bag and walked out. Mum was terribly upset, but Dad said she was a slut, just because she had a boyfriend.

After her sister left home, Edith began to realise why her sister had wanted to leave home. Her father started to turn his attentions to her, and would often come into her bedroom in the evening when her mother was out at work:

He was usually so bad tempered and nasty. But as soon as Mum went out he turned all friendly and kept laughing. He used to ask me about school, and my homework, and then he said it was time for me to go to bed and he'd help me to undress. At first I was surprised, since he'd never helped Mum with any of us before. He kept stroking me and saying what a pretty girl I was – it wasn't like him at all.

Edith found it very painful and embarrassing to go back over these memories, and describe her feelings about her father's behaviour. She felt guilty about admitting that at first she had been pleased, since previously her father had not paid her any attention. But she had also been very scared, particularly when her father also undressed himself, and persuaded her to lie down on the bed with him, and to touch his penis. Eventually, he was regularly demanding that they should have intercourse, which Edith felt powerless to refuse. She was never able to confide in her mother, and said she still wondered how much her mother knew. Edith needed a long time to work through her grief and shame about her experiences with her father, and her feelings of being betrayed by her mother, whom she felt should have protected her.

Slowly, Edith started to make connections between her earlier incestuous relationship with her father, and the way that this was being repeated in her adult relationships with her boyfriends. She described her feelings of disgust about her own body, which she felt was shameful, and simultaneously, not really part of herself. As a young girl she had enjoyed masturbating, but after her experiences with her father she denied to herself any feelings of sexual arousal. She said she hated the 'messiness of sex', but felt that she had to put up with it 'because that's what men want'.

It had obviously been extremely difficult for Edith to describe all of this. She told me how she had finally left home at 16, and only went back to see her parents at Christmas and for anniversaries. She had never felt able to confide in women friends, whom she felt would despise her for what happened, and the men friends she made were far from being willing or able to listen to her talk about herself. In addition, her subsequent problems in relationships with men seemed to confirm her fears that she was perhaps, after all, a 'slut'. She was therefore very worried that I, too, would reject her for what she had told me, and anxiously scrutinised my reactions in the following sessions. I was gradually able to convince her that I didn't blame her for what had happened, and listened attentively to her over the many weeks it took for her to tell and retell her story.

This lack of negative judgement, and my willingness to let her explore her feelings about herself and her past, was apparently what Edith needed. During our sessions together, she made considerable progress in self-acceptance and self-understanding. Not only did she make connections between her childhood experiences and her current choice of men friends, but she also realised that she allowed men to abuse her at work as well. Gradually she felt more confident and more able to stand up for herself when, for example, volunteers were asked for to work extra hours. She was very scared that she would lose her job, but after a while realised that her boss no longer picked on her once she ceased to be willing to be pushed around. By the time she no longer felt the need for sessions with me, she was feeling much more sure of herself, and confident that, next time, she would get involved with a man who would be able to give her affection, not abuse.

Sexuality in women's relationships

Sexuality is present in almost all intimate relationships, and can be an opportunity for the expression and experience of closeness, intense physical gratification, emotional fulfilment, and deep love. However, sexual intimacy can also be physically frustrating, tedious, thoroughly unpleasant, or even terrifying.

Psychologically, being involved in a sexual relationship has a number of consequences for both men and women, largely because sexuality so uniquely involves these extremes of emotional and physical experiences. But for most women, at least during their fertile years, it also involves the risk of pregnancy, or the annoyance (and in some cases, danger) of contraception. In addition, it carries for the vast majority of women the further complication of both social control, which is wielded over them by others, and constraints which are imposed by each woman on herself (see the discussion by Carol Smart and Barry Smart, 1978). Hence sexual intimacy can never be uncomplicated for women: alongside physical pleasure, it always also raises issues of scrutiny, control, danger, and risk.

In this chapter, we shall consider the meaning of sexuality in women's lives, initially by looking at some of the theories which have been advanced to explain women's sexuality and gender identity, and then by looking at a number of issues such as violence and incest which colour many women's sexual experiences. Following from this we shall consider male attitudes towards female sexuality, and the way in which these attitudes influence women's sexual experiences. Next we shall look at the development and varieties of women's sexual experiences and expression, including heterosexuality, lesbianism, and celibacy, and then we shall examine the way in which the conflicts which many women feel concerning their bodies affect their sexuality. As in previous chapters, we shall conclude by looking at some of the therapeutic implications arising from the preceding analysis.

Conventional theoretical approaches to women's sexuality and gender identity

Most conventional texts concerning human sexuality view it as a combination of skilled and instinctive behaviour, based on a physiological drive which is thought to be far stronger in men than in women. This 'drive' is assumed to be primarily concerned with the survival of the species, and is said to account for the desire by men to be as promiscuous as possible, while keeping 'their' women away from other men, who are seen to be rival sources of fertilisation. A woman's sexuality, according to many of these theories, is an add-on extra, serving primarily to tie the woman further to 'her' man. Any sexual pleasure which *she* might experience from sexual contact is therefore seen as a rather unimportant aspect of the process.

These very simplistic, male-oriented assumptions underlie many traditionalist theories of female sexuality, ranging from the theories of socio-biological writers such as David Barash (1979), Kevin MacDonald (1988), and Edward Wilson (1975), and learning theorists such as Glenn Wilson (1979), to the psychoanalytic theories of Sigmund Freud (1925) and his followers. Similar assumptions also underlie most conventional accounts of the process of gender identification. What is most striking about many of these theories is that they seem to have been developed with the man as the prototype, and as a consequence, a woman's experience is usually either seen as a 'lesser' version of the man's and hence not worthy of as much attention, or is simply misunderstood. For example, traditional psychoanalysts, from the early days of Freud onwards, have considered the development of women's gender identity and sexuality to be highly problematic, assuming it to be distorted version of male sexuality, and have therefore focused less attention on women's experiences.

From the point of view of socio-biology, both David Barash (1979) and Edward Wilson (1975) suggest that since men during their fertile years continuously produce millions of sperm, whereas women (normally) produce only one ovum per menstrual cycle, then male promiscuity and female fidelity are a 'natural' form of social organisation, which they claim also explains why women, not men, care for children. Of course, as Ruth Hubbard (1983) points out, this 'explanation' ignores the fact that most men do not produce millions of children, nor do more powerful men normally produce more children than weaker ones, which would follow logically from such a neo-Darwinist position. More importantly, they ignore the enormous variety in forms of social organisation which characterise human societies, and which very probably have a far greater influence on human behaviour than the contribution of biological propensities. (This is not to deny the reality of biological differences between men and women, but to suggest that they have been vastly overstated, often for clearly ideological reasons. See the work of Marian Lowe, 1983 and Joan Smith, 1983, for further discussion of this issue.)

Within a more behavioural framework, a number of theorists such as Glenn Wilson (1979) have tried to explain the development of female sexuality and femininity as being the result of appropriate social conditioning whereby little girls are rewarded for behaving in feminine ways, and eventually for displaying adult womanly behaviour, including female sexual responsiveness. According to views such as these, femininity is 'naturally' produced by the girl, and is then reinforced by a process of simple conditioning. Although useful in pointing to the contribution of social, rather than merely biological influences on behaviour, these analyses are, by and large, lacking in any critical analysis of the social context within which the behaviour occurs. In addition, such theories are totally unable to explain the enormous variety of women's experiences, or the ability of some women to behave in non-stereotyped ways.

Turning last to psychoanalytic theories, we see that rather similar and unquestioning assumptions concerning 'natural' female behaviour also underlie conventional Freudian views, although such theories often display much less appreciation of the contribution of social factors than do the behavioural theories. Briefly, the traditional psychoanalytic view of women's sexual development is that the girl's femininity and sexuality develop out of her gradual realisation of, and acceptance of, her apparent castration, which generates in turn her desire to produce her father's child as a form of compensation for her lack of a penis. In addition, psychoanalytic theorists believe that once the girl discovers that her mother also lacks a penis, she then turns against her mother, imagining that she, too, has been castrated. This anger with her mother then begins the young girl's

Oedipal attachment to her father, hence forming the debut of her path towards adult sexuality.

For this view to have any credibility, a number of questionable assumptions have to be made. The girl child must have been able to observe a naked boy child (as well as her naked parents), and have been able to notice the difference between boys and girls. She must then be assumed to have concluded that her body is physically inferior to that of a boy, and then must be assumed to be striving to deal psychologically with this painful lack. She must also be assumed to feel anger and resentment towards her mother, seeing her mother as an inferior, and must see the attainment of her father's baby as the only way in which she can be compensated for her own woeful inadequacy. All these assumptions were, of course, made by male theorists.

For a number of reasons, including the implausibility of some of the assumptions noted previously, this traditional Freudian approach has not been very helpful in explaining women's sexuality, especially given the fact that it is particularly difficult to separate theory from value-judgements on these issues. More helpfully, however, some women writers such as Juliet Mitchell (1974) have recently tried to adapt some of Freud's original ideas to include an awareness of the social and interpersonal context within which girls and boys develop their sexuality and gender identity. In a lengthy and often complex series of arguments, Mitchell reinterprets Freudian theories concerning a girl's psycho-sexual development using the perspective of the French radical psychoanalyst, Jacques Lacan.

A baby, Mitchell argues, has no sense of sexual difference, but is born into a family structure where its gender plays a prominant part, for example, as eldest daughter, or youngest son, or whatever. The thoughts that other family members have, even before it is born, will help to determine its later gender identity. Slowly the baby finds out not only about its mother but also about its father, and about itself in relation to these two powerful adults. Like Freud, Mitchell believes that a girl's envy of the penis, and the castration that she fears she has suffered, is central to the formation of women's gender identity. But rather than being a mere anatomical description, Mitchell follows Lacan in his cultural explanation of the symbolic power of the phallus. According to Lacanian thinking, the little girl's sense of inadequacy when she discovers that she does not possess a penis like her father or brother is based on an awareness of the symbolic power of the male organ. Hence the baby learns about being male or female, at the same time as learning about being a member of human society: and with that learning comes an appreciation of the balance of power between the sexes: a balance which is tipped heavily in favour of the male.

These arguments have been taken further by other Lacanian writers such as Vivien Bar (1987), who points out that 'the idea of the father is always present – even if he is physically absent, as in artificial insemination' (p.242), or indeed, as in divorce or death. Further, language and the law itself are assumed to be based on the male organ as symbol of authority: hence in Lacanian theory, the father holds an important symbolic function, mediated through the onset of language, which breaks into the mother–child dyad and initiates the child's separation from the mother. (The relative disengagement of many fathers, especially in their parental relationships with their daughters, may be one reason for the difficulties that daughters experience in separating from their mothers: an issue which we discuss in more detail on p.76.) Interestingly, these writers have had more influence on theorists and thinkers in the world of literature than on those in the world of psychological theorising, although in some countries, such as France, a number of psychotherapists involved in court cases have made use of these ideas concerning the role of fathers in separating mothers from their babies.

Athough Mitchell's reformulation of Freudian ideas have contributed something to our understanding of women's sexuality, in many ways object-relations theories have been more satisfactory in their explanatory power. Whilst not containing an explicit theory of sexuality, object-relations theorists such as Ronald Fairbairn (1952), Harry Guntrip (1971), and Nancy Chodorow (1978) view sexuality as but one aspect of the human capacity for relationships, which develops out of early childhood experiences. Thus these theorists reject the biological, deterministic aspect of both the Freudian theories of sexuality, which tend to stress innate drives and impulses over relational experiences, and the cruder, non-psychological pseudo-Darwinist theories of the socio-biologists. Instead, object-relations theorists consider the nature of the child's early personal relationships to be crucial to the development of the adult's sexuality. Nancy Chodorow (1978), for example, argues that a principal goal of adult sexuality is a return to the merging experienced by the infant with the mothering 'other'. She uses Michael Balint's (1968) notion of primary love to describe the emotionally intense feelings the child has in early infancy, before there is any experience of differentiation between itself and mother/other. She suggests that as adults, we strive to recapture this experience of being in a symbiotic relationship with another. When we seem to attain such a close relationship with another, we can then experience feelings of great love and security, physical pleasure, and immense emotional relief, almost as if we were recreating the merging bliss of relationships in infancy. But as we have already noted in Chapter 3, this may entail fears of loss and rejection, as well as a defensive denial of the merging experience.

The early development of sexuality and gender identity

Having looked at a number of conventional perspectives on women's sexuality and gender identity, we will now turn to an examination of how sexuality and femaleness develop in the first place. Because we have found it to be the most helpful approach to women's sexuality, we will continue to draw in this section very largely on material from the object-relations school of psychodynamics, although other sources will also be introduced where relevant.

Relationships with other people begin in infancy, when the child is being touched, stroked, talked to, suckled, and held – all experiences which occur in the early days following birth. As already noted, object-relations theorists believe that these sensations lead to infantile feelings of merging with the mother and of being contained by her, and that these feelings form the origins of sexuality. They derive from normal bodily experiences, such as being fed, cleaned, and changed, and their daily occurrence is therefore assumed to form a crucial part in the child's emotional, and hence sexual, development (for a discussion see Janet Sayers, 1986). It is also through these experiences of being cared for that babies begin to develop a sense of the boundaries between themselves and others, as they learn to distinguish between 'me' and 'not me'.

It is here, however, that women's conflicts over intimacy also have their origins. As we saw in Chapters 2 and 3, the legacy of early childhood experiences is different for women than it is for men. According to writers such as Nancy Chodorow (1978), the tendency for mothers to have a greater identification with their girl children than with their boy children means that the boundaries between mother and daughter are often less clear than those between mother and son: because of the similarity of sex, the mother may think she knows exactly what her daughter is feeling and wanting. As a result of the mother's projective identifications with her baby girl, the daughter's actual infant needs are however *less* likely to have been accurately perceived and responded to than are a son's, since the mother is responding to what she thinks the daughter ought to need, rather than to her real needs. Consequently, when they grow up, it remains difficult for many women to be able to identify correctly and know their own true needs, or to expect anyone to be able to meet them.

Nowhere is this more clearly apparent than in the expression of women's sexuality, since the intimacy of a sexual relationship is, in most cases, the place where the earliest conflicts concerning childhood emotional experiences are focused and displayed. For some women this means that the desire for nurturance, including physical holding and emotional connection, are mixed up with the fears of being misunderstood, submerged, and engulfed. Luise Eichenbaum and Susie Orbach have described the problems for women in merging with another in an intimate relationship, as follows:

A temporary psychological merger with another is especially precarious if one is unsure of the boundaries of the self in the first place. The merger is much wished for but may be felt to be dangerous for one may feel stuck in it. The falsely constructed boundaries between self and other so endemic in women's psychology hide an undeveloped and shaky sense of self-identity ... intimate relating, in providing a feeling, however brief, of being understood and met, can be excruciating for it can stir up all the longing that has for so long gone unmet and hence has been repressed and denied.

(Eichenbaum and Orbach, 1987:63–4)

From here on, the experiences of the girl and the boy are even more markedly divergent, since following her early experiences of being nurtured but also of

75

being frequently misinterpreted, the girl is then expected to give up her dependency and love for her mother and turn her attention to men in the process of gender differentiation. But as Vivien Bar (1987) has pointed out, the establishment of gender differentiation and a girl's sense of her own femaleness comes about not only through her experiences with her mother, but also in relation to her father. Yet because of the absence of the father in most of the child's daily experiences, both boys and girls have to develop their notions of maleness from images derived from how their mothers and society at large define masculinity, and hence they risk gaining mixed messages, both of men's power and importance, and also of their unreliability and significance. This can clearly have serious and negative implications for a girl's growing sense of who she is and who she will become. Further, in trying to become 'feminine' in the effective absence of a father, the girl may be forced into using the strategy of trying to be as different as she can be from her image of what men are supposed to be. Hence she will often learn to accentuate her femaleness, usually through prettiness, dependency, sexiness, and charm, which in turn may buy her attention from her father when he does eventually appear.

One other important component of the process of the development of sexuality out of early childhood experiences is that, of course, not every experience of physical contact with the mother has been a good one: the baby may sometimes not want the food that is offered, or may feel hungry, cold, wet, and misunderstood. As a result, the pleasurable aspects of contact with the mother comes to be contrasted with the painful ones, with the result that, as Melanie Klein's work has suggested (see, for example, Klein, 1935), the 'good' and 'bad' aspects of the mothering person are split off and separated in the child's reactions to being nurtured. The consequences for the child's developing sexuality are that he or she possesses powerful internal images of physical contact as both positive and negative, both sensations being largely out of conscious control. The results of this dynamic for the later development of a boy will be discussed in more detail on p.80. But for a girl, it means that she holds within herself certain influential notions of sexuality and femininity, which are both good and bad, and are not easily amenable to conscious or rational examination. These notions do not just apply to her mother of course, but also to her own developing sexuality. Hence a part of her may well believe that her own sexuality is bad and to be hidden, denied, and controlled if at all possible.

Issues which affect women's sexual experiences

Having looked at theories of women's sexuality, and the development of sexual and gender identity, we now turn to an examination of some of the issues which can affect how a woman experiences her sexual responsiveness. The first of these is the issue of the girl's separation from her mother.

As noted on p.71, most psychoanalytic, behaviourist and socio-biological theories pay scant attention to processes which, although crucial to women's development, are not also central features of men's development. A good example of this is the unique capacity of women to bear children, which we will discuss further in Chapter 7. But in addition, an adequate account of women's sexuality and gender identification should also pay attention to the mother–daughter relationship and the ambiguous nature of the girl's giving up of her mother. Here the feminist psychotherapists' reworking of object-relations theories have been particularly helpful, however. Luise Eichenbaum and Susie Orbach (1987), for example, have argued that the separation of mother and daughter is never quite complete, and as a result, women often find it more difficult than do men to abandon themselves totally to the experience of fusion in sexual intimacy. In the heightened intimacy of a sexual relationship, women seem to be seeking (as are men) a return to the fusion and merging experienced originally with the mother, yet because women are themselves often still unsure of their own boundaries, a secure sense of blissful completeness through sexual union can be more elusive for women than it is for men.

The second problematic issue for most women in their sexual intimacies is the relative inability of many men to provide women with a secure context within which to experience sexual fulfilment. Since women, by nature of their childhood experiences, tend to be more receptive and sensitive to the needs of others than do men, they are more likely than men to be able to fulfil the 'mothering' or 'surrounding' aspects of sexuality. Hence in heterosexual relationships the regressive aspects of sexual merging may well be less satisfactory for women than for men (Chodorow, 1978), so for this reason, too, the sense of fusion may be less easily attainable for women. Of course, this sense of fusion or completeness which can be experienced through sexual intimacy may be even more problematic for some women than for others. For example, women who have not had nurturing relationships with their fathers may find it even less easy to find satisfaction later with their male partners, since it will be even harder to establish a context of trust in which regressive feelings can occur. (See also Ursula Owen, 1983, for some women's accounts of their relationships with their fathers.) By contrast, other women may find that the desire to merge and be contained in fact leads them to reject sexual partnerships with men entirely, and to find greater fulfilment in sexual relationships with other women, through lesbian relationships: a topic which will be discussed later in this chapter.

Sex, pain, and violence

Another issue which any analysis of women's sexuality must address is the link which many writers claim exists for women between sex and pain, or sex and violence. This link is often taken by traditionalist theorists (for example, Havelock Ellis, 1913) as evidence of women's 'masochistic nature' which is said to be demonstrated by the fact that some women seem to enjoy and obtain sexual pleasure from pain or violence. At a slightly less dramatic level, this 'masochistic instinct', or 'trait' has been claimed by psychoanalytic writers such as Helene

Deutsch (1945) to underlie many women's ambivalent feelings about their sexuality.

However, what these more conventional theorists ignore is the fact that for many women sexuality *is* often associated with violence and pain, either the violence of actual rape, or the violence implicitly or explicitly contained in the sexual fantasies which are portrayed widely in films and in advertising images of sexually aroused women. This association is sometimes then described by women themselves in their fantasies as if they are being 'taken over' sexually by men (see Shere Hite, 1976). Yet many women's experiences of sexuality have only been those in which they have been required to be the passive victims of male brutality, hence they have only been able to experience their own sexuality through the eyes of men (see also Ann Burgess and Lynda Holmstrom, 1974; Del Martin, 1982). Indeed, as Carole Vance (1984) has argued, there is a powerful tension between sexual danger and sexual pleasure for women:

> To focus only on pleasure and gratification ignores the patriarchal structure in which women act, yet to speak only of sexual violence and oppression ignores women's experiences with sexual agency and choice and unwittingly increases the sexual terror and despair in which women live.
>
> (Vance, 1984:1)

In considering women's experiences of sexual intimacy, then, we have to be aware of these very real constraints within which their sexual expression develops.

The reality of male violence against women is not, however, the only reason for the existence of violence in some women's sexual fantasies, or the distaste which some women feel for any form of sexual contact. The desire for a merging with the other which is felt in a heightened manner during sexual contact, also contains powerful echoes from childhood, not all of which are pleasurable (see Luise Eichenbaum and Susie Orbach, 1982). A number of pre-verbal bodily experiences from early infancy can be stirred up by sexual contact, which can also make adult intimacy fraught with conflicts. For example, for some women, the experience of physical intimacy is one of being submerged or even almost extinguished; hence they may struggle at all costs not to lose control of themselves. For others, sexual contact may involve a sense of shame and disgust, which can remove all sense of pleasure from any form of sexual intimacy. But such experiences can only be understood within the interpersonal context of their origins, rather than being assumed to be caused by some underlying masochistic 'trait' or 'instinct'.

Incest and sexual abuse

Linked to the issue of sex and violence is, of course, the issue of incest. According to most psychological theories, the father's presence in a girl's early life has the effect of developing and fostering her awareness of her own femaleness, in principle, without gratifying her (or his) own sexual desires. But as Edith's story shows, however, some men are unable to distinguish between parental and erotic love, and hence engage in overt sexual contact with their girl children. Edith is by no means an isolated example: many women have recently 'broken the silence' that has surrounded the issue of incest within their families, and have poignantly described their own experiences (see for example, Sarah Davenport and Helen Sheldon, 1987; Florence Rush, 1980). Indeed, as already noted in Chapter 2, Karen Alter-Reid and her colleagues (1986) have pointed out that approximately 38 per cent of women report having experienced some form of sexual abuse during their childhood, of which between 3 and 10 per cent will have been incestuous.

With some honourable exceptions, the psychoanalytic and psychiatric professions have contributed very little to our understanding of the plight of incest victims. Rather than focusing on the father's deviant role in incestuous contact, traditional psychoanalysts have claimed that women generate fantasies of incestuous abuse; hence the victim is blamed for her own suffering, and the male is effectively exonerated from blame.

One of the exceptions, however, is the Swiss psychoanalyst Alice Miller (1985), who has devoted much of her life to therapeutic work with victims of child abuse, and who is highly critical of orthodox psychoanalysis for having viewed women's descriptions of sexual abuse by their fathers (or other men) as fantasy rather than as fact. For instance, Miller has described how in his early work, Freud discovered that many of his women patients had experienced incestuous relationships, which then led him to postulate that these very real traumas were the source of later adult neuroses. However, Freud subsequently abandoned this 'seduction theory', under pressure, according to Miller, from his defensive denial of his own memories of incestuous feelings towards his daughter Mathilde, and the shock and indignation aroused in his (male) critics concerning such ideas. This abandonment of the 'seduction theory' then led Freud to develop his Oedipal theories concerning male and female sexual development, and to describe sexuality between father and daughter as being the outcome of the girl's strivings to compete with her mother for her father's affections.

Although Alice Miller has not been alone in arguing for the reality of incest in women's lives, the 'seduction theory' account of women's sexual experiences is still widely rejected by conventional psychoanalysts, possibly for reasons similar to those which may explain Freud's self-deception. Women and girls are therefore still blamed for being 'seducers', and are often accused of lying when they do have the courage to report that they have been abused (Jean Moore, 1981).

However, therapists who listen closely to what their clients have to say and refuse to 'blame the victim' have become more and more aware of the prevalence of incest and other forms of child sexual abuse. As we saw with Edith, for some women a history of sexual abuse also affects all subsequent adult relationships, since it leaves victims particularly vulnerable to relationships where they are subject to repeated male sexual violence. For such women the dangers inherent in sexuality obviously predominate over the pleasures; yet they often see very little hope of finding a way out of their plight, as they often feel both demoralised and powerless. Karen Alter-Reid and her colleagues (1986) have summarised empirical research over the past decade concerning sexual abuse, and have reported that survivors of child sexual abuse often suffer a variety of long-term consequences, including suicidal attempts, sexual difficulties, marital problems, unwanted teenage pregnancies, anger towards themselves and other women, and feelings of isolation and depression. According to Alter-Reid and her colleagues, some of the fathers and 'uncles' involved in such abuse quite astoundingly defend their actions by saying that they wanted to introduce the girl to sex in a 'loving relationship'. Besides being extremely dishonest, this is obviously a tragic example of the 'protectiveness' of men, which is so harmful to so many women's lives.

Male attitudes towards women

It is perhaps relevant at this point to look in more detail at the sexuality of men, and their beliefs about women, since these beliefs clearly have a major impact on most women's sexual experiences. Whilst we reject the claims (for example, Andrea Dworkin, 1987) that all men are automatically sexual aggressors, or that all women are the innocent victims of male malevolence, nevertheless we do believe that some aspects of the psychological make-up of most men in contemporary society contribute little to the happiness and fulfilment of either women or men, and that an appreciation of this situation is needed if the two sexes are ever to live in greater harmony with each other.

Fundamental to an understanding of this situation is the fact that it is women who are primarily responsible for children. This has a number of far-reaching effects for both men and women particularly on the way in which subsequent relationships with others are structured. The effects of mother-rearing on men's images of and feelings about women have major implications for women's experiences, since all women, whether they have sexual relationships with men or not, are affected by the way that men view and treat them. The lesbian woman is no more protected than her heterosexual sister from the consequences of male psychology, unless she succeeds in isolating herself entirely from all contact with men.

We have already pointed to some of the consequences for women of the close identification which exists between mothers and their girl children. The consequences for boys are rather different, however. Because a mother is more likely to experience her son as a definite 'other' compared with her daughter (since her son is of the opposite sex to her), she is less likely to identify projectively with him and to think she knows exactly how he feels. Boundaries between mother and son are therefore likely to be less blurred, thus facilitating his autonomy and eventual separation from her. But in addition, she is less able to help him cope with the process of gender identification. In isolated nuclear families, a woman bringing up children will often spend long periods of time without adult company, particularly without her male partner, and so a son may become a 'stand-in' for his father, as the 'little man' of the household. Yet he knows very little about what men are supposed to be like, except that they are usually very busy and noticeable by their absence. Nancy Chodorow further argues that a mother's 'emotional investments and conflicts, given her socialization around issues of gender and sex and membership in a sexist society, make this experience of his particularly strong' (Chodorow, 1978:105).

As a consequence, boys have a difficult task: to carve out a male identity for themselves in the absence of a clear male role-model with which to identify. Hence boys have to use their fantasies of masculinity, as gleaned from media images, older boys, and their mother's projections, from which to forge their own sense of male identity. The male role thus assumed often then consists of many of the media's and his mother's fantasies about what boys 'should' be like.

In explaining the problematic nature of this situation, Joseph Pleck (1981) argues that boys have to live up to an image of masculinity, which includes aggressiveness, toughness, and above all else, superiority to women, all of which are actually quite difficult for a young boy to maintain in practice, since (obviously) little boys often feel far from brave, fearless, aggressive, and manly. Therefore, Pleck argues, everything that is perceived by the boy to be female has to be fiercely rejected through a process of over-compensation, since 'actual or imagined violation of sex-roles leads individuals to overconform to them' (p.145). In this process of over-compensation, the young boy attempts to act in a hypermasculine way, in particular by attempting to demonstrate his difference from all that is female. (Incidentally, Pleck further suggests that later on in life, rape and other types of male aggression may reflect this attempt by insecure and over-compensating men and boys to demonstrate their masculinity and power over women, in a frantic defence of their 'manhood'. Similar points have been made by Susan Brownmiller, 1975).

It is in this way that masculinity and sexual difference, which are the quint-essential Oedipal issues, become enmeshed with the young boy's attempts to become what the child understands is required of males. But these are not the only problems which boys have to face in becoming men: like Pleck, Nancy Chodorow suggests that boys typically react to the childhood task of gender identification by emphasising their differentiation from their mothers, but she also points out that boys simultaneously try to maintain a strong emotional bond with their mothers, since after all, mothers still represent the best hope of warmth and comfort. Ruth Moulton (1977) further suggests that boys are profoundly frightened of women's power, feeling inadequate and small next to their mothers, and yet in desperate need of their care and love. Added to this are the conflicting feelings which all children have about the 'good' and 'bad' aspects of their mothers, which as both Nancy Chodorow (1978) and Dorothy Dinnerstein (1978) have pointed out, lead to the polarisation of the powerful providing aspects of the mother's care from the inevitable frustrations and rejections involved in being cared for.

The long-term consequence of this conflicting set of feelings for male sexuality and men's relationships with women is that the sexual difference between men and women becomes the arena for a struggle for power and control. As they grow up, men retain the split internal image of women, which then leads them to revere and idolise what they see as the good, or 'madonna' in women whilst reviling, punishing, and attempting to control the castrating bad, or 'whore' in women. When this is added to the confused messages given to children about sexuality, that it is in some senses 'bad' and not to be talked about or done in public, then it becomes fairly easy to understand how it is particularly in the area of sexuality that these conflicts and confusions are expressed most clearly. Sexuality comes to represent all that is bad and yet desirable in women, hence requiring male control and containment; but at the same time, women are idealised as possessing all that is soft, desirable, and good.

Thus it is that men have frequently imposed a double standard on women's sexuality and autonomy, seeing them (in the memorable phrase) as 'temples built on sewers'. Women have been expected to conserve their virginity and sexual innocence until marriage, whereupon their chastity and fidelity are controlled, often under threats of physical or emotional punishment. 'Loose' women, on the other hand, who have demonstrated their sexuality, are expected to be unconditionally available to men. This logic allows for the brutal and degrading treatment of prostitutes and sexual attacks on women who are perceived to be acting in a free manner, as well as the stifling containment of daughters and wives in the name of loving 'protection' of their innocence and chastity (see Nicholas Groth, 1979). It also allows for the jealous double standards held by many men concerning the sexual fidelity of their wives.

Of course, in the example of Edith, described at the start of this chapter, her father's sexual possessiveness extended from his wife to his daughters. Whilst Edith and her sister were not allowed to have boyfriends and develop a normal adolescent sexuality, they were at the same time vulnerable to his sexual attentions. Fathers like this, who are unable to differentiate between erotic love and parental love, behave in such a way in their relationships with their daughters in order to gratify their own pathological needs. According to Alice Miller (1985), incestuous desires of this sort suggest a severe disturbance in the father's own early emotional experiences. The tragedy for women is that the cycle is then all too often repeated: for Edith, gratifying her father's incestuous lust was the only way she had experienced men's love, which then led her to enter into relationships with other men who similarly viewed her as merely an object for their own sexual satisfaction.

Women's experiences of intimacy

In this section we want to look at the range and varieties of women's sexual experiences. First, however, we want to point out that there are an enormous number of alternatives that women may opt for during the course of their lives, each of which may be expressed at different times through different types of relationships or forms of interaction. For example, a sexual life style that is appropriate during one stage of life, for instance in late adolescence, may be very different from the one adopted following the birth of a child. Neither is better or worse than the other. Relationships will also change over time, and sex may come to play a greater or lesser role in an individual's life. Further, at some time during her life a woman may choose or may have to become celibate. Each way of coping with sexuality can be fulfilling in its own way since there are clearly no 'correct' forms of sexuality which suit all people at all times of their lives.

In addition, it is important to note that, for many women, their sexual preferences are neither clear cut nor permanent. In fact, it may perhaps be best to see intimate relationships as existing as a spectrum, from 'straight' heterosexual relationships, through a whole variety of bisexual intimacies which may or may not be exclusive, to homosexual involvements. Further, women may have both heterosexual and lesbian relationships at different times in their lives, and find both forms of sexuality equally satisfying, or equally difficult.

Relating sexually to men

The majority of women in our society choose to, or find themselves, 'falling in love with' and feeling sexually attracted to men. A man's body feels, and is, very different from a woman's. It is more clearly 'other', which for some women may heighten the excitement of the contact, yet at the same time may make it more threatening. It may be rather puzzling to work out how a man's body – or this particular man's body – responds, and especially difficult to help a man to understand how a woman's body feels. At the same time, a heterosexual relationship can bring such a great sense of fulfilment and wholeness that for at least some women, it is the most central part of their lives.

In seeking to understand the details of sexual relationship between men and women, conventional psychological theorists and sexologists have not been very helpful, mostly providing over-simplistic formulations based on male-defined assumptions and practices. For instance, it is possible to detect a repeated misogyny on the part of the so-called conventional sexual 'experts', who have carried out their research largely from within the perspective of a masculine norm (see, for example, Havelock Ellis, 1913; Alfred Kinsey and colleagues, 1953). Of critical importance has been their acceptance of what Angela Hamblin calls 'the heterosexual ritual', whereby 'real' or 'normal' sex means penetration, penile thrusting, and ejaculation. This, she argues:

> renders the sexual pleasure of the woman irrelevant, and limits heterosexual practice to a series of repetitive acts which maximise the possibilities of pregnancy. It creates a male sexuality in which heterosexual men

learn to seek their sexual pleasure, almost exclusively, from (intercourse)
... at the expense of all other forms of sensual/sexual bodily awareness,
exploration or expression.

(Hamblin, 1983:108)

Such a definition of what constitutes 'real' sex is, she argues, internalised by
women so that other forms of sexual contact, which might in fact give them more
pleasure, are seen by both partners as being subsidiary, merely 'foreplay'. It may
also lead some men to believe that they have a 'right' to sexual intercourse in
sexual interactions, to the extent that they are entitled to use highly coercive
persuasion or even force to achieve this result.

Yet many women experience their sexuality very differently from this male-
oriented process, as was clearly shown some years ago by a survey of 3,000
American women carried out by Shere Hite (1976). The Hite Report covered a
range of women's sexual experiences, focusing on the ways in which the women
in the survey achieved orgasm, and including their preferred sexual activities,
their relationships, and changes in their sexual activity over time. One of the most
significant findings in this long and intricate report was the repeated account by
a large majority of women that their sexual satisfaction in terms of experiencing
orgasm was far stronger when they were masturbating or being manually stimulated by their partners, than during penetration. Whilst women sometimes
reported that they wanted to be penetrated for emotional reasons, to feel more
complete or to provide pleasure for their partners, their own pleasure was
frequently diminished or absent.

In a more recent British study, Sheila Kitzinger reported similar findings.
However, she was also aware that this very focus on orgasm as the most
important measure of female sexuality was also felt by many women to be
oppressive:

> Orgasm has been set up by our culture as something women should strive
> for, a gift men must offer women and the proof of sexual success for both
> partners. Sex researchers ... all assume that orgasm is the measure of
> sexual satisfaction ... For most women orgasm does not have this central
> role in life.

(Kitzinger, 1985:80)

The French psychoanalyst Jacques Lacan seemed to recognise this when he
considered the problematic nature of female *jouissance*, which can be translated
to mean the 'over the top' feelings associated with sexual climax. For Lacan,
women have what he called a 'supplementary' *jouissance* beyond the experience
with the phallus, a 'something more' which he found impossible, as a man, to
define (see Juliet Mitchell and Jacqueline Rose, 1982). His former colleague
Luce Irigary tried to describe the ways in which women are capable of sensual
feelings throughout their whole bodies, without focusing on so-called erogenous
zones, as follows: '... woman has sex organs just about everywhere. She

experiences pleasure almost everywhere ... the geography of her pleasure is much more diversified, more multiple in its differences, more complex, more subtle than is imagined' (Irigary, 1981:103).

Yet such a multifaceted analysis of sexuality is not experienced by most women. At a most simple level, women are often ignorant of basic sexual physiognomy. Female genitalia are hidden and unknown compared with the prominence of male genitalia, and girl children are often not even given names by which to begin to understand these parts of their bodies. Luce Irigary explains this absence:

> Moreover she has no 'proper' name. And her sex organ which is not a sex organ, is counted as *no* sex organ. It is the negative, the opposite, the reverse, the counterpart, of the only visible and morphologically desig-natable sex organ: the penis.
>
> (Irigary, 1981:101, emphasis in the original)

Hence most women have not been able to make full use of their sexual respons-iveness, nor do they insist on exploring their very considerable capacity for sexual enjoyment. Instead, a woman will often conform to the sexual needs of her male partner, almost automatically considering her own pleasure to be of less importance than his.

One way to try and understand how and why this happens is to consider the powerful impact of ideology concerning sexuality, which has changed surprisingly little over recent years. The availability of more effective contra-ception, and a number of social changes which took place in the 'swinging sixties', appeared on the surface to encourage the development of a culture of sexual exploration and permissiveness, which opened up numerous sexual possibilities for women. However, this permissiveness in fact co-existed with an ideal of chastity before and within marriage, especially for women, and this, together with recent developments such as the growing problem of sexually transmitted diseases, especially AIDS, means that the reality is actually somewhat different for most women. In fact, as the suffragettes of the early twentieth century found in their own experimentation with what was then called 'free love', fluctuations in ideology have relatively little impact on most women's difficulties in sexual relationships with men.

Indeed, as women discovered during the period following the first world war, sexual 'freedom' from constraints and prudery rarely brings a freedom for the experience of sexuality in women's own terms. Then, as now, many women felt under pressure to involve themselves in prescriptive sexual encounters, somehow believing that sexual intimacy should and could occur after minimal acquaintance (see also Myrna Lewis, 1983). As Lynne Segal has described in her own recollections of the liberated sixties and seventies:

> The ubiquitous symbolism of male conquest and female submission, built into almost every image of heterosexuality, depicted a strange 'liberation'

for women. And by the end of the 1960s many women were to recognise the male domination anchored in such a 'sexual liberation', as well as to express a deep dissatisfaction with the sexual experiences it had provided for them.

(Segal, 1983:30)

In this way, many women found, and indeed still find themselves caught up in a situation where they feel they should be sexual partners for men who are virtually complete strangers, despite feeling that this isn't quite what they really want. At the same time, media images of the sexually liberated woman portray her as enjoying this almost random sexuality, 'the zipless fuck' described by Erica Jong (1974), as much as men appear or claim to do. Yet the reality is often different, as the woman often feels she is somehow failing to find what she really wants through these encounters. In addition, an even deeper message is being conveyed through the ideals held by society: liberated sexuality should not in fact be practised by 'nice' women. As already noted, most men still want their wives to appear chaste, and if not virginal, then at least to be less experienced than themselves. This is clearly a double, if not a triple bind: it is not only that women may well not enjoy casual sexual relationships, but that there are ambiguous and contradictory messages about female sexuality. For not only are women in some senses expected to behave sexually according to a male model, but the images of women as either madonna or whore, which exist for the long-forgotten psycho-dynamic reasons (which we have already outlined), lead to a scapegoating of those women who are in fact acting like men. Women are expected to be sexually willing, but not too experienced or too available to threaten the male sense of power and superiority. In addition, they are not supposed to have clear ideas of their own about how they might enjoy sex more, as this might betray too greedy (and unfeminine) a sexual appetite.

Relating sexually to other women

Throughout history, a number of women have chosen to reject the possibility of sexual relationships with men, by whom they may feel oppressed and intimidated, and have chosen instead to relate sexually to other women. Whilst for most lesbian women their sexuality is entirely a private matter, lesbianism for some women has developed into a political as well as a personal choice. In attempting to understand their relationships with men, some women say they have become more clearly aware of subtle, but none the less real, aspects of sexism and violence which exist even within men who profess to be radical and non-aggressive. In translating this political awareness into personal change, many women who had not previously experienced lesbian relationships, or seen themselves as lesbians, have sought out sexually intimate contact with other women.

According to many lesbian women, the sameness of their bodies facilitates the expression of their own sexuality. This probably occurs because of the familiarity of another woman's body, which may be less threatening, more comforting, and more powerfully sensual than a man's. It may also occur because the sense of merger may be easier with another woman, who (as already noted) is possibly more able to offer nurturance and containment than a man. Sharing physical knowledge of oneself with another woman may also be simpler and less anxiety-provoking; she is, after all, an extension of one's self. There is often a greater sense of equality and less fear of violation, which may aid in the difficult task of being close and intimate with another person of either sex.

Although sexual intimacy between women has in the past been either patholo-gised or ignored by orthodox psychoanalytic and psychiatric theories, more recently, feminist psychotherapists have been constructively exploring the special dynamics involved in lesbian relationships. They have suggested that whilst for some women being a lesbian can resolve many problems in that it allows them to redefine their lives without men as sexual partners, nevertheless interpersonal relationship issues such as jealousy and dependency are present between lesbian lovers as between heterosexual couples. Indeed, lesbian relationships, like other sexual relationships, are still inevitably complex since they also involve two human beings bringing with them their own psychological and social histories. Some writers (for example, Luise Eichenbaum and Susie Orbach, 1982) have argued that the dynamics between lesbian couples can be understood in the same ways as those between heterosexual couples. Others, particularly radical feminists such as Adrienne Rich (1980) have argued that the negotiation of lesbian relationships is invariably easier and less wrought with issues of power, since by definition, it involves two women on an equal basis. Yet others such as Angela Douglas (1987) argue that these relationships are more complex, because no clear-cut social conventions exist to structure or bolster the relationship, as there are in marriage, and also because there is still much homophobia in society at large (see also Elizabeth Wilson, 1983). As Joanna Ryan (1983) has argued: 'For too long women have been "mother" to men – why should we now wish to be mothers to each other with all the connotations of powerlessness and dreaded omnipotence that this conveys?' (p.208).

Yet these infantile feelings, as Joanna Ryan goes on to consider, are fundamentally involved in all women's sexual relationships. She claims that often these emotions are 'even more overwhelming with women than with men, just because of where they "come from" (p.208). This means that issues of identity and anxiety about boundaries are likely to be even more salient for lesbian women than for heterosexual women.

From our reading of the evidence, we believe that to argue that gender factors alone account for difficulties in interpersonal relationships ignores all the other issues such as psychological history, educational background, political and philosophical values, and so on that influence the way in which people relate to each other. All of this means that the possibility of being open and intimate with another person is likely to be as difficult and threatening between women as it can be between women and men, but ultimately just as rewarding when it works.

Celibacy

Whilst we live in a society that accentuates the importance of sexuality in our lives, the reality for many women is that for large portions of time they may be sexually celibate. This may be through choice or imposed by outside circumstances following, for example, the loss of a partner, or a change in the nature of a relationship. We saw in Chapter 3 that Laura was deeply unhappy about the absence of her sexual partner, particularly as she was living in a milieu of apparently satisfied couples. Many women who are recently divorced or widowed express similar feelings, often experiencing shame about the strength of their erotic feelings, and guilt that these can be directed apparently indiscriminately towards others at a time when they are mourning their lost partner.

As Tricia Bickerton (1983), who has developed workshops to enable women to explore their feelings about being alone, has found, women without sexual partners often express feelings of failure and inferiority. She interprets these in the light of a woman's earlier experiences of rejection, and the feelings of dependency that being alone can generate.

> It is such past rejections which can prevent women from regarding their present aloneness with confidence. The nature of being on one's own arouses feelings of loneliness which resound in the psyche and recall some of the early feelings of loss or distance. No wonder there is a constant yearning for a sexual relationship that will fill the gap. Perhaps in someone else's arms there will be a totality of love, a unity and lost perfection.
>
> (Bickerton, 1983:161)

Yet women who actively choose celibacy as a temporary or permanent solution in their lives can experience a sense of power in being more in control of their own feelings and relationships. They can actively explore their own auto-erotic feelings without the pressures to perform or consider the sexual satisfaction of a partner. As long as it is possible to be physically close, be it with friends, children, or even pets, our desires for body contact can often be adequately met without an explicitly sexual relationship. Unfortunately, in many western countries, non-sexual body contact is relatively infrequently exchanged, so for many people the reality is that celibacy effectively means a severe reduction in touching and being touched. We shall discuss these issues further in Chapter 8.

Women's conflicts about their bodies

There can be no woman alive who does not feel that there is something she would like to change about her body. She feels that her breasts are too large or too small;

her legs are too fat or too thin; her skin is too spotty or too wrinkled; or her nose or feet are too long. Above all, she is not the right size: the vast majority of women feel that they are overweight despite any objective evidence to support this belief.

From childhood onwards, the rewards for being perceived as physically attractive by others are evident for both women and men. Attractive school children are more likely to be given good marks by their teachers, have more friends, and later on, attractive candidates are more likely to pass selection interviews (see Gordon Patzer, 1985). Work by Diane Hayes and Catherine Ross (1986) has shown that overweight people are generally disliked, and considered by others to be mean, sloppy, and stupid. This emphasis on attractiveness is a particular problem for women, since ideals concerning what is physically desirable for women in our society are highly restricted, and much more stringent than those applied to men. In addition, examples of the ideal are widely promulgated: young women's bodies are used commercially to sell products as diverse as cars and computers, breakfast cereals and political parties. Indeed, women themselves are frequently treated as a commodity, since much of their value is judged in terms of how they look. Yet the images we see of the 'perfect body' all bear a striking similarity: firm breasts; long, hairless legs; shining hair and clear skin. Such women show no signs of having borne and nursed children: there are no stretch marks or sagging breasts, no wrinkles from decades of laughing, crying, and living.

The consequences of this for women's sexuality can be very serious. If the image of what is attractive is unattainable by most women, then the majority of women probably harbour at least a nagging suspicion that they are not, in fact, very attractive, or very sexy. If she feels she has to 'compete' against a teenage model, the middle-aged woman or the ordinary-looking young mother is unlikely to feel particularly confident in her own sexiness. This will mean that she is very probably less free to enjoy her own sexuality, as she may well feel that by comparison with the ideal, her body is a bit of a let-down for her partner. This is an especial problem for older women, but it also applies to the vast majority of younger women too, who are not models, and do not have the time, energy, or money to make themselves resemble the ideal.

Tragically, some women do try to emulate the ideal, in order to become sexier, or more 'feminine'. As we have already seen in Chapter 2, one of the ways that women attempt to alter their body shape in order to become more like the emaciated models that the media project is to try to control their eating. Unfortunately, the pervasive phenomenon of dieting, and the consumer industry it generates, affects the vast majority of young women, and increasingly, girl children as well. The cult of the body beautiful has also extended into other areas of our lives, generating a plethora of 'fitness freaks' who compulsively exercise in the way that is reminiscent of compulsive dieting. Jean Mitchell (1987) has pointed out the relationship between obsessional fitness regimes and their similarity, psychologically, with attempts to control food intake. She maintains that excessive weight-training, or aerobics expresses yet another example of women trying to control their bodies and punish themselves. This, she argues, is increasing as women experience a decreasing ability to control other aspects of their lives.

Whether women impose strict regimes on themselves, or have them imposed by others, they rarely feel that their bodies are naturally acceptable to others, or that their expression is unproblematic. As a clear example of this point, it can be seen that women with disabilities are frequently denied the possibility of any form of active sexuality. As has been pointed out by Roberta Galler (1984), medical professionals rarely contemplate or plan for the eventuality of handi-capped people having sexual contact with others; for example, sheltered housing or specially adapted accommodation for the disabled hardly ever includes space for double beds. The idea of marriage between two handicapped people is often met by both horror and amusement amongst many of those who care for the mentally ill or handicapped. Legal battles over the compulsory sterilisation of young women with mental handicap also raise important issues concerning a woman's control over her own sexuality and fertility; once again, rather than shielding women from any unwanted or unprotected intercourse which might result in conception, it is the woman's body rather than the man's which is seen as being dangerous and in need of restraint and control.

Implications for therapy with women

As we have seen, sexuality for women represents a complex interplay between the fear of danger and being engulfed on the one hand, and the desire for pleasure and joyful fusion on the other. Both these aspects of a woman's experiences should be considered when working therapeutically with women's sexuality. But in particular, therapists need to be aware of the negative aspects of this interplay, and the possibility that the woman may in the past have experienced incest, rape, or sexual harassment of some sort. Whilst, as we have seen, early psychoanalysts turned away from the knowledge of the frequency of these events for women, we now know that from childhood onwards many women have experienced a variety of different forms of unwanted sexual attention. Any therapeutic work with women, therefore, must be based on this awareness, allowing women to express and work through their feelings, where necessary, even if the therapeutic or counselling aims are ostensibly focused on other issues. For those whose primary difficulty is the aftermath of rape, incest, or other sexual trauma, therapy at least initially needs to consist of a gentle reworking of the incident or incidents, in an accepting and supportive manner. Only when her traumas have been understood and accepted will a woman who has been the victim of some sort of sexual abuse be able to move beyond the trauma to work on other sexual or current inter-personal issues.

Contemporary sex therapy

The early sexologists, such as Havelock Ellis (1913) and Alfred Kinsey and his colleagues (1953) held highly conventional assumptions about the nature of sexuality between men and women, which then generated rather distorted data concerning women's sexual experiences and pleasures (see Sheila Jeffreys, 1985; Lynne Segal 1983). However, much contemporary sex therapy is based on the pioneering work of William Masters and Virginia Johnson (1966), whose research provided vital and much more accurate information concerning the anatomy and nature of men and women's sexual arousal. For example, Masters and Johnson made public the fact that the clitoris and vulva are important loci of women's sexual pleasure, and that women retain a higher sexual arousal plateau than men, being capable of multiple orgasms.

In brief, Masters and Johnson's therapy aims to provide sexual knowledge and techniques for 'sexually dysfunctional' couples, so that women and men can develop mutually satisfying responses in sexual relationships with each other. The therapeutic approach used is conjoint: that is, therapists treat both partners simultaneously, with the ultimate aim of producing a more sexually informed partnership. Using the techniques of sensate focusing and an early contractual ban on intercourse, the couple is taught gradually to reduce the level of anxiety which they usually associate with sexual contact, and to start to enjoy all of their bodily experiences together.

Many couples report having received enormous benefit from being treated by this form of therapy. However, from the point of view of women, the positive therapeutic implications of Masters and Johnson's work have been more limited, since therapists trained in these methods tend to focus on women's sexuality almost entirely within the context of achieving penetration and intercourse (see Barbara Dodd and Anthony Parsons, 1984). In targeting orgasm for the woman as well as for the man, they thus stress performance over the nuances of pleasure, retaining a male-defined view of women's sexuality. In addition, Masters and Johnson's theories are profoundly behaviourist, in that they assume that people can 'learn' or 'unlearn' their expression of sexual satisfaction, and even change their sexual orientation, more or less according to their conscious wishes. As with any mechanistic approach, this ignores the nature of the interpersonal relationship between the couple, and the dynamics of sexual desire. Further, the focus on heterosexuality means that the therapy is usually provided only for married, or at least 'stable' couples, frequently using male and female co-therapists to model 'appropriate' behaviours. In the UK at least this rarely includes the use of surrogate partners, which has been a source of considerable debate since the publication of Masters and Johnson's original approach, but which may be needed for the effective treatment of some single men and womena.

Developing on from the Masters and Johnson approach, there have recently been a number of important advances in thinking about women's sexuality, for example, the woman-focused sex therapies of Helen Kaplan (1974) and Lonnie

Barbach (1975). Nevertheless, many of these therapies still assume that the achievement of orgasm is the primary aim of sex. Yet, as we have seen, there are many other aspects of women's – and men's – sexuality which are equally as important. A truly women-centred theory and practice of sexuality should allow for women to develop individually their own range of experiences and sensations, acknowledging that these will change over their life span, and will alter depending on whether the woman is alone or with a male or a female partner. Perhaps we should in fact talk about women's sexualities in the plural, and adopt a therapeutic stance that allows for such diversity.

Alternative approaches to sex therapy: women alone

In recent years, a variety of alternative therapeutic experiences have been made available to women who wish to explore the possibility of an autonomous sexuality, particularly by using group therapy approaches (see, for example, Sheila Ernst and Lucy Goodison, 1981). These groups aim to help women explore and develop their 'own' sexuality by incorporating features such as massage and fantasy. These therapies are intended to encourage women to experience a range of sexual/sensual sensations by themselves, away from the pressures to perform or to consider the needs of a partner. Important aspects of such approaches are the 'permission' given for a women to be sexual, and the knowledge provided about her own body. For women who have been brought up to believe that sex is immoral and dirty, these can be profoundly valuable experiences.

Similar 'permission' can of course also be given in individual psychotherapy, in the context of a growing awareness of relational issues. In Edith's case, for example, her shame about her father's sexual advances had led her to 'disinherit' her adult body. She cut herself off from all sensual and sexual sensations, which allowed her to become the object of men's sexual pleasure and denied her any good feelings of her own. However, within a therapy relationship with a therapist who could talk openly about sexual feelings and acknowledge the traumatic nature of her earlier experiences, Edith eventually came to value and appreciate herself, making her less vulnerable to abuse. She was then slowly able to allow herself the possibility of having sexual relationships with people who were more sensitive to her needs and wishes.

Another issue of relevance to therapeutic work with women is the importance of sexual knowledge. As we have already noted, many women are unaware of their own genital anatomy; hence one important task for a therapist working with a woman on her own may be to provide the woman with straightforward education about her body, and thus to help her gain more confidence in talking about it. For only when a woman knows what her body looks like, how it feels, and how to talk about it, will she be able to decide how and when to share herself with others. Knowing about herself means that she is more likely to be able to communicate to others what she wants, although this does not of course guarantee that she will get what she wants. But knowing what she likes and how to talk about it is obviously a first step to asking for it, and hence to getting it.

Alternative approaches to sex therapy: working with couples

Following on from some of the points made previously, therapists working with couples often need to challenge the tendency of many women to feel reluctant about asserting their own needs in a sexual relationship. Many women still feel nervous of asking their partner to stroke or stimulate them in particular ways, and hope somehow that the partner will have the powers of a mind-reader. It may be that this relates to the romantic myth discussed in Chapter 3, which promotes the notion that the couple should be so perfectly in tune that they do not really need to discover anything about the other, let alone communicate about a topic such as sex. Yet this is obviously unlikely to be very successful, especially if the partner is a man, and hence can only find out what the woman wants or likes if she tells him.

One result of women's socialisation to be caring and nurturing, and hence sensitive to the needs of others, is that they will often try hard to adapt themselves to what their partners want. Many men, on the other hand, who have not usually had the same interpersonal experiences, are often unable to pick up subtle cues and nuances, and may be unpractised or unwilling to consider their partner's needs. In the absence of any information from the woman, a man will often assume that everything is all right and that no change is needed in their actions. Their women partners, hurt and disappointed that they are not getting what they want, may well then withdraw into silent isolation and sexual frustration. Ironically, in choosing to relate to men, women are in fact choosing to be close to people who are probably not so skilled in interpersonal sensitivity as they are themselves, or as their mothers used to be, and are hence increasing the chances of not being understood. Therapists working with couples must therefore help the partners to break this pattern of the man's dependency on the woman's emotional and sexual subservience. Most men initially find this rather threatening, but many eventually discover the greater pleasures that can come from shared sexuality, and developing their sensitivity to the needs and desires of their partners.

Earlier in this chapter we stressed that sexuality is not an aspect of human beings which is simply an 'add-on extra', separate and apart from other aspects of people's interpersonal relationships. Hence, any therapy which deals with sexual difficulties or dissatisfactions must also be concerned with emotional issues between the couple, such as unresolved childhood needs, dependencies, jealousies, and fears of intimacy. Emotional issues such as these are all revealed in a couple's sexual relationship, so that therapists must be concerned with these questions as well as with the mechanics of sex. Otherwise, therapy concerned with sexuality might as well be conducted from a 'how to do it' manual, whereby sex becomes a perfomance carried out by emotionless automata. Instead, therapy with a couple which is centred on sexual difficulties must also be concerned with the types of personal and emotional issues which we discussed earlier in Chapter 3.

Assertiveness in sexual relationships

We have repeatedly stressed how important it is that therapists help women in relationships to be able to negotiate their needs with others. Sometimes this involves being able to initiate sexual intimacy with the other person, but sometimes it involves being able to refuse that intimacy. For many women, being able to refuse is actually even harder than being able to initiate intimacy. It is sadly rare for men to supply nurturant caring for each other or for women, so that particularly for women working with male colleagues or superiors, there are many demands on them to be emotionally giving and available. Many women may then find themselves becoming sexually involved with men to whom they may have originally intended only to offer friendship and support. Hence a woman's ability to negotiate for what she does and does not want in relationships, is crucial, although in some situations it may involve acting in ways that seem to be 'ungenerous' or uncaring. Indeed, a man may often imply as much if a women does not respond to his sexual requests. A woman may then need considerable support in refusing to accept this form of emotional blackmail, and to assert her rights to control her own body and sexual involvements.

Adolescent girls are of course particularly vulnerable to this form of blackmail, when they are told that they can only prove their love for their boyfriends if they consent to intercourse. But adult women can also be pressurised in this way, and because their nurturing responses are so well established, they may find them- selves agreeing to sexual involvements which do not really suit them at all. Therapists may therefore have to encourage women to become considerably more assertive in the conduct of their sexual and non-sexual relationships. Assertion techniques such as those developed by Ann Dickson (1982) can be most helpful in this connection.

Concluding note

Earlier in this chapter we mentioned the difficulties which particular groups of women may have in feeling good about their bodies and their sexuality. The problems of middle-aged and elderly women will be discussed in more detail in Chapter 9, and those of women who are celibate will be examined again in Chapter 8, when we look at women who live without sexual partners. But there are also other groups of women who may need especial help from therapists, and these are the handicapped or disabled. For these women it may be appropriate to obtain very specialised forms of help, possibly in the form of prosthetic devices or aids. But even though this may be the case, the need for mechanical assistance should not blind the therapist to the existence of emotional or interpersonal difficulties, which are likely to be compounded by society's contribution to the plight of the disabled: shame, disapproval, and embarrassment. This group of women is often tragically neglected, and may have especial difficulties in obtaining access to therapeutic help.

While in this chapter we have considered the special form of intimacy that occurs through sexual contact with others, we want again to stress that there are of course other forms of intimate relationship, and some of the most important for women's lives are the relationships which develop between a woman and her children. This, then, will be the subject of Chapters 6 and 7. Next, however, we turn to look at the world of work, where women spend a high proportion of their time, and where, as we shall see, the fact of a woman's gender and her capacity for relating sensitively to others also has an enormous impact.

References

Alter-Reid, K., Gibbs, M.S., Lachenmeyer, J.R., Sigal, J., and Massoth, N. (1986) 'Sexual abuse of children, a review of the empirical findings', *Clinical Psychology Review* 6: 249–66

Balint, M. (1968) *The Basic Fault*, London: Tavistock.

Bar, V. (1987) 'Change in women', in S. Ernst and M. Maguire (eds) *Living with the Sphinx*, London: The Women's Press.

Barash, D. (1979) *The Whispering Within*, New York: Harper & Row.

Barbach, L. (1975) *For Yourself: the fulfilment of female sexuality*, New York: Signet.

Bickerton, T. (1983) 'Women alone', in S. Cartledge and J. Ryan (eds), *Sex and Love*, London: The Women's Press.

Brownmiller, S. (1975) *Against Our Will: men, women and rape*, London: Secker & Warburg.

Burgess, A.W. and Holmstrom, L.L. (1974) *Rape: victims of crisis*, Bowie Md.: Brady.

Chodorow, N. (1978) *The Reproduction of Mothering*, Berkeley: University of California Press.

Davenport, S. and Sheldon, H. (1987) 'From victim to survivor', *Changes* 5: 379–82.

Deutsch, H. (1945) *The Psychology of Women: a psychoanalytic interpretation*, Volume II, New York: Grune & Stratton.

Dickson, A. (1982) *A Woman in Your Own Right*. London: Quartet Books.

Dinnerstein, D. (1978) *The Rocking of the Cradle*, New York: Souvenir Press.

Dodd, B. and Parsons, A. (1984) 'Psychosexual problems', in A. Broome and L. Wallace (eds) *Psychology and Gynaecological Problems*, London: Tavistock.

Douglas, A. (1987) 'Feminist psychotherapy and lesbianism: implications for theory and practice', paper presented at the Feminist Psychotherapy Conference, Leeds, UK, April.

Dworkin, A. (1987) *Intercourse*, New York: Secker & Warburg.

Eichenbaum, L. and Orbach, S. (1982) *Outside In ... Inside Out*, Harmondsworth: Penguin.

Eichenbaum, L. and Orbach, S. (1987) 'Separation and intimacy: crucial practice issues in working with women in therapy', in S. Ernst and M. Maguire (eds) *Living with the Sphinx*, London: The Women's Press.

Ellis, H. (1913) *Studies in the Psychology of Sex*, Volume III, *Analysis of the sexual impulse, love and pain: the sexual impulse in women*, Philadelphia: F.A. Davis (first published 1903).

Ernst, S. and Goodison, L. (1981) *In Our Own Hands: a book of self-help therapy*, London: The Women's Press.

Fairbairn, W.D.R. (1952) *Psychoanalytic Studies of the Personality*, London: Routledge & Kegan Paul.

Foucault, M. (1978) *The History of Sexuality*, New York: Pantheon.

Freud, S. (1925) *Some psychical consequences of the anatomical distinction between the sexes*, in S. Freud (1977) *On Sexuality* Pelican Freud Library, Volume 7, Harmondsworth: Penguin.

Galler, R. (1984) 'The myth of the perfect body', in C. Vance (ed.) *Pleasure and Danger*, London: Routledge & Kegan Paul.

Groth, A.N. (1979) *Men Who Rape*, New York: Plenum Press.

Guntrip, H. (1971) *Psychoanalytic Theory, Therapy and the Self*, New York and London: Basic Books.

Hamblin, A. (1983) 'Is a feminist heterosexuality possible?' in S. Cartledge and J. Ryan (eds) *Sex and Love*, London: The Women's Press.

Hayes, D. and Ross, C. (1986) 'Body and mind: the effects of exercise, overweight and physical health on psychological wellbeing', *Journal of Health and Social Behaviour*, 27: 387–400.

Hite, S. (1976) *The Hite Report*, New York: Macmillan.

Hubbard, R. (1983) 'Social effects of some contemporary myths about women', in M. Lowe and R. Hubbard (eds) *Women's Nature: rationalizations of inequality*, New York: Pergamon.

Irigary, L. (1981) 'Ce sex qui n'en est pas un' (This sex which is not one), in E. Marks and I. de Courtivron (eds) (1981), *New French Feminisms*, Brighton: Harvester Press.

Jeffreys, S. (1985) *The Spinster and Her Enemies*, London: Pandora.

Jong, E. (1974) *Fear of Flying*, London: Secker & Warburg.

Kaplan, H. (1974) *The New Sex Therapy*, New York: Brunner/Mazel.

Kinsey, A.C., Pomeroy, W.B., Martin, C.E., and Gephard, P. (1953) *Sexual Behaviour in the Human Female*, London: W.B. Saunders.

Kitzinger, S. (1985) *Women's Experience of Sex*, Harmondsworth: Penguin.

Klein, M. (1935) 'A contribution to the psychogenesis of manic-depressive states', in M. Klein (1975) *Love, Guilt and Reparation and Other Works*, London: Hogarth.

Lewis, M. (1983) 'The history of female sexuality in the United States', in M. Kirkpatrick (ed.) *Women's Sexual Development*, New York: Plenum Press.

Lowe, M. (1983) 'The dialectic of biology and culture', in M. Lowe and R. Hubbard (eds) *Women's Nature: rationalizations of inequality*, New York: Pergamon.

MacDonald, K. (ed.) (1988) *Sociobiological Perspectives on Human Development*, New York: Springer-Verlag.

Martin, D. (1982) 'Wife beating: a product of sociosexual development', in M. Kirkpatrick (ed.) *Women's Sexual Experience*, New York: Plenum Press.

Masters, W.H. and Johnson, V.E. (1966) *Human Sexual Response*, Boston: Little Brown & Co.

Masters, W.H. and Johnson, V.E. (1970) *Human Sexual Inadequacy*, Boston: Little Brown & Co.

Miller, A. (1985) *Thou Shalt Not Be Aware*, London: Pluto.

Mitchell, J. (1974) *Psychoanalysis and Feminism*, London: Allen Lane.

Mitchell, J. (1987) '"Going for the burn" and "Pumping iron": what's healthy about the current fitness boom?' in M. Lawrence (ed.) *Fed Up and Hungry*, London: The Women's Press.

Mitchell, J. and Rose, J. (eds) (1982) *Feminine Sexuality*, London: Macmillan.

Moore, J. (1981) 'A family affair', *Community Care*, pp. 14–15, 11 June.

Moulton, R. (1977) 'The fear of female power – a cause of sexual dysfunction', *Journal of the American Academy of Psychoanalysis* 5: 499–519.

Owen, U. (1983) *Fathers: reflections by daughters*, London: Virago.

Patzer, G. (1985) *The Physical Attractiveness Phenomena*, New York: Plenum.

Pleck, J. (1981) *The Myth of Masculinity*, Cambridge, Mass.: M.I.T.

Rich, A. (1980) 'Compulsory heterosexuality and lesbian existence', *Signs* 5:191.

Rush, F. (1980) *The Best Kept Secret: sexual abuse of children*, New York: Prentice Hall.

Ryan, J. (1983) 'Psychoanalysis and women loving women', in S. Cartledge & J. Ryan (eds) *Sex and Love*, London: The Women's Press.

Sayers, J. (1986) *Sexual Contradictions*, London: Tavistock.

Segal, L. (1983) 'Sensual uncertainty, or why the clitoris is not enough', in S. Cartledge and J. Ryan (eds) *Sex and Love*, London: The Women's Press.

Smart, C. and Smart, B. (eds) (1978) *Women, Sexuality and Social Control*, London: Routledge & Kegan Paul.

Smith, J. (1983) 'Feminist analysis of gender: a critique', in M. Lowe and R. Hubbard (eds) *Women's Nature: rationalizations of inequality*, New York: Pergamon.

Vance, C. (1984) *Pleasure and Danger: exploring female sexuality*, London: Routledge & Kegan Paul.

Wilson, E. (1975) *Sociobiology: the new synthesis*, Cambridge, Mass.: Harvard University Press.

Wilson, E. (1983) 'I'll climb the stairway to Heaven: lesbianism in the seventies', in S. Cartledge and J. Ryan (eds) *Sex and Love*, London: The Women's Press.

Wilson, G. (1979) 'The sociobiology of sex differences', *Bulletin of the British Psychological Society* 32: 350–2.

Chapter five

Women and work

Clare's story

Unlike most of the other women whose stories are told in this book, Clare did not come to see either of us because she felt in need of help. Instead, she was an aquaintance of several years' standing. She had always appeared to us, and doubtless does so to many others, as a confident and well-organised woman, in her fifties, who loved her work and who felt fulfilled by her chosen path in life: that of an independent woman, doing a job that she believed in, and devoting most of her waking hours to her work.

When I first asked Clare about her work, we talked for some time about her job history, and about how she had decided very early on not to have children, but instead to maintain her own economic independence and pursue her career. I was therefore astonished when, towards the end of our conversation, she mentioned enthusiastically that 'there are only 230 weeks until my retirement!' I asked further, and she said, yes, for the past few years she had kept the number of weeks until her retirement written into her diary each week, so that every Monday she could cross one more week off. Despite the fact that she gained a lot of satisfaction from her work, she longed for the day when she could retire and do exactly as she pleased.

I therefore thought I really needed to look more closely at Clare's experiences of work, to try and discover the exact place of work in her life. I started by asking Clare to tell me about her schooldays:

I enjoyed school, although when I first went to grammar school, my mother was dead against it. She had nine brothers and sisters who all lived in the same village as us, and my mother's sisters – my aunts – all thought that girls shouldn't have an education. So there was a lot of pressure put on to the family: 'What are you sending Clare to grammar school for? It's not good for girls.' But my father always stood up for me, and I also stuck to my guns. I desperately wanted to go to grammar school, and I desperately wanted to go to college. So in the end I went to a girls' grammar school, in spite of all the opposition.

In those days, the 1940s, it was just becoming fashionable for girls' grammar schools to have a science sixth form. Now I was an all-rounder – I'm hope I'm not being arrogant, but I was fairly good at everything, so there was a battle for me between the english mistress and the chemistry mistress. The headmistress, in her wisdom, finally decided that I should be a chemist, because she wanted a science sixth, and I could have done either. So she pushed me that way, and I must have agreed, in fact I know I agreed, because at that time I was all churned up about religion. I wanted to know how things worked, and I thought, misguidedly, that I'd understand *why* if I knew *how*. I rather liked the idea of being a white-coated scientist too – quite an erroneous idea, but that was also behind it!

I then asked Clare how she had first experienced the world of work:

After school I went to college and did a chemistry course. At that time there was an enormous shortage of women science teachers – there still is – and so while I was in my last year at college, my old headmistress rang me up and said 'Our chemistry mistress is leaving, would you like to come back and teach when you've finished your course?' Now in those days you didn't have to have a teaching certificate, especially if you were a scientist, so you could go straight back and teach. By then I had also met my future husband, Ian, and he thought he wanted to teach too, although he never really did in fact. At the time I was very anxious to have a big 'together-ness' thing with him, so I said yes, I would go back, assuming that Ian would also get a teaching job. Ian had said he wanted to teach chemistry, although I at that stage had thought I wanted to be an industrial chemist. I had this vision of being like Madame Curie or something like that, but because he wanted to teach, I decided to accept the offer of teaching and go back to my old school. When I was 13, there were two things I wasn't going to do: I wasn't going to get married and I wasn't going to teach; but by the time I was 21 I'd done both!

So then I taught for two-and-a-half years while Ian was doing his National Service. But while Ian was away, he was in the education corps, teaching soldiers, and decided there that he didn't like teaching after all. So when he came out, he decided to go into industry, not teaching. Little wifey Clare then decided she'd work in industry too! So I then handed in my notice as a teacher and went to work for Browns, like Ian.

That was a terrible mistake. I had enjoyed being a teacher, although it's such a long time ago now that I can't be entirely sure. I was so undecided about all sorts of things then, not necessarily in a negative way, but open to all sorts of different experiences, that I didn't stop and analyse whether I enjoyed it or not, but I think I did, although I found the junior work rather boring. In fact I remember one of the things that influenced my decision to change to working in industry was when I sat down and marked 90 accounts of how to separate salt from sand, and most of them hadn't got the message and I thought, really I don't want to spend the rest of my life doing this! And also, at Christmas we had Christmas parties, and exams to mark, and reports to do, and at the same time I was trying to be a good wife and do all the Christmas things at home, and that was very stressful. So I decided I'd rather have a job which was more spread out over the year, without these horrific peaks when everything happened at once. So really the decision to give up teaching was partly me, but mostly following my husband, because we still had this vision that our marriage was going to be different. It was quite clear from the start that neither of us wanted children. Also, I was going to be what was in those days called a 'career woman', and we had this vision of developing our careers together, so therefore I wanted to be in the same sort of job as him. But of course it didn't work out that way at all, because he was a man. He was offered a year's graduate traineeship at Browns, in which he went round all the different departments working for three months in each – Research, Quality Control, Development, and so on, whereas I applied to Browns six months after him, and I was immediately offered a job in Quality Control and there I stayed. At the time I accepted that quite happily. I didn't even question it.

I then asked Clare what happened next: were her visions of combining happily married life and becoming another Marie Curie at Browns fulfilled?

No! Ian settled in the Research department after doing his graduate trainee year, and got on very well. I stayed in Quality Control and stuck there, and didn't get on well at all. There were a number of reasons for that. One was that Ian would bring work home, and do work in the evenings, while I would creep around in the kitchen making his sandwiches for the next day and keeping quiet, not having the radio on, and being supportive. I'm not actually blaming Ian, as this was my choice at that stage. I can remember when I went to Browns, I was employed on a temporary basis, because all married women were temporary, and I recall saying, 'That's fair enough, if there is a recession, obviously the women would have to go first.'

Then there was the issue of my pension. I was in the teachers' pension scheme but when I went to Browns one of the first things I said was, 'Can I join the pension scheme?' I don't know why, because obviously retirement must have seemed aeons away then, but I just knew that I ought to be in a pension scheme. Quite rightly, and it is galling to know that I felt like that then, because I am now about to suffer from what happened next, and it just wasn't my fault. I was told, 'No, you can't join the pension scheme, you're married.' So I wasn't allowed to join the pension scheme until I'd been with the company for twelve years, when they sent me a letter, an incredible letter, which said, 'It looks as if you really do mean to stay with us, you've been here 12 years, as a special favour would you like to join the pension scheme?' So I did, but by then I'd lost twelve years of service. I'm really resenting that now, as I approach retirement.

I was paid less than my husband, too, because my job was less responsible anyway. Not only that, but in Quality Control, when I first joined, men and women were paid differently. There'd be men and women working on the same bench doing the same job, and on the notice-board would be two scales, one for men, and one for women. This was bad enough, but then I realised the men were getting more holidays than I was. Now in industry, holidays are like gold dust and when I looked into this, I discovered it was because they were earning more. It was Catch 22. If you were a woman you earned less than a man, and therefore you didn't qualify for the extra holiday. I wrote to the personnel director about the holiday, and was invited to go and take afternoon tea with him, which I did. He was an old officer-type, and he said, 'We see you've been with us for 16 years, Mrs Hamson.' I said, 'I am still Temporary, you know'. He said, 'Are you really?', and buzzed his minion, who came with the records. He looked at my card and indeed it said 'Temporary' on it – this was after sixteen years – and he took out a gold ballpoint pen and he struck through the word Temporary. That was my only victory at Browns, but I thought it was a considerable one! But I'd realised by then that I didn't like chemistry and really hated Browns.

It had started to puzzle me very considerably why Clare had stayed at Browns for so long, even though she said she hated it, and clearly felt resentful of the treatment she received as a woman. I asked her why she had stayed:

Because I assumed that once you've got some training, and you want to earn your own living, there's no way out. At least I couldn't see a way of getting out. If I had my time over again, I'm quite sure I could have got out. And in the end, of course, I did.

I then wondered how working for so long at Browns had made her feel. Did she get depressed, or was she cheerfully resigned?

No, I didn't get depressed, that's the funny part about it, really. I just accepted it – sounds daft. I knew that I wanted to work, and I knew financial independence was important to me, and I accepted that I was trained as a chemist and therefore that was what I had got to do.

I then asked her if at the very least she obtained the satisfaction of doing the job well, although she didn't really enjoy it.

No – I got very little satisfaction from the actual job. It was ... status is the nearest I can get to it. The fact that I was working and financially independent was very important to me.

Feeling sad on her behalf, I asked her if she had at least looked forward to evenings and weekends.

No, because I wasn't doing the things I wanted to do then either. That was a bone of contention between Ian and me, because I was doing housework in the evenings and weekends, which I loathe. Ian and I liked different things, but we tended to do what Ian liked on holidays, until I objected. That is why holidays became so important to me, because I began eventually to do some of the things I wanted to do, although I still felt I'd got to have my fortnight's annual holiday with him!

So how had she got out of Browns in the end?

When I got my teeth into this holiday question, I went to my trade union shop steward, who was a man, and said, 'Why can't the union do something about this?' But he didn't want to know, he didn't think it was at all important. So I then started going to branch meetings, and in no time at all I was branch secretary, because you only have to open your mouth at a union meeting and you're elected, especially if you are prepared to do the secretarial work. And then I got very active in the union and as a consequence, did a day-release course, one day a week for 30 weeks, doing communication, economics, and industrial relations. This then led me to doing a certificate in industrial relations. I got release for these courses from Browns only with a great deal of hassle – I had to be really aggressive – rather than assertive! In fact, the only thing that really did mean something to me in all my time at Browns was the union. I felt I was doing something useful, and I got a lot of satisfaction out of that. I became very active in women's work – I felt very strongly about how women were treated in industry, so I was active in both local and national Women's Advisory Committees. I felt that was really useful. The time I got active was the time of the Sex Discrimination Act, so unions were bending over backwards to encourage women, and I'm quite sure that's why I made the rapid progress I did. If you were a women and you were interested, you were almost pushed, because they were so pleased to have you as their token woman. That's why I got on. And it was really because of my union work that it dawned on me that I could in fact get out of Browns.

Next I asked Clare about the way in which her career developed after leaving Browns.

I decided to go into adult education, which is where I am now. It is incredibly hard work: most days I'm busy all day and every evening, and I also have to work at least every other weekend. The bit I like best is the teaching, but I don't really enjoy all the administrative work. There is a lot of committee work, especially in the evenings – reinventing the wheel! A lot of it is sheer hassle. It makes me feel like I'm wasting a lot of precious time, but I like being busy and feeling I'm doing something useful.

Having been absorbed in the story, it then occurred to me that somewhere along the line, Clare and her husband had got divorced. I felt this was sure to be relevant, so I asked her about it.

We got divorced just after I left Browns. We were married when we were both 21, and I never really enjoyed being married. My husband was a very nice man and I won't have a word said against him, but he tended to be very domineering and I slowly realised I was being crushed by him. He wasn't very supportive, either, for anything I wanted to do, or think. So when I saw this job advertised in adult education, and realised it meant moving away from home, I didn't really mind. Basically we just drifted apart.

I wanted to know how much Clare felt, looking back, that the opportunities which had been open or closed to her were to do with being a woman. She replied that she felt that she had not personally experienced discrimination in teaching, although she knew that some of the other perfectly well-qualified women with whom she had worked had not got headships or other senior teaching posts, apparently because of their sex. However, she said vociferously that there had definitely been discrimination against her at Browns. She felt that it was just assumed she would do some lowly job: 'And I don't think it has changed now, it hadn't changed much by the time I left!

I also wondered what sort of conflicts had existed in the past, and existed now, between her employment role, and her role as a woman.

I do think there was considerable conflict when I was at Browns. I was still very much trying to be the caring wife, and therefore I was quite happy – no, I wasn't happy, but I just accepted it. I felt it right for Ian to bring work home while I did the domestic things. He was the big important man, doing his group's work, and although I couldn't easily have brought my work home, if I'd been more single-minded, I might have got on better. Still, I don't really know if it would have made any difference.

I then said to Clare that I felt that in some ways work must have played an important part in her life, in that she decided very early she didn't want children, and now she was living alone, spending much of her time on her job. For her, work was clearly not a part-time activity while real life went on with her husband or children. But she vociferously denied this, saying that work was just a way of earning a living for her, which then allowed her to do what she really did want to do. So finally, I asked Clare what it was that she really did enjoy in life.

Music and my home! If I had pots of money I'd spend a lot more time at concerts and recitals, and swanning around to festivals. I do a bit of that, but not as much as I'd like. Also, I'm now doing an Arts degree with the Open University, which I wanted to do when I was 18, until I got pushed into chemistry. It is so clear to me now that I should have done English when I was 18, as it's what I really love. But I did collude in the decision to go for chemistry, there's no question about that. But a few years ago it dawned on me that the Open University was there, and I always wanted to do a degree in English – may sound daft to you, but it's Everest to me! It won't do me much good by the time I do get it, if I ever do get it, but I do want to get it, because I do respect people with academic achievements! But work now seems to me to be something that just takes up too much of my time, when I would rather be doing what I really want to do. I've now worked for 34 years, and I think that is long enough for anybody, don't you?

Women in the workplace

Astonishingly, it is still the case, when over 40 per cent of the workforce in most advanced countries such as Britain are women, and when between 60 and 75 per cent of women are in part- or full-time employment, that women's work is not taken seriously. Most textbooks on employment, training, trade unions, or even unemployment, see work as a male domain, and consider the archetypal worker to be male, and quite probably employed in some heavy manual trade. In fact such an individual is in the minority, since most employees now work with the assistance of sophisticated machinery, or in the service, administrative, or leisure industries, where many of the demands are interpersonal rather than physical. Nevertheless, the image or stereotype of the workplace as a male sphere, and the home as a female sphere, persists.

For all women workers, there are a number of very serious consequences of this stereotype, for example, the poor training opportunities open to women, justified by seeing women's work as secondary to their 'main' occupation, and the consequent low levels of pay. For women who are mothers there is also the severe lack of provision of child-care facilities in the workplace, and the inflexibility of most employers regarding patterns of employment. But in parallel to the very real obstacles which exist to women's full participation in the workplace, and hence to the benefits of employment, there are also a number of psychological barriers. The vast majority of women are channelled, and to an extent accept channelling, into a handful of occupations, such as catering, sales, education, nursing, and semi- or unskilled assembly work (see Shirley Dex, 1985; Janet Holland, 1980; OECD, 1985). Many do not have the opportunity, skill, desire, or confidence to consider any other alternatives. Only a small number of women have 'careers', often in what are usually considered to be male domains, see their work as the central focus of their lives, and have reasonably satisfactory work experiences.

In this chapter, we seek to unravel some of the psychological components of women's working experience, although consideration of social and economic issues can never be very far away. Any discussion of psychological issues should only be undertaken with an awareness of the ever-present backdrop of deeply resistant practices of sexual discrimination, unequal pay, and unequal opportunity. It must also be noted that this backdrop has remained substantially unaltered over recent decades, despite attempts to bring about equality through legislation, for example, the UK Equal Pay and Sex Discrimination Acts, and numerous EEC edicts on the illegality of discrimination against women workers.

But it still remains the case that women workers earn on average 20 to 40 per cent less than men (OECD, 1985), meaning that, in the UK, for example, women in the labour force lose out on over £15 billion a year because of sex bias at work (Helen Hague, 1987). This is not a trivial problem: in many instances women's wages are economically essential to their families: in the UK, for example, almost two million women are the sole supporters of households, and the number of two-income familes on or below the poverty line would be trebled without the woman's earnings. The figures are similar in the United States (Janet Holland, 1980).

The structure of this chapter will be as follows: first we shall show how women's domestic responsibilities and personal commitments affect their involvement in the workplace, both by earning women the label of 'unreliable', and by reducing the amount of energy, enthusiasm, and resources which women may have to give to their jobs. We shall also examine some of the aspects of the working environment, such as sexual harassment and sex discrimination, which cause particular problems for women employees. Next we shall review theories concerning women's involvement in work, and see how far women are adversely affected by unemployment. We will also look at some of the psychological determinants of particular job choices, showing how even in the work sphere, personal and emotional concerns are never very far away. In concluding the chapter, we shall discuss the role of therapists in helping women to understand their ambivalences about work, and empowering them to operate more effectively in the working environment.

Women's work histories: women as 'unreliable' workers

The first, and perhaps most crucial issue in understanding women's working lives is that it makes little sense to talk about the pattern of women's experience of paid work without also talking about the domestic and family responsibilities almost always assumed by women. Even if a woman chooses a particular career, and makes every effort to pursue it, it is an extremely rare woman who does not have to modify or even radically alter her plans in response to overt or covert pressures from family or employers. As a consequence, women are often seen as unreliable employees. Even Clare, who had made it quite clear that she did not want children, was, because she was a married woman, treated as a potential mother or dependant, and hence seen as being 'temporary'.

But even more pervasive than discrimination from employers is the perception by the woman herself that her career does not matter as much as her husband's, or that doing what she wants for herself must come second to what is needed by her family. Until she and her husband were divorced, Clare followed her husband's career changes, so much so that it was impossible for Clare to tell the story of her own experience of work without describing her husband's history too. This she assumed at the time was quite natural, as were her lower wages and reduced opportunities for training. Employers often justify their discrimination against women by claiming that they are a poor risk, although in fact the time lost through illness and turnover by women employees is actually lower than that lost by men (Janet Holland, 1980). Nevertheless, women do not capitalise on this good record and are still seen as being 'unreliable' because of their loyalty to their families.

The major reason for a break in women's employment record is of course for child-rearing. Most women who have children do have a break of some sort in their employment history, and according to Heather Joshi (1987) rarely recover their position in the employment hierarchy in terms of pay, responsibility, promotion, and status. Certainly, the financial losses of full-time motherhood are substantial. In the UK, for example, most women (97 per cent) who drop out of paid work over and beyond the minimum maternity leave, do so for an average of six to seven years. Helen Joshi's analyses indicate that a typical British mother in bringing up two children loses earnings of over £122,000 during her lifetime. This is the case not only because of her loss of earnings from paid work in the early years of her children's lives, but also because of the fact that when women return to work, they are usually downwardly mobile, moving either into part-time work or to jobs at a lower level than their previous employment.

In addition to their difficulties in participating in paid employment, many women also find that combining their child-care responsibilities with social or recreational activities connected to work is equally problematic. The additional double-bind for women is that if they *do* organise alternative child care to enable them to participate in paid work or other activities, they are often faced with feelings of guilt and criticism from others that they are not with their children; yet those who are full-time mothers often feel equally guilty that they are not contributing to society at large and that they are somehow non-productive. These issues are discussed more fully in Chapter 7. But it is relevant to note here that this sense of responsibility for others, and automatic self-sacrifice can then, of course, be used by employers who will claim that women are not as ambitious and interested in pursuing careers as are men, and are therefore not worth promoting or training.

Women's double shift

There are a number of psychological factors underlying the pattern in women's working lives noted previously, some of which will now be outlined. The first reason for the fact that women as a group are less able than men to devote themselves unreservedly to their jobs is of course the responsibilities of women *outside* the workplace as well as within the workplace. Elsewhere in this book we discuss the major psychological consequences for women in the context of the family and interpersonal relationships, of their commitments to men and for children; but there are a number of important implications of these commitments for women in employment, too. As we have already seen in Chapter 3, women are far more likely than men to take responsibility for interpersonal and social relationships, and to respond to the needs of others by providing nurturance and care. These distinctions are clearly mirrored in the occupational choices made by men and women, whereby women are far more likely than men to be nurses, teachers, cleaners, or personal secretaries. But, more importantly, there are consequences for women, whether they are in part- or full-time employment, in terms of their performance at and dedication to work. Women are far more likely than men to take responsibility for the domestic and social aspects of family life, which has led some to describe women as perpetually working a 'double shift'. Jean Martin and Ceridwen Roberts, for example, in their survey of 6,000 British women carried out in 1984 have pointed out that more than half of all wives do all or most of the housework, and Jonathan Gershuny (1987) has reported that while women in the USA and Europe spend between 180 and 230 minutes per day on housework, including cleaning and food preparation, men spend between 40 and 70 minutes per day. Obviously, in this case, women have less time and resources available for work than men, and are less likely to see the employment arena as the only focus for their energies. At its most rudimentary, many full-time working women spend their lunch hours catching up on shopping, or popping home to see to the children, while their husbands may be consolidating social contacts at work, or simply relaxing.

This is not to say that this division of labour is imposed on all women under protest. Many women still feel, somehow, that they should do more of the cooking and cleaning than their husbands if they are to be good wives. Jean Martin and Ceridwen Roberts (1984) report that three-quarters of their sample of working women felt that the amount of housework done by their husbands or cohabitees was about right, and most thought that paid work was for them secondary to their family. In addition, many other writers have noted that most working mothers experience feelings of guilt and regret about their responsibilities for their children, a feeling almost completely unknown to working fathers.

Even highly motivated and reasonably well-paid professional women are much more likely than their husbands to undertake the major responsibility for domestic and family chores. The result for these professional women is the attempt to become a 'Superwoman', who performs the double shift faultlessly and without apparent effort. But the cost of performing the Superwoman role is normally exhaustion, and probably, unexpressed resentment. According to Alexandra Symonds (1979) who works therapeutically with many professional women, these women typically show enormous energy in combining professional and home-maker duties, but:

> there is a deeper and more significant struggle taking place . . . (which is)
> experienced daily many, many times at all stages of both her professional
> and wifely careers. Not only is she impelled to divide her time and energy
> to cover both home and work, but unlike the male professional, she is
> constantly beset with divided loyalties, a sense of guilt, and often a shaky

sense of identity.... As soon as a young man becomes inclined towards a profession, this system is built and maintained for him by the women in his life – first his mother, often his sisters, later his girlfriend and his secretary. When a woman becomes a professional she must most often provide her own support system. Many of my patients went into their careers without family support, and sometimes with the family's active disapproval. And, amazingly, when these same women got married, they automatically relegated their own professional needs to those of their husbands and families. Their own personal growth went underground without apparent resentment, although it took its toll in depression, unhappiness, and psychosomatic syndromes.

(Symonds, 1979:57–8)

Certainly, in the case of Clare, it was noticeable that she did not pay much attention to her own feelings about her working experience until after her divorce, never stopping to ask herself if she was happy or fulfilled. She assumed that a 'good' marriage, and an 'equal' partnership, meant that her employment aspirations were less important than those of her husband's. Doing most of the domestic work and following her husband's career just seemed to be something that she had to do, despite her struggle to become qualified in the first place. Her current state of resentment and regret seems to reflect years of having put herself, and her wishes, second to the needs and opinions of others.

The nature of women's work in the home

Of course, a crucial point in discussing women's double shift is to clarify exactly what is meant by the 'housework' that constitutes the second half of most working women's lives. The routine labour of cleaning, home maintenance, shopping, laundry, and child care was for many years 'invisible' to psychologists and sociologists of work, as it was entirely taken for granted and seen as boring both to do and to investigate. This probably also reflects the view, held by the wider society, that work is only valuable if it is paid. However, Ann Oakley (1974) drew the attention of researchers and women themselves to the immense labour performed daily in the domestic sphere, and its considerable economic value, and since then housework has been seen as a legitimate research area by at least a minority of psychologists and sociologists.

Despite this, however, housework is still seen as a low-status activity, which is assumed to be boring and of less merit than 'real' work. Yet this ignores the fact that the paid jobs performed by many women are routine and unskilled, and not particularly rewarding, whereas the tasks included in the term 'housework' may include some of the positive aspects of child care, and the opportunity for creative expression and social contact around the home environment. In this sense, the daily routine of many women without employment may in fact be more satisfactory, if less socially valued, than that of many employees, of both sexes.

Further, it may be that what the woman employed on the double shift is doing is declaring her refusal to be pigeon-holed into either one world or the other, and asserting her belief that doing things for the people she loves is at least as important as doing things for an employer who means little to her. In addition, although this may not be fully articulated, many women do not envisage their whole lives to be bound up with the notion of employment, as most men do. As such, women's identities as people may not be so fully dependent on paid employment as a man's, and consequently, they can 'afford' to detach themselves from over-identification with the world of work, and involve themselves in domesticity. In this way the greater commitment of a woman to the world outside the workplace may reflect her own set of values, which places human contact above the attainment of instrumental goals (see the distinction made by David Bakan (1966), and further developed by Rae Carlson (1972) between the agentic or instrumental modes of relating on the one hand, and the communal or expressive modes of relating on the other). As a result, many women may actually feel less comfortable than men in the world of employment, while many men may feel less comfortable than women in the domestic sphere (although this discomfort may of course be used by men as an excuse to avoid doing the domestic work).

Although based on an out-moded and inaccurate vision of the workplace, most people's stereotype of the worker does not include sensitivity to others or nurturance, but instead suggests control, competiveness, ruthlessness, and physical strength. This may then in part account for the unwillingness of both women and men to challenge the notion of the workplace as a male sphere: on a fantasy level, all the unharmonious and unwanted characteristics of the male world can perhaps be contained there, away from the peaceful harmony of the non-competitive, expressively oriented (female) home. But of course this stereotype is highly inaccurate, in that the skills needed by housewives and mothers include the ability to quantify, control, predict, and direct, as well as to comfort and support. Karen Howard (1986) has carried out a systematic job-evaluation exercise on the nature of housework, and reports that the skills needed in the home include those of negotiator, economist, electrician, cook, organiser, and decorator. In addition, there are some very clearly instrumental aspects to the role of a housewife: a number of writers have pointed out that the economic value of the labour provided in the home is enormous, such that insurance companies are now beginning to offer policies against the very substantial costs of replacing a wife's economic contribution in the case of her death. Simultaneously, it is being gradually recognised in the world of paid employment that a good manager in a whole variety of spheres from business to the service industries is one who possesses the ability to listen, to empathise, and to respond well to people (see, for example, Linda Micheli and colleagues, 1984); in other words, one who has the stereotypically feminine expressive and relationship skills.

Sexism and sexual harassment in unions and the workplace

Another reason for a woman's ambivalent attitude towards the workplace is that it can contain some very negative experiences for her. These experiences include sexism, sex discrimination, and sexual harassment. Sexism can be experienced in belittling comments and patronising or personal remarks about what women can or cannot do, and sex discrimination can be experienced through restriction by management of promotion and training opportunities. Trade unions are not immune from sexism or sex discrimination either, as was discovered by Clare when trying to pursue her holiday claim. The result of being on the receiving end of these practices is varied, but usually negative: the woman may simultaneously feel angry, confused, and powerless.

Sexual harassment, familiar to many women for many years, is at last becoming recognised and talked about. It can be defined as attention of a sexual nature which is unwanted and offensive. The servicing role that many women play in the workplace as nurses, secretaries, receptionists, and waitresses has all too often been used as justification for sexual exploitation, which varies from offensive sexual suggestions or touches to overt pressure to accede to sexual intercourse, under threat of dismissal or demotion. Women who object to such attentions are often seen as having no sense of humour, or as being prudes. This can be seen very clearly in the apparently trivial example of the woman who inadvertently 'strays' into an archetypal 'male' sphere such as a garage or work-shop, and can be acutely embarrassed and angered by the display of pornography which she often finds there. The workplace is seen by many men as their legitimate territory; hence women who complain about pornography are often seen as being either kill-joys, or frigid.

Indeed, one of the functions of sexual harassment and sexism in the workplace is to reinforce the notion of paid work as a male sphere in which women are unwelcome intruders who are best dealt with as sexual objects. Of course not all men respond in this way, but many men in work situations still feel under considerable pressure to conform to a form of male camaraderie, which reduces the potential threat posed by women's competence. It is not surprising, then, that most women are restricted to a very small number of occupational groupings, hence limiting the danger. In fact, in the UK, for instance, 60 per cent of working women are employed in three service and four manufacturing industries, and with one or two exceptions, are limited to the lower grades. In addition, many women, particularly those from the New Commonwealth, work outside the framework of the law, out of necessity or because of religious or cultural pressure. Such women may only find employment in closed, illegal 'sweatshops' in which there is no legal control on rates of pay or conditions of employment. All these factors again marginalise the contribution made by women in the workplace, and diminish the extent of their threat to the 'real' male worker.

Psychological and social issues in women's working experience

Having considered some of the difficulties encountered by women at work, we now turn to an examination of some of the more personal issues involved in the work experience. As we have seen elsewhere in this book, it is clear that both social and psychological influences are important in understanding the meaning of work in women's lives.

The psychological functions of work

A number of theorists have examined the functions of work in contemporary western society, where a high proportion of adults are covered by some insurance or welfare scheme, which although minimal, means that few people will actually starve unless they work. (Note, however, that this is not the case for many immigrant workers, or for any worker in some European countries where no social security payments are available after unemployment benefit runs out.) One of the most influential theories is that of Marie Jahoda (1981; 1986) which suggests that, apart from economic considerations, employment serves six distinct functions. Although the model of work used by Jahoda was not specifically designed for men or for women, we shall now illustrate it by using women workers as examples.

First, according to Jahoda, employment provides the individual with status and social identity. The employed woman no longer has to say 'I'm just a housewife', but can say that she is a barmaid, a teacher, or a telephonist. More importantly, employment outside the home gives her an existence separate from her parents, husband, or children. Second, employment imposes a structure on the day; it forces a pattern or routine on to her activities. Unemployed people frequently comment on their lack of ability to use their time constructively, because of this lack of structure. Third, employment requires the individual to meet and interact with people beyond the confines of the home; thus she makes social contact, and possibly, makes friends with other employees. Many mothers with young children comment that this is one of their major motivations for working, as the sole company of toddlers in the isolated family often seems insufficiently stimulating or interesting. Fourth, employment 'demonstrates that there are goals and purposes which are beyond the scope of an individual, but require a collectivity' (Marie Jahoda and Howie Rush, 1980). In other words, work offers the employee a sense of achievement as well as a sense of participation. Fifth, paid work enforces activity, and demands physical or psychological exertion. Freud commented that 'work is man's (*sic*) strongest tie to reality', and perhaps the participation in activity, however limited in scope, permits the expression or at least experience of self in contact with something 'real'. Last, Jahoda adds the function that employment serves of control, such that the individual senses that the responsibility for at least some part of every day is limited by some external figure or organisation.

Athough Marie Jahoda's theory seems fairly comprehensive (at least as far as the non-economic aspects of work are concerned), and was not designed with either sex in mind, many of the assumptions made by it, in common with most other academic accounts of employment, in fact imply that the individual in question is male. This is demonstrated, for example, by the assumption that it is work which imposes structure on the day, which of course ignores the domestic responsibilities of women outside work, in particular to provide meals and other aspects of caring for her family at regular times. Further, its applicability to many women's experience of work is not straightforward, for example, the idea that it is only paid work which keeps people in touch with 'reality': most mothers, for example, find the demands of their young children to be only too 'real'! As pointed out by Jean Hartley (1980), most women also have work experience in the home, whether as mothers or not, which although unpaid, certainly fulfils many of the functions noted by Jahoda. Work within the home, especially that which involves the care of children, imposes a structure to the day, enforces activity, and in many ways removes control or responsibility. What it may well not provide, however, is status, adult company, financial reward, or any great sense of achievement. Hence what Jahoda's theory can perhaps contribute to our understanding of the role of employment in women's lives is that, at least for mothers, paid work provides economic reward, and usually enhances the social and status aspects of her life.

Another model of the function and meaning of work in women's lives is that provided by Helen Astin (1984). She proposes that work motivations are the same for women as for men, but that because career choices for women are more restricted, and because of sex-role socialisation which rewards different types of behaviour for the two sexes, the experiences and expectations of women in the workforce are very different from those of men. In particular, she suggests, women's experiences at work are likely to be less satisfactory than men's, although not less important in terms of their contribution to the woman's own sense of psychological wellbeing. This is consistent with the evidence, which often appears surprising to most traditionally minded researchers in this field, that unemployment is at least as, if not more distressing for women than it is for men; and that the mental health of working women seems to be better than that of women who are not in paid employment (see p.114).

Women and unemployment

In order to understand the evidence referred to previously somewhat better, we shall now turn to an examination of these two related issues, first by considering the impact of unemployment on women. It is always difficult to obtain an accurate picture of the numbers of women who are unemployed at any one time, as women often fail to register as unemployed, or are persuaded not to 'use up' training places for the unemployed. Angela Coyle reports that in the UK, for example:

rising levels of unemployment in recession, now theaten the gains made by women in the post-war period ... the rate at which women are becoming unemployed is twice as fast as it is for men, and there is evidence that nearly one-half of unemployed women are not registered as such. It could be that women's unemployment is now double the official figures.

(Coyle, 1984:3–4)

Yet unemployment is still considered to be primarily a male problem. Lee Rainwater (1984) points out that in Europe, the majority of women not in the labour force would rather be working, while in her studies of unemployed teenagers, Christine Griffen (1985) reports the complex interplay of forces experienced by young women attempting to enter the labour force, including the demands of relationships, marriage, domestic responsibilities, and loyalty to friends, which means that the restrictions placed on women are enormous. This renders them even more liable than boys to periods of unemployment or very limited job opportunities.

It is sometimes assumed by traditionally minded researchers in this field, and politicians, that married women will not 'mind' being unemployed, as they can always return to full-time housework; whereas an unemployed man has the trauma of relinquishing his role as breadwinner. Yet as reported by Ian Miles and Jill Howard:

often married women treasure employment both as a means for exposing themselves to a world wider than that of the family, where they are expected to provide emotional support for their husbands; and as a means of legitimating their independence in personal financial matters, of establishing some right to a say in how family finances are accounted.

(Miles and Howard, 1984:4)

For women without families, of course, work may be the central focus for their energies and creative expression, let alone their way of earning a living. The consequences of unemployment can therefore be as devastating for women as for men: Michael Banks and Paul Jackson (1982), for example, have reported on the psychological consequences for young women of unemployment, which they found to be as emotionally damaging for women as for men, if not more so. Yet the responses of others to a woman's unemployment may not be at all sympathetic, since it may be assumed that an out-of-work woman can now return to being a 'proper housewife'.

Women's mental health and employment

Related to the issue of unemployment is the question of whether having a job is, in terms of her mental health, actually beneficial to a woman, and whether the psychological wellbeing of women who work outside the home is better than those who don't. This area has been summarised by Glenys Parry (1986; 1987), who points out that the results of a large number of research studies have been very mixed (for example, Ray Cochrane and Mary Stopes-Roe, 1981; George Brown and Tyrill Harris, 1978; Phyllis Newberry, Myrna Weissman, and Jerome Myers, 1979; Neil Krause, 1984). In brief, this work has shown that, irrespective of the economic issues involved, having a job does appear to serve some protective function for some women, in the face of life's adversities, although to an extent this depends upon the views of each individual woman and the age of her children. In other words, an employed woman, especially one with older children or no children, has better mental health than one who has no outside employment. However, Glenys Parry also reports that if she wants to be with her children most of the time, a mother is happiest without employment, whereas the woman who does not, is happier when she is also in employment (see also Chapter 7). But according to George Brown and Tyrill Harris (1978), for many women, having a job actually reduces the incidence of depression, anxiety, and general unhappiness. Being without employment can lead to feelings of apathy, depression, worthlessness, and frustration.

To assume that women can adjust with little trouble to being without employment assumes that their major function in life is the domestic one. Yet this ignores the capacity of many women for creativity, commitment to political, social, or organisational ideals, and activity outside the home. It also ignores the personal issues which may have inspired many women to choose their particular sphere of work, and which give energy and purpose to their daily activities.

Dynamic reasons for job choice

Having considered the role of employment in women's lives, and the consequences for some women of *not* being employed, we shall now turn to an examination of some of the psychological factors which lie behind women's choice of particular types of work, focusing on the dynamic, or unconscious reasons for women's particular choice of the work that they do.

As already noted earlier in this chapter, and in previous chapters, women's career choice is limited to a very considerable extent by lack of opportunity and numerous alternative commitments and obligations. Janet Holland (1980) actually concludes that occupational 'choice' as such does not exist for women: it is a misnomer. Nevertheless, for some women, especially those with more education and with some support, some degree of choice does exist, although this is often still constrained to women's sphere of work, such as nursing, secretarial work, or teaching. Yet parents and teachers often seek to circumvent that choice even further. Clare's story in this chapter and Lucy's story in Chapter 2 show how important it is that family and teachers listen to a woman's preferences for the occupation which is going to provide the structure for a large part of her life. For Clare, for example, the 'battle' that was waged between her and her teachers meant that it took her 35 years to discover what she really wanted to do, with considerable cost to her satisfaction and happiness in life.

In addition to parental or school pressures, however, there are also other, less conscious issues which influence people's choice of occupations. The questions with which individuals struggle in their interpersonal relationships are not left outside the factory or office door, but often come to be framed in terms of the issues which they choose to study and consequently practise in their daily lives. Anything which is really important, and relationships with others of course are, tends to prompt people to ask questions and seek answers. In part it is the perpetual struggle to find those solutions to internal conflicts which provides men and women with dynamic energy, driving them to act. Interestingly, therefore, people often put themselves into situations at work which raise some of the questions that also occur in their personal relationships.

This is well illustrated in an example provided by Robert Elliott (1983). He describes the case history of a woman whose dilemma was that she was nervous of entering into relationships in case she damaged someone else in the process. She expressed a considerable desire to help and care for others, but was also very frightened that the help or love she offered might hurt them along the way. What is particularly striking about this woman was the fact that she worked full time as a dentist, daily facing in her professional work some of the intrapsychic and interpersonal issues which she faced in her personal life, albeit in a highly symbolic form. This isn't surprising, as in their contact with others, people are always seeking to meet their needs and resolve their conflicts, no matter how damaging the results may sometimes be. This is one of the reasons why change is so difficult, and why people sometimes need the support of others who are not so involved, such as a professional counsellor or therapist, in order to be able to change themselves.

Another example of the interplay between personal dynamic issues and career choice can be seen in the way in which a woman may avoid choosing a career which might involve her in having to take charge of others, or needing to discipline workmates. This may well reflect her anxiety about her own ability to exercise power, having been taught very early in her life that any desire for control of others was wrong and dangerously unfeminine, and futhermore, that if she did behave in a powerful way, that she might destroy others in the process. Those who say that women only limit themselves by failing to seek promotion in the way that men do fail to take into account the long years of learning that women have had concerning the dangers and risks involved for women in the exercise of power.

A number of careers may provide the structure or context for women to deal with personally significant issues. For example, a career in the media may reflect a desire for public recognition, which comes from insecurity about parental recognition. Likewise, a career in the military or in the police may resolve anxieties about impulse control, or reflect a need for parental restriction, which for that particular woman is even more central than the fear of assuming authority over others. As a further example, a career in teaching may reflect a woman's desire to be in touch with the childlike parts of herself, or it may again reflect a need to gain control and authority over others.

Choosing a career in the helping professions is another very clear example of occupational choice which in some way resonates with personal issues. Alice Miller noted that an extraordinarily high percentage of the trainee psychoanalysts who came to seek her help and training originated from a similar background: they were the highly sensitive children of emotionally insecure parents who had developed the ability to respond to their parents' needs with uncanny perceptiveness and insight. She commented that:

> there existed an amazing ability on the child's part intuitively, that is unconsciously, to perceive and respond to this need of the mother or of both parents . . . this role secured 'love' for the child . . . he could sense that he was needed and this gave his life a guarantee of existence. This ability is then extended and perfected. Later these children become not only mothers (confidantes, comforters, advisors, supporters) of their own mothers, but also take over the responsibility for their siblings and eventually develop a special sensitivity to unconscious signals of the needs of others. No wonder that they often choose the psycho-analytic profession later on.
>
> (Miller, 1979:49)

A similar point is made by Luise Eichenbaum and Susie Orbach (1983) who, as we have seen elsewhere, argue that the mother becomes her daughter's first child, and that the process of becoming a woman *is* the process of providing care for others. Small wonder, then, that so many in the caring profesions are women.

The problem, as Alice Miller points out, is that individuals who choose to enter the helping professions for these reasons may have considerable difficulty in recognising their own needs. They have always been 'little adults', and have difficulty in relating to other people, except as clients or children. The social situation of women, in which they are expected to respond intuitively to the needs of others, clearly feeds into this dynamic, sometimes with sad consequences for their ability to understand and meet their own emotional and practical requirements. Since she is not in tune with her own needs, the individual woman may fail to find personal relationships for herself which are truly satisfying, and may instead seek the intimacy that she once desired with her mother by providing 'help' for others. This she may try to do by making use of the considerable empathic skills which she has developed through extensive practice, and which give her at least some emotional satisfaction. But the emotional satisfaction which she may gain from clients is likely to be rather limited, since clients, like young children, are needy, and are not in a position to give back much emotional support to their carers.

Another avenue for the expression of personal dynamic issues is of course in voluntary work, which may provide scope for an otherwise unemployed woman to care for others. Involvement in community activities such as Citizen's Advice Bureaux, church-based groups, play groups for deprived children, and so on, provide an extremely valuable contribution to community life, and it may also serve the function of making the volunteer feel needed and wanted. Some of the issues and problems brought by the users of such services may also resonate with the volunteer's own issues, thus permitting the volunteer to obtain some vicarious 'therapy' at the same time as providing a service. For example, a woman who feels neglected and disregarded by her own family and children may feel a special sympathy for, and indeed be able to give a great deal to, children or old people who have been rejected by their families. While this will probably benefit the woman and her clients alike, it may be important for those involved in running volunteer organisations to make sure that the volunteers do not neglect their own needs, nor impose their own solutions or 'need to be needed' on to their clients.

It is interesting to note in support of the points made earlier that it was just at the end of her relationship with Andy that Laura, whom we described in Chapter 3, decided that she wanted to change careers. What she wanted to do was to abandon her apparently 'useless' position as a student, and begin a career in social work. Without being particularly conscious of it, what she was attempting to do was to find a job in which she would be 'needed', and in which she imagined she would be welcomed and wanted by her clients on a personal basis. Whether this would be the case or not, a job as a social worker would serve the function, at least temporarily, of making her feel wanted again. It is certainly true that many people find that it does help to overcome losses by becoming actively involved in helping others, and that this desire to be needed can actually be a very positive and productive impulse. But Laura was not yet aware of her motives for such a sudden change in career. It was therefore important for Laura's therapist to help Laura become more aware of these feelings, so that she did not make the decision to move away from her studies for reasons of which she was not aware, which might then mean that she made the wrong decision in the long run.

Therapeutic implications

As we have seen in this chapter, for many women work outside the home is an essential part of their lives, bringing vital economic support, social contact, and an existence outside the domestic sphere. For others, it is central, bringing meaning and job satisfaction. Yet as we have seen, recognition and acceptance of the importance of work in women's lives by employers and by women themselves is limited. This has a number of consequences for women, since they may feel profoundly ambivalent about investing too much in the work sphere because of other commitments, particularly to their families, and because of the limited opportunities available to them. Employers in their turn frequently fail to recognise the contribution that is or could be made by women, and often impose on women poorer training, lower wages, and more limited prospects than are available to men. Yet work can bring many rewards to women, in terms of financial independence, opportunity for personal development, and control of their own lives, while unhappiness at work may be an important component of a woman's life stresses. Therapists have an important role to play, therefore, in helping women to resolve some of their ambivalent feelings about work, and in empowering them to perform more effectively and happily in the work sphere. It is most important, too, that therapists take any dissatisfactions with the work sphere as seriously as they would take problems in any other sphere of the woman's daily life.

However, few women will come to ask for psychotherapeutic help solely with occupational or work-related problems, since interpersonal and relationship issues are more usually the focus of any difficulties that women experience in their lives. Despite this, very real problems obviously do exist for women in the workplace, such as sex discrimination, low job satisfaction, excessive workloads, or lack of resources with which to do a job properly. But no matter how central these problems are, most women also bring to therapy their own emotional reactions to these situations, such as anger, guilt, or confusion, and it is often for these reactions that they will first seek help. Therapists must therefore be alert to the 'real world' difficulties at work which the woman may be having to face, but which she may interpret as being 'her' problem.

But in addition to discovering what are the 'real world' problems in the workplace, it is also important for therapists working with women who have employment-related difficulties to investigate whether there are any unexpressed conflicts which are preventing the women from developing a more effective strategy for dealing with such problems. Only then can the therapist act to encourage the woman to develop her abilities to deal with the situation outside herself which is problematic.

Problems for women in the workplace: competition, assertion, and power

A number of researchers have pointed out that one of the most commonly expressed conflicts amongst employed women is the anxieties which many women feel about being assertive and competitive at work. Having been systematically encouraged as a child to be nurturing and caring, and to consider the needs of others before her own, many women find it very difficult to insist that they, too, have rights, and can compete or achieve. To some women it can seem to run counter to their femininity to be able to do things better than others, especially men, such that many women will choose not to compete rather than to risk success. According to Christine Dunbar and her colleagues (1979), these conficts lead women to label competitive or assertive behaviour by other women, and by themselves, as 'castrating' or 'bitchy', while Matina Horner (1970) suggested that women actually fear success, perceiving that it can bring many unfortunate consequences for women, including rejection by other women and by men. Athough Matina Horner's research has not been clearly replicated, for many women her concept of 'fear of success' resonates with their experience of anxiety in the face of doing better than someone else. Many women, rather than win all for themselves, would rather lose, if by doing so they could avoid pain or humiliation for another person. Nevertheless, they may also feel frustration with themselves for reacting this way. Clearly, such conflicts are likely to interfere with a woman's ability to act effectively in the workplace.

A similar point is made by Ann Turkel (1980) who describes these conflicts as resulting from women's 'power dilemma', in which women feel uncomfortable about using power, despite desiring it. From childhood, Turkel argues, women have had less access to overt power than men have had, and consequently feel both powerless and angry about their situation. At the same time, men may feel very anxious about the use of power by women, feeling both unsexed and vulnerable, and will try to resist the overt use of female power by labelling the powerful woman as aggressive, unfeminine, self-serving, or castrating. This is then internalised by women, too, which further undermines their attempts to use power effectively.

Another analysis of the difficulties that women have in connection with power and authority is that provided by Jean Baker Miller (1976), to whom we have referred elsewhere. She has suggested that women do have some power, but it is only in those spheres which are permitted to them by men as the dominant group. According to Miller, the spheres where women are 'allowed' to be competent are in the expression of emotions and in the validation of men's masculinity. Thus women can have power in managing children – in the arts and in 'peripheral' areas such as fashion and nursing. But the overt use of women's power in other spheres, such as management, business, or politics, threatens men on a number of levels, and this in turn fuels women's fears that the use of their own power in these archetypally 'masculine' areas may be harmful. This can then lead the woman to feel highly critical of herself, while simultaneously reducing the chances of her being able to use her power and authority with confidence and skill. The result is often that a woman, attempting to use her authority in a 'male' sphere, may feel acutely anxious, and will then act precipitously, imperiously, unreasonably, or defensively, thus 'proving' the point that women cannot handle power or authority effectively.

Therapists can help women with these sorts of dilemmas by encouraging them to recognise their own anxieties about power, as well as their anger about their powerlessness, and to make use of these emotions in a more constructive way than by turning them back on themselves, or by acting ineffectively. Assertion training such as that described by Ann Dickson (1982) can be very helpful here, even for women who think they are quite capable of looking after themselves. Such training involves first, the identification of those situations where a woman feels she does not stand up for herself (for example, being given more work than a colleague is given), and second, a role-play, with a friend or therapist, of an alternative response which is not aggressive, but is clear and direct (for example, to refuse the extra work without endless explanation, tears, or anger). Christine Dunbar and her colleagues (1979) also suggest forming self-help groups, in which women can meet together on a regular basis to share some of their anxieties about work issues, which may include fears of competition and anxieties about handling economic and organisational success.

Of course, for some women these feelings may stem from a very basic sense of being unentitled, which we have already discussed in Chapter 3, and which is as evident in the world of work as anywhere else. For women who do feel extremely uncomfortable about their own sense of worth at work, despite evidence that their contribution is valued, more intense personal therapy may be needed. Both individual therapists and self-help groups can help women to challenge these feelings, and by providing support, can help the woman to dare to approach the working environment with feelings of confidence, and a greater awareness of the value of her own contribution.

Problems for women in the workplace: dealing with emotions

Another issue where therapists have a role to play can be in helping women to deal with their emotions in the workplace. For example, Kathleen Hooper-Dempsey, Jeanne Plas, and Barbara Wallston (1986) point out that women's emotional expressiveness, which is greater than men's, can sometimes cause them great embarrassment and frustration when, for instance, they start to weep in a professional situation, such as when an important request is turned down, or in response to an unkind remark. They suggest that rather than further berating herself for her 'weakness', the crying woman should acknowledge her tears, and use them productively. For example, they suggest that the woman could respond to an observer: 'My crying is a signal of the strength I feel behind my position. Let's not respond to the tears; they will take care of me in their own way.' Or: 'These tears are releasing a lot of tension for me; that will help this conversation quite a bit' (Hooper-Dempsey *et al.*, 1986:32). Working from David Bakan's analysis (see p. 109), they point out that this strategy asserts the value of both agentic and communal forms of communication.

Another related problem is that the emotional responsiveness of many women means that they find it hard to leave work behind them after hours. This can be a considerable problem for women in the helping professions who may find themselves worrying about clients long after they, or the clients, have gone home. Perhaps the clearest example of this difficulty is the emotional stress reported by many nurses, who regularly have to deal with pain, death, and bereavement. According to Kathy Parkes (1980), nursing is one of the most stressful professions, as shown by the extraordinarily high turnover. In the UK, for example, one in ten nurses leave nursing every year, meaning that the profession is constantly facing staffing crises (Jeremy Laurance, 1986). Yet very little is provided for nurses to help them to deal with stress, apart from appeals to their sense of loyalty and self-sacrifice. Elsewhere, one of us has argued strongly for the kind of help which nurses need to deal more effectively with stress at work (see Sue Llewelyn, 1984; 1989; Sue Llewelyn and Guy Fielding, 1987), including the establishment of support groups, the provision of trained counsellors, and the reorganisation of work patterns. Yet short-term financial constraints are often placed ahead of the welfare of nurses, meaning that few of these supports are made available to decrease the difficulties faced by this over-worked and undervalued group of workers.

Of course, it is not only nurses who experience these types of difficulties: social workers, teachers, junior doctors, psychotherapists, and local authority care workers are all examples of (primarily female) groups of workers who experience high levels of stress at work, and who too often receive little help in managing the resultant levels of stress. For these groups, self-awareness groups and training in different ways of coping with anxiety about work would be extremely helpful (see, for example, Harry Gray and Andrea Freeman, 1987). Even the provision of straightforward information about the nature of stress can be very useful, as a way of increasing women's understanding of their perfectly reasonable reactions to what are often unreasonable demands.

Concluding note

Work is not an additional extra to most women's lives. For some it is their only source of income, while for others it makes a substantial contribution to their economic position. But beyond this, work also allows at least some women to engage in activity that is important to them and provides them with both social contact and a way of meeting deep, intrapsychic needs. Therapists too often ignore the significance of work to women, themselves demonstrating some of the cultural assumptions that, in contrast to men, work is secondary to women. Yet the consequences of an unhappy working experience for women can be both destructive and debilitating, and is, in itself, worthy of considerable therapeutic time and attention. This does not mean, however, that those working therapeutically with women should forget the very real forces outside women themselves, which encourage women's feelings of frustration and powerlessness: after all, women still earn substantially less than men, have access to fewer training opportunities than men, and are considerably less likely to be promoted than are men. Any psychological intervention with women in the work sphere must therefore be seen as only one part of a struggle that working women still have to wage in seeking to attain satisfaction and reasonable treatment in their workplaces.

References

Astin, H. (1984) 'The meaning of work in women's lives: a sociopsychological model of career choice and work behavior', *The Counselling Psychologist* 12: 117–26.
Bakan, D. (1966) *The Duality of Human Existence*, Chicago: Rand McNally.
Miller, J.B. (1976) *Towards a New Psychology of Women*, Harmondsworth: Penguin.
Banks, M. and Jackson, P. (1982) 'Unemployment and risk of minor psychiatric

disorder in young people: cross-sectional and longitudinal evidence', *Psychological Medicine* 12: 789–98.

Brown, G. and Harris, T. (1978) *Social Origins of Depression*, London: Tavistock.

Carlson, R. (1972) 'Understanding women: implications for personality theory and research', *Journal of Social Issues* 28:17–32.

Cochrane, R. and Stopes-Roe, M. (1981) 'Women, marriage, employment and mental health', *British Journal of Psychiatry* 139: 373–81.

Coyle, A. (1984) *Redundant Women*, London: The Women's Press.

Dex, S. (1985) *The Sexual Division of Work*, Brighton: Basic Books.

Dickson, A. (1982) *A Woman in Your Own Right*, London: Quartet Books.

Dunbar, C., Edwards, V., Gede, E., Hamilton, J., Sniderman, M., Smith, V., and Whitfield, M. (1979) 'Successful coping styles in professional women', *Canadian Journal of Psychiatry*, 24:43–6.

Elliott, R. (1983) '"That in your hands...". Comprehensive Process Analysis of a significant event', *Psychiatry* 46: 113–19.

Eichenbaum, L. and Orbach, F. (1983) *What do women want?* London: Fontana.

Gray, H. and Freeman, A. (1987) *Teaching Without Stress*, London: Paul Chapman Publishing Ltd..

Gershuny, J. (1987) 'The leisure principle', *New Society*, 13 February.

Griffin, C. (1985) *Typical Girls?* London: Routledge & Kegan Paul.

Hague, H. (1987) 'Women at work "lose £15bn in wage gap"', *The Independent*, 19 May.

Hartley, J. (1980) 'Psychological approaches to unemployment', *Bulletin of the British Psychological Society* 33:412–14.

Holland, J. (1980) *Work and Women*, London: University of London Press.

Hooper-Dempsey, K., Plas, J., and Wallston, B. (1986) 'Tears and weeping among professional women: in search of a new understanding', *Psychology of Women Quarterly* 10:19–34.

Horner, M. (1970) 'Femininity and successful achievement: a basic inconsistency', in J. Bardwick *et al.* (eds) *Feminine Personality and Conflict*, Belmont, California: Brooks & Cole.

Howard, K. (1986) 'Managerial skills: they can be developed in the home', paper presented at the 2nd Women and Work Conference, Nottingham, May.

Jahoda, M. (1981) 'Work, employment and unemployment: values, theories and approaches in social research', *American Psychologist* 36:184–91.

Jahoda, M. (1986) 'Social psychology of the invisible', *New Ideas in Psychology* 4:107–18.

Jahoda, M. and Rush, H. (1980) 'Work, employment and unemployment', Occasional Paper Series, 12, SPRU, University of Sussex.

Joshi, H. (1987) 'The cash opportunity costs of childbearing: an approach to estimation using British data', London: Centre for Economic Policy Research, discussion Paper no. 208.

Krause, N. (1984) 'Employment outside the home and women's psychological well-being', *Social Psychiatry*, 19:41–8.

Laurance, J. (1986) 'Worst ever crisis faces nursing', *New Society*, 5 December.

Llewelyn, S. (1984) 'The cost of giving: emotional growth and emotional stress', in S. Skevington (ed), *Understanding Nurses: the social psychology of nursing*, Chichester: Wiley.

Llewelyn, S. (1989) 'Caring: the costs to nurses and relatives', in A. Broome (ed.)

Health Psychology, London: Croom Helm.

Llewelyn, S. and Fielding, R.G. (1987) 'Nurses: training for new job demands', *Work and Stress* 1: 221–33.

Martin, J. and Roberts, C. (1984) *Women and Employment*, London: HMSO.

Micheli, L., Cespedes, F., Byker, D., and Raymond, T. (1984) *Managerial Communication*, Glenview, Illinois: Scott, Foresman & Co.

Miles, I. and Howard, J. (1984) *Age and sex differences in the experience of unemployment*, Science Policy Research Unit, University of Sussex.

Miller, A. (1979) 'The drama of the gifted child and the psycho-analyst's narcissistic disturbance', *International Journal of Psycho-Analysis* 60:47–58.

Miller, J.B. (1976) *Towards a New Psychology of Women*, Harmondsworth: Penguin.

Newberry, P., Weissman, M.M., and Myers, J.K. (1974) 'Working wives and housewives: do they differ in mental status and social adjustment?', *American Journal of Orthopsychiatry* 49: 282–91.

Oakley, A. (1974) *Housewife*, London: Allen Lane.

OECD (1985) *The Integration of Women into the Economy*, Paris: OECD.

Parkes, K.R. (1980) 'Occupational stress among student nurses', *Nursing Times* 76: 113–19.

Parry, G. (1986) 'Paid employment, life events, social support and mental health in working class mothers', *Journal of Health and Social Behavior* 27: 193–208.

Parry, G. (1987) 'Sex-role beliefs, work attitudes and mental health in employed and non-employed mothers', *British Journal of Social Psychology* 26:47–58.

Rainwater, L. (1984) 'Mother's contribution to the family money economy in Europe and the United States' in P. Voydanoff (ed.) *Work and Family*, Palo Alto: Mayfield Publishing Co.

Symonds, A. (1979) 'The wife as the professional', *The American Journal of Psychoanalysis* 39:55–63.

Turkel, A. (1980) 'The power dilemma of women', *The American Journal of Psychoanalysis* 40:301–11.

Chapter six

Becoming a mother

Jeanette's story

The doorbell rang one summer afternoon, and when I went to answer there stood a short, fair, hesitant-looking woman. 'Hello', she said, 'I'm Jeanette. A friend told me you were running a pregnancy-support group and I'd like to join.' I took her into the garden so that we could talk in peace. Jeanette told me that she was five months pregnant and lived nearby with Ted. He worked as a graphic designer, and she had a temporary job in a travel agency which she said she was about to give up since it was both tedious and tiring.

> I'd really like to meet some other pregnant women, because none of my friends have babies so I've got no-one to talk to about it all. Ted isn't very interested, and anyway he doesn't get home till late because he doesn't work fixed hours – so he sleeps in late and gets to work around lunchtime.

I asked her what he thought about the pregnancy. She looked wryly at me. 'Well', she said:

> when I first told him, we had a blazing row, and he said it was nothing to do with him. In fact, things were so bad, I left him for a while and went to stay with a friend by the sea. But after a few weeks he came to find me, and I decided to move back in with him. I very much want this baby. It wasn't an accident you know.

Jeanette told me a lot about herself that first afternoon, as if she hadn't talked to anyone for a long time and she could now let things out for a new listener. We talked about where she wanted to give birth, and I told her about the choices available locally. I then explained how the pregnancy-support group worked, and that by then we were a group of eight women who met once a week. 'Will it be all right if I start next week?' she asked. I said it would be fine since we were looking for a couple of new members to replace those who were about to leave.

The following week she was the first to arrive, and seemed pleased to have some time to herself. She was particularly interested in my 6-month-old daughter, who obligingly smiled and enjoyed being played with.

I can't wait to see what my baby will be like. You know, I had an abortion three years ago, soon after I first left home, and I've always wondered what that baby would have looked like. Sometimes I look at little children when I go past a playground or am on the beach and I think how my baby would have been learning to walk, or starting to talk.

I mentioned the sadness involved in having an abortion, and how everybody expects that we act as if nothing had happened immediately afterwards. There was not much time to say anything else, as the other members of the group started to arrive. I introduced Jeanette and she soon seemed to be at ease with the other women, most of whom were also expecting their first babies. We had arranged to try some 'active birth' exercises, and so spent the next hour practising some of the positions that are helpful during contractions, and the various positions for delivery. As always there were mixed reactions and some of the women started talking about their fears of physical pain. Jeanette shared some of these anxieties.

'I keep thinking that it would be a lot easier to have a Caesarian and then it would be all over,' she said. One of the other women disagreed and argued that she didn't want to miss out on any of the experiences. Jeanette took up this idea and became more enthusiastic about the possibility of a natural labour.

Over the following weeks that she attended the meetings, Jeanette seemed to oscillate wildly between each of the opinions expressed, and seemed to lack a clear identity of her own. Two of the members were intending to have home deliveries, and Jeanette suddenly decided that this was what she wanted to do. We talked about the amount of support needed, both practically and emotionally, in order to organise a home birth. I asked her who she could rely on to be with her after the baby was born.

'Well definitely not my mother', she replied. She'd already talked about her strained relationship with her mother, whom she experienced as overbearing and interfering. 'There'll be Ted, of course, and I've asked an old school friend of mine who said she'd come and stay when the baby's due.'

I felt less than certain that Jeanette would get the support she needed, and was relieved when she said that she'd booked into a hospital. I was more concerned when I next saw her, with Ted, in one of the local shops. Apparently, Ted had come home from work early and announced that he had given up his job. 'I couldn't take any more from the boss,' he explained to me. 'He kept giving us impossible deadlines and refused to pay for the overtime. Besides, the work was a real bore.'

Ted and Jeanette were now finding it hard to make ends meet. The baby was due in a few weeks time and their relationship appeared to be increasingly strained. Jeanette said to the group one day:

I felt sure he gave up his job because he was jealous that I didn't have to go to work any more. But he does nothing in the house, he won't lift a finger. I keep asking him to decorate the spare room, but he refuses. The place is a real mess.

Of even greater concern were her haphazard eating habits. Although she was knowledgeable about nutrition and was very concerned about not eating anything that might be toxic for the baby, she had an over-riding fear of putting on too much weight. When we discussed food and weight-gain in the group, she spoke bitterly of her problem during adolescence of puppy fat, and how she had gradually starved herself slim when she was 16. Somehow the image of herself as pregnant reminded her of her adolescent fatness, and nothing could persuade her to eat regular, ample meals. She was still anxiously waiting for a letter from her school friend, who was supposed to come to stay to help out during the time of the baby's birth, but when at last she heard from her, the friend was away on holiday, touring Italy. Jeanette seemed to have no other close friends, and was very dependent on Ted, who was becoming increasingly moody and withdrawn.

Suddenly, one afternoon, the phone rang: 'I've got an appointment with the midwife and Ted refuses to drive me into town', Jeanette sounded breathless and tearful. 'Can you give me a lift? I've been having contractions all morning and can't face the bus.'

I said I'd pick her up straight away, and we drove to the antenatal clinic and waited for her turn to be examined. The midwife who greeted her told her she was starting to dilate, to go home and get some rest, and then to come in later when her contractions were strong and more regular.

Jeanette looked at me with an excited smile and edged herself down from the table. 'Oh well', she said, 'here goes.' We drove back carefully and I left her to patch things up with Ted, who had just started to paint the spare room. Later that evening the phone rang again. 'Can you come round?' whispered Jeanette in between gasps. 'I'm having lots of contractions and I'm not sure what's happening.'

When I arrived I found her rolling around on the floor, on her back – the exact opposite of the leaning-forward positions she had practised in the group to ease contractions. I helped her on to her knees and started to massage her back. 'That's better,' she sighed. 'It was hurting like hell before.'

After a while, in between contractions, she whispered that she hadn't had time to get a case packed. I showed Ted how to do the back massage and then put some nightclothes and baby things into a plastic bag. Since she had been having contractions since the morning, and by now they seemed strong and were occurring fairly frequently, I suggested they should start immediately for the hospital. This involved a half-hour's drive, and their car was far from reliable. When I said this to Jeanette, she responded anxiously: 'I don't want to go into the hospital. I wish I could have it here.' My heart sank – I didn't feel able to substitute for the midwife! I waited a few minutes more, then said again: 'If you wait too much longer, the journey will be uncomfortable.' 'OK', Jeanette replied, 'let's go, Ted.'

I waved them off, straightened out the room and went home. I kept wondering what was happening and at 6 a.m. there was a knock on the front door. It was Ted, face shining, who bounced into the room. To my relief, the birth had gone relatively well. To begin with, Ted had lost the way to the hospital, but they finally arrived in good time. Jeanette had found the contractions more difficult to manage once in the hospital, and she was given some pethidine, but finally at 4 o'clock in the morning the baby was born, a little boy.

'He's wonderful', said Ted, 'lots of black hair and jet black eyes.'

'How's Jeanette?' I asked.

'Oh – fine,' replied Ted.

Later that afternoon I went to visit her, and found her sitting up in the bed, looking tired, but pleased. She proudly showed me her son, sleeping in the cot alongside. 'He's rather dozy,' she said. 'He doesn't seem to want to suck very much.'

We talked a bit about establishing breast-feeding, which we'd often discussed before and with which she was very determined to succeed. She seemed to be getting some good help from the staff, although other visitors and people in the ward were saying contradictory things. Once again, she seemed unable to make up her own mind, particularly about how often to nurse her son and how to avoid any problems.

When I went to visit her a couple of days later, she had a large sore on each breast. 'I'm having to express the milk with a pump,' she said miserably. 'It's too painful when the baby sucks, and then he doesn't get enough milk and howls.'

I asked her what help she was getting, and again she seemed confused and unsure about what advice to follow. It seemed that the midwife was encouraging her to let the baby nurse as often as possible, and her doctor was telling her to give the breasts time to heal and meanwhile bottle-feed the baby. By now I was beginning to feel powerless in encouraging Jeanette to keep to one set of decisions, rather than oscillating wildly between different courses of action. Somehow she seemed to elicit advice from everyone in her uncertainty, but was unable to decide for herself what to do with the information. I tried to encourage her to follow the midwife's plan and ignore everyone else, but as I left the hospital I felt that I was being as directive and unhelpful as everyone else.

The next time I saw Jeanette was at a meeting of the group a week later. She had come out of hospital and Ted's mother had arrived to help out. Jeanette found her very supportive and seemed relieved to have someone around who could create some order for her. The baby was fine and gaining weight, but she still had one extremely sore nipple and was continuing to hand-express the milk from that side. During the meeting her baby started to cry and Jeanette groaned. 'Not hungry again, you greedy little pig!' she complained. 'He never gives me a rest.'

She picked him up out of his carrycot and sat back in her chair, holding him near the sore breast. He searched for the nipple and finally managed to get a part of the breast into his mouth. 'Ouch', she yelled, 'that hurts!' The baby started to cry again as he lost the milk that had just started to flow. I suggested that if she leaned forward as she nursed him, the baby could suck more easily without pulling on the sore nipple. 'That doesn't feel so bad.' Jeanette smiled and started to relax. The baby fed hungrily and dropped off to sleep.

Over the next few weeks Jeanette became increasingly confident about breast-feeding and her baby remained a relatively calm, settled infant. Despite this, however, Jeanette was anxious that he wasn't putting on enough weight, and felt increasingly irritated by the limitations of her new life being primarily responsible for the child. She felt exhausted by the broken nights, but unable to rest during the day while the baby slept. She appeared to be increasingly stressed by the demands made on her in looking after the baby, and became more and more angry, both with him and with Ted, whom she felt wasn't doing enough to help. He was still out of work, and not very energetically looking for a job, so was around the house a lot of the time. In the initial weeks he had enthusiastically bathed and changed the baby, and taken him for walks in his baby-carrier. Slowly, however, Ted seemed to lose interest, and Jeanette felt that she was more and more responsible for the baby's care.

Three months later, she suddenly visited one day and announced that she was leaving Ted. 'It's become impossible,' she said, 'he hasn't spoken to me for weeks, and completely ignores the baby. It's as if we didn't exist for him.'

Despite this, however, she was looking stronger and more confident than she had done for a long time. She told me that she planned to move into a house with two other women, and had started looking for part-time work. After this she contacted me less frequently, and as I was soon to move to another area, I had less time to visit her. I did, however, receive a short postcard on the anniversary of her son's birth, saying that the communal living with the two other women had not worked out, but she was now happily living with her parents. Her mother was looking after the baby so that Jeanette was now able to go back to work.

Mothering in women's lives

The issue of motherhood is, for many if not most women, one of the most central themes of life. Whether or not they are biological mothers, and whether or not they are currently caring for children, women are all deeply affected by the implications of reproducing and nurturing children. 'Mothering' is assumed to come naturally to women, and extends to all their other relationships too. As Adrienne Rich (1977) points out, if women refuse to 'mother' others, especially men, they are described as inadequate women, or as 'cold, castrating bitches'. If they decide not to have, or are unable to have children of their own, women are seen as selfish, barren, and unmaternal. The implications of mothering also affect women in the workplace: as we argued in Chapter 5, women's abilities to 'mother' others are made use of in their work as teachers, nurses, counsellors, social workers, secretaries, or cleaners. Even the potential for motherhood limits choice. Women's child-bearing capacity often forms a vicious circle in the process of choosing a career, when school subject choice is constrained by traditionally suitable options, and when qualified women are eased into disciplines considered to have more flexible conditions, allowing for child care. Furthermore, many high-risk (and high-pay) industrial jobs are de facto proscribed for women of childbearing age, and hence are closed to virtually all women of all ages.

In this chapter, we shall start by outlining the social context of women's mothering, and then consider some of the pressures which may influence a woman's decision to conceive. Of course, not all women *can* conceive, so we shall then consider the issue of infertility and its treatment. In addition, not all conceptions proceed to term, so we shall look at termination of pregnancy and miscarriage. Then we shall look at the experiences of pregnancy and giving birth, before considering some of the therapeutic implications of these different aspects of women's reproductive lives.

Pronatalism and choice

During the past half century, despite many problems (as outlined in Chapter 4), the development of contraception and in some places the relative availability of abortion have enabled at least some women to exercise a limited amount of choice over the number and timing of the children they bear. In western Protestant countries, women no longer have the physical and emotional burden of yearly pregnancies, which previously resulted in large families, and severely affected women's health and liberty. However, we would like to argue that the freedom of 'choice', to have or not to have children, is in fact almost as heavily limited by cultural constraints as by the availability of contraception and termination. We live in what has been called (Gimenez, 1984) a 'pronatalist' society which, for a variety of reasons stresses women's reproductive and mothering functions to the exclusion of virtually every other function. Martha Gimenez points to the extent to which parenthood is universally prescribed by a number of pronatalist assumptions. There are, she claims, 'no legitimate or socially rewarded alternatives to the performance of parental roles ... parenthood is a *precondition* for women's and men's adult roles' (Gimenez, 1984:288, emphasis in original). She quotes the work of sociologist Juliet Blake, who points out that even family-planning advocates and those who seek to bring about population control do not seriously consider the possibility of not producing any children at all (Blake, 1974). Within a pronatalist context, not only are women provided with a limited view of sexuality, which designates as proper the formation of a heterosexual husband-and-wife couple, but as soon as that union is publicly celebrated, demands that the woman starts to produce children. Both Gimenez and Blake also criticise feminist theory for having ignored the ideology of the compulsory nature of motherhood, in particular, the way that contemporary feminism stresses the 'do-both' syndrome, that is, that motherhood and careers are not an either/or option, but that modern women have the 'right' to combine both. Gimenez argues that we need to expand the concept of reproductive freedom to include not merely the choice of time of conception and overall number of children, but also the possibility of a child-free status as a legitimate option for women.

Nevertheless, at present, the vast majority of women will have, or want to have, children. What is the nature of the complex interaction of external pressure and internal motives that underlie a woman's 'decision' to become pregnant? There may be both active and passive reasons. The woman who decides to stop using contraception and 'see what happens' is making a different kind of choice from one who plots her morning temperature curve and examines her vaginal secretions to determine ovulation and hence her peak fertility; but it is a choice none the less. In a society which places contraceptive responsibility almost universally in the hands of the woman, governed by the technological/biological constraints of the contraceptive pill and the intrauterine device, any contraceptive 'failure' becomes largely her responsibility also. Thus all heterosexually active women of childbearing age continually have to face the possibility of conceiving, and hence have to make choices about their fertility.

Pressures to conceive

In strongly pronatalist societies, advertising and other media images representing images of bouncing babies and adorable toddlers are supplemented by statutory inducements, or payment for motherhood. Such is the concern about maintaining the population after the experience of heavy losses involved in two world wars, that countries such as France and the USSR provide extra child benefits or medals for women who produce large families. Conversely, of course, where the state considers the population to be too large, as in China, it is women again who are under pressure to control their fertility. In any case, there is much encouragement to conform to what the society concerned says it needs.

Much of the pressure is of course closer to home. Men, obviously unable to bear children themselves, must rely on women to do so. Although direct pressures by men for their women partners to have children may be somewhat attenuated in societies where children are not economically productive, but rather represent an emotional 'investment', nevertheless male desire for children often produces covert, if not overt, pressure. Once their children are born, and particularly once they have reached a reasonably interactive stage, male desires for their offspring are often very intense, as witnessed by the battles for custody that frequently ensue when parents separate. The involvement of the father varies according to individual interest, social class, and personal history (see Nigel Beail, 1982), although for many it heralds a time of reduced satisfaction with marriage (see Carolyn Cowan and colleagues, 1985).

Despite these social pressures, the desire to have a child is often experienced by many women (who have the choice), as an 'instinctive' and personal decision. Biological determinist accounts would explain these urges as deriving from women's innate reproductive ability. But, as Janet Sayers (1982) has more convincingly argued, such simplistic notions cannot adequately explain the range and complexity of women's experiences, particularly since some women with perfectly functioning bodies decidedly do *not* want to have children. In their book *Why Children?*, Stephanie Dowrick and Sibyl Grundberg (1980) have collected a number of essays by women describing what lies behind their decision to have or not to have children. What is clear from these essays is that women do not simply respond to a biological urge, but have a multiplicity of reasons for their choices, which are based on both psychological and social considerations.

In contrast to the biological approach, psychodynamic writers have tried to formulate the unconscious factors involved in wanting to conceive. Freud (1924) saw the wish for a baby as being the ultimate way in which women could resolve the castration complex and reduce their penis envy. A baby, especially a boy baby, he claimed, gives to the woman the phallus she lacks. This theory, of course, completely ignores the social pressures, as current now as when he was writing, to produce a male child, as well as being predicated on the debatable emotion of penis envy. The *symbolic* nature of women's envy of a male phallus, and its representation during motherhood have been supported by Freudian feminists influenced by the writings of Jacques Lacan, for example, Juliet Mitchell (1974), and Juliet Mitchell and Jacqueline Rose (1982). But such theorists ignore a woman's identification with her mother, rather than her father, in her conflicts concerning motherhood.

Object-relations theories have widened the issue, and have interpreted women's desires to have a baby in terms of their early experiences of being mothered. Nancy Chodorow (1978) has used this approach to describe women's longing for motherhood in terms of an attempt to recapture the psychic fusion they experienced with their own mothers. Luise Eichenbaum and Susie Orbach (1982) suggest that by representing the one idealised way in which women can create for themselves the perfect object, the baby is imagined to be the one person who will unconditionally love them. In that sense, in having a baby, women are wishing to reproduce for themselves a mother figure, who will provide them with nurturant love. As we will see, children, especially babies, are far from able to provide such emotional gratification, but according to these theorists, the fantasy nevertheless exists that they will be able to do so.

There can be other motives, too, of which the mother may not be entirely aware. In looking at Jeanette's story, for example, it appears that she was a young and poorly qualified woman, for whom having a baby gave a way out of a tedious and unfulfilling job. She had also hoped that the baby would patch up a precarious and unsatisfactory relationship with Ted, who was otherwise not making any clear commitment to her. We might assume, more profoundly, that her own poor relationship with her mother had left some deeply felt affectional longings that were not being met by any of the adults in her limited circle of acquaintances. To the extent that the baby became an emotional burden and the relationship with Ted was finally destroyed, the baby's arrival could not be said to have fulfilled these desires, although it did provide a justification to return to the parental home. Perhaps there Jeanette received some belated parenting, either directly, or vicariously through the care taken by the grandparents of their grandson, which may explain her apparent satisfaction with this arrangement.

Fertility and self-identity

For a young woman, the body's fertility may often be something she feels she has to battle against, rather than being something which is integrated easily into her concept of herself. Coming to terms with menstruation and developing a positive image of her own sexuality will usually take place within a framework that excludes the desire to conceive, although as is tragically common, many young women who are starting sexual relationships are especially likely not to take contraceptive precautions (see Sue Lees, 1986; Ann-Marie Coyne, 1986). As an inevitable result, some early pregnancies do occur. In the UK, for example, in 1983 there were 5,353 known conceptions amongst teenagers aged under 16 years old, which resulted in 1,249 live births (quoted in Coyne, 1986). Such a premature entry into the constraints and obligations of motherhood must be a disadvantage for young women, especially in a complex technological society that demands of its adults long years of education and a high awareness of social structures. It is therefore not surprising that some young women see their fertility as something to be feared and restricted, rather than welcomed.

Women who *do* want to become pregnant, then, have to face an abrupt reversal of their previous construction of menstruation and sexuality. If they are in a committed heterosexual relationship, sexual intercourse will take on an added dimension as it becomes part of a process involving procreation as an aim, rather than merely being an act in and for itself (some religious groups, of course, would argue that intercourse should always have procreation as an aim). Although for some women this may be erotically arousing, and they can feel themselves opening out and welcoming the possibility of fertilisation, for others it reduces sexual desire and makes them tense and inhibited (Sheila Kitzinger, 1978).

The act of conceiving has numerous psychological as well as physical consequences. In a culture which medicalises both sex and childbirth (see p.147) women are inevitably liable to have fears about pregnancy and parturition. Since most births take place in hospital settings, and are artificially managed along medical rather than midwifery principles, women are not likely to have witnessed any other woman's labour before their own. Some women may also be ambivalent about the changes that caring for a child will make to their lives, their relationships with their partners and their personal autonomy, given that conventionally, a major part of the child care will be their responsibility. Also, since in a pronatalist culture parenthood represents a *rite de passage* into adult status, a woman may be aware of the sensitive issues involved in 'replacing' her own parents. As Dana Breen (1975) has shown, there is often a discrepancy between how a woman remembers her own mother to have been, and how she thinks the 'ideal mother' should be. Particularly if her own experience of being parented has been unsatisfactory, she may worry that she will be unable to nurture a child, and hence may feel herself to be incapable of entering into motherhood. As we saw with Jeanette, there may be a strong desire to 'do better' than her own parents, whilst retaining a feeling of helplessness that this places demands on her that she would be unable to fulfil. Thus Jeanette was caught in the vicious circle having high expectations of herself (although she didn't really know how she wanted to behave and vacillated wildly between conflicting pieces of advice), while simultaneously blaming herself for her inevitable failure. As we have seen, Jeanette's solution, although perhaps temporary, was to reject her autonomous adult status for a while and return to her parents.

Infertility

Considering the elaborate contraceptive methods undertaken by most women to prevent an unplanned pregnancy, it comes as a great shock for some women to find that there are difficulties for them in conceiving. Traditionally, a failure to conceive has been seen to be the woman's problem, so much so that despite the fact that this is just as likely to be due to a problem with the male partner, many doctors do not even refer the man for diagnosis. As Michael Humphrey, a psychologist working in the field of infertility treatment, has stated: 'The male partner can be held fully responsible in some 15 per cent of couples investigated, and is diagnosed as subfertile much more frequently . . . yet technical advances in the treatment of infertility have been virtually confined to the female partner' (Humphrey, 1984:80).

In fact, infertility is solely attributable to the woman in only one-third of cases, the remaining two-thirds being attributable to the man, or to a joint difficulty. Sadly, inability to conceive is a problem which is confronting increasing numbers of people. For example, in the United States, it has been estimated that there are between 5–12 million people of childbearing age who are infertile (Ellen Cook, 1987). This represents about 10–15 per cent of all couples. The causes of an inability to conceive are many and varied. Iatrogenic problems induced by modern contraceptive techniques, whether by long-term use of the contraceptive pill or by infections due to intrauterine devices, may be one reason why infertility appears to be increasing. Another reason may be environmental and especially industrial hazards affecting the reproductive apparatus of both men and women. In addition, higher levels of sexual contact have meant that sexually transmitted diseases, which have relatively little effect on men, have had devastating effects on many women's reproductive systems. Another major cause is the absence of sexual intercourse, due to impotence or ignorance. Last, recent life-style changes have meant that many independent women, who have delayed the decision to have a child, find in their mid-30s that they are having difficulties in conceiving for age-related reasons. As Judith Stacey writes: 'Involuntary childlessness is one of the cruellest, unanticipated traumas.. . . Few among those of us who deferred childbearing decisions until the biological limits considered the possibility that an affirmative decision might be impossible to implement' (Stacey, 1986:239).

The discovery of infertility has been labelled as a crisis (Melvin Taymor,

1978) with enormous consequences for a woman's sense of identity and personal relationships. The woman may feel anxious, guilty, and estranged from others, and may also feel intensely angry with this cruel blow of fate. A frequent response is grief, but the grieving is often done in private, because of an overwhelming sense of guilt, shame, and failure. According to Kimberly McEwan and her colleagues (1987), about 37 per cent of women who receive a diagnosis of infertility are significantly psychologically disturbed by the information. Those most seriously affected seem to be women who felt that they were to blame for the infertility, and those with strong, non-Protestant religious beliefs. In their self-help book on the experience of infertility, Naomi Pfeffer and Anne Woollett describe the complex and changing emotions experienced when trying to conceive, both for the woman and for her partner:

> Infertility reveals itself in the attempt to create a particular relationship, that of mother and child. Not succeeding can affect all your other relationships to a lesser or greater extent.. . . The dilemma is that by devaluing or sacrificing relationships in the quest for motherhood, you may become more isolated. (Pfeffer and Woollett, 1983: 31)

This applies as much to a woman's evaluation and experience of her work as it does to her personal relationships. Previous achievements and interests may be felt to be worth nothing, given the tragedy of the inability to conceive. Simultaneously, strong feelings of envy may be felt towards women who are already pregnant or have children of their own, which are particularly stressful if the woman feels surrounded by friends with babies.

Although a failure to conceive may be successfully helped simply by careful counselling of the couple's sexual practices (for example, William Masters and Virginia Johnson in 1970 found that some of the couples they counselled were then able to conceive) there are a great many factors involved in the complex process of conception, which may or may not be susceptible to medical treatment. As with all other aspects of women's health care, the diagnosis and treatment of infertility is poorly developed and unevenly available in most countries. In the UK, for example, there are a limited number of NHS infertility clinics (often with long waiting lists), supplemented in some areas by private agencies or hospitals which provide medical advice and infertility counselling. Results are often far from satisfactory, with current estimates suggesting that only one-third of the couples seen are successfully treated (Michael Humphrey, 1984).

The possible physical causes and available treatments are well documented in a variety of sources, and will not be repeated here (see, for example, the women's health handbook *Our Bodies, Ourselves* by Angela Phillips and Jill Rakusen, 1978, which provides a clear idea of what is involved in treatment). But where current medical practice and women's health literature often fail women is in their underestimation of the role of emotional factors in the success or otherwise of infertility treatments. Emotional issues may affect not only specific functions, as seen, for example, in the suppression of ovulation due to stress found in women undergoing donor insemination treatment (Michael Vere and David Joyce, 1979), but also have a more global and yet indefinable reaction on reproductive processes. Although not substantiated by any large-scale studies, some psychoanalysts have also suggested that emotional conflicts may have profound effects on conception and successful pregnancy (see especially Karen Horney, 1967; Helene Deutsch, 1945). Unfortunately, because of the small number of adequately designed research studies, the psychology of conception and pregnancy is still poorly understood by health-care providers. Nevertheless, it is undoubtedly the case that the decision to become pregnant will generate many conflicts for some women, which are not easily resolved, and may well be linked in some way to difficulties in conception.

It is clear, however, that in addition to the psychogenic factors that might hinder conception, the very process of undertaking lengthy physical examinations to diagnose and treat infertility will have many emotional repercussions. From the precise timing of intercourse, to post-coital tests and laparoscopy, the progression of investigations may cause not only individual feelings of depression and grief, but profoundly affect the relationships of partners involved. Yet whilst the medical treatment inevitably focuses on these physical events, women's psychological needs, and the strong and often overwhelming feelings which accompany the physical treatments, are often neglected. Most women would benefit from a more psychotherapeutic approach during this time. This would enable them to acknowledge their fears and ambivalences, and if provided in a group context, would allow them to gain support from other women in similar situations. Yet such help is most notable by its absence.

Implications of reproductive technology for the treatment of infertility

Since the adoption of babies has become an almost impossible option for many women who are childless but want to become mothers, technological advances in artificial methods of reproduction have attracted much interest. But again, as with other aspects of their reproductive life, women often find that access to facilities is governed at least in part by medical authorities, and paradoxically in part by social criteria which actually have little to do with medical criteria. For example, it is often argued that fertility treatments should only be available to 'stable' married couples, which ignores the realities of everyday parenting, that because of divorce or desertion, many women do successfully raise children on their own without necessarily having chosen to do so. Here, as in so many other areas, the woman herself is not deemed to be able to decide for herself what is the best course of action for her own life.

There are a growing number of different forms of assistance potentially available to the childless, but here we shall discuss only two in some detail, artificial insemination (the placing of semen inside a woman's vagina or uterus by means other than sexual intercourse), and *in vitro* fertilisation (the replacement inside a woman's uterus of one or more embryos, usually but not always the result of the extraction of the woman's ripe ovules followed by fertilisation by her husband's sperm). Artificial insemination (AI) is a reasonably successful procedure, most inseminations occurring within the first three cycles of treatment (RCOG, 1976), whereas the success rate for *in vitro* fertilisation (IVF) is much poorer, with between 10 and 20 per cent of women being success-ful per treatment cycle (see Simon Fishel and Malcolm Symonds, 1986; Robert Edelmann, 1987).

The use of AI

Negotiation of the decision to opt for AI or IVF can be a difficult one for many couples for a variety of reasons. In the case of AI, the discovery that he is sub- or infertile can be traumatic for a man who associates his virility with his fertility, and unless this issue is faced by the couple who do decide to go ahead with AI, it can re-emerge later in the child's life, or in the couple's relationship. In addition, many AI couples express their intention of concealing from their children the knowledge of their true origins. Yet in the event of any problems, it is not unknown for parents to apportion blame on the unknown genetic factor rather than take responsibility of a child's development, or to use the 'secret' of the child's biological parenthood as a particularly potent weapon in family disputes. Further, in some instances, men who discover that they cannot have children will refuse to consider the use of donor sperm, rejecting social fatherhood in the absence of biological fatherhood. This is obviously highly distressing to a woman who does want to become a mother, forcing her to choose between a child and her partner.

The question of using AI is also complicated for women without partners. Although some agencies will accept single women, not all do so, and state-provided services are unlikely to be available to them. If treatments have to be repeated, the costs, both emotional and financial, can be very high. Furthermore, the medicalisation of the procedure can be unnecessarily distressing, and counterproductive. As a result, some women, as described by Lisa Saffron (1986) in her guide to alternative methods of insemination, have chosen to use self-help groups to practise self-insemination. Saffron outlines the practical, emotional, and legal issues involved, and suggests that for women who do want children without having to use subterfuge, unemotional sexual entanglements, or medical inter- ference, such a procedure is often preferable. As with childbirth, women's bodies can often function optimally when in familiar and recognised surroundings, which is now recognised by some private agencies, such as the British Pregnancy Advisory Service in the UK, who offer women the possibility of self- insemination at home with donor sperm, rather than attending a clinic. Yet it seems likely that, in the UK at least, the unregistered use of donor sperm will be declared illegal in the future, following the recommendations of the *Warnock Report on Human Fertilisation and Embryology* (see Warnock, 1985).

For single women, and particularly for lesbian women, who want to mother a child, and yet who do not want to have to have intercourse with a succession of men until they find themselves pregnant, such legal decisions merely reinforce feelings of powerlessness and loss. As with all forms of reproductive treatment, the need for counselling and therapeutic help is considerable, although rarely available.

The use of IVF

The other form of treatment for infertility which we shall discuss is *in vitro* fertilisation, offered to women who are unable to conceive because of damaged fallopian tubes (often as a result of infection, but sometimes caused iatrogenically in connection with intrauterine devices for contraception). It is a highly complex procedure, which involves extracting a woman's ripe egg follicles by laparoscopy, fertilising them with her partner's sperm in the laboratory, and replacing them a few days later in her uterus to implant and grow. At any stage of the procedure, the delicate biological response may not function optimally, and the cycle will have to be abandoned. As already noted, the success rates for the procedure are relatively low, although this depends on the place where it is carried out and the stringency of the criteria used before the whole procedure is attempted. For example, some private agencies may put women through an entire treatment cycle (involving the induction of ovulation through the use of at least two different fertility drugs, two operations usually carried out under general anaesthetic, considerable expense, and an enormous investment of emotional energy and time), even though the likelihood of successs in that particular menstrual cycle is low, because (for example) of an inadequate response to the first dosage of fertility drugs.

In addition to the problems noted previously, it is also the case that IVF treatments in particular are still in their early stages, and anxieties about possible side effects or complications may well confound the emotional strain for those undergoing the procedure. Despite recommendations of the Warnock Committee (see Warnock, 1985), counselling is not automatically available to women during this time, and levels of emotional distress are often very high, especially as every day brings yet another chance of failure (see Tim Appleton, 1986). As with all other forms of fertility treatments, couples may be loath to confide in friends or family members, particularly when the chances of success are low. If unsuccessful, they may have to bear their grief and disappointment alone without being able to explain the cause of their distress to others. In addition, because of the nature of the technology involved, women undergoing these procedures also often feel passive, powerless and out of control of forces, both biological and technological, which seem to be controlling their lives. It has been argued (for example, by Naomi Pfeffer, 1987) that the procedures involved in IVF place woman and children at a certain risk, a consideration which has been under-estimated in the race for technological advance.

As yet there have been only a few follow-up studies of IVF children, although some do exist (for example Maria Barreda-Hanson, David Mushin, and John Spensley, 1987); and even fewer studies of the implications for the parents of having undergone the procedure. However, those studies which have been done suggest that both children and parents do not differ in any significant way from 'normal' parents and children (see Alexina McWhinnie, 1986). On the other hand, Robert Edelmann (1987) has described a number of studies of couples who have attempted the procedure, and found evidence of a relatively high level of anxiety in many of the couples, especially those who attempt the procedure more than once. In addition, the practice of implanting more than one fertile embryo, which increases the chances of the success of the procedure, also increases the likelihood of multiple births, which is hazardous for mother and children alike.

Problems associated with the use of reproductive technology

It seems that on the one hand, the use of reproductive technology offers tremendous hope and opportunity for otherwise childless couples, and as such opens up choices for men and women which must be welcomed. On the other hand, the very possibility of achieving a pregnancy in this way, for some people, merely delays recognition of and acceptance of their infertility, besides being an enormous drain on their financial and personal resources. In some cases, there may also be unresolved issues centring on the previous infertility which may rebound on any children conceived in these ways.

Apart from those individually concerned, it has also been argued that the scientific experimentation required to achieve AI and IVF births has serious implications for women as a group (see, for example, the collection of essays edited by Rita Arditti, Renate Klein, and Shelley Mindon, 1984). Julie Murphy (1984) in her essay on reproductive technologies expresses fears that development of techniques such as egg recovery and embryo replacement or transfer involves the separating out of the various stages of human reproduction with the possible implications of control and selection at each of these stages. She argues that women run the risk of being viewed increasingly for their reproductive function, for example as 'egg donors' or 'egg hatchers', and that it is only a small step from here to greater social control over women's independent choice over their fertility.

It is certainly not unknown for medical advances to be used in this way. For example, some diagnostic procedures such as amniocentesis (where a sample of the amniotic fluid is extracted from the pregnant woman's abdomen to screen for genetic disorders such as Down's syndrome) have been abused by some families to pressurise expectant mothers to abort girl foetuses (see Betty Hoskins and Helen Bequart Holmes, 1984). Besides the ethical issues involved, such a misuse of technology could have enormous implications for family dynamics: where girls do exist they may always be second or later-born siblings and thus are even more firmly placed in an inferior position. While men as a group may feel threatened by the increasing use of procedures such as AI, and that their role in reproduction could become negligible, the greater likelihood is actually that reproductive technology will be used to control women and *their* reproductive freedom.

The ultimate use of a woman's body solely for reproduction is, of course, surrogate motherhood, whereby a woman becomes pregnant by arrangement, agreeing to hand over the child after the birth to the biological father and his wife. This procedure is in many ways alarming, not least because many of the agencies which have been set up to carry out this procedure fail to provide adequate information, counselling, and legal advice to women prepared to undergo surrogate parenthood (see Susan Ince, 1984). Many of the mothers in question are poor, and have few resources on which to draw in controlling what happens to them or their children. Athough of dubious legality in most countries, it seems unlikely that the use of surrogate motherhood will decline in the future. A moving and very telling description of the issues raised by surrogate motherhood can be found in Margaret Atwood's futuristic novel, *The Handmaid's Tale* (1987), in which environmental pollution has rendered most women infertile, leaving a small group of potentially fertile women obliged to 'service' a politically oppressive elite.

Termination of pregnancy

For those who are able to conceive, reactions to the conception will vary enormously. In some cases, especially where the pregnancy is unplanned, there may be a denial by the woman herself that she is pregnant, especially if she continues to menstruate, albeit in a modified form. An unplanned pregnancy brings a marked crisis in a woman's life, for which decisions have to be made rapidly. Depending on her financial and emotional security, the number of children that she may already have, and her feelings about abortion, she will have to decide whether or not to continue with the pregnancy. Abortion in most countries is governed by law, and is only permitted under various conditions, although the interpretation of the law varies widely. In the UK, for example, a woman has to have the agreement of two registered doctors who will decide whether continuing the pregnancy would involve a greater risk to the woman's life, injury to her physical or mental health, or injury to the health of her existing children, than if the pregnancy was terminated. In these circumstances termination is legal, although there are continuing pressures to lower the time limit. The vast majority of terminations are carried out before the tenth week after conception, although in some circumstances (usually involving the discovery of malformation of the foetus, although sometimes resulting from delays in detecting, reporting, or referring on the pregnancy), terminations may be carried out well after the twentieth week. Many relatively late terminations are due to the time inevitably taken to process the results of amniocentesis (the removal and culture of a sample of amniotic fluid which can determine the presence of some foetal abnormalities). Attempts to lower the time limit on abortions have so far allowed for later terminations in the case of such procedures. But the traumatic nature of the decision for the woman involved cannot be underestimated.

However, while abortion in some circumstances is legal in the UK, there is considerable evidence that facilities are still inadequate, and that there is a wide variation in provision throughout the country (Lane Committee Report, 1974; David Paintin, 1985). As a consequence, many women have to use private services, which are costly. However, in the private sector there have been isolated examples of innovations of provision, particularly in the organisation of day-care clinics which reduce waiting times and do not over-load gynaecological facilities. Some women (such as Lena Jega, 1978) have argued that an even more effective innovation would be for women to act independently of medical authority, using technology which already exists, such as the procedure of menstrual extraction, which requires no medical intervention. This procedure has been pioneered amongst women's groups where access to abortion is limited or illegal.

Despite frequent short-term emotional distress, there is not much solid evidence that a termination of pregnancy leads to a great deal of long-term serious psychological disturbance in most women who have had to choose this alternative (see Sue Llewelyn and Rachel Pytches, 1988). For some women, however, emotional upheaval immediately following the termination may be pronounced. Whilst much of the stress concerns the practical business of making the arrangements for the termination itself (see Angela Neustatter and Gina Newson, 1986), the ensuing feelings of guilt and grief may, for at least some women, be experienced intensely. Private agencies arranging for termination will generally provide at least one pre-operation counselling session by an experienced person who is not the doctor making the medical referral; however, in the UK state service the counselling is usually provided by one of the doctors responsible for making the recommendation to terminate. This, of course, puts both doctor and client in an ambiguous position, as the woman is not likely to admit to any ambivalence to the doctor whom she must convince of her need for a termination. Seldom are any post-termination counselling sessions provided, yet the decision to abort a pregnancy is almost always a painful one, being a choice between two potentially traumatic alternatives.

In some centres, however, post-abortion counselling has been made available to women, and has been found to be extremely helpful. Mira Dana (1987), for example, has described the post-abortion groups she has run, which are often attended by women many months or even years after the event. Women who have denied their emotional reactions at the time of the termination may have found that their feelings re-emerge at a later date, especially if social disapproval at the time led them to conceal their feelings of grief. Even amongst feminists who have campaigned for freer access to abortion, there has often been a denial of the conflicts and moral issues involved, giving the impression that any ambivalence expressed is a vote against women's rights. These women, then, may be particularly distressed by their feelings following terminations.

There is a wide variety of responses in a woman's reactions to the loss incurred in abortion. Generally, if the woman is able to express her feelings of grief, the experience of loss and sadness will be lessened, and she will be able to resume her pre-conception life, often with relief and a renewed sense of purpose. However, if this process is blocked, either by herself or by significant others, feelings of depression, emptiness, and anger may be exacerbated (see Mira Dana, 1987). Women who intend to have children at a later date and women with strong religious convictions are those who tend to have a magnified stress response to the abortion, as do those who are highly ambivalent about their decision.

It is very clear that a woman's current relationships also determine her reaction to termination. Numerous studies have shown that women with few close friends, without personal support, and with absent or disturbed relationships with their partners tend to be hardest hit by termination. This also has long-term consequences. Annabel Broome (1984) has shown that whilst most women adjust well after their initial distress, unsuccessful adjustment because of unresolved grief, guilt, or reactions from others is likely to have serious implications for future pregnancies. In addition, Mira Dana (1987) has suggested that many women express a fear of sexuality following a termination, and because the reaction of at least some male partners who learn of an unwanted pregnancy is to reject the woman, some women have to cope with a lost relationship as well as with a lost baby. The result may be a well-concealed envy of other mothers and their babies, exacerbated by a society which views motherhood as women's 'real' task.

Miscarriage

There is much evidence to suggest that an early, well-planned, and supported termination is less emotionally distressing than a spontaneous abortion, or miscarriage (see Annabel Broome, 1984). Although the pattern of grieving that needs to be initiated is in many ways similar, the shock of miscarriage may be greater, particularly if there were no warning signs giving the woman time to prepare for the loss before the event, and hence robbing her of any sense of control. Until recently, even amongst women, there has been a reluctance to describe and discuss experiences of miscarriage, echoing the silence of the medical and nursing profession, who often have great difficulty caring for a distressed woman after a miscarriage. Yet the experience is an extremely common one; Gillian Lachelin (1985) suggests that it is possible that more than 75 per cent of all human conceptions are lost. Of course many of these take place before the woman is aware that she is pregnant, but for those who have had their pregnancy confirmed and have begun to form a relationship with their developing baby, a miscarriage comes as a tremendous shock. In their book describing their own and other women's miscarriages, Ann Oakley, Ann McPherson, and Helen

Roberts (1984) consider the range of physical and emotional reactions. Whilst each woman will react in her own particular way, a large number initially blame themselves for the miscarriage, often attributing overwork or excessive activity as the cause. Insensitive attitudes on the part of medical and nursing staff greatly intensify the trauma, especially when staff deny the necessity of coming to terms with the loss as with any other bereavement.

Women also cope with their loss in many ways: some will want to become pregnant again as soon as possible, while others feel the need to adjust to the loss before conceiving again. According to Ann Oakley and her colleagues, support from family and friends was perceived to be especially important, but many women described how even after a very short time the event was forgotten by others, although not by the woman herself. Significant dates, particularly the expected date of delivery, often triggered off new bouts of mourning, and while some women said they had buried their thoughts and feelings, others continued to fantasise about the lost baby long after subsequent children were born.

As we will discuss later, the successful resolution of these loss experiences depends in large part on how successfully they are dealt with at the time. Yet there is often little help available to many women, and little knowledge about the best way to help. As Jacqueline de Gier (1987) writes: 'A miscarriage is likely to be one of the saddest and most traumatic experiences a woman can have ... for a woman who wanted a baby and lost it, it is the ultimate failure.'

Experiences of pregnancy

Having discussed some of the problems involved in becoming or staying pregnant, or choosing to terminate the pregnancy, we now turn to the more positive processes of the experience of taking a pregnancy to term, and giving birth. Yet in many ways, not much is known about these processes, either. Despite the fact that pregnancy and childbirth are major life events which are experienced by almost all women, irrespective of race or class, orthodox psychology has virtually ignored them, which means that there is much still to be understood about the range of experiences and reactions. Once again, they are developmental events which do not figure within the 'psychology of man'.

Yet it is clear from talking with and counselling pregnant women and mothers that most women do undergo profound changes in their emotional, physical, and social states around the time of pregnancy, which deserve attention. It is important to note here that whilst focusing on psychological issues, we cannot ignore the fact that the economic position of many expectant women is precarious, with severe limitations being imposed on the receipt of maternity benefits, restrictive practices denying job protection for many pregnant women, and a refusal by most governments to consider seriously the granting of parental leave. This is especially true for Britain, which is the only EEC country steadfastly to ignore this issue. All of this means that whilst having to come to terms with their bodily changes, emotional responses, and personal relationships, many pregnant women are also facing the possibility of severe economic hardship.

Psychological aspects of pregnancy

In this section we shall consider some of the common psychological experiences of pregnancy. However, as with other bodily changes, it must be recalled that each woman responds differently to the stages of pregnancy, so what is true for one woman may not be so for another. For example, whilst for some women early signs of pregnancy are welcome, if sometimes unpleasant, for others there will be a sense of debilitation and lack of control, as if they were being invaded by a foreign body which has taken them over. In addition, while some women are aware of being pregnant from the time that they conceive, others will only slowly realise that they are pregnant after missing one or more periods. The experience of one pregnancy may also be very different from another. Many women report being more aware of second or later pregnancies at an earlier stage than with their first one, when bladder sensitivity, uterine tensions, and general sensations of bloatedness and nausea may be similar to and hence confused with pre-menstrual feelings.

Like all transitional phases, pregnancy triggers in many women the return of unresolved conflicts and anxieties. Confusing fantasies may emerge. For example, a woman might feel that her insides are just one large cavity and that at birth everything will come pouring out (see Joan Raphael-Leff, 1980), or that the baby will never stop growing. These images may be linked with fears of pain, and that under duress she will lose adult control and become childlike in her need for relief and reassurance. According to Sheila Kitzinger (1978), emotional changes often take place during pregnancy, particularly a heightening of emotional sensitivity in which reactions of sadness, joy, anxiety, or depression may become much more intense than usual. For women who have previously felt in charge of their emotions and perhaps not shown them very openly, this can come as an immense shock, both to themselves and to their partners, work colleagues, and others. More frightening still, for women who already have experienced large swings in their emotional stability, such experiences may rekindle fears of emotional precariousness.

Some psychodynamic descriptions of women's emotional reactions to pregnancy have stressed the way in which the woman's relationship with her own mother will affect her feelings during this time. For example, Dionora Pines (1982) focuses on the regressive feelings that may be triggered, in that the newly pregnant woman may be aware of the feelings and fantasies of early infancy. She may identify with the foetus, and feel as though she is herself a baby in her mother's womb. If she feels that she was loved and cared for by her own mother, Pines argues, she is likely to experience positive feelings for her own developing child. If, however, her own mother was ambivalent about being pregnant and was rejecting of her as a child, then feelings of ambivalence and conflict are likely to emerge. Above all, as Luise Eichenbaum and Susie Orbach (1982) have also pointed out, pregnancy may raise again the question of a woman's separation from her mother. The fact that the daughter in her turn has become pregnant heightens the similarity between the two women, which may increase the feelings of dependence which the daughter has towards her mother, as well as the identifications which the mother has with her soon-to-be-mother child. On the other hand, some daughters may use this situation to assert their autonomy, being determined to 'do it differently' and push their mothers away. For older women, a daughter's pregnancy can generate a range of feelings; joy in anticipation of having a new baby in the family, envy that the daughter is somehow replacing her, or fear that the daughter will not be able to cope with the experiences and responsibilities. Whilst for some women, mother/daughter conflicts can be greatly resolved, or at least some rapprochement felt during this time of sharing in their joint experience of motherhood, for others the stresses involved may heighten angry or rejecting feelings.

Although we are primarily focusing on the pregnant woman's experiences, the reactions of her partner are also relevant as they will influence how she feels. For some couples, pregnancy is a time of increasing closeness, while for others, previously concealed tensions will emerge. Heightened needs for dependency and intimacy, often mixed with alternating desires to be alone, focusing on her own internal processes, seem to be common. Such powerful feelings inevitably change the dynamics of the relationship to which considerable adjustment is required by both partners. Such adjustment does not always occur: George Brown and Tirril Harris (1978) found a decline in husband/wife intimacy following the birth of a first child, especially amongst working-class couples. On a sexual level, some women may feel an enhanced sense of their sexuality during pregnancy, but others may feel completed by the foetus inside them and not in need of anyone else. They may particularly fear penetration, anxious that this may somehow harm the baby physically or psychologically, or feel spied on by the foetus (see Lesley Saunders, 1983). These feelings of anxiety may be particularly heightened following a previous miscarriage.

Complex emotions will be aroused for the partner, who may share in and empathise with the pregnant woman's experiences, or who may feel cut off and deny any interest or responsibility. When the partner is a woman, and particularly if she has not had children herself, these may be strong feelings of envy and jealousy (see comments by lesbian couples in Lisa Saffron, 1986, and Jill Brown, 1983). When the partner is a man, such feelings may be tinged with intense regret that he will never be able to undergo the magical experience of childbirth. Eva Kittay (1984) has examined in detail the concept of 'womb envy', earlier developed by Karen Horney (1967), claiming that there is both anthropological and psychoanalytic evidence to suggest that from young childhood, boys envy and wish to possess for themselves the procreative powers of women. We saw earlier how Jeanette's partner, Ted, resented her increased dependence on him during pregnancy, and reacted to her retreat from the world of work by giving up his own job too. He continued to deny any responsibility or interest right through the pregnancy, but having experienced the birth of 'his' son, became jubilant and ecstatic as though he himself had given birth. Eva Kittay (1984) outlines some of the common defences shown by men against such envy, including both idealisation of the pregnant or labouring woman and devaluation of the significance and complexity of pregnancy and childbirth. Male appropriation and control of the process of birth can also be seen as a powerful defence which greatly reduces control held by women during these events. For whereas the imminent mother is experiencing, perhaps hesitantly, feelings of adult responsibility and separateness, the medicalisation of pregnancy and childbirth often entails humiliating infantilisation, which could be a way for some men of dealing with their otherwise unexpressed envy.

Medical aspects of pregnancy

As soon as the pregnancy is confirmed, previously healthy women find that they become patients, subject to hospital routines under the authority of medical staff and procedures over which they have little control. To a large extent they are expected to submit passively to these procedures and routines. For many, this can be an intensely alienating experience. In their research into women's experiences of medical treatment during pregnancy, Hilary Graham and Ann Oakley (1981) interviewed women about their experiences of pregnancy and childbirth, and compared their comments with views held by the doctors involved. They found that the women's own knowledge and expertise about their pregnancies were undervalued and underestimated by doctors, who often refused to discuss treatments or tests, answered questions in a condescending manner, and generally saw decisions as resting entirely with the medical personnel.

As with other areas of medicine, information is often withheld from pregnant women who may be unable to find out results of tests, or to assess realistically the benefits or side effects of interventions or treatments. One example is the widespread use of new technologies such as ultrasound scanning to check on foetal development. This is now used so commonly that it has become difficult to plan controlled trials to assess side effects or contra-indications, including long-term follow-up, since there is not a large enough control group of women not receiving scans (see AIMS, 1986). Yet this intervention has not been rigorously tested, and known side effects on animals are not mentioned to women before-hand. There are undoubted benefits to ultrasound scans, such as the detection of foetal abnormality, but women themselves have little choice in the matter. As Maureen Ritchie (1984) reports, it is difficult to avoid exposing one's unborn baby to standard medical procedures. For example, when one of us tried to discuss with an obstetrician her reasons for not wanting a routine early scan by describing some of the research findings, the doctor replied angrily, 'I don't believe in research'!

Despite increased technological surveillance, women's inevitable fears and anxieties that they may be carrying a deformed or poorly developed baby are seldom adequately addressed. Viewed primarily as a medical event, the psychological aspects of pregnancy and childbirth are often ignored. Childbirth preparation, which could be offered during the whole length of pregnancy and which should ideally include a consideration of psychological issues, rarely takes place more than a few weeks before delivery and tends to focus on physical rather than emotional preparation. The classes which are provided tend to accentuate the separation of roles in the management of childbirth, and may mitigate against women getting to know their birth attendants before labour. Important as appropriate exercise and accurate information are for women about to give birth, these cannot be properly made use of if women are not emotionally able to use them. If, like Jeanette, their underlying lack of confidence and their conflicts concerning their own personal autonomy are not addressed, information presented at a rational level will be either ignored or followed automatically, rather than incorporated into the woman's total responses.

Labour and childbirth

Women often report that the birth of a child, particularly perhaps the first child, was for positive or negative reasons, the most significant event in their lives. When it goes well, birth can represent a 'peak experience' far in excess of any other. As Eva Kittay has described:

> the actual experience of childbirth, at least when carried out in favourable circumstances, is par excellence an experience of merger and continuity with all of creation. I speak now of an unproblematic birth for the woman who is willing, awake and aware, and not terrorized by fear. During her labour and especially in its final moments, the labouring woman feels herself at once overtaken by and working along with overwhelmingly powerful forces – to bring about the birth of the child. We know that the sexual act can overwhelm us and introduce to us new possibilities of our physical and emotional selves ... but childbirth is still more powerful – the uterine contractions that are needed to expel the baby are far more intense than orgasmic contractions; and the tiny head emerging from within us remains a magical conjuring act which discloses our continuity amid discreteness as completely as any sexual encounter.

> (Kittay, 1984:118)

Yet, as Kittay goes on to point out, childbirth is more often painful, difficult, and potentially hazardous to mother and child. In this case, it can remain a dark memory which disturbs the early relationship with the child and colours women's feelings about their bodies and their femaleness.

In recent years, there has been increased academic interest in childbirth, particularly since the sociological work of Ann Oakley (1980). Fundamental to the discussion about how to optimise the positive experience of childbirth for women is the issue of the changing nature of obstetric practice. Until very recent times, labouring women were attended by other, experienced women who offered a range of services from contraceptive advice to abortion and delivery. Barbara Ehrenreich and Deirdre English (1979) have documented the history of woman-centred care by such 'wise women', the forerunners of the midwife. They show convincingly how the increased professionalism of the practice of surgery, heightened by the invention of the obstetric forceps, led to the gradual demise of the role of the midwife and her replacement by the medical attendant (originally always male, since women were barred from obtaining medical training). As the instrumental aspects of obstetric practice increased, midwives were deemed to be 'incompetent' since they rarely had access to the new technology. This has reached such proportions that in many western countries, midwives have become merely obstetric nurses. Similar points have been made by Jean Towler and Joan Bramall (1986) in their book describing the historical 'conflict' between midwives and doctors. In looking at the move from midwifery-based community care to obstetrically controlled hospital care in the UK, Rona Campbell and Alison Macfarlane (1987) have shown that whereas in the 1940s over half of the babies born were delivered at home, by the 1980s the number has dropped to fewer than one per cent. Nowadays, the illness model of pregnancy extends inevitably to childbirth, which is rarely seen as a normal event. If allowed to proceed it need not pose complications but becomes instead a medical procedure requiring careful monitoring and surgical intervention.

This change in orientation from what Barbara Rathbone (1982) calls the 'midwifery' to the 'medical' model has profound implications for women's psychology. Instead of having confidence in the normal functioning of their bodies, women are surrounded by fear-inducing procedures, which can lead them to believe that only doctors can 'deliver' them. The passive role of the patient, and the iatrogenic complications resulting from medical interventions mean that the fear of childbirth can become a fearful event, a self-fulfilling prophecy. For example, a woman in labour may often be attached to a foetal monitoring machine, which means that her mobility is severely reduced, often contrary to her felt needs. She may be given artificial oxytocins to speed up labour, which lead to strong and closely spaced uterine contractions. Unlike the normal rhythmic flow of contractions which are easier to respond to, these induced contractions often leave a woman feeling out of control, and hence increase the likelihood that she will be given pain relief. This in turn reduces awareness of the changing nature of her contractions, so that she is less likely to be able to give birth to her baby without yet more interventions such as episiotomy, delivery by vacuum suction or forceps, or eventually, a Caesarian section. The natural analgesics produced by the woman's nervous system during labour are flooded by artificial chemicals, which in turn cross the placenta and affect the baby's nervous system. This produces a less active and unresponsive baby who is often slower to initiate rooting and sucking reflexes.

Hence, as we shall discuss in the following chapter, optimal conditions for mother–infant development can be rarely met following technologically intrusive births. (see Jill Rakusen and Nick Davidson, 1982, for a fuller account of the iatrogenic consequences of an interventionist approach). This is not to deny, of course, that in some instances, complex technology may be vital to save the life of both mother and baby, but simply to point out the importance of being aware of the psychological as well as the physical needs of both mother and baby, *especially* when an interventionist birth is necessary.

Analysing the psychodynamic reasons for the need of medical staff to exercise such control over childbirth, Joan Raphael-Leff (1985) argues that a birth presents a situation unique in medical practice. Not only may the 'patient' insist on being conscious and concerned with decision-making, her partner and perhaps other family or friends may be present, participating as well. The emotions generated, intimacies shared, and the woman's expression of feelings may be embarrassing and arousing to the staff. According to Joan Raphael-Leff:

> Staff are forced to risk being discredited by joining in her abandon or else have to enforce their defences to minimize the threat of contamination. Repeated exposure to a deeply arousing primitive experience is liable to stir up archaic fantasies and unresolved emotions in the observer.... The graver the deliverer's personal doubt and need for reparation – the more intense the need to control.
>
> (Raphael-Leff, 1985:17)

Where hospital procedures are less defensively authoritarian and hierarchical, as Janet Sayers (1987) has shown, women are more likely to experience some measure of autonomy over their confinement. But in order to take advantage of this, women must be prepared to give up their longings for a consultant/father figure who will make decisions for them. Such points have also been made by Helene Deutsch (1945), who suggested that women in labour transfer feelings related to their father's authority on to the obstetrician, whilst transferring on to the midwife rivalous and ambivalent feelings related to the mother. It must, however, be remembered that this is a two-way process, and that maternity staff often project uncontrolled feelings and attitudes on to their patients too. We shall return to this issue in the next chapter when discussing the early relationship between mother and baby, in particular the effects of institutional factors on the establishment of breast-feeding.

Implications for therapy

A psychotherapeutic understanding of the importance of reproduction in women's lives is crucial for all those working with women. However, most women who are not in contact with a psychotherapist or counsellor at the time of their pregnancy, or who do not seek or obtain psychotherapeutic support in the event of a crisis in their reproductive lives, have to rely on the understanding and care provided by other health professionals. Yet whilst the salience of the emotional as opposed to the merely physiological changes involved in conception, pregnancy, and childbirth is becoming increasingly recognised by some midwives, doctors, health visitors, and other professionals involved in maternity care, there is very little training provided to enable them to deal effectively with the psychological aspects of their work. Instead, patronising reassurance is often given instead of careful attention to a woman's expression of her feelings. Just as hazards at work have been used as a reason to bar child-bearing women from certain industrial jobs instead of improving working conditions for all, the emotional upheavals of pregnancy are used as evidence for women's basic 'feminine instability' rather than as a positive indication of the sensitivity of their procreative abilities and the need for change to be made in the nature of the services provided.

Three very different aspects to therapeutic work with women are potentially necessary. One involves preparing for motherhood, which may include specific information-giving as well as therapeutic support for the psychological issues brought to the surface as a result of pregnancy. The second involves dealing with loss, which will be necessary in situations which do not result in the birth of a live, healthy baby. The third involves approaches to the actual birth itself.

Preparing for motherhood

Ideally, preparation for the meaning of motherhood should start long before this becomes a reality. Although at school girls may receive classes on 'baby care' and learn to wash dolls and pin nappies, there are very few opportunities for young women to think about whether or not they actually *do* want to have children. Indeed, orthodox psychiatric advice has often involved prescribing motherhood for emotionally unsure women (providing of course that they are married). Rather than an event which takes place at the height of a woman's adult maturity, when there are well-developed emotional and perhaps financial resources to deal with the stresses of creating a new person, younger women are usually dealing with pregnancy, childbirth, and motherhood before they themselves have successfully severed the umbilical cord with their own parents. Teachers, social workers, and others involved with young women could provide alternative images of womanhood to that of automatic motherhood, and increased opportunities in education and training need to be created to provide valid alternatives.

Once pregnant, most women find that apart from medical surveillance, they are left on their own to deal with the complex emotional issues that arise. They may traditionally turn to their mothers for support, although for some, pregnancy can be a time of intense conflicts in the mother–daughter relationship, and a more neutral source of information and counselling is therefore required. Pregnancy-support groups, such as the one attended by Jeanette, could be offered at doctors' surgeries or similar locations to cover not only nutritional advice (for example, Gail Brewer and Tom Brewer, 1977), exercises to enable women to participate actively in the various stages of labour and birthing (for example, Janet Balaskas, 1983), but also a chance to describe and discuss the fears, joys, and excitement of producing a child. Awareness of issues important for early infant development and the mother–child relationship would also prepare women for the psychological as well as physical aspects of caring for a child, especially feelings about breast-feeding, motor and cognitive development, attachment, and so on (see, for example, Penny Stanway and Andrew Stanway, 1978; Penelope Leach, 1980 for useful books accessible to the general reader).

In the UK, organisations such as the National Childbirth Trust offer meetings of this nature, where women who are already mothers offer to share their experiences and provide support for first-time mothers, but these are not widely available to all women. Most hospital-based 'mothercraft' courses seem to fall far short of these objectives. As with any group, complex dynamics will emerge to which the group leader will need to be sensitive. With women sharing an experience of pregnancy in common, issues of competitiveness, rivalry, envy, and the contagion of shared fears and anxieties will emerge as well as encouragement and support. A leader who has had successful and positive birth experiences herself may be able to enhance confidence and encourage assertiveness in group members. But she will have to guard against being impatient with or insensitive to those who are more dependent on an authority figure such as a doctor to see them through their confinement. As we saw with Jeanette, negotiating pregnancy and childbirth is sometimes the first independent event that a young woman has to face, involving complex decision-making concerning life and death issues for herself and her baby. This may leave her unable to make up her mind clearly and cause her to lean on stronger people, or people who express firmer ideas. The rivalry and envy of birth educators and attendants who have not had positive experiences or who are themselves childless (especially perhaps in the case of men) will obviously affect the experiences of pregnant women, something about which professional staff need to be particularly aware.

Coping with loss

There are repeated occasions during women's reproductive lives when they may have to come to terms with loss. Even when a live, healthy, longed-for baby is born, there can be a profound feeling of loss of the foetus inside, which if not dealt with can affect the relationship established with the baby who is now outside. In addition, there is the loss of the child-free self, which seems likely to be linked to feelings of post-natal depression (see Paula Nicolson, 1988). Some women are often surprised to find that after delivery they feel in some sense empty without the continual company of their 'bulge', despite at the same time having feelings of relief that the constraints of late pregnancy and the anxiety of labour are behind them. However, as we will see in the next chapter, many women find that the intimacy they establish with their babies, particularly when breast-feeding, enables them to make the transition between the baby-in-the-womb to the baby-in-their-arms. But women who have had frightening, painful, or complicated deliveries, especially if these resulted in an emergency Caesarian section, often feel cheated and deprived of the positive experiences of birth. For them in particular, a period of grieving is necessary, which if not resolved can reassert itself, perhaps at a future pregnancy.

When the process of labour results in a baby who is stillborn, or who dies in the perinatal period, the giving up of the pregnancy without the recompense of a baby involves a more obvious loss. The long-term as well as the short-term effects can be devastating (see Brian Tew, Jenny Morris, and Michael Laurence, 1985), especially if the mourning process is not resolved. Maternity and paediatric staff are now more aware of the needs of grieving parents, who if they want can usually see, touch, and acknowledge their dead baby before having to part with it finally. Parents who have been denied this contact, or who were too ill or distressed to undergo it, often express profound sorrow that they never knew their babies. When the baby lives, but is handicapped in some way, parents have to face not only the responsibilities of lifelong care for a child who will not develop normally, but also the loss of an idealised perfect baby (see Joan Bicknell, 1983).

Finally, as we discussed earlier in this chapter, the loss involved in miscarriage, termination, the final acceptance of infertility, or the decision not to have a child are often less socially recognised but profoundly important. In all of these situations, both for the woman herself, her partner, and wider family, it is important that the necessary time and support are found for the process of grieving to be accomplished. The mixed emotions of anger and sadness which are involved in grief are but the normal reactions to loss. As Janet Mattinson (1985) has pointed out in describing these feelings, emotional health is not an absence of conflict but the ability to deal with it:

> it is psychologically healthy to be able to experience a variety of emotions normally, or uniquely, pertaining to a stressful event *at the time*, or soon afterwards when the dulling effect of shock has worn off.... Those in emotional trouble later in their lives are often those who fail to do their grieving at the time it is needed ... when one major loss is not mourned at the time, a subsequent loss rebounds on the first and then the double grief ... can then be quite overwhelming, out of proportion and unduly persistent.
>
> (Janet Mattinson, 1985:167, emphasis in original)

While we have primarily focused in this chapter on women's experiences, for most women these take place within the context of a partnership. As a family therapist, Janet Mattinson (1985) has described the emotional conflicts of couples who were unable to grieve earlier losses, for example, of an abortion or a stillbirth, which later affected a new loss such as the death of a parent or unemployment. She points out that the loss of a baby, whether before, during, or after birth, involves much guilt as well as the pain of loss. As Lily Pincus and Christopher Dare (1978) have shown, families often attempt to avoid such guilt and pain by maintaining family secrets which prevent the event from being exposed and dealt with: often with serious long-term consequences for all concerned.

We have argued throughout this chapter that more psychotherapeutic help should be freely available to women facing reproductive crises. This should take the form not only of improved training of medical personnel, but also of easier access to skilled therapists and counsellors who understand the importance of the normal emotions surrounding pregnancy. Especially important is an understanding of the phases of grieving after loss, so that staff can recognise when these are delayed, denied, or intensified in either partner (see Colin Parkes, 1975). As Lily Pincus has suggested:

> Each crisis of loss that can be overcome will help towards the overcoming of future losses; the giving up of the familiar need not be experienced merely as a loss but, through the acceptance of the new situation, as a challenge, with the potential for growth.
>
> (Pincus, 1981:33)

Management of the birth itself

Within recent years, some women who are the consumers of maternity services have initiated a movement towards woman-centred care which is beginning to challenge accepted maternity practice. Some of these practices are far more sympathetic to the psychological needs of pregnant women, and as such are to be welcomed. In the UK, for example, campaigning groups such as the Association for Improvements in the Maternity Services (AIMS) and the National Childbirth Trust (NCT) are providing information and support for women who want to give birth in as natural a way as possible without risking the hazards of unnecessary interventions. Pressure from such groups is leading to changes in practice within hospitals, too, such as the encouragement of mobility during labour, the reduction of routine episiotomy and analgesic use, and the active choice of birth positions. Mothers are now more likely to be able to hold their babies immediately after birth, who can then be encouraged to suckle and can more frequently be kept alongside their mothers rather than relegated to night nurseries (see Sheila Kitzinger, 1983). Partners or other chosen relatives or friends are now normally able to attend and participate in the labour and in some hospitals, can cut the umbilical cord and bath the baby after delivery. In many hospitals, women's ideas concerning the management of their labour are filed in their notes, so that such 'birth plans' can be used by staff on duty to tailor their interventions to the birthing woman's stated expectations. However, it must be noted that whilst this gives informed (and therefore probably middle-class) women a greater chance of participating in the decision-making, the statement is in no way obligatory and is therefore subject to staff interpretation. Nor do such 'permissions' necessarily fundamentally change hospital routines (see Kitzinger, 1978).

Furthermore, despite these advances, it must also be noted that the overall rate of change in many hospitals has been slow. This has led some women to set up alternative care in the private sector. For example, throughout the UK, there are a growing number of birth centres staffed by sympathetic midwives to provide a birth environment that is more attuned to women's – and babies' – emotional and physical needs. Whilst these may offer radical sources of childbirth practice, they will be unavailable to those women who cannot afford to pay. Statisticians are attempting to analyse the poorly available data on the safety of different places on birth, and are finding evidence to suggest that births at home or in family doctor units involve no greater risks than those in consultant units (see Margaret Tew, 1985; Rona Campbell and Alison Macfarlane, 1987). Whilst some obstetricians such as Frederick Leboyer (1977) and Michel Odent (1984) have been at the forefront of the movement to create hospital environments for birth which are of maximum advantage to the natural process of birth, others in the medical profession have fought to maintain medical authority and control. For example, when the British obstetrician Wendy Savage tried to institute a more community-based, woman-centred obstetric practice in London, she found herself to be charged with professional malpractice, this instigated by her male colleagues who disagreed with the degree of choice she gave to women over childbirth (Wendy Savage, 1986). With rare and honourable exceptions (for example, the Association of Radical Midwives' proposal for future midwifery-based childbirth services, and the World Health Organization's documents on women's rights in childbirth, AIMS, 1987) professional attendants have generally de-skilled women's child-bearing abilities and produced instead a dominant ideology which denies the role of the woman's own expertise and capabilities, rendering birth an abnormal rather than a normal process.

References

Appleton, T. (1986) 'Caring for the IVF patient: counselling care', in S. Fishel and E. Symonds (eds) in *In Vitro Fertilisation: past, present and future*. Oxford: IRL Press.

Arditti, R., Klein, R., and Minden, S. (eds) (1984) *Test-tube Women*, London: Pandora Press.

Association for Improvements in the Maternity Services (1986) 'Ultrasound: reassurance or whitewash?' *AIMS Quarterly Journal* pp. 3–4, Autumn.

Association for Improvements in the Maternity Services (1987) 'Birth is not an illness', *AIMS Quarterly Journal* pp. 1–2, Spring.

Atwood, M. (1987) *The Handmaid's Tale*, London: Virago.

Balaskas, J. (1983) *Active Birth*, London: Unwin.

Barreda-Hanson, M., Mushin, D., and Spensley, J. (1987) 'In Vitro Fertilisation: a psychosocial and developmental study', in H. Dent (ed.) *Clinical Psychology: research and developments*, London: Croom Helm.

Beail, N. (1982) 'The role of the father during pregnancy and childbirth', in N. Beail and J. McGuire (eds) *Fathers: psychological perspectives*. London: Junction Books.

Bicknell, J. (1983) 'The psychopathology of handicap', *British Journal of Medical Psychology* 56:167–78.

Blake, J. (1974) 'Co-ercive pronatalism and American population policy', in E. Peck and J. Senderowitz (eds) *Pronatalism: the myth of Mom and Apple Pie*, New York: Thomas Y. Crowell.

Breen, D. (1975) *The Birth of a First Child*, London: Tavistock.

Brewer, G. and Brewer, T. (1977) *What Every Woman Should Know: the truth about diet and drugs in pregnancy*, New York: Random House.

Broome, A. (1984) 'Termination of pregnancy', in A. Broome and L. Wallace (eds) *Psychology and Gynaecological Problems*, London: Tavistock.

Brown, J. (1983) 'The daughter is mother of the child: cycles of lesbian sexuality', in S. Cartledge and J. Ryan (eds) *Sex and Love*, London: The Women's Press.

Brown, G. and Harris, T. (1978) *The Social Origins of Depression*, London: Tavistock.

Campbell, R. and Macfarlane, A. (1987) *Where to be Born? The debate and the evidence*, Oxford: National Epidemiology Unit, Radcliffe Infirmary.

Chodorow, N. (1978) *The Reproduction of Mothering: psychoanalysis and the sociology of gender*, Berkeley: University of California Press.

Cook, E. (1987) 'Characteristics of the biopsychosocial crisis of infertility', *Journal of Counselling and Development* 65:456–70.

Cowan, P.C., Cowan, A.P., Hemming, G., Garrett, E., Coysh, W.S., Curtis-Boles, H., and Boles, A.J. (1985) 'Transition to parenthood: his, hers, and theirs', *Journal of Family Issues* 6:451–81.

Coyne, A.M. (1986) *Schoolgirl Mothers*, London: Health Education Council, Research Report 2.

Dana, M. (1987) 'Abortion: a woman's right to feel', in S. Ernst and M. Maguire (eds) *Living with the Sphinx*, London: The Women's Press.

De Gier, J. (1987) 'Miscarriages and myths', *New Society* pp. 20–1, 13 May.

Deutsch, H. (1945) *The Psychology of Women*, vol. 2, New York: Grune & Stratton.

Dowrick, S. and Grundberg, S. (1980) (eds) *Why Children?* London: The Women's Press.

Edelmann, R. (1987) 'Psychological aspects of in vitro fertilization', paper presented at the Annual Conference of the British Psychological Society, Brighton, Sussex.

Ehrenreich, B. and English, D. (1979) *For Her Own Good: 150 years of the expert's advice to women*, London: Pluto Press.

Eichenbaum, L. and Orbach, S. (1982) *Outside In ... Inside Out*, Harmondsworth: Penguin.

Fishel, S. and Symonds, E. (eds) (1986) *In Vitro Fertilisation: past, present and future*, Oxford: IRL Press.

Freud, S. (1924) 'The dissolution of the Oedipus complex', in S. Freud (1977) *On Sexuality*, Penguin Freud Library, vol. 7, Harmondsworth: Penguin.

Gimenez, M. (1984) 'Feminism, pronatalism and motherhood', in J. Trebilcot (ed.) *Mothering: essays in feminist theory*, New Jersey: Rowman & Allanheld.

Graham and Oakley, A. (1981) 'Competing ideologies of reproduction: medical and maternal perspectives on pregnancy', in H. Roberts (ed.) *Women, Health and Reproduction*, London: Routledge & Kegan Paul.

Horney, K. (1967) *Feminine Psychology*, New York: Norton.

Hoskins, B. and Holmes, H. B. (1984) 'Technology and prenatal femicide', in R. Arditti, R. Klein, and S. Minden (eds) *Test-tube Women*, London: Pandora Press.

Humphrey, M. (1984) 'Infertility and alternative parenting', in A. Broome and L.

Wallace (eds) *Psychology and Gynaecological Problems*, London: Tavistock.

Ince, S. (1984) 'Inside the surrogate industry', in R. Arditti, R. Klein and S. Minden (eds) *Test-tube Women*, London: Pandora Press.

Jega, L. (1978) 'What the Abortion Act has meant for women', in *Abortion Ten Years On*, London: Birth Control Trust.

Kittay, E. (1984) 'Womb envy: an exploratory concept', in J. Trebilcot (ed.) *Mothering: essays in feminist theory*, New Jersey: Rowan & Allanhead.

Kitzinger, S. (1978) *The Experience of Childbirth*, 4th edn, Harmondsworth: Penguin.

Kitzinger, S. (1983) *The New Good Birth Guide*, Harmondsworth: Penguin.

Lachelin, G. (1985) *Miscarriage: the facts*, Oxford: Oxford University Press.

Lane Committee Report (1974) Report of the Committee on the Working of the Abortion Act, London: HMSO.

Leach, P. (1980) *Baby and Child*, Harmondsworth: Penguin.

Leboyer, F. (1977) *Birth Without Violence*, London: Fontana.

Lees, S. (1986) *Losing Out: sexuality and adolescent girls*, London: Hutchinson.

Llewelyn, S. and Pytches, R. (1988) 'An investigation of anxiety following termination of pregnancy', *Journal of Advanced Nursing* 13:468–71.

McEwan, K.L., Costello, C.G., and Taylor, P.J. (1987) 'Adjustment to infertility', *Journal of Abnormal Psychology* 96:108–16.

McWhinnie, A. (1986) 'Test-tube babies: the child, the family and society', in S. Fishel and E. Symonds (eds), *In Vitro Fertilisation: past, present and future*, Oxford: IRL Press.

Masters, W. and Johnson, V. (1970) *Human Sexual Inadequacy*, Boston: Little Brown & Co.

Mattinson, J. (1985) 'The effects of abortion on a marriage', in R. Porter and M. O'Connor (eds) *Abortion: medical progess and social implications*, London: Pitman.

Mitchell, J. (1974) *Psychoanalysis and Feminism*, Harmondsworth: Penguin.

Mitchell, J. and Rose, J. (eds) (1982) *Feminine Sexuality: Jacques Lacan and the Ecole Freudienne*, London: Macmillan Press.

Murphy, J. (1984) 'Egg farming and women's future', in R. Arditti, R. Klein and S. Minden (eds) *Test-tube Women*, London: Pandora Press.

Neustatter, A. and Newson, G. (1986) *Mixed Feelings: the experience of abortion*, London: Pluto Press.

Nicolson, P. (1988) 'The social psychology of "Post-Natal Depression"', unpublished PhD Thesis, University of London.

Oakley, A. (1980) *Women confined: towards a sociology of childbirth*, Oxford: Martyn Robertson.

Oakley, A., McPherson, A., and Roberts, H. (1984) *Miscarriage*, London: Fontana.

Odent, M. (1984) *Birth Reborn*, London: Souvenir Press.

Paintin, D. (1985) 'Legal abortion in England and Wales', in R. Porter and M. O'Connor (eds) *Abortion: medical progress and social implications*, London: Pitman.

Parkes, C. (1975) *Bereavement: studies of grief in adult life*, London: Tavistock.

Pfeffer, N. (1987) 'Artificial insemination and infertility', in M. Stanworth (ed.) *Reproductive Technologies: gender, motherhood and medicine*, Cambridge: Polity Press.

Pfeffer, N. and Woollett, A. (1983) *The Experience of Infertility*, London: Virago.

Phillips, A. and Rakusen, J. (1978) *Our Bodies Ourselves*, Harmondsworth: Penguin.

Pincus, L. (1981) *The Challenge of a Long Life*, London: Faber & Faber.

Pincus, L. and Dare, C. (1978) *Secrets in the Family*, London: Faber & Faber.

Pines, D. (1982) 'The relevance of early psychic development to pregnancy and abortion', *International Journal of Psycho-analysis*, 63:311–19.

Rakusen, J. and Davidson, N. (1982) *Out of Our Hands: what technology does to pregnancy*, London: Pan.

Raphael-Leff, J. (1980) 'Psychotherapy with pregnant women', in B. Blum (ed.) *Psychological Aspects of Pregnancy, Birthing and Bonding*, New York: Human Sciences Press.

Raphael-Leff, J. (1985) 'Fears and fantasies of childbirth', *Journal of Pre- and Peri-Natal Psychology* 1:14–18.

Rathbone, B. (1982) *In Labour: women and power in the birthplace*, London: Junction Books.

RCOG (1976) *Artificial Insemination: explanatory booklet for patients*, London: RCOG

Rich, A. (1977) *Of Woman Born*, London: Virago.

Ritchie, M. (1984) 'Taking the initiative: information versus technology in pregnancy', in R. Arditti, R. Klein and S. Minden (eds) *Test-tube Women*, London: Pandora Press.

Saffron, L. (1986) *Getting Pregnant our own Way: a guide to alternative insemination*, London: Women's Reproductive Rights Information Centre.

Saunders, L. (1983) 'Sex and childbirth', in S. Cartledge and J. Ryan (eds) *Sex and Love*, London: The Women's Press.

Savage, W. (1986) *A Savage Inquiry*, London: Virago.

Sayers, J. (1982) *Biological Politics*, London: Virago.

Sayers, J. (1987) 'Women confined: psychoanalytic perspectives', paper presented to the Oxford History Workshop Conference 'Women, Reproduction and Technology', Oxford.

Stacey, J. (1986) 'Are feminists afraid to leave home? The challenge of conservative pro-family feminism', in J. Mitchell and A. Oakley (eds) *What is Feminism?*, London: Basil Blackwell.

Stanway, P. and Stanway, A. (1978) *Breast is Best*, London: Pan.

Taymor, M.L. (1978) *Infertility*, New York: Grune & Stratton.

Tew, M. (1985) 'Safety in intra-natal care: the statistics', in G. Marsh (ed.) *Modern Obstetrics in General Practice*, Oxford: Oxford University Press.

Tew, B., Morris, J., and Laurence, M. (1985) 'Some long term effects of stillbirth upon a mother and her family', paper presented at the annual conference of the British Psychological Society, Swansea, March.

Towler, J. and Bramall, J. (1986) *Midwives in History and Society*, London: Croom Helm.

Vere, M.F. and Joyce, D.N. (1979) 'Luteal function in patients seeking AID', *British Medical Journal* ii: 100.

Warnock, M. (1985) *A Question of Life: The Warnock Report on human fertilisation and embryology*. Oxford: Basil Blackwell.

Chapter seven

Bringing up children

Margaret's story

The women's therapy movement has generated a great many innovative ideas for introducing women to therapeutic experiences who might otherwise not seek help from such a source. Alongside individual counselling, a wide range of theme-centred groups have been developed on topics found to be particularly pertinent to the lives of women. It was whilst running such a group one Saturday that I first met Margaret. The theme for the day was 'Our Mothers, Ourselves', and we were a group of eight women exploring the ways in which we were similar to, and different from, our own mothers. All of the women that day had children themselves, and all were struggling to get to grips with the complex feelings about being mothers, and of their relationships with their children in the light of their own memories and experiences of childhood.

Margaret expressed most clearly the feelings felt by the whole group, that they were continually having to act as adult, responsible care-givers when they themselves felt at times a desperate need to be looked after and protected.

'Sometimes,' she explained:

I feel so dreadful I just can't get up and get the children ready for school. Thank goodness Dick doesn't have to go to work until they leave, because he can organise their breakfast and take them to school on his way. After they've left the house I feel a bit better, but I get so depressed about letting them all down. They're too young to understand what's wrong.

Margaret explained during the course of the day that she had two children, aged 9 and 7 years, both girls. She had married when she was quite young, at the age of 20, a man who was her first real boyfriend. Her mother had disapproved of her going out with boys, and Margaret and Dick had finally married secretly in a registry office so that she could leave home and join him in his digs. He was working as an infant school teacher but Margaret did not have a paid job as her mother was against her leaving their rather isolated farm, which she would have had to have done to find work.

Although Margaret felt that overall she was feeling much better now that the children were at school, she expressed a profound fear that she might at any time lapse into the terrors and anxieties she experienced when her children were little. 'With Clare, the eldest,' she said:

I just couldn't believe what was happening to me. I so enjoyed being pregnant, and very much wanted to have a baby. But the birth was very long and difficult, I had a forceps delivery, and afterwards I just couldn't seem to cope. Mum came to stay when I came out of hospital, and for the first couple of weeks I hardly touched Clare at all. Then when Mum went back home, I somehow found the strength to feed and change the baby when Dick wasn't around, but otherwise he did most of the work. I never went out of the house for weeks. The neighbours were surprised when they eventually saw me out with the pram, and Clare was so big – they didn't even know she'd been born!

Margaret's doctor had diagnosed post-natal depression, and prescribed for her some medication which had made her feel very lazy and light-headed. After several weeks she stopped taking the pills as she felt that they made her worse rather than better. Her memories of her first year of motherhood were of exhaustion and fear that she would break down completely:

Just as I was beginning to feel a bit better, I discovered that I was pregnant again. I felt desperate. I'm a Catholic, and don't believe in abortion, but for weeks it was in the back of my mind. Clare was still so young, and still sleeping very badly. Somehow I got through the pregnancy all right, but I dreaded going into hospital, as I was terrified that I'd crack up after the baby was born. Luckily Becky's birth was easier, but afterwards I had the same panic. I hardly stopped crying all the time I was in hospital – I didn't even want Clare to come and visit me, which I know was hard for her.

During the course of the group session, Margaret wept a lot as she relived her initial experiences of motherhood. She described her chronic fatigue and her feelings of rage which would overwhelm her when the children were young. She described also her fears that she might hurt them or damage them, and the depression that overcame her each time she lost her temper. Other members of the group also talked about the extremes of love and hatred that they felt for their children, and Margaret listened attentively and appeared to be astonished at what she heard. At the end of the day she said that she was relieved that no-one was critical of her 'failure' as a mother, and that she was surprised that other women had similar feelings. She left looking drained but somewhat calmer than at the beginning of the group.

Several days later, a letter arrived for me from Margaret. In it, she wrote thanking me for having organised the group, and then asked if she could continue to see me individually, as she felt she had a lot more to sort out about herself. I arranged an appointment, and we started what turned out to be a series of meetings which lasted for over a year. During the initial sessions, she talked a great deal about her own parents. She wept often as she recalled the battles that were waged between her mother and father, and of her desperate attempts to stop them arguing.

'I wish Dad would stand up to her more,' she said:

He just lets her get away with all her bad moods and tempers. He'd just stand there while she ranted on at me for something I'd done wrong. I never seemed to be able to do anything right. None of us did.

Alongside her descriptions of her mother as being cold and nagging, Margaret expressed a longing that some day her mother would show her some warmth and love: 'Every time I go to visit her, I hope that this time it will be different. But it never is. And when I get back home I feel dreadful. It takes weeks to get over each visit.'

Gradually, Margaret seemed to need to talk less about her childhood, and focused more on her current family. It was as though she had emptied herself of a lot of pain, and could begin to move into her adult self. She became less critical of her mother, and started to comment on how difficult it must have been for her to shoulder so much of the responsibility for the farm, since Margaret's father was often ill. But as she reached a stronger sense of herself, Margaret's relationship with Dick reached an all-time low.

Everyone I know tells me how lucky I am, and that he's a perfect husband. I suppose they're right. I don't know how I could have managed without him, especially when the children were little. But he's so quiet and distant. It's as if he's not really there. When I'm feeling really bad and can't do the cooking or the housework, he just gets on with it. He never shouts at me or anything. But it's like a heavy weight, crushing me. I feel so guilty, but I can't talk to him about it.

On describing her relationship with her husband, in the context of her experiences of her own parents, Margaret began to make links between them. She realised that she was seeking in Dick a 'good mother', who could support her in the way that she had never experienced with her own mother. Yet at the same time she resented his acceptance and complicity with this role. She was angry with him when he seemed to become too much like her own father, passive and emotionally absent. She had an overwhelming fear that she would somehow ruin her love for her own daughters, and become as estranged from them as she was from her own mother. As babies and toddlers she had found them demanding and exhausting, and was much relieved that they had both finally settled in at school. But in looking towards the future she felt extremely anxious and protective, finding it difficult to accept their blossoming independence and potential maturity. She desperately wanted to show them the love and caring she felt she had missed herself, but in forcing herself to do this she felt unreal and depleted.

Over the months, Margaret was able to accept the therapeutic 'caring' that I offered her, in being regularly available for her, and she slowly found that she could respond more naturally to her children's needs, without striving to be the all-loving 'perfect mother'.

There came a time, however, after a few months, when Margaret began to feel that although she had made many changes, she was feeling locked into her old ways of being by the nature of her relationship with Dick. She talked for a while of leaving him, but felt unable to part him and the children. Then she asked if I could see him as well. It seemed clear that now that Margaret was feeling more confident and sure of herself, the dynamics of their relationship would have to change. Dick would need to stop being the protective partner and learn to tolerate a more equal relationship with Margaret. But I was not the right person to help him in this task, bound up as I was in Margaret's own experiences. I suggested they contacted a family or marital therapist, and gave them some addresses. This they did, arranging for a number of joint sessions. Some weeks later they both came to see me. Margaret was looking healthy and cheerful, while Dick, whom I hadn't met before, was quiet but seemed calm and relaxed. The marital sessions had been quite stressful for them, as they had both been confronted with many important issues in their relationship with each other. But overall they were feeling confident and optimistic. Margaret spoke positively of the future and of her plans to look for a part-time job. There was a sense that they felt less burdened by their responsibilities as parents, and had ceased to see life as such a struggle.

Caring for children

Finding a way to meet the needs of children without sacrificing the needs of those who care for them is a complex and difficult task. In clinical work we have often met women who are in desperate need of help, feeling torn apart by their responsibilities as mothers, guilt-ridden about not living up to their own idealised images of what motherhood should be, and yet desperate for some time to be themselves. Wanting to retain their independent identity, most women are also aware of the needs of their children, and as daughters of their own mothers, many of them carry within them conflicting memories of their own childhood. The anger and sadness of feeling rejected, over-protected, abused, or manipulated often remain alongside the warm and comfortable memories of being nurtured, mothered, and contained. These conflicts, past and present, are often confusing and may even feel overwhelming to the woman concerned, although they may also be the source of many women's hopes and ideals about providing a better life for their own children.

All of this occurs against a backdrop of change in thinking about the rights and responsibilities of parenthood, and an evolving understanding of the needs and developmental processes of children. In particular, there is nowadays an increasing awareness of the emotional needs of young children, which has considerable implications about the way in which we think about what should be provided by parents. There have also been recent massive swings in the way that societal expectations define the nature of childhood and hence the ways in which children are cared for. In this chapter we will consider the ways in which motherhood has traditionally and more recently been defined, and then look at how women as mothers themselves experience this stage of their lives. We will see that women differ enormously in their reactions to motherhood, so that pressures to be either full-time mothers or to 'do both' and maintain a working role outside the family will be differently perceived and acted upon by different women. We will also look at just what is involved in mothering, by discussing the psychological needs of growing children. We shall then discuss the different ways in which both women and children could gain from a widening of society's obligations to its young, before looking at some of the therapeutic implications.

It must be noted at the outset that at present, whether as the biological mother or as her substitute, it is women who are still providing most of the care for young children. Hence, whether we use the terms 'mothering', 'nurturing', or 'caring', we are inevitably describing women's work. We are well aware of the debate that surrounds the use of these terms. Many writers have argued that by retaining the word 'mothering' there is an implication that only women, and particularly only biological mothers, could or should be involved. Many prefer to use the term 'parenting', which implies the possibility at least of the job being shared between both parents. But as Susan Peterson (1984) has argued, the term 'parenting' does not represent what actually happens. Children are still considered to be the mother's responsibility, and thus talking about 'parenting' changes the language but not necessarily the actions. It also devalues the important and vital nurturing and caring skills that mothering involves. Hence where we use the term, we do so to reinforce these positive connotations, and refer to a process, not a particular person.

The construction of 'motherhood'

Historians of the family, such as Lawrence Stone (1982), have argued that motherhood, as we know it, is a relatively recent phenomenon. In other centuries, and currently in other cultures, childhood is short-lived and children are quickly expected to become productive members of adult society. In these circumstances, mothers are expected to continue their productive work, which is likely to be home-based, without absenting themselves for the process of reproduction. In many cases they may not have intimate and total responsibility for their children.

In describing the social and economic changes that have led to childhood in most 'advanced' cultures becoming a distinct and lengthy dependent state, Barbara Ehrenreich and Deirdre English (1979) show how the pre-industrial child was in effect an apprentice, working and learning alongside the other productive workers of the family unit, and being cared for in the process. With industrialisation, and the gradual separation of work from home, childhood became a separate and distinct phase, involving the care of mothers. As Ehrenreich and English show, this special nature of childhood was, however, not granted to children of working-class families since their labour, and that of their mothers, was initially very profitable for the repetitive and routinised work of the new industrial age. Nor, incidentally, was motherhood the work of upper-class women, most of whom employed lower-class women to act as wet nurses and nannies to care for their children. Gradually, however, liberal protective values predominated and child labour (in richer western countries) became illegal. Education outside the home also became widespread. But while state educational provision began to take over the training of older children for the skills required by industry, the responsibility for babies and young children was left to the individual family, in most cases the mother.

However, twentieth-century motherhood no longer involved the preparation of children for a simple, rural, home-based existence; hence educational experts and psychologists were called in. Barbara Ehrenreich and Deirdre English (1979) describe in detail how successive changes in theories of child psychology and education have generated changing ideologies about child management and in particular the mother's role. From 'scientific motherhood' (which exhorted mothers to instil 'good habits' into children from birth and which was supported by the burgeoning technical advances of behaviourism) to the more permissive 'child knows best' regime (popularised by Benjamin Spock, 1957), 'expert' advice went through rapid reverse-turns. Between generations, and even between successive babies, women were advised to adopt completely different attitudes towards their children.

Underlying all of these new theories was the assumption of the existence of 'mother love', (note, not 'father love' or 'parental love') which continued to be biologically defined. Using the influential instinct theories of ethologists such as Konrad Lorenz (1966) and Robert Hinde (1961), attempts were made to locate the source of this maternal instinct in women's physiology. The supposed natural and spontaneous love that mothers were assumed to feel towards their babies came to be considered so important that it was soon claimed that *only* biological mothers should look after their children. However, this view conveniently fluctuated according to economic necessity. Whereas during wartime mothers were encouraged to join in productive work, and state-run nurseries were provided to cater for their children, the return of the combatants meant that much female labour was now surplus, and the importance of the biologically based maternal instinct was reasserted.

In the second half of this century, the belief that it was crucial for women to remain at home was supported by John Bowlby's (1951) WHO Report on conditions in wartime children's homes. He described the shocking conditions that prevailed and argued that it was the lack of affectional care which led to the sickly, apathetic babies whom he observed. But in transferring his analysis from institutions to conditions in the home, and in generating the concept of 'maternal' rather than 'affectional' deprivation, his research became the justification for condemning those women who, through necessity or choice, continued to work outside the home after their children were born. Despite more relevant evidence showing that, under appropriate conditions, children can form satisfactory attachments to a number of caretakers, none of whom need be the biological mother (for example, Michael Rutter, 1977), women are still criticised for making alternative child-care arrangements, on the faulty assumption that anything less than full-time biological mothering will harm the child. We will see later in this chapter that such an assumption affects both the quality and availability of provisions for young children, as it does the conditions of work and financial status of women with children.

Psychiatry, psychology, and mothering

In some respects psychology has not been particularly helpful to our understanding of mothers. Until very recently, psychological accounts of women's mothering have tended to focus simply on the damaging aspect of the mothering role. For example, Barbara Ehrenreich and Deirdre English (1979) have traced the history of the concept of the 'pathological' mother, who, whether through her malignant presence or by the trauma of her absence, was held to be responsible for a wide range of childhood disturbances. Using an analogy from medicine, Rene Spitz (1965), for example, had claimed that there were what he called 'psychotoxic' diseases of infancy, in which the mother's personality acts as the 'disease-provoking agent'. In addition, psychoanalytic understandings of childhood disturbances, rather than being used to help those women (and men) who *did* have problems in their relationships with their children, tended to lead to victim-blaming, *mal de mère* theorising. Ehrenreich and English document how mothers were over-simplistically labelled as being either too 'rejecting', or too 'over-protective', or even both, with women becoming increasingly guilty and filled with self-doubt about their mothering abilities.

From being held responsible for neurotic and psychosomatic disturbances, such as bed-wetting or asthma, it was then but a short step for mothers to be held responsible for psychoses. The concept of the 'schizophrenegenic mother', introduced by Gregory Bateson and colleagues (1956) and popularised by Ronald Laing (1960), did at least represent an important step forward from oversimplistic biochemical theories of psychosis. But locating the cause of fundamental personality and relationship problems almost solely within the mother's behaviour simply increased the tendency for mother-blaming, and overlooked the multidetermined nature of psychological development. Whilst more recent systems theories of family functioning have refined these definitions and now dismiss linear causality as an explanation of the disturbance of family members (see, for example, Arlene Vetere and Anthony Gale, 1987) the major responsibility of mothers for their children's emotional as well as physical welfare is still a tacit assumption made by many child health and mental heath professionals.

One psychoanalytic writer, whose work can be seen as attempting to emphasise the positive aspects of women's mothering, was Donald Winnicott. As a practising paediatrician, he had a wealth of experience of mother–child relationships, and was seemingly aware of women's guilt about their mothering abilities and of the damaging nature of mother-blaming theories. He claimed that mothering need only be 'good-enough' (Winnicott, 1965) for children to thrive and develop normally. Yet as Sheila Ernst (1987) has pointed out, even 'good-enough' care is not achieved in our current society without great costs for the woman herself. Frequently isolated and economically impoverished, often without adequate adult company or support, even such good-enough mothering is difficult to sustain, especially when required for 24 hours a day, seven days a week, over a prolonged period of time. In not commenting on these problems, Donald Winnicott's understanding of the realities of motherhood shows important limitations.

Understanding women's experiences of mothering

In the following three sections, we shall look in detail at the experience of mothering children as they grow older. It will become clear that although demands differ at different stages, some of the underlying conflicts remain, in particular, how to maintain a satisfactory balance between the needs of mothers and the needs of children.

Young babies

The birth of a child is an event that will significantly alter a woman's life, whatever happens over the ensuing months and years, and however she decides to define her motherhood. When labour and birth are positive experiences, a woman is likely to feel an overwhelming sense of achievement and emotional wellbeing, as Sheila Kitzinger's (1988) collection of women's birth experiences illustrates. But these accounts also show how a distressing or insensitively managed labour in which the woman has been unable to give birth to her baby herself (for example, if the delivery was made by forceps or Caesarian section) may leave the woman feeling cheated, and that she has somehow failed. This was certainly the case for Margaret, who had felt drugged and out of control of her first child's birth, the memories of which echoed throughout the early years of her motherhood. Suddenly, after all the months of waiting, a woman is expected, and expects herself, to make the transition and become a competent and fulfilled mother. Yet common reactions for many first-time mothers in facing up to the eventuality of caring for a newborn baby are those of anxiety and awe. The foetus that had previously been carried within her, automatically nourished and contained in the womb, becomes a separate, fragile little baby, whose needs have to be understood and whose very life seems precarious. As Maya Angelou wrote about the son she gave birth to when she was 16:

> I had a baby. He was beautiful and mine. Totally mine. No one had bought him for me.... Totally my possession, and I was afraid to touch him....

Suppose I let him slip, or put my fingers on that throbbing pulse on top of his head?

(Angelou, 1984:280)

The immaturity of a human newborn, who is totally dependent on being cared for and who will remain dependent for many years, can indeed be a frightening responsibility for which many women feel unprepared.

Women who give birth in hospital often experience the attitudes of medical staff to be crucial in affecting their early feelings of confidence about their abilities to care for their babies. Ann Oakley (1980) has described how the women she interviewed were often dissatisfied with their post-partum care, either having to fend off the intrusions of a busy hospital routine or conversely, feeling unsupported when they needed advice. This is particularly apparent for the establishment of breast-feeding, the success of which appears to be highly dependent on staff attitudes and routines (see, for example, Peggy Thomas's survey carried out in 1987 of women's early breast-feeding experiences).

Despite increasing knowledge of the physiological and emotional benefits of breast-feeding for both mothers and babies (see, for example, Penny Stanway and Andrew Stanway, 1978), the taboos against nursing even newborn babies still tend to be culturally prevalent. In western societies, a woman's breasts have an erotic significance, which has very largely obliterated the primary function of lactation. Many women themselves feel that offering the breast to a baby is 'dirty' or in some sense incestuous. In addition, their partners' reactions have been shown to be a determining factor in successful breast-feeding. Harriet Lerner (1979) has described how many men feel a sense of 'ownership' of their wives' breasts, and many cannot cope with the regressive jealousy that they feel on watching their infants being nursed. Sensitive counselling rather than criticism or mere instruction is clearly needed in such situations to help women and their partners, so that they do not deny themselves what Niles Newton (1978) has described as a crucial and psychologically powerful aspect of their reproductive lives. Newton shows how women who do breast-feed successfully view this as a highly positive experience, especially since the special nature of such contact with the baby can be seen to bridge the transition between the baby-inside and the baby-outside.

Another issue of current concern to both mothers and to those who provide maternity services has been the quality of the very early relationship between the mother and her child. Ethological theorists, arguing from analogy with animal research, have suggested that there is a biological attraction between mother and child which is dependent upon intimate contact immediately after birth (see, for example, Marshall Klaus and John Kennell, 1976). Such theories lead to the argument that if mother and baby are separated for too long, for instance due to the baby's absence in intensive care, a 'bond' will not be established beween them, precipitating later rejection of the baby by the mother. It is certainly true that concern about 'bonding' has led to significant improvements in the way that mother and baby are treated, particularly in limiting the separation of newborn babies from their mothers during their hospital stay. But such a biologically determined concept totally ignores the complexity of women's reactions to their infants. As Ann Oakley points out:

> It is ... deeply interesting that the discovery of bonding came only after childbirth had been medicalized and removed to the hospital. The unmonitored bonding of mothers and babies in home deliveries had never evoked comment from the medical profession – nor, significantly, did the invention of the need for mother–baby bonding in hospital give rise to the reply that mothers and babies might be better off at home.
>
> (Oakley, 1986:141)

Ann Oakley argues that there are numerous methodological flaws in the mother–infant bonding studies, and that their uncritical acceptance has encouraged medical staff to appropriate mothers' feelings towards their babies: 'the domain of motherhood deemed relevant to medicine was extended, and there was now something else that mothers could not do by themselves, but only with medical help' (Ann Oakley, 1986:141).

For whilst many women *do* experience immediate positive feelings towards their babies, often described as a 'falling in love' which can be overwhelming and passionate, other women may experience an initial state of shock, or even feelings of rejection and disgust. To assume that all women should joyfully 'bond' with their babies immediately after birth ignores the context in which their babies were conceived, gestated, and born, together with the new mother's awareness of the likely struggles to come in rearing the child. Whilst for some women the pleasures of intense intimacy with their newborn babies is a part of their recurring desire to have more children, others may be simply filled with anxiety and despair.

Object-relations theorists have argued that women who have not been adequately cared for in their own infancy may feel overwhelmed by the demands made by a small baby (see Luise Eichenbaum and Susie Orbach, 1982). Newly delivered mothers may experience a resurgence of their own infantile needs, and deeply resent and envy their own baby's helplessness. Indeed for *all* women, however secure in their ability to provide nurturing care for their babies, the support that they receive during this time is of vital importance. According to Donald Winnicott (1982), the intense feelings of being bound-up with the baby (which he called 'primary maternal pre-occupation') involve immense amounts of emotional and physical energy, and highlight the woman's own needs to be cared for herself. Winnicott saw the father as being responsible for providing this support, but in fact all who care for the new mother, especially maternity staff and community services, should be aware of how vulnerable she feels. Not all women have the baby's father available to support them, and those that are present may not be able to offer such care because of the limitations of their own nurturing abilities.

As Sheila Ernst (1987) has commented, this preoccupation with the baby, which Winnicott describes as being like an illness that overcomes women in late pregnancy and gradually wanes as their babies mature, can more accurately be seen as a fundamental characteristic of women's pyschology. It is a chronic, not an acute state, which can involve a lifelong emotional involvement with the needs of others, particularly children, and is also something that some women may have to resist in the struggle to survive intact themselves.

When a mother does not immediately feel closely involved with her baby, her feelings are often explained as being the result of a physical dysfunction, usually assumed to be hormonal in origin. However, the psychological and social determinants of post-natal depression are ignored by such a physiologically based account. A number of studies have linked several vulnerability factors to post-natal depression, for example, poor social support, housing problems, a segregated marital role, and little previous contact with babies; with the risk being intensified by a technological birth (see Ann Oakley, 1980; Sandra Elliott and her colleagues, 1988). In addition Dana Breen (1975), in her intensive study of the psychological impact of the birth of the first child, has suggested that poor post-natal adjustment is more likely to occur in women who over-idealise motherhood and femininity.

However, in focusing on either social or psychodynamic factors, there is a tendency to ignore the multidetermined nature of women's reactions to motherhood. Joan Raphael-Leff (1985) has suggested that a range of factors can precipitate maternal distress, which she claims results from women feeling prevented from 'actualizing (their) own specific expectations about motherhood' (p.152). Although arguing that each woman has individually distinct reactions towards being a mother, she has described two different general approaches to motherhood. Whereas for the first type of woman motherhood is a much desired state of self-realisation, the second type of woman sees motherhood as a role which can be assumed and relinquished, not an essential part of her core self. In the first group, the woman looks forward to motherhood, expects it to be rewarding, and sees her task as adapting herself to the baby's needs. In contrast, the second style of mothering occurs where the mother sees her task as training the baby to fit into her routine, since the woman's aim is to reinstate her pre-natal life style and personal identity, to which the baby is expected to adapt. Joan Raphael-Leff suggests that those who are ready to adapt to their babies are more likely to feel at ease with the baby's dependence on them, whereas those who need to regulate the baby's demands feel threatened by an infant's fragility and helplessness. Here, the baby's incessant needs are more likely to be perceived as being overwhelming, and therefore the mother is apt to turn to someone else – her partner, her own mother, or a baby-minder – to perform the day-to-day care. Whereas for the second type of woman a return to work is psychologically beneficial, for the first type of woman, who feels that she is a vital part of her baby's world, the economic necessity to work is perceived as a cruel separation. We can compare the following accounts:

This is the dreadful knowledge that you have embarked on a course of action which is beyond your capacity to cope with emotionally ... the year following (the birth) was probably the most emotionally crippling of my life.... I had no patience to amuse or stimulate my baby. I was bored and tired by turn, and as the months wore on, increasingly frustrated by the lack of mental stimulus that had been so much a part of my daily life before.... In my case, a full-time nursery place was found which provided a happy, carefree environment for my son with other children.... For me there was the freedom to return to a working environment, which I so badly needed as an individual.

(Megan Johnston, 1987:57)

and:

She was a miracle to me, but when she was eight months old I had to leave her daytimes with the woman downstairs to whom she was no miracle at all, for I worked or looked for work.... I would start running as soon as I got off the streetcar, running up the stairs ... when she saw me she would break into a clogged weeping that could not be comforted, a weeping I can yet hear.

(Tillie Olsen, 1980:12–13)

Accounts like these suggest that it is vital that individual differences in women's reactions to motherhood are considered and understood, since they affect the sort of child care which is then needed. Current expectations that women can happily combine having children with other forms of employment ignore the individual ways in which women define their motherhood, as well as the problematic nature of finding adequate child care (which we shall discuss later).

Whereas single mothers have to create support systems for themselves to help them in their mothering, women in partnerships face a different task of renegotiation. For the birth of a first child by definition means giving up the exclusivity of a two-person relationship and reforming a more complex dynamic. Whilst for many women the intimacy of the couple may be replaced, at least temporarily, by intimacy with the newborn child, for the partner there may be a gap or sense of loss. This is so whether the partner is a man or a woman, as accounts from lesbian as well as heterosexual partnerships have shown (see, for example, Jo Chambers, 1983). Lily Pincus and Christopher Dare (1978) argue that the couple face the task of creating a new three-person relationship, and that difficulties can occur if one of the partners refuses to allow a third person into the relationship. Both adults need to come to terms with their own baby needs, which may be triggered by the presence of their own real infant. A woman may look to her partner, or to her own mother, to provide the support she needs, but these solutions can be problematic if the people available are unable to deal with their own conflicts. A partner who feels envious will be unable to share freely in caring for the baby or providing support for the mother.

Difficulties in the couple's relationship concerning different styles of caring for the child, or conflicts involving envy of the nurturance provided, are often most clearly seen in their sexual relationship. As Lesley Saunders (1983) has described, sexual demands made soon after childbirth can be felt like yet another task of mothering. Especially in the early months, when women may be recovering from an episiotomy or Caesarian birth, and having sleepless nights followed by many claims on their bodies by nursing babies, the desires of a partner for physical contact and intimacy may be difficult to meet. This can be perceived as deeply rejecting by a partner whose needs for reassurance and intimate contact may be particularly heightened. Advice that pressurises women into remaining sexually attractive, and stern warnings to mothers not to 'let themselves go' are particularly unhelpful. Much more helpful is sensitive counselling, and help for the partner to be patient about the process of adaptation to motherhood.

Mothering toddlers

We have focused so far on women's experiences during the initial stages of mothering, since it is here that the transition from non-motherhood to motherhood poses the most acute change. Yet women's responsibilities and caring for their children extend over a great number of years. The complete dependence of the newborn changes into the strivings for independence which are characteristic of toddlerhood. The type of care provided has to change continuously in response to the developing needs of the child, and for the person with day-to-day responsibility, this can be a source of both pleasure and pain, as the seemingly endless energy of the child engages with the boundaries of patience and tolerance of the care-giver. Increasing language abilities make the child a more sociable companion, but the limited conversation of a toddler and the repetitive questions of a young child can exhaust an adult who has no other company. Furthermore, the toddler is essentially self-centred. Adrienne Rich has described some of the difficulties of perpetual motherhood, as follows:

> It began when I had picked up a book or began trying to write a letter, or even found myself on the telephone.... The child might be absorbed in (playing); but as soon as he felt me gliding into a world which did not include him, he would come to pull at my hand, ask for help, punch at the typewriter keys. And I would feel his wants at such moments as fraudulent, as an attempt moreover to defraud me of living even for fifteen minutes as myself.... I could love so much better, I told myself after even a quarter-hour of selfishness, of peace, of detachment from my children.
>
> (Adrienne Rich, 1977:23)

Adrienne Rich also writes about the exhaustion of caring for young children, compounded by the loss of sleep due to children's different sleep rhythms. Lack of sleep is one of the major problems for mothers of young children, whether or not they work outside the home during the daytime, the results of which can reduce women's psychological resilience and make them more liable to feelings of depression, anger, and hopelessness. In this connection, Rich also raised the issue of women's violence against their children. She considers not only the stresses of isolated motherhood, and the effects for women of having unplanned or unwanted pregnancies, but also the nature of women's relative powerlessness. For, as Linda Gordon (1986) has argued, women's position in the family means that they can only victimise those less powerful than themselves; that is, their own children. However, despite their overwhelming responsibilities for children, women are not proportionally responsible for the abuse:

> Given that men spend on the whole so much less time with children than women, what is remarkable is not that women are violent towards children but that men are responsible for nearly half of the child abuse. But women are always implicated because even when men are the culprits, women are usually the primary caretakers who have been, by definition, in some ways unable to protect the children.
>
> (Linda Gordon, 1986:69)

Although there are undoubtedly many pleasures and joys invoved in caring for young children, these years can be highly problematic for some mothers, especially when they are unable to structure any time off. In her study of mothers of pre-school children, Mary Boulton (1983) found wide variations in the ways in which motherhood is experienced. Whilst some mothers felt generally 'satisfied', in that they had a sense of purpose, and on balance enjoyed looking after children, others felt 'alienated', in that they were irritated by the tasks of child care. Boulton was looking for social-class differences, but found that these were not a predictor of who would be satisfied or alienated. However, she did find a group of women who were neither satisfied nor dissatisfied, who were more likely to be middle class, and who felt in 'conflict', in that they had a positive commitment to their children but did not enjoy child care or the life style of being with pre-school children. She concludes that 'motherhood is neither "naturally rewarding" nor "inherently frustrating" but, rather, a woman's exper-ience as a mother is the product of a complex set of social and psychological factors' (Boulton, 1983:62). Interestingly, George Brown and Tyrril Harris (1978) did find social-class differences in alienation from motherhood: in their study, 42 per cent of working-class mothers with at least three children under the age of 6 were depressed, compared with only 5 per cent of middle-class mothers. Similar findings were obtained by Hannah Gavron (1970) and Ann Oakley (1974).

Inevitably, dealing sensitively with toddlers and pre-school children over an extended period requires sustained powers of patience, tact, and physical energy. Care-givers without adequate psychological resources (both in their own past history and their current life situation) can only react by imposing inflexible restrictions on the child's vitality. The caring tasks at this stage involve an ongoing set of negotiations between the child's push towards development and the carer's need to preserve safety and some sense of equilibrium. Such 'loving authority' is as necessary during childhood as in adolescence, since the child needs to feel contained by the caring strength of another person. Where this is lacking, children will push against the absence of containment until they meet a barrier, and in doing so may place themselves in dangerous, self-abusing situations, and will most certainly exhaust those trying to provide the care. Whilst conventional theories of child development see the temper-tantrums and the negativity of the young child as being a natural property of the growing process, we would suggest that, as in infancy, the child's reactions are very largely dependent on the transactions occurring between child and carers. If the carer herself is exhausted, demoralised, and isolated, her ability to deal creatively with the endless, recurring conflicts involved in child care will be severely limited.

Mothering school-age children

Once the intense dependence of early childhood gives way to greater strides towards independence, many women find, as did Margaret, that they are able to care for their children with much less conflict. In particular, when the child is able to start school, full-time mothers no longer have around-the-clock responsibility. For some, this will provide an opportunity to reintegrate themselves into the wider world of employment, although demands of the workplace and the structure of the working day do not fit easily with the much shorter school day. In addition, children at the start of their school lives are more likely to come into contact with a wider variety of illnesses and infections and hence may be irregular attenders requiring someone available at home to look after them. It is still generally women who act as sick nurse in such situations, requiring time off work, which in turn gives women the reputation of being 'unreliable' in the eyes of employers (see Chapter 5).

However, handing over a child to someone else's authority and value system may be a very ambivalent experience (see, for example, Mary Kelly, 1983). Despite the fact that most infant and primary school teachers are women, the structure and regime of most schools is a very 'masculine' one, reflecting the values of the outside world rather than those of the home. The philosopher Sara Ruddick (1984) describes this conflict as resulting from what she calls the 'preservative' love of mothers for their children. In this 'preservative' love, there is a conflict between mothers wanting to continue to raise their children in the nurturant way they treated them as babies, yet realising that the real world demands that they be tough and able to make their own way. This is perhaps particularly marked when raising boys, who are required by the world outside the home to become 'masculine' and to repress the gentler and more sensitive sides of themselves. Judith Arcana (1983) has shown how the school years, television, and social expectations profoundly challenge and mould boys' development by demanding their conformity to the expected male role. This is of special concern to women alone bringing up sons, as they are often criticised for not providing a male 'role-model' for their sons. Some feminists have argued that this is not a problem, since socialisation into traditional masculinity is something their sons can well do without. However, a solution used by many other single mothers has been to seek out nurturing men as friends for their children, and this introduces children to the notion that men can be caring as well as 'masculine'.

Women's feelings about bringing up daughters will be discussed in detail in subsequent sections of this chapter. But it is worth noting here that a mother's pleasure in her daughter's developing helpfulness and sociability may easily slide into a reliance on her daughter to help out and support her. As Susie Orbach and Luise Eichenbaum (1987) have pointed out, the mother may become the daughter's first child, as the daughter begins her long apprenticeship in caring for others. The values of school are unlikely to challenge this particular dynamic, however, as it is also useful to teachers. The process can of course be profoundly harmful both to the young girl's ability to separate from her mother, and to her capacity to develop an adequate sense of self.

As we shall see in Chapter 9, being a mother does not end, even when a child reaches legal adulthood. Mothers, as Sara Ruddick describes, must 'foster growth and welcome change' (Ruddick, 1984:218). For women whose lives seem to be standing still, this can create many stresses. For those who are open to new events and the inevitable unfolding of the years, there can be much satisfaction in letting go and seeing how the people they have created from their own bodies live their own lives. But that is not always easy, as we shall see in Chapter 9.

Meeting children's emotional needs: the psychological work of child care

There are, as we have already described, continuously changing fashions concerning the responsibilities of parents for their children. But no matter what the current fashion, as psychologists, and particularly in our work as psycho-therapists, we are regularly confronted by people who, despite being adequately nourished and cared for physically, demonstrate the impoverishment of their emotional upbringing. Whilst it is unlikely that any single event can be said to be responsible for adult distress, we would nevertheless argue that there is abundant evidence to suggest that the adult personality is constructed to a considerable extent from childhood experiences, and that those who care for young children determine and define the nature of these experiences. We shall focus in the rest of this section on describing the psychological needs of young children, and will consider how far their needs are met by those who care for them, not forgetting that those looking after small children generally find that this is but one of a number of tasks they perform, since all the routine home-maintenance tasks usually have to be dealt with at the same time. For reasons of space, we shall only look in detail at the first two or three years of life, and the 'mothering' required at this time.

Babies who are healthy and born at or near term are generally very good at communicating their needs. Premature or brain-damaged babies may be more difficult to understand, since their responses are frequently less well organised.

Adult carers who can tune in, listen and respond uncluttered by their own emotional distress or by advice about what the baby *should* be needing, will usually be able to interpret accurately what ought to be done for the baby. Initial misinterpretations can usually be reduced as the parents get to know the individual reactions of 'their' particular baby. Detailed observations of babies from birth show that they have a repertoire of organised responses which enable them to interact with the world. Jerome Bruner and his co-workers have studied a range of these responses, covering the baby's sucking actions, different cries, body movements, and eye-contact (for an overview see Kenneth Kaye, 1984). Object-relations theories of infant psychology share this perspective, arguing that far from being governed by undifferentiated and basically asocial drives, as both Sigmund Freud and Melanie Klein believed (see, for example, Melanie Klein, 1937), babies are from birth predisposed to respond to social relationships. Despite the human baby's immature developmental state, he or she is able to react positively to those who provide care, with what Michael Balint (1965) has called 'primary love'.

At first, babies' cortical limitations mean that they are unable to distinguish themselves from their surroundings. During this period of symbiosis, unaware of boundaries between 'me' and 'not-me', the baby has been described as still being in a 'merged' state with the mother. The caring required by such a sensitive creature involves structuring the environment so that the child is protected from physiological insult. Hence the most important quality of care in the early weeks is in providing what Donald Winnicott (1965) described as a secure 'holding' environment, initally through physical holding and gradually through extending these feelings of security to the way the baby's world is structured. The 'holding' environment is therefore one in which the child feels comfortable and contained. Winnicott argues that: 'Being and annihilation are the two alternatives. The holding environment therefore has as its main function the reduction to a minimum of impingements to which the infant must react with resultant annihilation of personal being' (Winnicott, 1964:47).

The empathy required to produce such security for the baby, the ability to ask the question 'What are you going through?' and to attempt to provide for the baby what he or she needs, involves considerable sensitivity to the changes in the baby's growth. In the early weeks and months of life there will be day-to-day developmental changes, which mean that different care-givers need to be aware of the baby's new responses. Fathers who share care or take over at weekends need to know, for example, that the baby now hates being bathed, having previously enjoyed it. Good two-way communication is also required between child-minders and parents so that the person who knows the baby best can interpret what the baby is 'saying'. Donald Winnicott argued that when the infant is repeatedly misinterpreted and the care-giver is unable to sense the baby's needs, the result is a form of despairing compliance, which is the earliest stage of the development of what he called the 'false self'. The infant then reacts to environmental demands through this aquiescent false self, which leads to the build-up of a false set of relationships. Rather than growing up to be him- or herself, the child complies with what the care-giver needs. Such a child therefore lacks spontaneity, and lives merely by imitation of others.

In her accounts of child-care practices, Alice Miller (1987a) has analysed the cases of many individuals who have been coerced to develop in ways that are determined by their parents' needs, rather than their own. She quotes in particular the example of Sylvia Plath, whose poems and novel *The Bell Jar* (1963) speak eloquently of the conflict between real and false selves. Alice Miller comments:

> Many parents are like Sylvia's mother. They desperately try to *behave correctly* toward their child, and in their child's behavior they seek reassurance that they are good parents. The attempt to be an ideal parent, that is,... not to give too little or too much, is in essence an attempt to be the ideal child – well behaved and dutiful – of one's own parents. But as a result of these efforts the needs of the child go unnoticed.
>
> (Miller, 1987b:257, emphasis in original)

Winnicott has suggested that normally the baby protests against being forced into such an imposed existence and becomes irritable, showing feeding and other bodily disturbances. If not recognised, these disturbances may eventually disappear under the pressures of compliance to what is required by the care-giver, only (Winnicott argues) to reappear at a later stage. These, then, may well be the beginnings of psychological disturbances that we see in later childhood and adulthood.

Psychotherapeutic work with adults and children has enabled what Alice Miller (1987a) has called 'the drama of being a child' to be pieced together and understood. In her study of child-rearing practices, Miller points out forcefully the effects of the harshness that has frequently been a feature of adults' 'care' for children. She also describes the defensive mechanisms by which children remain unaware of the nature of their upbringing, making it more likely that they in turn will repeat the process with their own children:

> The former practice of physically maiming, exploiting and abusing children seems to have been gradually replaced in modern times by a form of mental cruelty that is masked by the honorific term *child-rearing*. Since training in many cultures begins in infancy during the initial symbiotic relationship between mother and child, this early conditioning makes it virtually impossible for the child to discover what is actually happening to him. The child's dependence on his or her parent's love makes it impossible in later years to recognise these traumatizations, which often remain hidden behind the early idealization of the parents for the rest of the child's life.
>
> (Alice Miller, 1987b:4, emphasis in original)

Whilst for some care-givers, responding to the needs of young children is delightful, if exhausting work, which enables them to get in touch with the nurturing they received as infants and to identify with the baby. For others, it is a frightening time of feeling overwhelmed by a complex bundle of demands which do not make sense and cannot be satisfied. Of course, the baby's own temperamental character will interact with those of the caretaker. Babies who startle easily and who are more difficult to feed and settle, or who have erratic sleep patterns are often experienced as being more problematic. Premature babies and those with brain damage continue to show disorganised patterns of responses, which are often difficult to interpret (see Susan Goldberg and colleagues, 1980).

One of the ways in which babies slowly begin to differentiate themselves and achieve a separate identity is through the extent to which their actions and gestures are reflected back to them, especially through the faces of those that care for them. Winnicott (1974) considered such 'mirroring' to be a crucial experience for young infants; those who are not in close enough contact with another person's face, or who are cared for by people who can only reflect back their own distress, miss out on this crucial opportunity for self-development. Certainly, searching for eye contact is but one of the ways that the infant elicits and expresses sociability. Baby researchers from a variety of perspectives have provided a wealth of information concerning the active nature of infants' attempts to engage others in dialogue (see, for example, Kenneth Kaye's (1984) studies of the way that infants' sucking patterns affect mothers' jiggling movements as they are feeding them).

The rapid development that takes place in an infant who is provided with a responsive environment – who is picked up, talked to, smiled at, sung to, and so on – means that very soon the state of merging leads on to the beginnings of individuation. Responding to the child's need to individuate and separate is one of the most crucial and difficult tasks of caring for children. A 'merged' baby may at times be difficult to 'interpret', but once he or she is successfully fed, warm, and comfortably occupied, the baby will not put him- or herself in any danger. A 'separating' baby, however, is one that is becoming mobile and fascinated by the wider world. The carer therefore continuously has to monitor the baby's environment and make rapid decisions about the baby's security. For example, can the baby be left on the floor and continue to explore or will he or she find one of the marbles left by an older child, or try to unplug the radio?

The lengthy process of separation and the struggle towards individuation have been the subject of particular study by Margaret Mahler and her colleagues (1975). Based on their observations of mothers and their young children in a laboratory nursery-group setting, Mahler argues that there are clear signs that the baby is tentatively beginning to move towards separation and individuation as early as 6 months of age. At this stage, Mahler describes the baby as having 'hatched', in the sense that rather than drifting in and out of sleep, the baby becomes more alert and aware of the surroundings. The baby's brain is also developing rapidly, so that at around this age memory has developed sufficiently to be able to distinguish between familiar and unfamiliar faces. It is at this point that the baby begins to show the 'attachment' which John Bowlby (1971) has described, and which has also been of interest to ethologists who have looked at imprinting in animals. But unlike animals, human babies do not attach themselves in a straightforward way to the first, moving mother-figure they find. Instead, they are far more discriminating, tending to prefer people who interact with them in an empathic and responsive manner. As Michael Rutter (1977) has shown, babies will attach themselves to a number of people – to mothers, fathers, older siblings, kind neighbours – and may not necessarily attach themselves to the person providing the primary care if that person is cold and unresponsive. Babies and young children may also change their preferences and show greater attachment to one person rather than another in a seemingly unpredictable way. In addition, they start to be able to maintain relationships over time. Before the second year, babies do not have sufficient cognitive ability to understand that the people or things which they cannot see still continue to exist, and so they will react with panic and grief when they cannot find the person they want. But by the time they are toddlers they can begin to cope with short absences, or are mobile enough to follow people around.

Margaret Mahler's research also showed that in the early months of the second year the two processes of separation and individuation develop independently and not always at the same rate. A child who is developing the cognitive skills of memory, perception, and reality testing, which allow the achievement of a sense of self and which in turn determines the process of individuation, may not at the same time develop the boundary formation and distancing from a preferred person which is required for separation. Mahler suggests that this may be particularly the case for children who walk late, and also for children whose caregivers have a difficulty (for emotional or practical reasons) in putting a distance between themselves and their infants. Conversely, other children start to separate by making wild dashes away from 'home base' before they have the cognitive skills to integrate the experience.

By the middle of the second year, Mahler found that there was often an increase in anxiety about separation, following a period of relative unconcern about being left:

As the toddler's *awareness* of separateness grows – stimulated by his maturationally acquired ability to move physically from his mother and by his cognitive growth – he seems to have an increased need, a wish for the mother to share with him every one of his new skills and experiences.

(Mahler, Bergman, and Pine, 1975:76–7, emphasis in original)

Mahler calls this the period of *rapprochement*, more commonly recognised as the 'clinginess' of the toddler. This seems to reach a crisis just before the second birthday, after which, the children in Mahler's study appeared to differ enormously in their rate of development towards individuation.

These findings hold immense significance, both for the way that the mothering person behaves, and in the way that child care is provided. Mahler argued that optimally, carers need to provide a 'quiet availability', which enables children to come and go at their own rate. She agrees with Winnicott that children need to be given a 'gentle push towards independence' (Mahler *et al.*, 1975:78) whenever they appear ready to make the transition. But neither Mahler nor Winnicott consider the wider context that facilitates or hampers this task. Isolated mothers with no family or friends with whom to share child care, and insufficient income to pay for baby-sitters or nursery care (should these be available), cannot provide alternative environments for the child to gain separation experiences. Conversely, the inevitable planned changes in carer that occur for children whose mothers work outside the home are determined by schedules over which the child has no control. Hence separation cannot be structured at the child's pace, and no allowances can be made for the child's vacillating needs for closeness and distance. We will return to these issues when we consider options in child care, in the final section.

Whilst we have discussed separation issues for young children generally, it is important to note how especially complex this is for girls. Susie Orbach and Luise Eichenbaum (1987), following on from Nancy Chodorow (1978), have argued that these developmental tasks are more difficult for girl children, whose mothers may be more ambivalent both about the symbiosis of early attachments and the distancing involved in letting go. This dynamic between mothers and daughters, they say, results in a more complex and often protracted separation experience for girls, which indeed may never be fully completed. Their therapeutic work has led them to conclude that many adult women continue to feel unseparated from their mothers. However, in describing unconscious processes rather than observable actions, it is difficult to assess how strong such feelings are. Certainly many children retain what Ronald Fairbairn (1952) described as an 'infantile dependence', or reach merely a 'transitional' form of dependence which leaves them prone to continued anxiety over separation, but it is hard to say whether this is more common in girls than in boys.

We have focused here on the young child's emotional development, to the exclusion of cognitive and motor development, since it is likely that an environment which is responsive to the child's emotional needs will also provide the necessary context for growth in other areas. This is because all of the interactive tasks that make up child care, from feeding and bathing to soothing and entertaining, necessitate a sensitive adaptation of the carer's behaviour to the child's developmental level. Hence, in the absence of other factors such as developmental or physical handicap, cognitive and motor development are likely to proceed reasonably satisfactorily if the emotional caring is satisfactory.

Child care and women's autonomy

We have discussed the psychological needs of children in such depth because the needs of children should properly structure our understanding of the nature of the care that ought to be provided for children. It should have become clear from this discussion that good-enough parenting requires energy, enthusiasm, and skill (see Bruno Bettelheim, 1987). However, it should also have become clear from this and previous chapters that these qualities are not likely to be present if the child's carer is tired, lonely, and feels undervalued. Yet that is precisely the situation experienced by many mothers who are having to care for their children, both because of the limitations of their own early experiences, and the nature of the current context of mothering.

One way of resolving at least some of these problems would be the sharing of child care, for the sake of mother and child alike. But as we have seen throughout this chapter, mothers are expected to be primarily responsible for their children's care. In examining their experiences of caring for young children, we have argued that women vary enormously in terms of how much they are prepared, or can afford to be involved in full-time care. Yet at the present time, women do not always have the opportunity to exercise choice. As we have seen in Chapter 6, a pronatalist culture encourages motherhood for many women who, were they not so pressured, might on mature reflection decide this was not the right option for them. Some women may be ill-prepared for the realities of child care, and find that after their children's birth they do not want to be full-time mothers. Yet other women, in contrast, may very much want to be involved in the day-to-day care of their children, but for financial reasons are forced to provide alternative care whilst they are in paid work. For all these women, some form of child care by others is then necessary, and desirable.

Varieties of child care

Good quality child care is a prerequisite for women's continued participation in the world outside the home. Whether on a full-time, part-time, or occasional basis, all of those who are responsible for young children need to have safe, caring environments where their children can be looked after. This is, of course, fundamentally an economic and political issue which is dealt with differently in different countries. In the UK, for example, there is virtually no state-provided child care until children reach school at the age of five years. This, as we have seen, is an arbitrary starting-point, not based on any consideration of the child's developmental needs, since most children would benefit from collective experiences at a much younger age. In France, on the other hand, as well as the wide availability of subsidised crèches, free nursery education is provided in most parts of the country from the age of 3 years, and is becoming increasingly available from the age of 2. These French nursery schools are usually attached to primary schools and staffed by trained teachers with paid assistants to help with the extra demands of young children. (Also in France, single parents are entitled to a small wage, less than the minimum wage but enough to survive on, if they choose to look after their children at home, and mothers with three or more children are now provided with a wage for two years to allow them to care for their children, providing that they meet certain criteria of previous employment.)

However, in the UK, as Sandra Scarr and Judy Dunn (1987) show in their survey, state-run nursery and pre-school provisions are derisory, and diminishing. Here, the vast majority of babies and young children are cared for in individual homes, either their own or other people's. According to the Women and Employment Survey (Jean Martin and Ceridwen Roberts, 1984, quoted in Sandra Scarr and Judy Dunn, 1987):

> about 65 per cent of the under-fives whose mothers work full-time are looked after by relatives (44 per cent by grandmothers, 13 per cent by fathers). 23 per cent are cared for by childminders, 6 per cent by babysitters and 3 per cent in exchanges with friends. 9 per cent are in day nurseries. Of the children whose mothers work part-time, an even higher percentage is looked after by family members.
>
> (Scarr and Dunn, 1987:183)

Further, unlike in France and some other European countries, such as Finland, there are no tax concessions for the cost of child-care in Britain, so that this takes up a large proportion of the mother's or family's income. Workplace nurseries, which are well placed to provide high-quality care at the mother's or parent's place of work, are taxed, unlike company 'perks' such as cars or subsidised lunches. Hence for many British mothers, whether in paid work or not, child care often depends on haphazard arrangements relying on the goodwill of friends and relatives or the employment of other, poorly paid women who will 'mind' their children for them often because they have no other job prospects.

Child care within the family

As we have seen, the British child-care statistics show that within the family, it is frequently the child's grandmother who provides the day-to-day care when the mother is not available. Where the three generations are in close proximity and are able to deal with the conflicts that this arrangement may generate, this can be a good solution for children. As Caroline New and Miriam David (1985) argue in their book on child care, those who care *about* children are likely to be better able to care *for* them. Yet as for any method of shared care, it depends on good communication between carers and healthy family dynamics. One of the dangers of such an arrangement is that it will infantilise the mother. An extreme example of this is where the children of a young single mother are brought up 'as if' they were their grandmother's, a process in which both women, consciously or unconsciously, may collude. Other dangers include the imposition of the mothering task on to older women who thought they had completed this stage of their lives. While for some older women, caring for their grandchildren can provide an intimacy which is less stressful than their experiences had been with their own children, this is not true for all grandmothers. Increasing numbers of 'young' grandmothers are in paid employment themselves, or have other elderly dependants requiring care. Most importantly, many may feel that they have done their share of child care and have no desire to start all over again.

Despite the increase in lone parenting and women-headed households (see Chapter 8), the statistics noted on p.179 show that in the UK at least, 13 per cent of children with full-time working mothers are cared for by their fathers for some portion of their time. Both Nancy Chodorow (1978) and Dorothy Dinnerstein (1978) see shared parenting between mother and father as being the ideal solution, both in terms of freeing women from the sole responsibility of child care and in giving girl (and boy) children an alternative model of nurturance provided by a man. On the other hand, while this idea has been welcomed, and in some measure implemented by many with liberal persuasions, cultural feminists such as Adrienne Rich (1977) have argued that men do not have the skills to care adequately for babies and young children. In addition, many of those who have tried to implement shared parenting accept that it is usually only a privileged, usually middle-class solution. It normally depends on flexible working hours, or the possibility of living on two part-time incomes, or one job-sharing income. Working-class solutions tend to be even more stressful, involving at least one of the partners working unsocial hours. Some women, for example, work in the evening or at night so that they can be at home during the day to look after their children. Here, the stresses of lack of both sleep and time for the couple or family to be together are a serious drawback. Despite all its other destructive aspects, unemployment offers another possibility for shared parenting, although women with out-of-work husbands rarely find that these men increase their participation in housework or child care (see Lydia Morris, 1987).

Many other women have found that a previously egalitarian relationship created before children arrived, alters significantly once domestic work is stretched to involve child care. Diane Ehrensaft (1984) describes vividly the conflicts involved and the effects of different sharing arrangements. If men are to be more involved in their children's upbringing, she suggests, they have to move from a more peripheral 'fathering' role to a central 'mothering' one. As Ehrensaft points out, this can be easier to achieve when dividing up the physical tasks, such as feeding and bathing, than for the psychological work of child care, which includes being emotionally available to the children's needs, and also the ongoing logistic planning involved in catering for children's emotional and physical growth. Men, she claims, carry less of this mental load (such as who remembers to book the dental appointments or when the children are likely to need a bigger size of shoes). Significantly altering commitments to the two worlds of work and home means that fathers involved in child care would have to give up work rewards; middle-class men would see others promoted above them, for example. Equally, women have to be prepared to give up their one area of control, that of the family. Sometimes, even when the woman is prepared and able to do this, the child will not accept the change. Couples who have decided to take it in turns to be primary care-giver on a one-year-on/one-year-off basis, for example, often find that since the mother is often 'on' during the child's first year of life, she becomes psychologically more important, which makes her subsequent comings and goings more problematic.

Undoubtedly, as suggested by Adrienne Rich (1977), many men *are* unskilled at looking after young children. They have not, after all, been brought up to see this as an integral part of their adult existence, as both Dorothy Dinnerstein (1978) and Nancy Chodorow (1978) have pointed out. Learning practical skills like changing nappies is one thing. But, as Diane Ehrensaft has described, developing traits of 'empathy' and 'nurturance' necessary for good mothering is a far more challenging task. 'These are the very traits that often remain undeveloped or atrophy in the man's life history and are not easily reinstated at a later developmental period' (Ehrensaft, 1984:55).

Whilst some fathers soon seem to be able to tune into the needs of babies and young children, others will interpret the job merely as 'baby-sitting', either trying to get on with whatever interests them more or somehow not adequately attending to the child. Others are unable to perform simultaneously all the other tasks that need to be done by the home-bound person. As Graeme Russell (1983) discovered in his study of care-sharing fathers, many of these arrangements collapsed because working mothers found that they had to do all the shopping, cooking, cleaning, and laundry on their return from work, plus respond to their children's demands to spend time with them.

Child care outside the family

Where child care is not available from the immediate or more extended family, more formal arrangements have to be made. In the UK, as we have noted, very few places are available for babies in local authority nurseries, and these are generally restricted to children considered to be 'at risk' by local authority social workers. Such limited provision means that mothers who need to work for financial reasons receive no state-supported child care. Additionally, women who seek time away from full-time motherhood would have to admit to being abusive or severely negligent, with all the risks of being so labelled in the long term, before their children can even be put on a waiting-list. Again this situation compares very unfavourably with countries such as France, where crèches are more widely available, staffed by trained personnel and receiving state subsidies.

In the private sector, one alternative has been the creation of workplace nurseries. These have been developed by employers such as universities and colleges of higher education, who usually have more articulate and educated employees. Staffed by trained nursery nurses and subject to legal requirements in terms of staff/child ratios, these can enable parents to participate in their child's care during the working day, which is particularly helpful for children being breast-fed. However, in the UK, recent government decisions to tax workplace nurseries have led to many closures or prohibitive costs for those parents continuing to use them. Like any other social organisation, the atmosphere and philosophy of a nursery will depend on the values and training of the staff. Of course, as long as nursery care is considered to be low-status work with poor pay, the quality of care may be less than optimal. Carers will often find it difficult not to project back on to the children in their care the negative feelings and low self-esteem engendered by such a poor evaluation of the job. The emotionally, intellectually, and physically demanding work of caring for young children demands adults who are cared for themselves, both in terms of adequate financial rewards and conditions of work, and of the value placed on that work by others. Although often given lip-service, such levels of reward and recognition are, in practice, notable primarily by their absence.

This poor evaluation of child care is nowhere more clearly seen than in the individualised solutions of baby-sitters and child-minders. For a small proportion of affluent families, this role has been elevated to that of 'nanny', who may be provided with lodging and food, and will also be expected to conform to the family's expectations of her behaviour outside working hours. More usually, however, baby-sitters and child-minders are working-class women who have either already raised their children and seek work outside the home but have no qualifications other than their own experiences of child care, or are women with pre-school children who seek work in their own homes whilst they care for their own children. Both pay and conditions of work for child-minders are often abysmal; very few child-minders are salaried, so that they usually only get paid for the hours that the children are actually in their care, and this at a very low rate. One result is that child-care provision is often haphazard, leading to frequent changes in care arrangements, and consequent insecurity for the child (Janet Sayers, personal communication), and anxiety for the mother.

Implications for therapy

We have focused in this chapter on caring for children during the early years, since it is at this time that women's responsibilities are most clearly apparent. We have argued that the way in which child care is currently organised, relying on individual women caring for their own or other people's children, in isolated homes with little or no financial reward and minimal support, generates a situation in which it is very difficult to provide consistently good care. This is detrimental to both women and children. Women suffer emotionally, as well as socially and financially, often manifesting feelings of depression as they struggle to cope with their anger, anxiety, and loneliness (see George Brown and Tyrril Harris, 1978). Children suffer, because instead of being cared for by responsive, loving adults who can react positively to their needs and provide an environment of warmth, security, and interest, they find themselves often being ignored, emotionally abandoned, or grudgingly cared for by one tired and over-burdened person. Psychodynamic accounts of mothering have frequently shown how in the long run this can lead to the destructive fantasies about women often held by adult men – and indeed by women as well. Harbouring feelings of being let down and inadequately loved in infancy, unhappy and neglected children project their feelings on to other women in adulthood. They then often instigate a lifelong search for a 'real' mother, whose image inevitably fails them in all later relationships.

The need for structural changes

The therapeutic implications of what we have been saying in this chapter are vast, both on a personal and on a wider social level. The primary consideration is a structural one, allowing for a greater societal commitment to children's care. Age-appropriate crèches and nursery schools would enable young children to have a wider range of experiences necessary for their social, emotional, and cognitive development and provide a network of support for those who primarily care for them. Babies and toddlers, whilst needing to be with familiar people with whom they feel secure, do not have to be with the same person all the time. Indeed, we have argued that it is impossible for one adult to provide good around-the-clock empathic care. Child-carers, whether of their own or other people's children, need time to renew their energies and replenish their emotional resources. In our analysis of women's psychology, we have constantly seen that women are brought up to expect that they should be able to provide 'tender loving care' on an unlimited basis. Many women come to believe and demand this of themselves, and feel guilty and inadequate if they cannot meet this idealised requirement of femaleness. This is nowhere more clearly seen than in the ideology of motherhood, which represents ever more stringent demands on women to be responsively available to their children, keeping them not only clean and well-fed but also educationally 'stimulated', at the same time as being household managers, competent workers, and supportive and seductive partners. The image of 'Supermum' is all-pervasive, and many women tend to measure themselves – always unfavourably – against an impossible target. In fact, given a freer choice, women vary enormously in the way that they construe motherhood. Whereas for some it means desiring the intimacy of being the primary care-giver, for others it means wanting to continue to function in a pre-child manner, and hence delegating child care to others. Men have always been free to define the extent of their contact with their young children, and most choose to limit this to a few minutes at either end of the day (see Sandra Scarr and Judy Dunn, 1987). Whereas some 'new men' are reversing this trend, becoming more involved with daily aspects of child care, the majority still see this as 'women's work'.

It seems at the very least reasonable and psychologically sound to argue that children should be cared for by people who have actively chosen to be with them, and who have a commitment to their development and wellbeing. This means improving the conditions of work and financial rewards for all who care for children. Mothers who choose to stay at home with their young children need an adequate income and community child care resources to support them. Drop-in play centres and crèches with reliable and trained staff, good staff–child ratios, and safe, attractive facilities would allow young children to be well cared for in the absence of their mothers or other primary carers. Those who take extended leave to care for young children need adequate employment protection so that they can return to work when their children are older. Significant changes are required in working hours so that home and employment are less unequally divided. Women who choose to continue in paid employment need subsidised child care so that the carers they employ can be adequately paid and have appropriate conditions of service (including paid holiday and sickness leave, pensions, and normal-length working days).

The need for a greater understanding of children's needs

Any structural changes of this nature must incorporate a wider awareness of the importance of psychological factors in providing for children. Caring for babies and young children should involve, as we have seen, a willingness to empathise consistently with and respond to each individual child's needs. Women's ability to do this depends in large part on experiences of being cared for themselves, and the current emotional and practical resources they are able to draw upon. For those adults who have benefited from loving care when young, it will be possible to find satisfaction in the task of babycare which recompenses for the difficult times. A toothless smile or a hand clutched to guide the first faltering steps can reward the carer for the exhaustion of disturbed sleep and conflict-ridden negotiations with a toddler. But for those who have not experienced sufficient loving care themselves, the demands of providing a nurturant environment may deplete already limited emotional resources. As we said earlier, Alice Miller (1987b) has pointed out that harsh treatments 'for the child's own good' still form the consensus of opinion about child management. There is a need, therefore, for all of those involved with the care of children to be helped to overcome their defensive reactions to their own early experiences. Doctors, psychologists, health visitors, and others providing professional advice to mothers, child-minders, or nursery nurses could do much to create a climate of opinion that truly attempts to meet each child's developmental needs. Careful selection and training of those who work with children should emphasise personal warmth and a knowledge of the psychology of childhoood, while ongoing support should be available to all child-care staff who may need it.

The need for therapy for individuals

Individual or group psychotherapeutic support is so rarely available, and so often expensive where it exists, that few mothers or carers of young children are able to afford either the time or the money to attend. Yet this is the very point in their lives when women may most need to have their own infantile needs recognised. For some women, access to such help may come about only if there is a crisis, for example, if they are in severe difficulties in relating to their infants, or if their children are developing serious psychological disturbances. Ideally, psycho-therapy for those caring for young children would provide a containment for the feelings of anxiety over separation and fear of abandonment that frequently resurface when faced with responsibilities for children. Women who feel overwhelmed by a baby's demands can be helped, not only through making structural changes in their lives, but also in being nurtured themselves so that they feel less drained by the emotional demands on them. 'Maternal love' from a therapeutic relationship can provide the equivalent of a 'holding' environment for the carer. In a less stressed state, many mothers may then find that it is easier to respond to children's needs, and to reach solutions to regularly occurring child-care problems which previously appeared to be unresolvable.

Whilst some women can make use of self-help groups and other relatively informal forms of support provided by organisations such as the National Childbirth Trust, others may benefit from more professionally run forms of group help. One good example of this is the work of Sandra Elliott, Marion Sarjack, and Tessa Leverton (1988), who run groups for women who have few other sources of support available to them. Their groups are open to mothers from several months before the expected birth of the baby, and have been shown to reduce significantly the chance of depression and other problems occurring during the early stages of parenthood.

Other women, like Margaret, feel unable to admit to the extent of their distress and blame themselves for feeling incompetent and inadequate. For such women, individual therapeutic help may be needed. For example, Margaret was only able to make sense of the disorganising nature of her experiences of early motherhood once her daughters were older and she started therapy. In recognising the significance of her feelings about her own mother, she was then able to make use of the therapeutic relationship to help prevent similar conflicts occurring with her own separating daughters. In letting them grow away from her at their own pace, she was also able to start to free herself from her dependence on her husband. Almost inevitably, her emotional growth precipitated a crisis in the marital relationship, hence the need to continue their therapeutic work together.

Couple therapy can also be more appropriate when partners are unable to resolve feelings of jealousy generated by the presence of children in their lives. Partners who felt rivalrous about younger, or preferred siblings, for example, may find it especially difficult to make a place for children in their own adult family. Family therapy may also be indicated here (see, for example, Salvador Minuchin, 1974), as the whole family has to adapt to its changing structure.

Finally, whilst we have emphasised therapeutic work with adults, it is important to note that psychotherapy with children can allow for the expression and reparation of childhood distress should the adults responsible be unavailable, unwilling, or too numerous for therapeutic support. Children who have been taken into care to protect them from abusing parents, for example, will need sensitive therapeutic help to enable them to start to repair the damage to their emotional development. Nowhere is this clearer than where there is some evidence of sexual or emotional abuse occurring within the family. Sadly, as we have seen in Chapter 2, this seems to be currently on the increase. Therapy with children is beyond the scope of this book, but is often essential if the burdens of a disturbed childhood are not to be re-enacted in the adult's life, through interactions with partners and any subsequent children.

In this chapter, we have discussed some of the dilemmas and difficulties experienced by many women when trying to provide adequate care for their children. We have stressed the importance for the woman herself to be adequately nurtured and cared for, if she is to be able to provide for her own dependants. This is often hard enough for women who have supportive, stable relationships, but it is often (but not always) even harder for those who are trying to bring up children on their own. In the next chapter, we shall look at women without partners, some of whom will be mothers, and who are likely to be especially vulnerable. Their difficulties and satisfactions, as well as those of single women without children, will therefore form the substance of the next chapter.

References

Angelou, M. (1984) *I Know Why the Caged Bird Sings*, London: Virago (first published 1965).

Arcana, J. (1983) *Every Mother's Son: the role of mothers in the making of men*, London: The Women's Press.

Balint, M. (1965) *Primary Love and Psychoanalytic Technique*, London: Tavistock.

Bateson, G., Jackson, D., Haley, J., and Weatland, J. (1956) 'Towards a new theory of schizophrenia', *Behavioural Science* 1:251–64.

Bettelheim, B. (1987) *A Good Enough Parent*, London: Thames & Hudson.

Boulton, M.G. (1983) *On Being a Mother: a study of women with pre-school children*, London: Tavistock.

Bowlby, J. (1951) *Maternal Care and Mental Health*, Geneva: WHO. Abridged version, *Child Care and the Growth of Love*, Harmondsworth: Penguin, second edn, 1965.)

Bowlby, J. (1971) *Attachment and Loss, vol. 1: Attachment*, Harmondsworth: Penguin (first published 1969).

Breen, D. (1975) *The Birth of a First Child*, London: Tavistock.

Brown, G. and Harris, T. (1978) *The Social Origins of Depression*, London: Tavistock.

Chambers, J. (1983) 'Struggling to change, changing with struggle', in S. Cartledge and J. Ryan, (eds) *Sex and Love*, London: Virago.

Chodorow, N. (1978) *The Reproduction of Mothering: psychoanalysis and the sociology of gender*, Berkeley: University of California Press.

Dinnerstein, D. (1978) *The Rocking of the Cradle*, London: Souvenir Press.

Ehrenreich, B. and English D. (1979) *For Her Own Good: 150 years of the expert's advice to women*, London: Pluto Press.

Ehrensaft, D. (1984) 'When women and men mother', in J. Trebilcot (ed.) *Mothering: essays in feminist theory*, Totowa, N.J.: Rowman & Allenheld.

Eichenbaum, L. and Orbach, S. (1982) *Outside In ... Inside Out*, Harmondsworth: Penguin.

Elliott, S., Sarjack, M., and Leverton, T. (1988) 'Parents' groups in pregnancy: a preventive intervention for post-natal depression', in B.H. Gottlieb (ed.) *Marshalling Social Support: formats, processes and effects*, Beverly Hills: Sage.

Ernst, S. (1987) 'Can a daughter be a woman?', in S. Ernst and M. Maguire (eds): *Living with the Sphinx: papers from the Women's Therapy Centre*, London: The Women's Press.

Fairbairn, R. (1952) *Psychoanalytic Studies of the Personality*, London: Tavistock.

Gavron, H. (1970) *The Captive Wife*, Harmondsworth: Penguin.

Goldberg, S., Brachfeld, S., and Divotto, B. (1980) *Feeding, fussing and play: parent–infant interaction in the first year as a function of prematurity and perinatal medical problems'*, in T. Field, S. Goldberg, D. Stern, and A. Sostele (eds), *High Risk Infants and Children: adult and peer interactions*, New York: Academic Press.

Gordon, L. (1986) 'Feminism and social control: the case of child abuse and neglect', in J. Mitchell and A. Oakley (eds) *What is Feminism?*, Oxford: Basil Blackwell.

Hinde, R.A. (1961) 'The establishment of the parent–offspring relation in birds, with some mammalian analogies', in W.H. Thorpe and O.L. Zangwill (eds) *Current Problems in Animal Behaviour*, London: Cambridge University Press.

Johnston, M. (1987) 'The myth of motherhood: the pressure to conform', *Spare Rib* 184:57, November.

Kaye, K. (1984) *The Mental and Social Life of Babies: how parents create persons*, London: Methuen (first published 1982).

Kelly, M. (1983) *Post-Partum Document*, London: Routledge & Kegan Paul.

Kitzinger, S. (1988) *Giving Birth: how it really feels*, London: Victor Gollancz.

Klaus, M.H. and Kennell, J.H. (1976) *Maternal–infant Bonding*, St. Louis: Mosby.

Klein, M. (1937) 'Love, guilt and separation', in M. Klein (1975) *Love, Guilt and Separation and Other Works 1921–1945*. London: Hogarth Press.

Laing, R.D. (1960) *The Divided Self*, London: Tavistock.

Lerner, H. (1979) 'Effects of the nursing mother–infant dyad on the family', *American Journal of Orthopsychiatry* 49:339–48.

Lorenz, K. (1966) *On Aggression*; New York: Harcourt, Brace and World.

Mahler, M., Pine, F., and Bergman, A. (1975) *The Psychological Birth of the Human Infant*, London: Hutchinson.

Martin, J. and Roberts, C. (1984) *Women and Employment: a lifetime perspective*, London: HMSO.

Miller, A. (1987a) *The Drama of Being a Child*, London: Virago (first published 1979).

Miller, A. (1987b) *For Your Own Good: the roots of violence in child-rearing*, London: Virago (first published 1980).

Minuchin, S. (1974) *Families and Family Therapy*, London: Tavistock.

Morris, L. (1987) 'The no-longer working class', *New Society*, 3 April.

New, C. and David, M. (1985) *For the Children's Sake*, Harmondsworth: Penguin.

Newton, N. (1978) 'Completing the female sexual cycle: intercourse, childbirth and breast-feeding', *Sexual Medicine Today* 2:34–40.

Oakley, A. (1974) *Housewife*, London: Allen Lane.

Oakley, A. (1980) *Women Confined: towards a sociology of childbirth*, Oxford: Martyn Robertson.

Oakley, A. (1986) 'Feminism, motherhood and medicine – who cares?' in J. Mitchell and A. Oakley (eds) *What is Feminism?* Oxford: Basil Blackwell.

Olsen, T. (1980) 'I stand here ironing', in T. Olsen (ed.) *Tell Me a Riddle*, London: Virago.

Orbach, S. and Eichenbaum, L. (1987) 'Separation and intimacy: crucial practical issues in working with women in therapy', in S. Ernst and M. Maguire (eds) *Living with the Sphinx*, London: The Women's Press.

Peterson, S.R. (1984) 'Against "parenting"', in J. Trebilcot (ed.) *Mothering: essays in feminist theory*, Totowa, N.J.: Rowman & Allenheld.

Pincus, L. and Dare, C. (1978) *Secrets in the Family*, London: Faber & Faber.

Plath, S. (1963) *The Bell Jar*, London: William Heinemann.

Raphael-Leff, J. (1985) 'Facilitators and regulators: vulnerability to post-natal disturbance', *Journal of Psychosomatic Obstetrics and Gynaecology* 4:151–68.

Rich, A. (1977) *Of Woman Born*, London: Virago.

Ruddick, S. (1984) 'Maternal thinking', in J. Trebilcot (ed.): *Mothering: essays in feminist theory*, Totowa, N.J.: Rowman & Allenheld.

Russell, G. (1983) *The Changing Role of Fathers*, Milton Keynes: Open University Press.

Rutter, M. (1977) *Maternal Deprivation Reassessed*, Harmondsworth: Penguin.

Saunders, L. (1983) 'Sex and childbirth', in S. Cartledge and J. Ryan (eds) *Sex and Love: new thoughts on old contradictions*, London: The Women's Press.

Scarr, S. and Dunn, J. (1987) *Mothercare/Othercare*. Harmondsworth: Penguin.

Spitz, R. (1965) *The First Year of Life: a psychoanalytic study of normal and deviant development of object relations*, New York: International Universities Press.

Spock, B. (1957) *Baby and Child Care*, New York: Cardinal/Pocket Books.

Stanway, P. and Stanway, A. (1978) *Breast is Best*. London: Pan.

Stone, L. (1982), *Family, Sex and Marriage in England, 1500–1800*, Harmondsworth: Penguin.

Thomas, P. (1987) *Encourage the Mother*, London: Association of Breastfeeding Mothers.

Vetere, A. and Gale, A. (1987) *Ecological Studies of Family Life*, Chichester: Wiley.

Winnicott, D. (1964) *The Child, the Family and the Outside World*, Harmondsworth: Penguin.

Winnicott, D. (1965) 'The theory of the parent–infant relationship', in *The Maturational Process and the Facilitating Environment*, London: Hogarth.

Winnicott, D. (1974) 'Mirror role of mother and family', in *Playing and Reality*, Harmondsworth: Penguin.

Winnicott, D. (1982) 'Primary maternal preoccupation', in *Through Paedriatrics to Psychoanalysis*, London: Hogarth.

Chapter eight

Women alone

Sally's story

Sally asked if she could come and talk with me, not because she was in the midst of any particular crisis, but because she felt she would really like to understand herself better, in order to prevent the recurrence of a 'bad patch', which had occurred several years previously. Sally was a cheerful woman in her late forties, who lived on her own. She felt that the 'bad patch' was so out of character for her, that some sort of self-examination was called for. She started by telling me about a relationship which had broken down some time ago, since she was worried that the problems that she had experienced might be somehow connected with living alone:

I've been on my own for about five years now, after living with Clive for about ten years. Clive and I split up quite amicably, although for the first eighteen months or so we lived quite near to each other, only a couple of streets apart. I used to go round and get him his breakfast and we'd have the evening meal together. He used to cook or we did it between us; he didn't like living alone. I felt sort of responsible for him, because I knew he really wanted to get married, although *I* didn't since I'd been married before and I didn't want to go through all that again. We actually got along all right, and of course there was my son, from when I was married before, and Clive was quite fond of him, although in fact my son wasn't there much. Because we got on quite well, for the first eighteen months after we split up we actually lived apart, but together in a way. Every Sunday I would go to his place, and he would wash my car, operate the automatic washing machine (I'd take my sheets and towels), and I'd do his hoovering – until he met the women who is now his wife, and at that point he said, 'I think it better that you don't come on Sundays – because I don't want her to see your car outside.' So that was that. Unfortunately that was the start of the 'bad patch', when I also lost my best girlfriend and another relationship broke up. Everything sort of went that year – and that was really awful!

Sally looked rather sad as she recalled the past, although her obvious liking for

Clive seemed to me to be a cause of satisfaction and pride to her, and not the main source of her recent distress. However, I thought I needed to know some more about why her previous marriage had broken down, as well as why she had split up from Clive:

> Donald and I were married when we were both 19. Our son was born very shortly afterwards. I don't know if it would have worked if I'd been a bit different. Sex had a lot to do with it, it was the fact that I resented the fact that sex was expected. I think it was the marriage situation that totally upset things for me – at least that's the way I've rationalised it – I might be quite wrong – but I didn't like the fact that sex was a duty, or I saw it as a duty – and therefore I resented it and it all went wrong, and then he felt bad about it, and the whole thing was very painful. It was getting to the stage where he felt he'd got to ask, and I felt I'd got to say yes, and it was all very uncomfortable. Eventually he got involved with another woman. I felt very bitter about the whole thing at the time, although I don't now. It is such a long time ago.

Then Sally told me that she and Donald had got divorced after three years of marriage, when she was about 22, and their son Peter was a baby. Donald soon remarried, and they lost contact. Sally and little Peter lived on their own for quite a few years, which she apparently enjoyed, although it was hard work and financially very difficult at times. Then she met Clive, and they all moved into a place together. This arrangement worked fairly well, although Sally said she felt very divided in her loyalties between her son and Clive, as if she was being pulled in two different directions. Then when Peter was in his teens, he joined the Navy as a cadet and was away abroad most of the time; it had apparently always been an ambition of his. It was also about then that Sally realised that she didn't really like living with Clive: 'I just wanted more space. And I certainly wasn't going to consider getting married again.'

Next I asked Sally how she and Clive had split up:

> Oh, very peacefully, and mostly at my request. I simply said I would never consider getting married again, and that I wanted more time on my own. As I said before, for the first eighteen months after we split up, we lived very near to each other, and actually saw each other quite a lot. Then my father died, and left me his cottage, which is where I live now. My mother had died some time previously; she had committed suicide when she was 60, and before that, she was in and out of mental hospitals for about ten years. Her problems all started to happen when I was in college. She was depressed, had ECT, and was severely arthritic. She just decided life wasn't worth living. So after my father's death I moved in temporarily to their cottage. And of course having moved in, I discovered I loved it – except during that awfully bad year.

Gradually, Sally approached the subject of the time which was worrying her.

She said it was more like six months, than a year, but that she had felt really close to suicide, like her mother:

> It was over Christmas. I had just lost Clive because he had married again, like Donald had. I'd also lost Annie, my best girlfriend, at that time (because she moved in with someone I really couldn't stand). My son Peter was miles away at sea, and wouldn't be home for at least six months. At the very same time I'd been building up a wonderful (I thought) relationship with another man, which all suddenly went completely to pot. This all happened within about a week; I felt nobody loved me, there was nobody important in my life anymore, and I'd got nobody to talk to. I felt absolutely bereft, unloved, and unwanted. This went on for about six months – I was living on my own – it was quite tough, I was waking up in the middle of the night, sobbing, and hitting the whisky bottle, and actually did feel seriously suicidal. I don't think I'd have actually done it. I wouldn't commit suicide because I'm too much of a coward, but I was seriously thinking about it. I did feel very, very bad that year.

I wondered how she had managed to move on from there:

> Well, first I changed my name, back to my maiden name, I had my ears pierced, decided it wasn't going to get me down, and then I met a man who made me feel good. That was only a one-night stand but you know, it was just what I needed at the time. Then at the end of that year I met yet another man, George, and had a two-year relationship with him, and that helped. I was made to feel loved and wanted again. And – but then – I couldn't cope with that either, because ... it was taking up too much space, I resented the time I spent with him, I resented the fact that I couldn't sleep. He wasn't living with me, he only slept with me one night a week, but I couldn't cope with it, and I was bored. When the sex had worn off, I thought, 'What the hell am I doing in this relationship?' and in the end it took me one whole year to psyche myself up to tell him it was over. One year was good and one year was, 'How the hell can I get out of this?' Having got out of that, I've been very careful what I've got into again. In fact, I've not been involved with anyone else since then.

I asked Sally what she felt now about splitting up from George, living on her own without a partner:

> I feel I've drawn back from a dreadful abyss which I might have fallen into, not that there was ever any question of George moving in with me because he was married anyway, but it made me realise how much I do hate having anyone else around, even for one night a week. It really made me realise I must never ever get into that situation again, because it wouldn't work. It would be OK if someone came and lived next door! Nevertheless ... I do get scared that my needing to be loved so much will get me back into the

kind of situation I don't want. That's why I worry about the bad patch coming back again.

Trying to find out more about the issues which concerned Sally most about this bad patch, I felt I needed to understand what lay underneath her anxiety about needing love so much, together with her fear of a commitment such as marriage. I therefore asked Sally a bit more about herself as a person, and her feelings about relationships. She answered me after some hesitation:

> I don't need people just for company. I'm very introspective, and I need to think a lot about life, and people, where I'm going and so on. I like the time to think – and I'm with people a lot at work, so it's a tremendous relief not to have to listen to people at home. I don't like people in general very much, apart from certain people, and then I do like *them* a great deal. People are important to me, but only a few people like my friends Vera and Paula – I'm not a sociable type. My son Peter is important, too, but he's away at sea so much that he is not really a big part of my life now. But yes, I need to feel I belong to someone, that I matter to someone. I suppose I'm scared that I'll end up mattering to no-one. But marriage, no. That just made me feel suffocated. I suppose I saw too much of my parents' marriage ever to feel that it could work for me. And being married to Donald wasn't much fun.

Gradually, Sally told me more about herself, and about her early childhood. Her parents were apparently very badly suited to each other, and there were constant arguments at home. Sally was an only child, and always felt rather a disappointment to her mother, who had wanted a son, and who had suffered numerous miscarriages. Her parents had disagreed about almost everything, and especially about Sally's future: Sally's mother had wanted Sally to get married as soon as possible and have lots of children, while Sally's father had encouraged her to get a job and earn money as soon as possible. Sally's mother's illnesses and depressions meant that Sally had spent a lot of time trying to keep up the family's spirits, as well as taking a great deal of responsibility for the housework and other domestic chores. Sally had had very few boyfriends before marrying Donald, and had got married in part to get away from the pressures of home, and in part because she was pregnant: hence in a way doing what her mother wanted, but also displeasing her by very shortly afterwards splitting up from Donald:

> Being married to Donald never suited me, although my mother thought I should have stuck with him, no matter what. But after we had split up, I was so much happier living on my own than I had ever been in my life before. I felt exactly the same after I split up from Clive: I was doing what I wanted, not what my mother or anyone else wanted me to do.

This led me to wonder exactly how Sally felt now about living alone:

> I really love the total freedom. If I want to get up in the middle of the night,

I can. If I'm reading on Saturday afternoon and it gets round to 6 o'clock and another hour will see the book finished, I can go on for another hour without having to break off and get a meal for anybody. I don't have any responsibilities for other people. I don't do the housework like I used to – I used to clean the house thoroughly every week when I was married and when I lived with Clive, but now I clean about every two months – so there isn't any conflict any more. But of course there are plenty of problems, too. Managing financially as a single person is difficult: you've got to pay for your telephone, which is essential for a woman living alone, and heating, rates, gas, electricity. I think I'm going to be struggling when I retire – I really do, it worries me.

I then asked Sally about some of the other negative things about living on her own. For example, what about warmth, cuddles, and sex.
Sally grinned ruefully:

Ah, that's really interesting. The thing I *have* missed is touching somebody, not sex itself. One does miss touching. It *is* quite important, and it is something you don't get if you are not a member of a family, and haven't got young children that you hug – yes – I'm conscious of not touching anybody, and it is a deprivation. It is a good job you mentioned that, because I'd forgotten it. It isn't bothering me so much now, maybe I'm just getting used to it.

Despite the financial drawbacks, and the physical deprivations, it was none the less clear that in recent years, Sally was being able to control her own life in a way that had always previously been denied to her. So what was the anxiety underlying her fear of a recurrence of the bad patch?

Perhaps it has got to do with my fear that, after all, I shouldn't be so happy. My mother told me that it was selfish not to want lots of children, and not to want to stay at home looking after my husband. When I first split up from Donald, and before I met Clive, she told me that it was unnatural and cold for a woman to live on her own. She always pointed to the single women who lived near us when I was little, and told me that unless I was careful, I would be poor and lonely like them. She told me they were all a little odd, and rather dangerous. It was nonsense of course, but I suppose I've been influenced by her. I did feel like that at first, during the bad patch, until I found out that living alone really suited me. At that time, I didn't have any friends, and really, I suppose I *was* very lonely.

Then I asked Sally if she was ever lonely now:

No, never, I never – I don't know ... I was much lonelier when I was married. In the sense I felt that I couldn't talk to my ex-husband or to Clive about things that were worrying me, because they didn't listen. Even with Clive I used to go to bed and cry because I felt so lonely. That doesn't happen now. I know I can talk to people, and I never ever feel lonely. I just feel very peaceful, appreciate the quiet, and lack of hassle. You know, (smiling) people always ask that. They say, 'You must be lonely,' and 'Aren't you bored?' and 'Wouldn't it be nice to have someone to come home to?' and that's one thing that I always find quite amazing, because when I walk through my door, and lock it behind me, I always think, 'Oh bliss! I don't have to talk to anybody, it is so peaceful!' The idea of wanting someone to come home to is totally alien. I used to resent that about living with Clive, because he would come home and tell me all his troubles, and I'd have to be sympathetic, and then when I tried to tell him my troubles, he'd say, 'Well you should give it up if you don't like it,' or something like that. He used to have what I call folding ears, and I could see when his folding ears came down he wasn't listening to what I was saying anymore. I never really found a man who will listen to what I'm saying. Maybe – Prince Charming might suddenly appear over the horizon one of these days, but I doubt it! I'm not saying that in a regretful way – I don't think I'd want Prince Charming even if he did appear, I don't think I could be bothered with him, the disadvantages outweigh the advantages when it comes to having a man around the place!

Sally suddenly stopped, and smiled again. 'Yes,' she said:

I've just listened to what I said. I really do feel that. I've been much happier living alone. For me, being a single woman *is* fulfilling, despite what my mother said. It's lovely to get up in the morning and think, I can do just what I like, don't have to explain to anybody. I think one of the most difficult things is other people – people all think, 'Poor Sally, can't we find her a man?' and that's the last thing I want, a man to live with. 'It must be dreadful living on your own' they say, and at Christmas, I practically have to fight people off ... it was a difficult one, that was, because after that first Christmas they couldn't believe that I actually wanted to be alone at Christmas – and now I do, it's lovely. It's the freedom. Loss of autonomy is too big a price to pay, as far as I'm concerned, for the dubious benefit of having the occasional cuddle, which is really all I miss, and I miss that less as I get older. I do have close women friends to talk to, like Paula, who's very much like me, although she's quite a lot older than me. She understands how I feel about work, because she felt exactly the same. I've got another close friend, Vera, who has also been married before, and we can talk to each other about sex, is it all worth it, and all that sort of thing. And I feel at the moment very happy with these two close friends. I suppose.

Sally paused, and then smiled again, rather sadly:

What may be underneath all my anxiety about a re-issue of my bad patch is probably my worries about losing these friends, too, like I've lost people in the past. I'm particularly worried about losing the one who I can talk to about sex – Vera – because if the man she is seeing at the moment suddenly decides that she is *the* woman in his life, then things might go wrong for our friendship. Our special relationship would be destroyed – I'd still want to know Vera as a friend, but it would be a different relationship, because she'd have much less time for me. And I do feel a bit insecure from that point of view. It would be an inevitable betrayal. Another worry I have is that my other friend, Paula, is getting older, and she's been quite ill recently: I suppose I'm a bit frightened about losing her for ever. But I suppose that's inevitable sooner or later. Also, I would like it if I could see more of Peter.

Having had the chance to talk things out in this way, Sally said she felt much happier, and because she was aware of what was really bothering her now, felt more in control of her feelings. She had realised that the social image of 'the single woman' from her childhood was no longer so powerful, and was sure that she was right to live alone. In discovering that, she felt considerable relief, since to her it meant that she was stronger than she had thought. She did not deny the problems and disadvantages of living alone, but felt more convinced that she had made the right decision for herself. She also resolved to go and talk to her friend Vera about her fears of loss, as well as to spend some more time with Paula, and to make more effort to see her son Peter. Now that she had taken the plunge to talk to me, Sally said that she felt less afraid to come back and talk again if she started to feel herself getting depressed again. I pointed out that there were lots of issues connected to her fear of being unloved which we had merely touched upon (such as her unsatisfactory relationship with her mother), and offered her an open invitation to contact me again as and when she needed to do so.

Being single

The vast majority of women will, at some point during their lives, live on their own. For some it will be a way of life which has been chosen freely, while for others it will happen only by necessity, through the death of a husband, or the failure of a relationship. Being single is far more common than is usually supposed by a society which assumes that people normally live in households of two adults and two children. For example, the UK General Household Survey of 1985 showed that 23 per cent of all households consisted of one single person only. Also in the UK, surveys carried out in 1984 showed that while 68 per cent of adults were married, 27 per cent had never been married, and 5 per cent were divorced (*New Society*, 1986). Meanwhile, in the United States, the US Bureau of Census (1984) showed that the majority of women between the ages of 65 and 74 were single: either divorced, separated, widowed, or never married. Of course we realise that these figures are not straightforward, since some of these figures concerning marital status conceal the fact that many people, although technically single, do not actually live alone, but may be cohabiting with a partner; and in addition, data about people's domestic arangements also conceal the fact that many single women may be sharing a house with friends or with children.

In this chapter we shall be concerned primarily with those who are living without an *intimate* partner, for reasons of separation, divorce, death, or personal choice. We shall not exclude those who are living with friends or dependants, therefore, as we are interested in the psychological position of those who define themselves, and are defined by others, as single women, even if they do in fact live with friends or dependants. We shall open the chapter by looking briefly at popular images of the single woman, although as we shall show later, these images often differ widely from the reality of being single. In order to understand why the idea of the single woman is so threatening both to herself and others, however, we shall then examine the process of attachment, to see why, at least for some women, and for society at large, being single can seem problematic. Following this we shall look at the psychological, social, and practical consequences of being single, and then at the varieties of the single state: from being 'between relationships' and being celibate by choice, to being single because of divorce or widowhood. As elsewhere, we shall conclude with a section on the therapeutic implications of the issues that we have discussed.

Popular images of the single woman

Although it is a state which will happen, or has happened to virtually everybody, being single is still seen as somewhat 'abnormal' by most people. Women on their own are, on the whole, perceived by others as odd, frustrated, dangerous, unfortunate, to be pitied, or to be avoided. The very words used to describe the unmarried woman, such as 'spinster' or 'maiden aunt' themselves carry connotations of a wasted and barren life in contrast to those used to describe single men; the image of the bachelor conjures up notions of excitement, experience, and naughty independence. Likewise, divorced women are seen as far more threatening and dangerous than divorced men, and as being more desperately in need of another partner. These negative images do not seem to apply so much to widows, since living alone because of widowhood is much more 'acceptable' than living alone out of choice; nevertheless, in some cultures the word for 'widow' is identical to the word for 'relic', while in others, a widow is expected to retire gracefully from any form of public life, and to hand over responsibility for herself to her sons or brothers. In yet others, she is actually expected to commit suicide (see also Sheila Jeffreys, 1985).

The importance of these negative images of singlehood in women is that they have considerable impact on the ways in which the single woman sees herself, and they also affect the way in which single women are treated in social, legal, and economic terms. Later in this chapter we shall look at some of the evidence concerning the reality of women's experience of being single, which is often very different from, and much more complex than, this popular negative image. But we shall also look at the social and economic consequences, which often *are*, unfortunately, very negative. Initially, however, we shall look at some of the developmental issues which form the basis of our anxieties about the state of being unattached, and which underlie the negative images inspired by the idea of women on their own.

Attachment as the basis of the development of personality

As noted, in order to understand why being a single woman is seen both by many women themselves, and by men, as such a problem, we need to spend some time looking at the issues which underlie this anxiety. Probably the best place to start doing this is to examine some of the issues which constitute the process of attachment, which is the opposite of being single or separate. This means we have to look at the processes of relationship development, and at personality formation. As elsewhere, we have found some of the ideas of object-relations theorists to be particularly helpful in this respect, although we shall also draw on other material in our analysis, where appropriate.

As we have seen in previous chapters, people are not born as formed personalities, but are instead, as in the words of Ronald Fairbairn (1952), born as 'potential' human beings, who become individuals through their particular experiences of human relationships. The most crucial relationships that an individual will ever form are those which develop in the early weeks and months of life, for upon them the baby's physical and emotional survival depends. The mutual relationship between parents and child has become known as attachment, and as we have already seen in Chapter 7, this process of attachment, besides being essential to survival in babyhood, has been seen by many psychodynamic writers such as John Bowlby (1969) as the origin of all later psychological development. As described in Chapter 7, numerous studies of the maturation of young children have demonstrated the great distress experienced by little children when forcibly separated from their primary care-giver(s); while other studies have demonstrated the very gradual way in which children will tolerate increasing distance from their parents. Fear of strangers, which first occurs during toddlerhood, only starts to dissipate by the fourth year, and indeed for many people, never totally disappears. For example, approximately 17 per cent of children are said to be so shy that they need professional help (J. Asendorpf, 1986), while work by Philip Zimbardo (1977) suggests that 42 per cent of college students still describe themselves as shy when with strangers.

For young children, being with the mothering, or attachment figure is closely associated with safety and pleasure, while separation is associated with danger, fear, and distress. Parents, too, form very close bonds with their children, and tend to encourage children to stay nearby, often emphasising to their children the dangers of the world outside the immediate family circle.

Attachment to a parent does not only serve the purpose of keeping the child close to the source of food and warmth, but it also permits the development of emotional relationships, which themselves form the foundation of the child's personality. As we have said elsewhere, children become themselves through the medium of both the positive and negative consequences of being emotionally close to other people, but more fundamentally, also develop their unique personality structures through coping with any deprivation or lack in those early relationships. These deprivations may occur as a result of either real, physical separation for which children are unprepared, or psychological separation, in which their carers are absent emotionally, although present physically. In the case of serious deprivation, the child may conclude that emotional relationships are essentially risky and painful, and if possible, to be avoided. As we have already suggested in Chapter 3, these are the children (and eventually, the adults) who find it hard to cope with close relationships, and will seek to avoid getting close to others, or, alternatively, may feel so desperately unhappy about being on their own that they will cling to any relationship rather than risk being alone.

Hence children develop a variety of reactions when separated from the person or people to whom they are attached: they may tolerate quite long separations reasonably well, or they may become very distressed even at the shortest separation. Which reaction predominates will depend a great deal on their early experiences of attachment. But in addition to their own feelings about separation, the child also learns from the reactions of others about whether it is safe and desirable to be alone. Here, the feelings of the carers themselves about being alone have an enormous impact on the child. If, for example, the mother feels anxious about the whole idea of separation, either because she herself is not entirely confident in the strength of her attachments to others, and whether these attachments will survive separation, or because she is frightened of what the world outside might do to her or to the child with whom she identifies, then she will convey a message of danger to the young child.

This message is given far more strongly to girls than to boys, especially as mothers often tend to identify much more closely with daughters than with sons, simultaneously wanting to protect them from the world, and to keep them close in order to meet their own unmet needs (see Nancy Chodorow, 1978). Numerous studies have shown that from babyhood onwards, girls are encouraged to stay much closer to their mothers than are boys; for example, they are encouraged to return more frequently to their mothers, and are rewarded much more positively for evidence of dependency (see Sue Sharpe, 1976). As we have argued earlier, because of the mutual identification between mother and daughter, boundaries between them may also be somewhat blurred, which again leads to problems over separation (see also Luise Eichenbaum and Susie Orbach, 1983).

Hence the dangers of separation are made extremely clear to the girl child, while at the same time emphasis is placed on her relative weakness and inability to look after herself physically or morally. In particular, as she grows older, she learns that her sexuality is a precious commodity which renders her especially vulnerable to being abused or led astray, and hence that she must be protected, usually from dangers which are not clearly specified, but have something to do with men and sex. On the other hand, most boys and men are portrayed to her both by her parents and by stories, films, and other media as being strong and brave protectors who will guard her from all hazards, and will guide and structure her life for her own good, against the minority of wicked seducers before whom she is helpless, given the weakness of her sex. Her father, in particular, is portrayed as the source of protection and safety (even if in reality this is far from the case) and as being the one to safeguard her from her own nature as well as from others. Further, the girl child is also promised that at some point in the future, another man will arrive and take over the parenting and protecting role, and to symbolise this, she will abandon her father's name, and take her new husband's.

The psychological consequence of this for the developing child is to confirm her own anxieties about being separated, and further to underline the fact that she cannot, by herself, be truly safe, since unlike a boy, she does not have the strength to defend herself against the physical, sexual, and moral threats that exist outside her family. Moreover, the girl rarely has the chance to discover that in fact she could look after herself quite adequately, since she is infrequently left on her own or sent out by herself, and receives little training in the practical skills of life such as how to unblock a sink, how to do even simple car maintenance, or how to negotiate with officialdom (see also Sue Sharpe, 1976). As we have said in previous chapters, there is of course a paradox here, as the girl child often has considerable responsibility for looking after others, such as younger siblings; yet as a girl, she is judged as being in need of protection and care by others who are seen as being stronger and more competent than she is. In addition, she often has the burden of looking after her own mother emotionally, which further bolsters her fears of separation from her mother, because of the hurt that this might cause to her mother. Conversely, a little boy is often encouraged to be his mother's protector although he is a small child and she an adult woman, while paradoxically, he is usually given less real responsibility for other children or domestic matters than his sister, takes little emotional care of his mother, and is often actively encouraged to break away.

Psychological consequences of being a single woman

We shall now turn to an examination of some of the psychological, social, and practical consequences of being single. The psychological consequences of the attachment process that we have described on p.197 is that as adults, few women feel fully confident in their ability to look after themselves without some recourse to others. Some women feel unable to remain alone by themselves at all, and will go to enormous lengths to avoid spending a night in their own homes by themselves. Others will refuse to go out of the house on their own, and will feel painfully conspicuous unless with another person. Few women feel totally comfortable eating a meal in a restaurant by themselves, or going out to the cinema alone. Yet being alone and feeling entirely comfortable with it is not at all unusual in men.

There are at least two major reasons for this. The first is quite straightforward, which is that most women are aware that there are very real dangers for them when they are on their own, of unwanted attention, harassment, and even rape, as we have discussed in Chapter 4. The second (which we shall look at in more depth) is more psychological in nature. As already noted, early childhood experiences of separation and the anxiety surrounding them are restimulated when in adult life the woman finds herself temporarily or permanently 'unattached'. Irrespective of her own feelings about her ability to cope, or her enjoyment of being independent, she is very likely at some point to re-experience some of the fears which first occurred in childhood, especially if the period of being unattached is prolonged. The result is a feeling of submerged (or even overt) panic, a sense of being folorn and unloved, and a distinct awareness of impending danger. None of these reactions may be appropriate to the true adult situation of the woman, but they nevertheless emerge from deep within the woman's early emotional experiences. This is likely to be the case, even for women who have chosen to be single because relationships seem to be too costly and difficult.

Even if a woman is aware of all these issues, and does feel reasonably confident both in her ability to establish good personal relationships with others if she so chooses, and also in her ability to live by herself, nevertheless she is likely to be aware that if she lives alone, she is doing something which is not really expected of women. Because of the widespread assumption (which we discuss further on p.203) that all women will be connected to a man, a woman who does not choose to do so, or who has not yet found anyone with whom she does wish to live, is likely to feel, at the very least, somewhat uncomfortable with her state. Further, since parents usually expect their daughters to get married, they may express their disappointment when this does not happen, often discounting other achievements in their daughters' lives. Parents may also express their sadness about a lack of grandchildren. As we saw with Sally, the woman's resultant discomfort may stand in strong contrast to some of the positive experiences which she has of living alone, such as being fully in control of her spare time, her money, and her home.

In some instances, there may also be a very real regret that personal relationships are so difficult, as shown by a deep sense of sadness or loss. This is particularly the case when the woman has withheld from intimate relationships because of a fear of hurt and loss if and when a relationship ends. In addition, as women approach the end of their childbearing years, there may be an intense need to develop a relationship within which parenting is a possibility.

However untrue or irrelevant any of these issues may be for an individual woman, by choosing to be, or having to be on her own, a single woman is, in addition, having to face and cope with issues of personal and sexual identity which are not faced by most women safely 'in a relationship'. For a start, a single woman is unable to rely on a partner to meet some very crucial emotional needs, besides those of practical help and some degree of companionship. In particular, the single woman does not have the constant 'mirrorring' or feedback which a permanent relationship provides, and which, like the prototype which occurred in early infancy with her mother, can supply the woman with ongoing validation and confirmation of her identity and value within the relationship. This is not to say that the mirrorring process is always positive: in some relationships it may be destructive and hurtful. Nevertheless it exists, and helps the woman to maintain some sense of daily connection with her emotions and senses. For while in a warm, loving relationship the partners are able to provide each other with reassurance and confirmation, and in a cold or antagonistic partnership the couple provides at least a hard image of inadequacy and hurt to each other, the absence of a partner means that *nothing* is automatically provided, which can sometimes seem even worse.

This then means that the single woman must rely heavily on her own resources to provide herself with confirmation and validation, using resources such as her friends, her work, and her leisure activities to meet some of this need for confirmation of self. If she has a reasonably strong sense of identity and self-love, this absence of another will not be too troublesome; however for some women, especially following divorce or bereavement, the loss of this 'mirror' will be totally devastating, until another way of meeting her need for psychological and emotional validation has been found.

A tragic example of a woman who is unable to summon up any internal or external resources when she is left alone is that provided by Simone de Beavoir in her novel *The Woman Destroyed*. In this story, de Beauvoir describes with great sensitivity the pain and emptiness of the wife whose husband leaves her for someone else, and who is then unable to find any other source of meaning for herself. Towards the end of de Beauvoir's story, the unhappy wife is unable to summon up any internal resources, and, unwilling to look outside herself either, remains hollow and utterly demoralised:

> Before, I used (not) to come out of my burrow very often, but when I did I was interested in everything – the countryside, people, museums, the streets. Now I am a dead woman. A dead woman who still has years to drag out – how many? Even a single day, when I open my eyes in the morning, seems to me something whose end I can never possibly reach. In my bath yesterday the mere act of lifting my arm faced me with a problem – why lift an arm: why put one foot in front of another? When I am by myself I stand there motionless for minutes on end at the edge of the pavement, utterly paralysed.
>
> (de Beauvoir, 1971:219)

Either by necessity or choice, therefore, the single woman has to develop a stronger sense of self than her married sister. For some this will be quite simple, as having a very clear sense of their own self-worth, they will not need any bolstering of self that can come from living with an intimate partner. Others will be able to develop emotionally rich relationships with friends or children, which will meet most of their needs as effectively as a relationship with an intimate partner could have done. But for others, this will be a relatively difficult task, and only achieved with pain and immense effort.

Social consequences of being single

In previous centuries, single women were seen as a considerable economic burden, and parents went to great lengths to ensure that their daughters obtained suitable husbands who could provide for them. Of course this was a problem of society's own making: a society which paid women very substantially less than men, or even forbad them economic independence, inevitably meant a society in which women were seen to be economically draining. Finding a husband in these circumstances then became the understandable preoccupation of many young women and their parents. In poorer cultures, where the discrepancy between the positions of men and women were even greater than in the affluent countries, women were effectively given away only with the inducement of a dowry. (This is still the case in some parts of the world today, with tragic consequences for some young women who have been murdered because their in-laws have considered their dowries to have been insufficient.)

In western cultures, the search for a suitable husband is, of course, the substance of many romantic novels, and is an added component of the 'romantic myth', described in Chapter 3. But seeing women's need to find a husband as the central issue of romance in fact conceals the social prescriptiveness of marriage, based largely on society's pressure towards stability, and which is actually a more important basis of the romantic genre of literature. An additional fact which is often overlooked is the man's requirement to find some way of meeting his dependency needs. To this day, many people assume (wrongly) that men are not really interested in marriage, but must be 'trapped' into it by women, who are then assumed to be the prime beneficiaries of the marital state. Yet plenty of evidence exists that men benefit enormously from marriage, in terms of mental and physical health (see, for example, Michael Argyle, 1987; Jessie Bernard, 1975; Elisabeth Douvan and Richard Kulka, 1979; Julian Hafner, 1986), besides the economic and social benefits that men gain from having an unpaid housekeeper, social secretary, entertainer, and child-minder often constantly available at home.

It is perhaps worth commenting further here on the apparent reversal of popular image and reality when it comes to the respective value of marriage to men and women. Jean Baker Miller (1976) points out that dominant classes are most successful if they can convince subordinate classes that the subordinate class's inferior position is in fact the best one open to them, and that the dominant class is actually doing the subordinate class a favour by engaging in relationships with them. This conceals the need that the dominant class in fact has of the subordinate class, and ensures that the subordinate class will continue to ask to be subordinated. It is clear that men as a group have been extremely successful at convincing women that it is women, not men, who want and benefit from marriage!

No matter how absurd this reversal, the consequences of the emphasis on the importance of marriage for women is to make a women without a man feel as if she is violating some strong and natural law, and is in fact, socially a failure. It is of course the case that social changes mean that a woman living alone today is more acceptable than she would have been many years ago, but the sense of social awkwardness often experienced by many single women still remains. At the same time it was understood in previous years that if a women was single, to a certain extent it was not her fault, since wars and colonial expansionism meant that there was a real shortage of marriageable men. Now however, when the numbers of each sex is more or less equal, to be single is assumed to imply some perversity or other personal fault; hence the single woman is more likely to be blamed personally. The woman may then turn this back on herself: because she is aware that she is violating social expectations, which suggest that all women should if at all possible get themselves a man, and that those who do not do so must be unattractive, perverse, too choosy, or even, rather masculine, she may come to doubt her own femininity and worth to the rest of society.

In virtually all societies, the nature of a woman's connection to men is very carefully marked. Her married name immediately indicates the man to whom she is primarily attached, and her title also indicates whether she is married or not. Conventionally, she also wears a ring, which in an often unrecognised way symbolises her bondage in marriage, and which confirms publicly her marital status. None of this applies to men, clearly demonstrating the lesser importance to society at large of ascertaining a man's connection to a woman. Interestingly, many women today are refusing to change their name upon marriage, and although this is tolerated, it is often seen as a slight upon the husband and as evidence of poor commitment on the part of the wife to the marriage. In British law, for example, people may call themselves whatever they wish: a person's legal name is simply what he or she is commonly known by. Yet this is not appreciated by many women, who are discouraged (mistakenly) from being able to retain their own name, by fear of the legal complications which are said to follow, and by strong social disapproval. The refusal by other women to indicate publicly their marital status (as either Mrs or Miss) is also greeted by extraordinary heat, indicating that this apparently simple matter conceals a suprising degree of threat to existing patterns of social dominance and control.

Even if her singlehood is actively chosen, as in the case of Sally, the single woman may find the assumptions readily made by others extremely irksome. For example, she may be at the receiving end of numerous questions such as 'Where is your husband?' or 'Have you got a boyfriend?'. For the woman who is longing to form an intimate relationship, such questions can be extremely painful, as she finds in them evidence of her inability to attract the sort of man she wants, while for the woman who is reasonably happy in her single state, they can be impertinent and insulting. In addition, some women will be at the receiving end of some rather obtrusive match-making by their friends, whether it is wanted or not, while others may find that they are never invited to social occasions except, perhaps, when a 'spare' woman is needed to balance the numbers.

Positive aspects of being single

Having pointed to some of the psychological and social problems involved in being single, it is crucial also to point to some of the very real benefits for women from staying, or becoming single. For many women, being independent and totally responsible for themselves is far preferable to the dubious privilege of being an unpaid housekeeper and source of sexual relief to a man who offers little in terms of affection or company in return. For some, it is simply an easier way of life, without the emotional or sexual complications which restimulate earlier pains and hurts. For others it is a way of dedicating themselves to their work, or some cause or belief system without the distractions of an intimate personal relationship. But whatever the reason for choosing to remain unattached, it is undoubtedly the case that the single life can have some very positive benefits for women, ranging from a greater sense of self-respect, to the opportunity to practise an increased range of practical skills and abilities. Throughout history, pioneering single women from a range of disciplines have made significant contributions to the life of their communities – as teachers, doctors, explorers, and so on. Indeed, until recently, many of the professions have been closed to married women.

Another positive consequence of being unattached is that the single woman is likely to develop herself in ways which are not open to the woman in a long-term relationship. Single women who are reasonably adapted to or happy with their state are more likely than their married sisters to be psychologically andro-gynous, that is, to possess both traditional masculine and feminine psychological characteristics, and hence to be capable of acting or feeling in stereotypically masculine ways (such as being self-reliant, independent, assertive, and emotion-ally resilient), as well as in stereotypically feminine ways (such as being emotion-ally responsive, kind, and imaginative). The androgynous woman thus has many more psychological resources upon which to draw, and hence has the scope to become more effective than the stereotypically 'feminine' woman in a wider range of situations (see the discussion by Jeanne Maracek, 1979). Her emotional and personal life is therefore likely to be somewhat richer, and based on a more secure personal foundation. In fact, a number of studies have shown that, in a whole variety of situations, the androgynous woman is happier, mentally healthier, and more in control than the stereotypically feminine woman (see, for example, Sandra Bem, 1974; Janet Spence, 1979; Jenny Williams, 1984).

In addition, research has shown that the self-concept of many single women belies the social image of the unhappy or bitter divorcee, spinster, or widow. Lynn Gigy (1980) compared the ways in which two groups of single and married women over the age of 30 saw themselves, and found very few differences between the two groups except that the single women placed more value on personal growth and assertion than the married women. Beverly Hoeffer (1987) also looked at the outlook of different groups of women in mid-life, depending on their present and past marital status, and found that never-married women were healthier, less lonely, and more positive about life than widows. There were, however, few differences in outlook between the married women and the never-married women. Sophie Loewenstein (1981) and her colleagues studied the satisfactions and stresses of single women in mid-life and found that the majority were highly satisfied with most aspects of their life. Only 15 per cent, a figure comparable with the general population, had low life satisfaction. However, there were some specific areas of dissatisfaction (such as being celibate), a point to which we shall return later.

Another interesting point which contradicts many familiar assumptions about unhappy, disappointed single women is the evidence that in terms of mental health, single women are relatively favoured. They are less likely than married women to suffer from depression or agoraphobia (see Julian Hafner, 1986). Conversely, as has already been noted, single men are significantly less mentally and physically healthy than married men, again suggesting that marriage is particularly beneficial to men, but has some serious psychological drawbacks for women (see also Jessie Bernard, 1975; William Gove, 1976). Married women also have less legal protection than single women in some spheres: for example rape in marriage is not a crime in most western 'developed' countries.

Practical consequences of being single

Few *married* women can be unaware of the frustrations and annoyance resulting from institutional discrimination which occurs against them on legal, economic, and social grounds, for example, when their husbands are assumed to be the head of the household and therefore responsible for all legal and economic matters connected with the home. Yet single women also suffer discrimination; for example, it is much harder for a single woman to get a mortgage than a single man, and single women who are parents and claiming social security payments are the subject of considerable scrutiny, often amounting to harassment from state officials in order to ensure that they are not illicitly cohabiting. This is because it is assumed that if a woman has a sexual relationship with a man, he must be supporting her economically, and hence she must be claiming social security payments fraudulently. If she is assumed to be cohabiting, her payments will be reduced or even abolished completely.

There are other costs, too. Single people of both sexes are subject to the financial penalties of not being part of a couple: hotels and holidays are much more expensive, as are single portions of food. For those who live entirely alone, normal household expenses such as standing charges for fuel or the telephone are much greater because they are not shared. Although this obviously applies to both men and women, the fact that women earn so much less than men (see Chapter 5) means that it is primarily single women who suffer financially. Most single-parent families are headed by women, and they and their children make up the majority of people living below the official poverty line (see Mary Langan, 1985). There are consequences for retirement too: quite obviously, never-married women will not benefit from a husband's pension in their later life, while divorcees may receive only a reduced pension, even if they have devoted the majority of their lives as unpaid housekeepers for and assistants to their ex-husbands.

On the other hand, single women are often far more competent and skilled in practical matters than their married sisters. Because there is no-one else around to write to the taxman, to change the fuses, to make decisions about purchases for the house, and so on, a single woman has to be more self-reliant. For newly widowed or divorced women, the sudden need to deal with the practical aspects of life can be experienced as a terrible shock, occurring at the same time as having to adjust to the loss or departure of a loved one. Yet after the initial jolt, women on their own often display a far broader set of personal abilities than that shown by single men, and have the opportunity, denied to many women in relationships, of developing their abilities in a wide variety of fields from car maintenance to family financial adviser (see the excellent self-help manual for newly single women by Jean Shapiro, 1985). Like the single women we considered earlier, women who find themselves alone after the end of a relationship are often then able to develop a range of competencies rarely fostered in married women.

Different reasons for being single

There are a variety of reasons for being single, which have somewhat different consequences for each woman involved. We shall now look at some of the main forms of the single state which, although not always the case, tend to be linked to the age of the woman involved: for instance, widowhood is statistically far more common in older than younger women. The majority of the examples that we shall discuss concern heterosexual relationships, although it is quite clear that the experience of the loss or death of a lifelong lesbian partner is just as emotionally devastating as divorce or widowhood: in fact the lack of social recognition of the loss of a lesbian partner can sometimes make the process of grieving even more difficult to accomplish. Likewise, adapting to the single life is likely to be just as hard for a lesbian who really wishes for a partner as it would be for a heterosexual woman, with the added complication of social disapproval, and lack of easy access to places in which she can find a partner.

Being 'between' relationships

In her study of poorly qualified teenage school-leavers, Sue Lees (1986) reports on the enormous pressures on girls, coming from each other and from their families, to 'find a boyfriend', and eventually, to settle down in marriage and motherhood. Lees reports that the girls often viewed marriage and household drudgery as inevitable, to be accepted with cheerful resignation. Most of the girls hoped that the boy in question would not be exactly like their own fathers, and would help with the children and housework, but most of them did not question the need to gain the apparent status of 'having a steady boyfriend' and eventually, a husband. Although this study looked at young women with almost no educational qualifications, with few career prospects ahead of them, not dissimilar feelings are often expressed by young women with far more opportunities open to them. For at least some young women, having a boyfriend is seen during the teenage years as a goal in itself, such that being 'between boyfriends' is a cause of regret and shame. As already mentioned in Chapter 2, relationships with other girlfriends may in many ways be more rewarding, but the young woman is aware that she ought if at all possible to find herself a boyfriend. This is not to deny that some of the heterosexual relationships which develop at this time can be enormously positive too, especially when the young couple become sexually involved, but we want to emphasise that conforming to social pressures at this time can be at least as important for some young women as the real emotional commitment to a particular young man.

Even for the young unattached woman in higher education, there is often a sense of panic towards the end of her college years if she has not yet found a permanent relationship. She may see her friends getting married (there is often a spate of weddings in the year after a group of friends from college disband, following graduation) and wonder what is wrong with her. She (and other women of her age, from all sorts of social and educational backgrounds) may well have had a series of boyfriends, but none of the relationships have lasted for any length of time; alternatively she may have had one steady relationship which ended at the same time as college ended. In either case, she may well feel that although there is still 'plenty of time', she must be alert to all the opportunities open to her. Some women at this point may feel somewhat cautious of all relationships, but at the same time, may long for some emotional stability in their lives. Yet others may simply enjoy a period of sexual and emotional experimentation.

The majority of women do get married at some point during their lives, although a growing proportion live with their partner before getting married, and a greatly increasing number are likely to get divorced. The age of a woman's first marriage has been steadily decreasing over the past decade: for example in the UK in the 1970s it was 23.6 years, while in 1984 it was 22.6 (*New Society*, 1986). But remarriages are also more common, such that 35 per cent of all marriages now involve at least one partner marrying for the second time. What this means is that for those who do *not* get married, live with someone, or have a permanent relationship, as the years go by there is a growing awareness of being someone rather unusual. For those who have chosen to devote their energies to their career or some other enterprise, this decision will have fewer negative consequences than it will for those women who suddenly feel very lonely and anxious about their ability to establish the sort of relationship they would like. An additional problem is that the number of unattached men suddenly drops: the average age for British men to get married for the first time is now 24.7 years, hence the numbers of never-married men in their thirties is very small. One of the consequences of this is that, as we saw with Ann in Chapter 1, a single women over the age of about 30 is more likely to find herself involved with a man who is already married, with all the heartbreak that can result from such a situation, or with a man who is divorced and may already have children from a previous marriage, than with a man who has no previous commitments.

For a woman who really wants to find someone with whom she can establish a home, and possibly have children, being 'between relationships' can be very distressing. Although she may have a large number of supportive friends, and a very interesting job, she may well feel rather lonely, and aware that she is lacking the sense of being physically and emotionally special to someone. For some women, this sense of loneliness can be highly distressing, such that they may feel utterly worthless, and that their whole existence is futile. They may find themselves getting involved in a number of highly unsatisfactory and damaging relationships, just in the hope that someone might turn out to be the right one. The lack of physical comfort and sexual closeness can also be experienced as a very significant loss, leading to feelings of uselessness and unhappiness. Some women may even seek psychiatric treatment, believing they must be sick to feel and behave as they do. Others may turn to various forms of alternative therapy, feeling that perhaps they do not exude sufficient sexuality, or that they are too demanding upon men. Yet others may decide to avoid men altogether, simply concluding that 'all men are bastards anyway'.

It must, of course, be noted that by no means all women without a permanent relationship feel this way. Some women are very happy with their independence, and feel no need whatever to tie themselves down with a man and children. They may decide that there is plenty of time to find the right person in the future, or, like Sally, that life is much more tolerable if conducted without any permanent ties at all. If they have just ended an involvement with someone which has lasted for any length of time, they may simply feel delighted that they are now 'free' to live life as they please. They may wish for some casual relationships from time to time, but do not want anything which might involve commitment.

Chosen celibacy

Some women decide that the costs of intimate relationships with other people are too high, and opt for celibacy instead. This may be a decision taken early in life, before any sexual contact has happened, or later, after the end of a relationship or following bereavement. For many women, the decision to remain celibate is an enormous relief, freeing them from a miserable round of attempts to find a suitable partner, with apparently inevitable hurts and humiliations. For others it is a relatively difficult decision, as it means renouncing the pleasures of sexual relationships, but nevertheless, allows other aspects of life to develop. For yet others, it isn't really a choice, but just happens because of the lack of suitable partners. However, in none of these cases does a life of celibacy mean that the woman is without sexual feelings; rather that sexuality with another person no longer has a place in her life. For example, Sally, whose story we told at the beginning of this chapter, felt very strongly that celibacy was currently right for her, even though she had enjoyed sexual contact with men, and still felt attracted to some men on some occasions. But on the whole she found that the consequences and complications of becoming sexually involved were too great, and distracted her from other, more important aspects of her life. In a similar vein, Marjorie Calow wrote in her account of her decision to remain celibate:

> Now that I have realised my time is finite, I know other things are more important ... now I am no longer willing to spend time and money on men. I am finding more and more that I prefer friendship to sex – and friendship with women. So many men are pompous and there are a lot of interesting women around that I want to get to know better.... Because I *know* the pleasure that sex can give, I *also* know that my decision to lead a celibate life is a decision made in full possession of the facts.

> (Calow, 1984)

Celibacy does not mean that the woman has no sexual life at all however, since as we discussed in Chapter 4, she may still gain considerable enjoyment from masturbation. Indeed, for some women this will be more satisfactory than was their experience of sexual relationships with others. Through masturbation, a woman may be able to attain greater sexual pleasure than ever before, without any of the need to adapt to the needs of others, or to submit to sexual practices which she may not have enjoyed. Nevertheless, the absence of a regular sexual partner was one of the regrets mentioned by the single women in the study by Sophie Loewenstein and her colleagues (1981) mentioned earlier. This was found to be especially so for women without young children, probably because being alone means having little physical contact with others, whereas having young children normally also means giving and receiving plenty of physical affection.

One last reason for staying celibate is that a woman simply may not feel attracted to men, and yet does not have the courage, in a prejudiced society, to explore her sexual attraction to women. Such women are tragically paying the price for the limitations of tolerence in our social world. Therapeutic work with women in this situation is sometimes needed so that they can explore their feelings and gain the courage to discover whether sexuality with another woman is what they really want. Often it is sufficient, however, if they are able to meet other lesbians who can help them to take the risk of openly acknowledging their sexuality.

Divorce

It is a commonplace observation that divorce is becoming more and more frequent. American statistics suggest that over 40 per cent of new marriages are likely to end in divorce, while in the UK, one in three marriages are likely to end in this way. The time taken to divorce varies according to whether or not there are children involved, and social class: couples with children stay together twice as long as those without children, while unskilled or manual workers get divorced sooner than those in the professional classes (*New Society*, 1986). It is very hard to estimate the pain and distress involved in the growing divorce rate: no divorce or separation is painless, in that it involves at the very least the disappointment of hopes and the disruption of quite a number of subsidiary relationships. Some divorces are totally devastating, and result in bitter feuds which can last for decades. Nevertheless, it is also the case that untold misery exists between couples who cannot divorce for moral, social, or religious reasons, or because one partner effectively vetoes it. In addition, for some women, especially those who married young or have no children, divorce can be an immense relief, as well as an opportunity to learn more about themselves.

However, it also remains true that for most women, divorce is costly in a number of senses. It hits women especially hard, because of both the financial penalties and the burden of emotional failure. In the UK, for example, there are about one million single-parent families, nine out of ten of which are headed by women. Over 50 per cent of these are poor, and in the case of divorced families, the majority are considerably less well-off than when the family was together. Jackie Burgoyne (1987) describes in her study of single parents how much of the effort and energy of these parents (usually women) is spent, first, in obtaining an adequate standard of living, and second, in trying to create as normal a family life as possible, in part through the acquisition of material goods which are often assumed to be necessary for successful family life.

Even more demanding than this, however, is the practical struggle to be in at least two places at once: to hold down a job and yet to fetch the children from school; to develop some kind of independent social life and yet to be constantly available to the children; to do the housework and yet to play with the children as much as children from two-parent families are played with. In a study of recently divorced women, Mavis Hetherington and her colleagues (1978) found that a central problem was the sheer number of tasks to be completed on a daily basis: the women felt worn out by simply keeping the household going. In addition to the practical problems of dealing with children, there are also the emotional difficulties that can occur, especially if single mothers experience increased difficulty in parenting their children with confidence and enjoyment (see also the discussion in Chapter 7, p. 179).

Emotionally, divorce hits very hard too. Taught since early childhood to be responsible for the emotional happiness of others, women tend to try much harder than men to keep relationships going, even if they are painful and difficult, and to take the blame when things go wrong. This does not mean that women are faultless in their relationships; like men, they may cheat, lie, deceive, and seek to avoid responsibility. However, women are much more likely than men to initiate marital counselling or to seek personal therapy if a relationship is not working, and will persist in trying to understand and talk about the problems much longer than their husbands or lovers. It is true that women are much more likely to be the ones to sue for divorce; nevertheless, this may result from an agreement between the couple to preserve the woman's social position (that is, to save her from the label of 'jilted woman') than because it reflects the true state of their relationship. Alternatively, it may reflect the fact that women tend to suffer more emotionally when the relationship does finally go wrong, and are hence more eager to make a clean break. Yet another explanation could lie in the fact that men are actually more dependent on the conveniences provided by marriage than women, and are more reluctant, when the crunch comes, to risk the end of the relationship. This last explanation is supported by the evidence that a divorced man is much more likely to get married again than a divorced woman.

Divorce or separation also causes a change in the way the woman views herself. She loses her identity as a married woman, and has to rediscover herself without the prop of a recognised social status. This is especially difficult for women who have been married for a long time. Mavis Hetherington and her colleagues (1978) reported that despite an initial burst of frenetic activity and an ebullient sense of freedom during the first few months following the marital break-up, the newly divorced women whom they studied saw themselves as less physically attractive and competent than before the divorce, and as more helpless and apprehensive. They also tended to feel more apathetic and depressed about the future. Nevertheless, Hetherington reports that as she develops new interests and intimacies during the years after the divorce, the woman gradually feels better, although periods of gloom and self-blame recur, especially after contact with her ex-husband, or when she learns that he has remarried or started living with someone else.

Some of the other emotional issues involved in the break-up of a relationship have already been discussed in Chapter 3, as well as in the section p.206 on 'being between relationships', so they will not be repeated here. But one common thread which is worth restating is how clearly the pain which the woman feels in the present recapitulates her distress when faced with losses which occurred earlier in her life. Marriage or cohabitation is usually undertaken in a spirit of hopefulness and trust, so that even if the relationship has caused her considerable pain, the loss of the relationship leads inevitably to a sense of betrayal and disappointment. This sense of loss resonates very clearly with earlier senses of loss and betrayal, and as we have shown repeatedly, adult responses to loss will be attenuated when earlier losses have been unresolved. Especially if the marriage or relationship has ended because of the man's involvement with someone else, the woman is likely to feel rejected and insecure. She most probably entered the marriage with the hope that her needs for security and emotional closeness would be met, and yet this has not happened. Instead, she has been betrayed, and as may have happened in her infancy, the person she depended upon and loved most has turned their attentions to someone else. She may feel that early childhood fears that she is a worthless, valueless creature who is undeserving of love, have been only too clearly confirmed. As a consequence, her anxieties about being separate will re-emerge, which both confirm her sense of her own worthlessness, and cause her to feel anxious and desperate about her ability to cope in the future. This sense of failure is, of course, even more marked for someone who has found herself caught up in what appears to be a repeating pattern, as we noted with Ann in our opening chapter. Of course the current trend towards serial monogamy is likely to increase the numbers of people who spend some of their adult life on their own in this way, and hence to increase the amount of self-doubt that can result, although there may also be an increase in greater self-knowledge gained after the struggle to regenerate a sense of stability, which usually occurs when people are on their own.

Such feelings are, of course, less common if it is the woman herself who has initiated the split. Nevertheless, issues of dependency and the need for emotional closeness are still highly relevant. The woman may have found that, despite her initial hopes, this particular relationship has not met her needs, and she has turned to someone else. Alternatively, her anxieties about her own ability to be separate have led her to choose a partner, who, in the long run, suffocates her and fails to allow her to develop in the way she wishes. Hence, she has had to leave the relationship because she no longer feels in charge of her own life, and may then also doubt her own ability to form other more satisfactory relationships. In either case, the balance between the desire for intimacy and separateness has been lost, such that the woman's emotional needs are no longer being met within an existing relationship, which then leaves her with considerable emotional uncertainty about the future.

Widowhood

Most married women will eventually be widowed, both because they live longer than their husbands, and because they tend to marry men older than themselves. Emotionally and practically, widowhood usually has an enormous impact on a woman's life. First and foremost, the widow has lost the person who has probably been closest to her: her life companion, lover, and friend. Even if the relationship has not always been fulfilling to her, she is nevertheless likely to feel her husband's loss as an absence of something very important, which gives structure to her life. Her reaction is likely to include feelings of intense sadness, loss, resentment, and grief, which may last for the rest of her life (although for some women it may be relatively short-lived). Younger women are usually the most severely distressed by widowhood, probably because the death was unexpected, and seems particularly unjust.

The grief process has been ably described by many writers, such as Colin Murray Parkes (1970) and Elisabeth Kubler-Ross (1969). It is seen by most theorists as consisting of a number of discrete stages of emotional experience, developing from numbness and denial, through a stage of yearning and 'searching', to a stage of gradual acceptance. A study of 72 widows by Peter Marris (1958) showed that a number of problems were common, such as difficulty in sleeping, obsessive attempts to keep the husband's memory alive, and a terrible fear of going insane because of the severity of the grief. A common observation is also the prevalence of health problems in the newly bereaved, as well as the fact that many older widows die within a few years of their husbands' death.

Together with her grief at the loss of her husband, the woman may also feel intensely lonely. She may be actively avoided by her family and friends who don't feel able to cope with her grief, or she may simply find she is no longer invited out, since she is now a 'spare' person around the dinner table. Helena Lopata (1970) has described widowhood as an event resulting in a loss of social roles, as the woman loses the status of being part of a couple, and becomes an object of pity and guilt. The study by Peter Marris (1958) mentioned earlier also found that a widow often becomes much more isolated after the death of her husband, seeing much less of her husband's family, and surprisingly, no more of her own. One myth of widowhood is that a solution to the problem of loneliness would be for the widow to get 're-attached'; yet Marris's study also found that the majority of widows did not want to remarry, feeling that another marriage might betray the loyalty and love they felt for their husbands. Interestingly, however, widowers are much more likely to remarry, although this may simpy reflect the greater numbers of older women than men.

Widowhood also brings considerable economic problems. There may be a legacy of bills because of the husband's terminal illness, plus the costs of his funeral. For many women, pension arrangements will be barely adequate, while for those whose husbands die young, maybe leaving dependent children, there may be no financial provision left at all. Sudden poverty is therefore added to the woman's grief. But in addition, many women who had not taken an active role in the running of the practical side of their lives, perhaps seeing this as a 'male domain', or having been actively excluded by their husbands, are suddenly thrown into a world which they may not fully understand. They may be faced for the first time with the need to deal with the tax and social security systems, plus the economics of the household, all of which their husband had previously handled.

The importance of these issues is supported by a study conducted by Carol Barrett (1979). She asked a group of American widows what advice they would give to other women whose husbands were still living. Their replies fell into two categories. First they urged other women to learn financial management and to become familiar with the economic side of life. In addition, they advised keeping occupational skills alive, so that the women could earn a living independently if they so chose. Second, the widows urged other women to stay as psychologically independent as possible, to develop their own friends and hobbies, and to have a life which they could enjoy on their own. This suggests that those women who maintain their own skills and interests in life cope much better with bereavement than those who are totally dependent upon their husbands. The problems faced by most widows thus reflect the problems faced by women in other spheres of life; that is, the stereotyped woman who shows all of the socially desired feminine traits (for which she may have been rewarded) such as dependence and subservience to her husband's needs, is singularly ill-equipped to cope with life on her own.

In addition to all of the psychological difficulties posed by separation, which we have discussed previously, widowed women have the same psychological problem of social stigma as other single women, in a couple-oriented society. Most widows hate the term 'widow', seeing it as a constant reminder of death, and as an indication of their status as a no-longer-complete person. However, it must also be noted that for some women, widowhood allows a degree of freedom not experienced before. Carol Barrett (1979) in her study described finding the occasional widow who was jubilant in her personal growth and ability to cope on her own. Some widows are able to build supportive networks between themselves, and hence to find fulfilment in relationships with other women in similar circumstances, which was simply impossible earlier in their lives. Such women are actually happier and more fulfilled in widowhood than marriage, although this does not necessarily mean that they do not miss and grieve for their dead husbands.

Of course it is not only married women who have to face the loss of their lifelong partners. In particular, lesbian women who lose their partners through death suffer not only the same intense grief as widows, but, for many, there is little understanding by others of the extent of the loss, especially if the relationship has been concealed. For some relatives and friends who disapprove of the relationship, the death of the woman's lover may remove an embarrassment, which hardly helps the grieving woman. Some women may obtain sympathy and understanding from their friends, but the bereaved woman is unlikely to be allowed the same tolerance from employers or officials that a widow might. In addition, some cohabiting lesbians who have failed to register their joint home in both their names may face eviction on the death of their lover, at the same time as coping with their emotional loss. Others may have to face disputed wills, and possible financial ruin.

Therapeutic implications

Single women may enter therapy for any number of reasons, which may have little to do with their unattached status. For others, however, being single can be an issue in therapy, and it is upon these women that we shall concentrate in this section. It may be that the woman is finding it difficult to deal wih loss, following divorce, separation, or bereavement. Or she may want to understand why she is unable to find the kind of relationship which she feels would make her happy. Alternatively, she may seek help with one of her children, being aware that the absence of the child's father may be a significant factor in family functioning.

As in all therapies with women, key issues are likely to be concerned with separation, the importance of the recognition of emotional needs, and the development of autonomy. Many traditional therapies, however, ignore these underlying issues, and have assumed that the problems of single women can invariably be explained by the lack of a man, so that the answer to her unhappiness should be to increase her physical attractiveness and social skills, or to decrease her supposed hatred for or fear of men. Such therapies misunderstand both the complex nature of the evolution of feelings about intimate personal relationships, and deny the woman the opportunity to make an informed decision *not* to form a couple relationship with someone else.

Therapy with women who find relationships difficult

In therapy with a single woman who is unhappy, the therapist must be alert to the woman's current experiences of singlehood, and be careful not to make assumptions about the cause of any unhappiness about her situation. Like Sally, many women do not consider that 'finding a man' is what they want, but instead want to improve the quality of their relationships with others. Nevertheless, it is often helpful to explore, with the woman, the nature of her early experiences in relationships, in order to discover what intimacy means to her. As we said in Chapter 3, important issues from childhood tend to re-emerge in later relationships, and a woman who becomes aware of repeating patterns in her relationships (like Ann in Chapter 1, for example, who always chose men who were married or otherwise unattainable) may find that there are some issues from the past which need some exploration. It may be, for example, that because of conflicts with her mother or father during the process of separation in infancy, a woman who finds herself in a relationship is very frightened of losing her hard-won sense of independence, and hence chooses men who cannot threaten this because they are unavailable most of the time. Yet this can also cause her great unhappiness, as she longs for more of their company, and regrets the pain that she is causing her lovers' wives. Therapy must therefore consist of disentangling her fears about intimacy and reassessing what she does and does not want from her relationships.

Because of the social pressures which have always surrounded her, and which convey the message that a woman is not really complete without a man, it is sometimes hard for an unattached woman to feel comfortable about her single state. Luise Eichenbaum and Susie Orbach (1983) point out that 'women's second class position in patriarchal culture is reflected in their psychology' (p.139); hence women alone often fail to feel whole in themselves, and easily feel insecure and rather abandoned. These issues are readily uncovered in therapy.

Yet particularly if she is in therapy with a woman therapist, the single woman may feel apprehensive about her growing feelings of dependency on her therapist, as this experience may well recapitulate earlier conflicts of emotion with her own mother. Further, the woman may fear that her dependency signals her immaturity and inability to attain autonomy. The therapist has to help the woman to learn, through the therapy relationship, that feelings of dependence are not harmful, that engulfment need not result, and that maturity comes from acknowledging, not denying, her feelings. Furthermore, therapy can help the woman to learn that mature dependence does not mean either loss of autonomy, or a failure to establish personal boundaries. Nor will it mean that she can never separate from her therapist. When the woman has been able to learn this, through her relationship with her therapist, she becomes able to separate and to terminate therapy, without pain, and is then more freely able to choose whether or not to commit herself fully to an intimate relationship, rather than to avoid too much intimacy at all costs. A therapist who assumes that the answer is 'to find a man' risks ignoring the woman's own wishes for her future, and fails to pay sufficient attention to the deeper concerns that the woman may have about herself and her adequacy as an autonomous person, irrespective of the relationships which she chooses to establish.

Therapy with bereaved or divorced women

Although issues of separation are still salient, conflict over the ability to maintain intimate relationships are unlikely to form the basis of the concern expressed by a woman who is single because of recent bereavement. She may, however, seek help in order to assist her in coping with the stress and pain of her loss, which she may find very hard to bear. She may feel that without her dead husband or lover, life is no longer worth living, and that she would be happier dead. Similar concerns may of course be expressed by women whose husbands or lovers have left them. These are not trivial problems: suicide attempts are not uncommon amongst both bereaved women and deserted women (see David Lester, 1983).

Therapists may therefore be approached for help by bereaved women who want to rediscover meaning and purpose in their lives. It is crucial, however, that this search for meaning does not replace the need for the woman to grieve for her loss. One recent therapeutic approach for bereaved people has been the work of Frederick Melges and David Demaso (1980), who offer therapy which centres on issues of loss and death for those who have failed to grieve adequately for their loved one, and who need to repeat the grieving process in therapy with the support of a secure relationship. Other developments have included cognitive therapy with the elderly bereaved, who no longer feel that life is worth living. As we shall also note in Chapter 9, therapists such as Dolores Gallagher and Larry Thompson (1982) and David Cooper (1984) have developed ways of working specifically with elderly people, which aim to help them to rediscover joy in life, despite their losses.

It is essential that therapists who make use of any of these therapeutic aproaches also take into account some of the psychodynamic issues which we have already mentioned, as well as recognising both the pervasiveness of the social disrespect which exists towards widows and single women, and their economic problems. Additional pharmacological help should only be used with caution: medical professionals are often somewhat unhelpful with bereaved people, by an over-eagerness to prescribe tranquillising drugs, which can actually delay the process of coming to accept the loss.

Family therapy with single women

Some single women come for help, not for themselves, but for their children. For example, a recently divorced or bereaved woman may find that her son or daughter has suddenly started to behave disruptively at school, or has recommenced bed-wetting. Some family therapists, for example Anita Morawetz and Gillian Walker (1984) have developed forms of family therapy specifically for single women and their children. Such therapists believe that the absent father is a crucial member of the family, even if he has had no contact with his children since conception. Working on the need to strengthen the family structure, and give more confidence to the mother, these therapies can be very helpful to women on their own, as they do not insist that the only effective family is one with a father present. Of course there are some family therapists who may make this assumption, and these are likely to be profoundly unhelpful to single women (see the discussion by Rachel Hare-Mustin, 1978). But by acknowledging the nuclear-family oriented social world in which these single-parent families exist, family therapists can help the woman and her children to establish satisfactory ways of living for themselves which meet the needs of both children and mother.

Being a lone parent involves assuming both financial and emotional responsibility for children. Whether chosen or not, such responsibility is often hard to sustain, especially in a society which tends to pathologise single parents, and views the single-parent family as an unnatural and undesirable form of family organisation. Women who seek therapeutic support in their parenting often need to be convinced that they are doing a good job, since they frequently feel criticised and unable to assess how competently they are managing. Women bringing up sons alone may be particularly anxious about the lack of a male parent, especially at times when their sons begin to question their authority, and express extreme disobedience or even violence. Therapeutic support here may require showing women ways to strengthen their authority without having to resort to male authority figures. Sometimes, however, a male family therapist may be able to perform this function, allowing the mother time to regenerate her own strengths, as long as in doing so he does not undermine her own position. On the other hand, mothers of daughters may be concerned about how to provide positive images of men, especially if their own relationships with men have been unhappy. They may also be fearful for their daughter's safety, and need another adult with whom to discuss ways of achieving a balance between over-protectiveness and abandon when caring for their daughters.

Despite the stresses involved, many single women find that they appreciate the special relationship which they can develop with their children when they are the sole adult in the family, particularly following the end of a turbulent relationship with another adult who may not have contributed much towards, or disagreed about, parenting the children. Problems may then arise for the woman in allowing her children to separate, and here again therapeutic support can provide the woman with a context within which to explore her feelings about being left by her children.

Group work

Other therapies which can be helpful to single women include group therapy or support groups for women who are facing similar problems, for example, the discussion groups held by Carol Barrett (1979) for widows. She reports that such groups help widowed women to develop self-confidence, and to learn about the practical side of coping alone, as well as to forge new networks of intimacy. Similar groups have been established elsewhere for single parents and newly divorced women. For example, Tricia Bickerton (1983) has reported on groups for women alone in which she has helped them to explore the strengths and weaknesses of their position. She claims that it is particularly difficult for a single woman 'to discover her own self-esteem or separate from another, to enjoy her aloneness, to care for and nurture herself' (p.160), and has devised a series of exercises to help women to re-examine where their sources of support actually can come from, as well as to uncover their inner strengths.

By sharing their experiences in this way, single women learn above all else that they are not abnormal, and that relationships apart from those with a husband, lover, or cohabitee can be satisfying and fulfilling. They can then learn to build a sense of self-esteem which comes from within, and is not entirely dependent on the presence of another.

Concluding note

As we have said, being alone is something that most women will face at some stage of their lives, particularly as they grow older. For older single women, therefore, the difficulties of being alone can be almost indistinguishable from those faced by all older women, in a society which is not only couple-dominated and patriarchal, but is also youth-oriented. In the next chapter, therefore, we shall look in more detail at the experience of women in their middle and older years, as well as considering the therapies which are available for them.

References

Argyle, M. (1987) *The Psychology of Happiness*, London: Methuen.

Asendorpf, J. (1986) 'Shyness in middle and late childhood', in J. Kagan and J.S. Reznick (eds) *Shyness: perspectives on research and treatment*, New York: Plenum Press.

Barrett, C.J. (1979) 'Women in widowhood', in J.H. Williams, (ed.) *Psychology of Women: selected readings*, New York: Norton.

Bem, S. (1974) 'The measurement of psychological androgyny', *Journal of Consulting and Clinical Psychology* 42:155–62.

Bernard, J. (1975) *Women, Wives and Mothers: values and options*, Chicago: Aldine.

Bickerton, T. (1983) 'Women alone', in S. Cartledge and J. Ryan (eds), *Sex and Love: new thoughts on old contradictions*, London: The Women's Press.

Bowlby, J. (1969) *Attachment and Loss*, vols 1 and 2, New York: Hogarth Press.

Burgoyne, J. (1987) 'Material happiness', *New Society*, pp. 12–14, 10 April.

Calow, M. (1984) 'The five ages of woman', *The Celibate Woman* 2:31–2.

Chodorow, N. (1978) 'The Reproduction of Mothering: psychoanalysis and the sociology of gender, Berkeley: University of California Press.

Cooper, D. (1984) 'Group psychotherapy with the elderly: dealing with loss and death', *American Journal of Psychotherapy* 38:203–14.

de Beauvoir, S. (1971) *The Woman Destroyed*, Glasgow: William Collins.

Douvan, E. and Kulka, R. (1979) 'The American family: a twenty-year view', in J.E. Gullahorn (ed.) *Psychology and Women: in transition*, Washington, D.C.: Winston Holt.

Eichenbaum, L. and Orbach, S. (1983) *Understanding Women*, Harmondsworth: Penguin.

Fairbairn, W.D.R. (1952) *Psychoanalytic Studies of the Personality*, London: Routledge & Kegan Paul.

Gallagher, D. and Thompson, L.W. (1982) 'Treatment of major depressive disorder in older outpatients with brief psychotherapies', *Psychotherapy: Theory, Research and Practice*, 19:482–90.

Gigy, L.L. (1980) 'Self-concept of single women', *Psychology of Women Quarterly* 5:321–40.

Gove, W. (1976) 'The relationship between sex roles, marital status and mental illness', in A. Kaplan (ed.) *Beyond Sex-Role Stereotypes: reading toward a psychology of androgyny'*, Boston: Little Brown & Co.

Hafner, R.J. (1986) *Marriage and Mental Illness*, New York: Guilford Press.

Hare-Mustin, R. (1978) 'A feminist appproach to family therapy', *Family Process* 17:181–94.

Hetherington, E.M., Cox, M., and Cox, R. (1978) 'Stress and coping in divorce: a focus on women', in J.E. Gullahorn (ed.) *Psychology and Women: in transition* (1979), Washington, D.C.: Winston Holt.

Hoeffer, B. (1987) 'Predictors of life outlook of older single women', *Research in Nursing and Health* 10:111–17.

Jeffreys, S. (1985) *The Spinster and Her Enemies*, London: Pandora Press.

Kubler-Ross, E. (1969) *On Death and Dying*, New York: Macmillan.

Langan, M. (1985) 'The unitary approach: a feminist critique', in E. Brooks and A. Davis (eds) *Women, the Family and Social Work*, London: Tavistock.

Lees, S. (1986) *Losing Out: sexuality and adolescent girls*, London: Hutchinson.

Lester, D. (1983) *Why People Kill Themselves: a 1980's summary of research findings on suicidal behaviour*, 2nd edn, Springfield, Illinois: Thomas.

Loewenstein, S.F., Bloch, N.E., Campion, J., Epstein, J.S., Gale, P., and Salvatore, M. (1981) 'A study of satisfactions and stresses of single women in midlife', *Sex Roles* 7:1127–41.

Lopata, H. (1970) 'The social involvement of American widows', *American Behavioural Scientist* 14:41–58.

Maracek, J. (1979) 'Social change, positive mental health and psychological androgyny', *Psychology of Women Quarterly* 3:241–47.

Marris, P. (1958) *Widows and Their Families*, London: Routledge & Kegan Paul.

Melges, F.T. and Demaso, D. (1980) 'Grief-resolution therapy: reliving, revising and revisiting', *American Journal of Psychotherapy* 34:51–61.

Miller, J.B. (1976) *Towards a New Psychology of Women*, Harmondsworth: Penguin.

Morawetz, A. and Walker, G. (1984) *Brief Therapy with Single-Parent Families*, New York: Brunner/Mazel.

New Society Database (1986) 'The marriage stakes', *New Society*, 2 May.

Office of Population Censuses and Surveys (1983) *General Household Survey*, London: HMSO.

Parkes, C.M. (1970) 'The first year of bereavement', *Psychiatry* 33:444–67.

Shapiro, J. (1985) *On Your Own*, London: Pandora Press.

Sharpe, S. (1976) *Just Like a Girl*, Harmondsworth: Penguin.

Spence, J. (1979) 'Traits, roles and the concept of androgyny', in J.E. Gullahorn (ed.) *Psychology and Women: In transition*, Washington, D.C.: Winston Holt.

United States Bureau of Census (1984) *1980 Census of the population* (PC 80-1-DI-A), Washington D.C.: U.S. Government Printing Office.

Williams, J. (1984) 'Women and mental illness', in J. Nicholson and H. Beloff (eds) *Psychology Survey*, 5, Leicester: British Psychological Society.

Zimbardo, P. (1977) *Shyness: what it is and what to do about it*, Reading, MA: Addison-Wesley.

Chapter nine

Older women

Peggy's Story

I finally met Peggy after she had cancelled three previous appointments, saying she felt too unwell to make the journey across town to see me. Her doctor, who felt that Peggy needed to be 'counselled' rather than have medication prescribed, had originally advised her to make the appointment. I was, in a sense, a last resort, since the doctor felt that if Peggy's symptoms became any worse she would have to be given a course of antidepressant medication, or else hormone replacement therapy. For Peggy, aged 50, was experiencing very distressing menopausal problems and was becoming depressed.

At first it was difficult for Peggy to talk about herself: she somehow couldn't find the words she needed and was obviously unused to talking about her own problems. So I asked her to start by describing the main events in her life. She told me how she had left school at the age of 15 and had gone to work in the upholstery section of a large car factory. Here she met the man who was to become her husband, and who worked in the paint shop. She was married at the age of 19 and had four children in fairly quick succession, two boys followed by two girls. She continued to work part-time until the youngest girl went to school, when she took up a full-time job again. Her mother had looked after the children while she was at work. 'She was a real blessing,' said Peggy, 'I couldn't have managed without her. My husband never helped much around the house or with the children, apart from taking the boys out to watch a football match sometimes.'

Peggy's mother had obviously provided her with a lot of support, especially when, after about fifteen years of marriage, Peggy had finally decided to leave her husband. 'He'd been running around with other women for years', explained Peggy, 'probably ever since I met him. Once the kids were old enough to look after themselves a bit, I decided I'd had enough.'

Peggy described the ending of her marriage as if it were a closed book, and it certainly didn't seem to be the cause of her current distress. For now it was Peggy's mother, Amy, who was causing Peggy the most problems. Amy was in her eighties, and until recently had apparently been a sprightly and energetic woman who had always helped out with her many grandchildren. But two years ago her husband, Peggy's father, had died. 'After that she seemed to go to pieces,' said Peggy. 'She didn't do her housework properly, wouldn't eat regular meals, just had little snacks in front of the television. The neighbours complained because of the noise, as her television was on very loud all the time.'

Peggy looked exasperated as she recounted how hopeless she felt her mother's condition was becoming:

I finally decided that she must come and live with us. Our house was big enough, now that the three eldest had left home. There was just Tina, the youngest, who'd just left school and was unemployed, and Bill.

I asked who Bill was. 'He's the lodger,' said Peggy, looking embarrassed. 'Well, you could say that. Mum calls him my boyfriend, but it's not like that. He has his own room.'

Bill had moved in with Peggy five years ago when his own mother had died. He was a bachelor, and had been devoted to his mother. He had lived around the corner, and Peggy explained how they had become friendly when he was made redundant. They had often met when out shopping, and Peggy described how she felt sorry for him when he was left alone after his mother's death. She had eventually offered him a place in her house, as the rent he contributed helped to pay her bills. She was also glad of the company, although at times she found him rather irritating. But Peggy's mother had refused to accept this relationship. She had been a practising Catholic all her life, and although she had helped Peggy through her divorce, claiming that Peggy's husband had 'never been up to much good', she would not accept Bill.

So Peggy's home life was complicated and stressful. There was Tina, her youngest daughter, unemployed and bored, who also seemed to be rather resentful of Bill, and about whom Peggy worried a great deal. There was Amy, Peggy's mother, who ignored Bill's presence and complained to Peggy that she was 'living in sin' and setting a 'bad example' for Tina. Then there was Bill, who despite Amy's treatment of him, was kind and gentle, and treated Amy like his own mother, bringing her tasty food to eat and finding the right TV programme for her.

I asked Peggy who she went to when she needed to talk about all of these stresses, or about her physical problems. 'There's no-one really,' said Peggy:

I couldn't talk to Bill about when I feel bad. I'd be too embarrassed. He's never been married, and he doesn't know anything about women's problems. My mother isn't interested in anyone but herself. And Tina tells me I'm imagining it all, and that I'm going soft in the head.

It was, apparently, this last taunt that had finally persuaded Peggy to come and see me. She initially thought I was a psychiatrist and would be able to tell her if she was really going mad. I explained to her that I wasn't a doctor, but a psychotherapist, and together we might be able to sort out what could be causing her physical symptoms by talking through her current life situation. Peggy agreed that she didn't really have anyone else to talk to, but for a long time she was very reticent about unloading her worries on to me. For a while she seemed to treat me like one of her own daughters, although there was hardly ten years' difference in our ages. She even found it difficult to describe her bodily symptoms to me, although she was very worried about still having very irregular but heavy periods. She was also concerned by bouts of hot flushes and night sweats, which she said would overcome her sometimes two or three times a week. In the night she was drenched, and would have to change her sheets, sometimes several times a night. Although talking about these symptoms embarrassed her, she found it easier to discuss them than to talk about her other problems.

Eventually I asked Peggy to try to think if there was any relationship between the tensions at home and her physical symptoms. At first she couldn't see any connection, but after she had been coming to see me for a couple of weeks she said that things did seem worse when her mother or Tina were 'playing up'. I asked her what they did that was so problematic.

'My Mum's beginning to lose her memory,' she explained:

She gets very confused. Sometimes she thinks Tina is me and tells her off for being around the house and taking so much time off work. This sends Tina crazy. She shouts at Mum and calls her a silly old fool. Then Mum gets all upset, and talks to me as if I was Gran, that's her mother, who's been dead for over thirty years.

Peggy said that she felt desperate at times. She often felt so ill herself that she couldn't cope with all the bickering at home. Bill didn't help much either, as he would often mope about how much he missed his own mother. I pointed out to Peggy that she was very busy being everybody else's mother – not only for her own children, especially Tina, but also for Bill by replacing the companionship of his lost mother, and now she was having to mother her own mother too. I added that she had even been trying to mother me by protecting me from the worst of her problems. Peggy laughed wryly as she denied this, but agreed that she did feel very responsible for everyone.

Over the next few sessions Peggy and I decided that there were some practical things that she could initiate to try and improve her situation. First, I told her about a group for menopausal women which met regularly at a local health centre, which Peggy agreed to find out about. Then she decided to arrange a meeting with a social worker to enquire about the possibility of finding sheltered accommodation for Amy. In the event, Peggy felt that she couldn't go to the group meetings. 'I can talk to you', she said 'but I wouldn't want to talk about my problems to a whole load of strangers.' Nevertheless, she did succeed in persuading the social services to look into the possibility of some sheltered accommodation for Amy, and she also came away from the health centre with lots of information about coping with menopausal problems, especially concerning dietary changes and the use of vitamins, such as vitamin E. She was impressed by the dietary advice, and started to make sure that all the family ate more wholesome food. 'I've never eaten very well,' she said. 'My ex-husband always wanted chips and pies, things like that. But eating well doesn't cost much more really, we can afford it if it makes us healthier.'

Indeed, it did seem that the vitamin E and healthier food eased her symptoms, and her hot flushes were occurring less regularly. She also said she felt better for having someone to talk to, although she was still finding it difficult to talk about her own feelings.

A shift in our relationship finally occurred when one day I unexpectedly had to cancel an appointment. One of my own children had become ill at school, and I had to go and collect her. When I next saw Peggy, her attitude towards me seemed to have changed. 'I didn't know you had children,' she said. 'You don't wear a ring or anything.' Her knowledge that I was a mother myself, and therefore somehow of an equal generation to her, seemed to release her from the responsibility of 'mothering' me and protecting me from her distress. She visibly relaxed, and for the first time was able to talk about her own childhood.

'I was only a little girl when the war broke out,' she explained:

Dad was called up straight way and sent out east. We hardly saw anything of him for six years. When he came back, he was like a complete stranger. He frightened us children sick. He was very thin, and spoke in a loud voice. Often he'd have nightmares, and scream out loud and wake us all up. I can't say I was ever very close to him. I was just glad to leave home and get married, although that turned out to be a big mistake.

Peggy spent a long time talking about her husband, and the fact that he, like her father, but for different reasons, was 'absent'. 'He was a big man,' she said:

I suppose I wanted someone I could depend on. But in the end I found out that he was weak and selfish. He couldn't resist a pretty face, and didn't really care about me and the kids. Since we've been divorced, he's never sent a penny, and never been to visit the kids. They say 'good riddance'. But I worry about how it will affect them. My boys have got kids of their own now and I worry a lot that they won't be good fathers themselves. There're like me, they've never really known what a 'Dad' was.

Slowly, Peggy was able to express the pain of her losses, especially the absent father and absenting husband. She was also able to grieve for her father's death. 'At the time I was just worried about how my Mum would cope,' she said:

I was right to worry, because she just went to pieces. But because I had to busy myself with her I didn't really have time to think for myself about my Dad going. I just had to make all the arrangements; she couldn't do anything.

Peggy's concern about her mother had also led her to cover up a lot of anger, which she allowed no-one to see:

When I get really mad with her, I take myself off to the park. Sometimes my Mum really makes me see red. If Bill and I are in the same room together, she won't even let us talk to each other. And he won't say a word against her! Sometimes I wish we'd never offered to have her. I really hope the social services comes up with some sheltered housing for her soon.

Expressing this anger in sessions with me initially made Peggy feel very sad, and guilty. But the resurfacing of her feelings about her father, together with the release of her anger towards her mother, gradually allowed her to find a balance. 'I've lost my Dad', she said, 'in fact I never really had him, so I suppose I might as well make the most of Mum before she dies too.' Hence it was that when the social services department finally said that there might be a place for Amy in some sheltered accommodation nearby, Peggy decided to turn it down. 'She's looked after me and the kids all these years,' she said, 'it's the least I can do, to look after her now.'

Fortunately, at the same time, a number of other significant changes also took place in the family that considerably relieved the tensions at home. Peggy's improved health seemed to help Tina to make more effort to take decisions about her own life. It was as if Tina had been unable to make the decision to separate from her mother until her mother was more settled, and only then was she finally able to decide she wanted to leave home. She had found a job as an au pair in Canada, and although Peggy was intially unsure about Tina travelling so far away, it was all finally agreed when Peggy found that a cousin of hers, who lived in Canada, would be near enough to be able to be in regular contact with Tina. With just three of them in the house, Peggy, Bill, and Amy, life slowly became less stressful. Peggy felt more able to cope with her mother's lapses of memory, and now that Tina was no longer at home, Amy herself was less critical of Bill's presence. Bill continued to provide companionship and support for Peggy, and helped her to care for Amy.

Peggy then decided that she no longer needed to see me, but continued to write me a letter each Christmas to give me news of herself and of her family. The last letter I received said that Amy had died, peacefully, and at home, following a serious attack of 'flu. Peggy described how relieved she was that she had been able to look after her mother right up to the end.

Women in their later years

In writing about older women, we have now reached what is perhaps for us the most difficult part of our work in this book. For whereas between us we have lived through or are currently having a good number of the experiences described in previous chapters, we are only just approaching that stage of our lives known as middle age, and old age is still in the future. We can no longer therefore describe or analyse the information from first-hand experience, and will have to rely more heavily both on academic research and on how other women describe their lives.

However, there is unfortunately a remarkable lack of material, either academic or personal, on which to draw. Although an enormous amount has been written about the first half of the life span, until very recently it seems as if there has been a conspiracy of silence about growing older, suggesting a widespread view of the second half of life that it is somehow less valuable or important than the first half. Athough it is in the middle and later years that the prejudices and problems of women reach their zenith, so far even feminism has done very little to combat the ageism of society at large. We are aware that we, too, are guilty of reflecting these assumptions about women's lives, since we have devoted almost the whole of this book to younger women, and most of this chapter will concern the middle-aged, rather than the elderly. But this dearth of critical writing about older women will hopefully change, partly because many academic researchers and writers are now beginning to recognise the importance of old age, and partly because those of us who were young in the 1960s and 1970s are now approaching our middle years, and are therefore beginning to describe and research the physical and emotional changes that ageing will bring to us.

In this chapter, we shall examine some of the social and psychological factors which structure women's lives in their later years. We shall start by looking at the demographic, economic, and social position of women in these years, before turning to a discussion of some of the restrictions on women's personal development which frequently occur during middle age. These restrictions take two main forms: first the continuing levels of responsibility for others often shouldered by middle-aged women for their teenage children and for their own ageing parents; and second, issues relating to women's health, especially the bodily changes associated with the menopause. We shall then turn to an examination of the effects of retirement from paid work, and some of the psychological issues likely to concern women in the middle and later years. It will become clear that emotional and personal development is as crucial at this point of life as at any other, even though the opportunities and support for such personal change is often limited. Next we shall look at some of the more positive aspects of later life, such as the opportunity it may provide for spiritual and emotional exploration. Then, as in other chapters, we shall conclude by suggesting some of the therapeutic implications that follow from our analysis.

The demographic and economic position of older women

It is now widely recognised that demographic changes are leading to a growing proportion of older compared with younger people in the population of most advanced countries: the 'greying of the nation' as Lily Pincus (1981) has called it. For example, it has been estimated by the UK Central Statistical Office that in 1982, there were more than 8.4 million people in the UK over the age of 65 years, a figure which is likely to increase by the year 2000 to 9.5 million. Meanwhile in the United States, the number of elderly people is likely to reach over 32 million by the year 2020 (see B. Pesznecker and E. Zahlis, 1986). Since women on average live longer than men, they account for the majority of this ageing population.

Robert Woods and Peter Britton (1985) point out that the number of over-80s is also likely to increase very dramatically, and that this may result in 'specific problems for the elderly woman left on her own, in accommodation which had previously contained a family' (p.6). As a group, elderly people are much more likely than younger people to have problems with their housing, mobility, and financial security, and this is especially true for the elderly woman. For example, 47 per cent of women over the age of 75 live on their own, compared with 27 per cent of elderly men; and 31 per cent of women over the age of 85 living on their own need help to go out, compared with 16 per cent of men (see Woods and Britton, 1985).

Demographic and economic changes have also affected middle-aged women. Increasing divorce rates, the growing acceptability of one-parent families, the decreasing birth-rate, and increased family mobility have all meant that women are more likely now than in other eras to be living on their own in their middle years, or at least to be living without any dependent children (see Carol Nadelson, Dereck Polonsky, and Alice Matthews, 1979). For the single middle-aged woman this means that she is more likely to have to rely solely on her own income, and, as we shall see, that often means a life of comparative poverty. For others, however, especially if married, the freedom from the demands of children can mean that the mid-life is a time of relative affluence. But middle-aged women as a group are nevertheless likely to be considerably poorer than are middle-aged men (see also our discussion in Chapter 5).

The social position of older women

Alongside economic marginality, for many older women there is a feeling of being socially marginal. Although this is obviously a generalisation, modern western society could be said to be characterised by a glorification of youth, combined with a lack of esteem for the accumulated experience and the wisdom of age, particularly if this is in the 'domestic' sphere of relationships and caring for others. The older woman may therefore feel that she is no longer wanted or needed by the rest of society, and that she does not have a valued place in the world around her. In addition, rapid technological changes can often induce her to feel anxiety or even panic, as she may not fully understand the increasingly mechanised and computerised world around her. Even the smaller routines of life may no longer feel safe. Corner shops and attended buses are rapidly giving way to the hypermarket and the private car, neither of which may be easy or possible for her to access. These experiences can add up to feelings of despair, in which the older person shuts herself off from new experiences, and as a consequence feels even more lonely and socially marginalised.

Even when societies face slower changes of life style, the contribution of older members is not always recognised. In her survey of anthropological data on old age as it is experienced in different societies around the world, Simone de Beauvoir (1977) has described the disparate nature of the attitudes and behaviours of the young towards the old. Whereas in some societies the older person is treated with respect and kindness, so that older people continue to fulfil important social functions such as handing on skills and knowledge, or using their position to advise, heal, or comfort younger members, in other societies those past their most productive years are rejected and despised. It is interesting to note that even in societies where the older generation is valued, elderly people are still dependent on the good will of those in their prime, who are usually those involved in productive work or paid employment, to maintain them in their position of respect. In a busy, competitive world, it is all too easy for this respect to vanish almost entirely, as it has done in many 'advanced' cultures today.

In addition to prejudice against them on the grounds of their age, older women, of course, also face prejudice on the grounds of their sex. In a society which places a relatively lower value on women than on men anyway, what positive attitudes there are towards the female sex can be seen to be reserved for younger women, at least when they are both healthy and beautiful. As a consequence, there is a tendency to ignore and oppress older women, who are often seen as being redundant, useless, and repugnant. Common stereotypes of older women include those of the 'old hag' the 'wicked witch' the 'stupid old bag', and the 'wittering old woman', images explored by Nancy Mayer Knapp (1984). Conversely, the older man, especially if he is rich and powerful, can generate an aura of virility, wisdom, and charm. Sexism, which operates throughout women's lives, therefore has a particuarly cruel effect on women as they get older.

Not surprisingly, as Susan Sontag (1979) points out, these attitudes encourage a climate of deceit: many women over the age of about 30 find themselves feeling both defensive and intensely uncomfortable when they are asked their age directly, and the vast majority will feel tempted either to lie or to deduct a few years when answering. Such defensiveness and embarrassment reveals very clearly the negative value that our culture places upon age, especially for women. Many women also attempt a number of subterfuges which allow them to 'pass' as being younger than they really are, a tactic vehemently denounced by Barbara MacDonald (1984). In particular, older women are often encouraged to make extensive use of expensive and totally ineffective cosmetics such as anti-wrinkle creams in order to try to conceal the natural changes of ageing. Yet the aggressive commercialisation of these so-called beauty products to eliminate wrinkles or restore hair colour, together with painful surgical interventions to remove sagging skin or unwanted layers of fat, merely encourage the fantasy of an elixir of youth.

Barbara MacDonald argues that the only healthy alternative for older women is to take pride in their years and to refuse the oppression of ageism. She describes the attempts to 'pass' as younger and the denial of one's age as entirely understandable, but as a most serious threat to women's self-identity:

> We attempt, of course, to avoid the oppressor's hateful distortion of our identity and the real menace to our survival of his hatred. But meanwhile, our true identity, never acted out, can lose its substance, its meaning, even for ourselves. Denial to the outside world and relief at its success ... blurs into denial (of ourselves).
>
> (MacDonald, 1984:55)

Restrictions on women's personal development in middle age

Although middle age could be a time for extensive personal development for many women, freed at last from early adult worries about identity, the duties of childrearing, or anxieties about possible pregnancy, the reality is that many women appear to have more, not fewer problems at this stage of their lives. We shall now examine two of these sources of worry: the continuing domestic responsibities of most women; and their health problems. Before we do so, however, it must be noted that not all women experience these events or changes as unreservedly bad: some will find the developments of middle age as positive and life-enhancing. For example, for some women like Peggy, taking responsibility for an elderly parent can be an extension of their mothering skills, allowing them to reciprocate the love they experienced as children. Unfortunately, this is not true for most women, however, because as we shall show, the economic, social, and emotional consequences of taking on this caring role are both punitive and restrictive.

Responsibilities at home for adult children and elderly parents

Earlier in this chapter we described how Amy, Peggy, and Tina, three generations of women in one family, experienced some of the conflictual developmental crises of adult womanhood. Tina was struggling to launch herself as an independent young adult, and at the other end of the life span, Amy was having to give up her autonomy and be cared for by her daughter Peggy. As the middle person in this triangle, Peggy seemed to be the one who was most stressed by the ambiguity of their intergenerational roles, which in turn often affected how she saw her therapist within the transference aspects of the therapeutic relationship. To begin with Peggy treated the therapist as her daughter, to be protected and shielded from the realities of life, like Tina. Later on, Peggy was able to rely on her therapist as more of an equal, since she recognised that as a mother herself, the therapist could probably understand the problems of mothering a teenage daughter. Finally, when her own mother, Amy, became more frail, and their relationship grew more problematic, Peggy could allow the therapist to care for her by giving her in therapy the space to express her grief for her lost parents: both her dead father and her ageing mother who was no longer strong enough to depend upon, and whom she would probably soon lose too.

Like many women during their middle years, Peggy was feeling responsible both for her children and her mother. Women in their mid-lives frequently carry not only the complexities of their children's ambivalent feelings about their independence, but they may also, like Peggy, have to take care of their own ageing parents whose dependence poses different limitations on their lives. As with all other aspects of women's family responsibilities, it is generally expected that women provide this service, not only for their own parents but often for their partner's parents as well. We shall now look at each of these responsibilities in turn.

Caring for grown-up children

Mothering teenage children and young adults poses particular difficulties for women, who are increasingly having to carry these parenting tasks single-handedly. Economic uncertainties and high unemployment, particularly amongst young people, are now affecting families from all parts of the socio-economic spectrum, in most developed countries. The unpredictability in the employment market and the continuing problem of inadequate education and training provision for young people, especially women, means that many teenagers, like Tina, are forced into continued dependence on their parents long after this is emotionally or socially desirable for either party. The consequence of this for the mother in particular can be a sense of frustration, coupled with feelings of loyalty and concern for the wellbeing of her children.

Often disparagingly called the 'empty nest syndrome' (Marjorie Lowenthal and David Chiriboga, 1972), the conflicts that some women feel about their young adult children leaving home can play a crucial role in determining the ease with which this transition is negotiated. Whereas in some families sexual rivalry and differences between adolescents and adults may provide an explosive mixture that results in young people being ejected from the parental home before they are ready, for others, the relative safety of the mother–father–child triangle or mother–child couple may hinder autonomous adult development. In such families, the children may feel unable to leave, both because of their own anxieties, and because of a sense of responsibility for their parents. In particular, young women may feel unwilling to leave their mothers. For example, like many children of lone parents, Tina felt both dependent upon and responsible for her mother, especially once her elder brothers and sister had left home. Young women in this position could be said to be mothering their own mothers, as Luise Eichenbaum and Susie Orbach (1982) have suggested.

It is sometimes claimed that women who do not work outside the home are more likely than working women to 'suffer' from the empty nest syndrome. Such women are then assumed to be to blame for retarding their children's transition to independent adulthood. However, there is no clear evidence that this is the case. The empty nest syndrome does not appear to be universal, and some women actually experience much more stress when their children return home (perhaps following domestic crises of their own, or because of unemployment) to create what Nancy Datan (1980) has called the 'crowded nest'. This suggests that for some women at least, far from being something which they cling on to, their domestic responsibilities for grown-up children are increasingly experienced as burdensome and restrictive.

Caring for the elderly

Possibly even more problematic for middle-aged women than the task of caring for grown-up children is the task of caring for aged relatives. The vast majority of elderly people in most western countries either live on their own, or with their families, and contrary to popular myth, are not dependent on the state for care. Some of those elderly people living with their families are in need of a very high level of support. In the UK, for example, Chris Rossiter and Malcolm Wicks claimed in 1982 that there were well over one and a quarter million people providing full-time care for dependants who were either elderly or handicapped. Further, many of those elderly people who *were* living on their own or with an elderly spouse were also in receipt of regular assistance from younger relatives, usually in the form of frequent visits and financial help.

What is perhaps most significant for our purposes about the figures provided above by Rossiter and Wicks is the fact that most of these elderly and handicapped dependants are almost solely the responsibility of women. It is quite clear, as one of us has pointed out elsewhere (Sue Llewelyn, 1989) that 'the burden of care is not equally distributed amongst family members; caring is predominantly a female occupation'. Again taking the UK as an example, in 1980 the Equal Opportunities Commission reported that over 70 per cent of carers of the elderly mentally infirm were women, while Muriel Nissel and Lucy Bonnerjea (1982) provided evidence which shows that over 50 per cent of wives looking after elderly relatives (who may actually be the husbands' parents) spent more than three hours per day in providing care, while their husbands did nothing at all. The economic cost to individual women can be enormous: the UK Equal Opportunities Commission showed that while 60 per cent of carers also have jobs, most of these jobs are part-time, while Nissel and Bonnerjea's study showed that any financial help available from the state did not compensate in any realistic way for loss of earnings or for the increased financial cost of looking after a dependent relative.

Even more significant, however, is the emotional cost of looking after a dependent relative. Alan Walker (1983), for example, has claimed that one in six women currently caring for the elderly at home in the UK are suffering from both physical and emotional stress, very probably with negative consequences for those who are receiving the care. Numerous studies (for example, those by Enid Levin, 1983; Dorothy Thompson and David Haran, 1985; Mary Gilhooley, 1984) have also provided evidence to show that many of those looking after a dependant themselves suffer from serious psychological distress. Results from one study in particular (Chris Gilleard and colleagues, 1981) showed that between 57 per cent and 73 per cent of carers themselves suffered from psychiatric symptoms which were sufficiently serious to warrant psychiatric help. Both the studies by Mary Gilhooley and by Chris Gilleard also found that those carers who were women suffered from more serious symptomatology than those carers who were men. Typically, men found it easier than women to go out and leave their dependant for short periods of time, and were thus more able to maintain their links with work or friends outside the home.

Caring for others can clearly be a very stressful business. But it is important to realise that there are many different sources of stress as experienced by carers, which obviously vary from person to person. Stress can best be defined as a transactional process (see Tom Cox, 1978) in which there is an imbalance between the demands made upon an individual and the resources that the individual has with which to meet those demands. The physical and emotional demands of caring for a dependant relative are very high, especially if that person is a spouse or parent (see, for example, Kristina Cooper, 1985, who describes very vividly the pain of caring for a loved one whose mind has deteriorated as a result of Alzheimer's disease). Feelings of guilt, anger, and hopelessness are likely to mingle with feelings of love, grief, and exhaustion. The resources with which to meet those demands are, however, limited. As we have already noted, carers and their families are often in economic hardship, and due to complicated bureaucratic procedures, they often fail to claim all the help to which they might be entitled (see the Equal Opportunities Commission, 1980). Many carers are also isolated from others; for example, Enid Levin (1983) found that 25 per cent of carers never left their elderly relative or spouse alone, while 50 per cent never left them alone for more than three hours. In addition, caring is often perceived as never-ending, with the only respite on the horizon being the death of the dependant, even though this death may bring the loss of a dearly loved one.

These conflicts are well described in Joan Barfoot's novel *Duet for Three* (1986). Here, Aggie, feeling betrayed by her ageing, increasingly incontinent body reminisces about her life, whilst June, her daughter, feels a mixture of loathing and concern in caring for the mother she never got along with or understood. June's desperate resignation to the fact that her life is passing her by as she rushes from work to home to care for her mother is contrasted with Aggie's feelings of youthfulness inside an ageing body. Joan Barfoot captures well the ambivalent feelings of both carers and cared-for, particularly the way in which earlier unexpressed resentments can influence the nature of the relationship. In this instance, June has never forgiven her mother for the disaster of her parents' marriage and her father's early death, which poisons the tender feelings she sometimes now has for her mother. Aggie has long retreated into gluttony to escape from facing up to painful disappointments in her life, which compounds the strains on her ageing body.

It is not surprising, therefore, that many women in their middle years do suffer from high levels of stress. The issue is similar to that posed by the problem of child care, which, as we have seen in Chapter 7, is generally performed by women who are paid either very low wages, or more usually, not paid at all. However, caring for young children, although demanding, is probably considerably less so than caring for an ageing, possibly dementing, relative or spouse, especially as the physical strength needed to lift and toilet a full-sized adult is obviously so much greater than a little child, and the rewards are often so much smaller. Yet even less help is available to women caring for dependent adults than to those caring for dependent children, and the job may go on, unchanging or deteriorating, for years.

Caring and loss

One of the most distressing aspects of caring for an older person is that the end of the task of caring often only occurs through that person's death. Death is a constant issue to be faced once a person has entered the middle years, since slowly, increasing numbers of loved ones are inevitably dying. This is likely to be particularly distressing when the lost person is a parent for whom the bereaved person has been providing care. Melanie Klein (1940), in writing about the process of mourning for lost loved ones, describes the way in which, as adults, this loss reactivates the earlier, infantile mourning that centred around what she has called the 'depressive position'. According to Klein, the child has to come to terms with the loss of the mother's breast or the comfort of the bottle in order to carry on with emotional development. But in addition, as we argued in Chapter 7, children's feelings of being securely 'held' emotionally, and then allowed to separate at their own pace, seem to be important determinants of how, as adults, people deal with loss.

Yet as we have seen in Chapter 7, many women have not consistently had this positive experience, and hence may suffer high levels of reactivated grief upon bereavement. The situation was more fortunate in the example given at the start of this chapter: Peggy's ability to come to terms with her mother's dependence upon her, once her grief about the loss of her father had been assimilated, was no doubt greatly helped by the basically good relationship she had always shared with her mother in the past. In Melanie Klein's terms, Peggy had a good 'internalised' mother that she could call upon to sustain her, and which she was able to make use of even after her 'external' mother, her real mother, was no longer able to perform this function. In addition, Peggy could make use of the 'mothering' provided by her therapist. But not all carers are in this position, and for them the job of caring is especially demanding, and ultimately, profoundly distressing.

Issues relating to women's health

The ending of women's reproductive cycle

The second of the restrictions which frequently limits the psychological development of women in their mid-lives is the onset of problems which occur as a result of physical ageing. For many women, these coincide with changes in their reproductive capacity, signalled by the menopause. In previous chapters we have discussed how women's lives are deeply affected by reproductive events, or transitions, and although we agree with Janet Sayers (1982) that a simplistic biological determinism is an inadequate theory on which to base descriptions of women's psychology, nevertheless we also recognise the influence that these bodily events have on the way in which women experience their lives. The menopause can be seen as the ultimate reproductive transitional experience, since it marks the ending of women's fertility. Emotionally, the menopause is likely to bring about a complex and ambivalent set of reactions. There may be relief from the threat of unwanted pregnancy; sadness at not being able to produce any, or any more children; anxiety about sexuality and attractiveness to others; and fears about the effects of ageing and the health risks associated with advancing years.

Like other aspects of women's biology, the menopause has been, until very recently, a taboo subject. Often considered to be 'unclean' during their menstrual periods, women have also been repudiated during the menopause. This negative view of the experience of a crucial phase in women's life cycle, and one which may last for many years, has often been internalised by women themselves, as the menopause is still a subject which is infrequently discussed openly. Like menstruation, childbirth, and lactation, women have been encouraged to conceal these physical events and not make their experiences public. However, in recent years, some women have tried to examine these issues more openly. For example, many self-help groups have been formed, focusing on menopausal issues, which have allowed numerous women to become more familiar with the psychological and physical effects of the menopause.

Besides providing a forum for the sharing of experiences, and the dissemination of information, these groups have also revealed a gap between much medical thinking on the subject, and women's own subjective experiences. Describing her findings from setting up such groups, Rosetta Reitz (1985), for example, has reported on the way in which women's experiences often differ from conventional medical descriptions. For instance, she has found that only about half of the women that she studied during the menopause ever experience the sudden rise in blood vessel dilation that results in what are called 'hot flushes', and fewer still experience the sudden perspirations that are known as 'night sweats'. Those women who do, she claims, can often be more effectively helped by dietary changes than by medical intervention, as was found by Peggy.

But of possibly greater significance is the way in which the 'medicalisation' of the menopause has made it appear as a pathological, rather than a normal process. The parallels with pregnancy and childbirth, indeed with all aspects of the female reproductive cycle, are all too clear and incontrovertable. Like pregnancy, the menopause is now conventionally viewed from a pathological perspective, such that the very language of current medically based descriptions of the menopause, such as 'vaginal atrophy', 'ovarian dysfunction', or 'hormone deficiency' irrationally compares the physiological state of older women with some 'normal' youthful average, or even worse, with the supposed equilibrium of the male. The pre-pubertal girl, for example, is not described as having ovarian 'dysfunction' or 'deficiencies' while she does not ovulate, she is merely at a normal stage of her development. Yet the same is not said to be true of the post-menopausal woman, who is seen as being 'deficient' because of her hormonal changes.

Rosetta Reitz (1985) argues that the bodily changes associated with ageing could be more helpfully seen, and described, as part of women's normal development. The fears engendered by a pathological approach, Reitz suggests, do much to exacerbate the symptoms of the menopause which, she claims, need not be as discomforting and unpleasant as is widely suggested. However, the predominant approach to the menopause remains the medical one. As with current practices in pregnancy and childbirth, the pathological perspective has lead to the widespread use of medical treatments, which are in many ways at variance with Reitz's developmental approach. In particular, the argument that menopausal women are 'deficient' in vital hormones such as oestrogen (the levels of which diminish once the ovaries cease monthly ovulation), has led to the development of hormone replacement therapy (HRT). Because lower levels of oestrogen are seen to be a problem, in HRT regular doses of artificial oestogen are given to women approaching the menopause in an attempt to mimic pre-menopausal hormone balances. Whereas the contraceptive pill artificially induces the hormone levels of pregnancy and hence inhibits ovulation, oestrogen replacement renders a woman's body perpetually in a 'normal' cyclic pre-menopausal state, for as long as the hormones are continued.

Whilst some women have undoubtedly found relief from menopausal symptoms by using this method, others have unfortunately found that the side effects of the therapy are as unpleasant as their previous symptoms. In addition, increased risks of endometrial cancer following hormone replacement therapy have led to concern over the possible iatrogenic effects (Barbara Seaman and Gideon Seaman, 1977). Hence HRT remains a highly controversial form of treatment.

As well as chemical treatments, surgical interventions are also being performed increasingly frequently to relieve women of menopausal symptoms, so much so that hysterectomy has become the most commonly performed major surgery in the USA, and recent estimates point to its increased use in the UK too (John Kincey and Thomas McFarlane, 1984). Most hysterectomies are performed on women under 50, for reasons which are not life-threatening. It is therefore of great concern that many women report feelings of depression and other signs of emotional disturbance afterwards, which might have been avoidable had the hysterectomy not been performed. For example, Donald Richards (1973) found that depression, defined in terms of doctors' prescriptions of anti-depressants, was more frequent and longer lasting amongst a group of women following hysterectomy than amongst a group of women of similar age who had not undergone the operation. This problem appears to be widespread, since as Kincey and McFarlane (1984) point out, higher levels of emotional distress are generally seen in both hysterectomy and other gynaecological patients, than in women of the same age undergoing non-gynaecological surgery.

Strong reactions to gynaecological problems are understandable from a psychological viewpoint. Loss of the uterus, as Beverly Raphael (1972) has argued, can been seen as a form of bereavement which needs to be adequately mourned like any other significant loss. Women who deny this loss or who in other ways defend against experiencing their grief, might therefore be expected to suffer more profound after-effects. All gynaecological problems are likely to have emotional repercussions, especially since issues of femininity, sexuality, and fertility are all concerned whenever women's reproductive capacity is being affected. Yet these factors are rarely taken into account when gynaecological surgery or intervention is being contemplated.

Interestingly, the question of whether the emotional distress precedes or follows the gynaecological problems often remains unclear. As we have seen with younger women (Chapter 2), converting emotional distress into bodily symptoms may in some sense be an 'easier' and more acceptable way of expressing pain than psychological suffering. Hence the middle-aged woman in distress may be more able to express her unhappiness through her physical symptoms than through the overt expression of emotion, such as depression, anger, or anxiety. Just as anorexia and bulimia are now understood to have considerable psychological components rather than being merely medical problems, so the psychological dimension of gynaecological disorders is now gradually being recognised (see Annabel Broome and Louise Wallace, 1984). Indeed, in considering the psychological effects of hysterectomy, John Kincey and Thomas McFarlane (1984) suggest that emotional problems seen after hysterectomy often reflect pre-existing difficulties, rather than the operation itself being a major cause of the subsequent emotional problems. They conclude:

> These findings lead to interesting speculation about the nature of the relationships between psychological problems, gynaecological symptoms and the subtleties of the decision-making process which leads the patient and her doctor to conclude that hysterectomy is appropriate for her.
>
> (Kincey and McFarlane, 1984:156)

This very clearly implies that a psychological understanding is vital before complicated and painful surgery or intervention is embarked upon. It also suggests that counselling should be available to all women involved in such surgery, should they wish for it.

Life-threatening illnesses

In the relatively small number of gynaecological operations that *are* performed because of malignant diseases of either the uterus or ovaries (which Kincey and McFarlane (1984) estimate as being the case in about 16 per cent of all hysterectomies) the woman concerned has to face the possible crisis of cancer. Psychological factors in the development and evolution of cancer have recently been the focus of much attention (see, for example, Cary Cooper, 1982; Martin van Kalmthout and Marina Kuyper, 1987; Paula Taylor, Dominic Abrams, and Miles Hewstone, 1988). Most research suggests that defensive attitudes and feelings of hopelessness are more marked in those people whose cancers progress more rapidly than in those whose cancers progress more slowly or remit. This has been highlighted in studies of women with breast cancer, where women who show high levels of defensiveness, who deny what is happening to them (for example, by indulging in comforting daydreaming), or who manifest feelings of helplessness, have a poorer outcome than women who confront and attempt to come to terms with their condition (see, for example, Mogens Jensen, 1987).

Cancer of the breast is one of the most serious illnesses likely to be suffered by women in their middle years. Treatment for this condition often, but not always, involves mastectomy, or removal of the breast. Women with breast cancer usually find that they have little time to prepare themselves for the consequences of having a mastectomy, nor do they usually receive much support in coping with the emotional reaction to the operation. Yet like hysterectomy, mastectomy is a mutilating operation which can significantly alter a woman's self-identity and self-image. Coming to terms with the loss of a breast involves for many women a major readjustment of their sense of who they are, and this will often involve renegotiations in personal relationships. In a society in which a woman's breasts are considered to be a vital part of her femininity, many women post-mastectomy are fearful of sexual contact with their partners, or of entering into new relationships. Unfortunately, women are usually encouraged to engage in a subterfuge which disguises the fact of the mutilation, which in itself may hinder psychological adaptation by encouraging the woman to maintain a defensive silence about her experiences. As with other cancer patients, a difficulty in openly confronting the event has been found in mastectomy patients (Colette Ray, 1977) which cannot be alleviated by treatments that focus on medical and surgical interventions alone. However, various forms of therapy have been designed to enable women to develop less defensive attitudes and actively confront their cancers, for example, that by Jo Spence (1986). We will discuss the contribution of psychologically based interventions further in the last section of this chapter.

Women's retirement from paid work

The shift from middle age to old age is often marked for men by their retirement from paid work. But despite the increasing proportion of women in the workforce, 'retirement' is still seen as a predominantly male phenomenon. The reasons for this are twofold: first, that the importance of work in women's lives is still often seriously underestimated, so that its termination is not seen as being a particularly important step; and second, that women after retirement from paid work often simply continue with their other unpaid job, that of housekeeper (see also Chapter 5). Their 'official' retirement is therefore often less visible than a man's. As a consequence, women are less likely than men to experience their retirement as a shock, and hence they may suffer less from some of the most immediate problems of retirement, such as boredom and feelings of uselessness. But they are also less likely than men to be able to enjoy the leisure and relaxation which the end of a working life could bring.

In addition, there are a number of significant differences between men and women in the resources available to them after retirement. Besides inequalities in pay and conditions of service throughout their working lives, even the age of retirement has in the past differentiated women from men, meaning that women have had to cope with the economic problems of retirement for much longer than do men. Further, private pensions are often lower for women than for men, and because they may have taken several years out of employment for child-rearing, women are often entitled to substantially less benefit than men. As we saw in Clare's case in Chapter 5, even those women who have not had time off to have children may have been excluded from company pension schemes, simply on the grounds of their sex.

For most men and women, retirement represents a marked reduction in income, particularly for those without the benefits of a private pension. Most people halve their income on retirement, which is of course especially hard on women who tend to have lower incomes in the first place. According to Paul Nathanson (1984), for example, less than 10 per cent of single retired women in the USA get any kind of private pension, while four-fifths of all single black women, and half of all single women over the age of 65, live in poverty. To take another example: in the UK, the 1978 report of the Diamond Commission showed that over half the retired are poor. Women, as at other stages of their lives, are over-represented in this category.

Although retirement could be experienced as a gain in terms of freedom from the constraints and pressures of working life, sadly it is more often perceived as a loss (see, for example, the personal account by Felicity Kaplan, 1982). Apart from financial penalties, retirement often brings about a loss of status, a lack of structure to the day, and the disappearance of friendships and regular contact with others. In a series of interviews with women aged over 60, Janet Ford and Ruth Sinclair (1987) found that, particularly for women on their own, retirement from work generated fears about loneliness and isolation. Many of the women felt unprepared to deal with this, and had not devised any effective strategies to improve their situation. Many were afraid to go out, and the majority were too poor to afford transport or leisure activities. Only those who were well served by local community resources, such as clubs and outings for pensioners, found that they could maintain some social contacts. Like women who give up work to stay at home with their young children, retired women who do not plan actively how to cope with their isolation risk facing empty days which they can only fill with repetitive domestic chores. Hence they may lose an important part of their self-identity and self-confidence, and eventually, their emotional and physical health.

In addition, for women who are married, retirement may place new strains on their marital relationship. When both partners retire, the couple will inevitably have more time together, and as Aleda Erskine (1987) points out, any emotional or sexual incompatibilities in the marriage which have previously been masked by working routines, may become inescapable after retirement. Of course this is not always the case, as some couples may in fact become closer after retirement, and can at last enjoy the time and opportunity to spend more time together. But according to Carol Nadelson and her colleagues (1979), for a significant number of women, especially those in blue-collar families, marital satisfaction decreases as the years go by.

In many ways, women could be *better* placed than men to make use of these years for individual growth and discovery. Less constrained by habits engendered by the routine of non-stop employment, many women could well be better able than men to make use of the leisure and freedom that can come after retirement and children leaving home. In fact some women do actually report these years to be amongst the happiest in their lives (see Norval Glenn, 1975), but sadly, these women are probably in the minority. Some evidence suggests that those women who do get the most out of their later years are those women who have maintained independence during the majority of their lives before retirement: JoEllen Nolan (1986), for example, suggests that those women who are most at risk of mid-life developmental problems are those who have not been involved in work outside the home for most or all of their lives, although this does rather depend on the type of work. Women whose jobs have been unskilled and poorly paid may be even unhappier and less prepared to structure their own time than those who have not worked at all.

The psychological development of women in the middle and later years

In keeping with the lack of attention paid to older people in most spheres of life, most conventional texts on developmental psychology concern only the years of childhood and adolescence. Yet the majority of our life span in fact occurs after these years, and the opportunities for development throughout life are immense. Despite this, we have very little idea of how best to understand the developments which do occur at this time. Rosalind Barnett and Grace Baruch (1979) note that there is a marked lack of sound theoretical work concerning the psychological development of women beyond early adulthood, and, as we have already noted in previous chapters, most male models of development (for example, those of Eric Erikson, 1959, and Daniel Levinson, 1979) tend to exclude women, or to assume that issues of identity are resolved much earlier merely through a woman's choice of her marital partner. Hence they ignore the numerous other ways by which women may establish their identities.

Yet this lack of attention to the way that older women live their lives ignores the very wide variety of opportunities for self-development open to women in their middle to late years. For example, many women (like Clare, whom we described in Chapter 5) take up educational opportunities, such as evening classes or correspondence courses, partly for reasons of interest and personal growth, but also for the sense of achievement which such activities can bring. Other middle-aged and older women become deeply involved in their communities, caring for others or developing their friendships and commitments to relatives and neighbours. Yet others develop their hobbies and interests, such as poetry-writing, gardening, or travel.

Based on observations such as these, a number of writers have tried to formulate theories of women's identity development which are more sensitive than the conventional male-oriented theories to the wide variety of activities and goals often pursued by middle-aged and older women. For example, as we pointed out in Chapter 2, Carol Franz and Kathleen White (1985) have tried to extend Erikson's theory of development, which they believe emphasises the individuated (male) personality, to include the importance of the 'attached, interpersonally connected, care-oriented (female) personality'. Other writers, such as Phyllis Katz (1979) and Rosalind Barnett and Grace Baruch (1979) have suggested that women's identity may take longer to develop then men's, or that it may change more drastically over the life span, given the wider variety of roles often undertaken by women during their lives. What is quite clear is that even in mature adulthood, women often have to battle very hard indeed against negative attitudes, poverty, and stereotyping in order to take effective control over the development of their lives. Nevertheless, the potential is considerable, if the very serious obstacles in the way of self-determination can be overcome.

Sexuality in older women

Another area of women's psychological development which is often shrouded in mystery is the sexuality of older women. The emphasis in our culture on youth and beauty is nowhere so pernicious than in the widespread judgement of older women's sexuality as inappropriate, undignified, or depraved. Yet according to Helen Kaplan and Clifford Sager, (1971) many women only reach their full sexual potential in their middle or later years. For some women, not having to worry any longer about becoming pregnant brings opportunities for sexual expression that have not previously been possible, while for others, greater leisure time and fewer responsibilities for young children can open up areas for sexual development which were not previously contemplated.

However, as B. Genevay (1982) points out, to be able to enjoy their sexuality fully, older women do need to have plenty of self-esteem and often, encouragement, so that they can transcend the stereotyped images which surround them of the sexual woman as someone with flawless skin and a firm, taut body. Sadly, not all women (or particularly their partners) are able to ignore these stereotyped images, and some women give up regular sexual activity after the menopause. Not all women have a choice in the matter, and for women who no longer have a sexual partner, perhaps following the death of a spouse, there may be considerable problems in maintaining a sexual life. As Susan Sontag (1979) points out, cultural values dictate that it is much harder for older women to take lovers or husbands younger than themselves, than it is for men to become involved with younger women. Given the unequal numbers of older men and women in the population, this means that many older widowed women will not remarry, or find new lovers. Many women may then have to renounce intimate sexuality with others for the rest of their lives. In addition, for some of these women, attitudes to masturbation, which were pervasive in their youth, may well have been much more repressive than those current today, meaning that for them this opportunity for sexual expression is closed too. Further, prevailing homophobia may prevent their sexual attachment to other women. For those who do find another partner, there is often considerable disapproval from grown-up children, who may find the sexuality of their parents hard to accept.

Moving into old age, sexuality becomes effectively a forbidden topic. Most people assume that elderly people have no sexual feelings at all, with the possible exception of 'dirty old men', whose sexuality is then seen as being pathological. This attitude is widespread within the helping professions: Janet Finch and Dulcie Groves (1985) point out that in the UK, for example, social work provision for the elderly tends to 'infantilise' clients, and nowhere is this clearer than in the complete denial of their sexuality. As a consequence, many older women (and men) suffer acutely from a deprivation of any form of physical contact. The provision of segregated sheltered housing for many elderly people, and the absence of double beds in those few homes where couples can live together, is possibly one of the clearest indications of society's verdict on sexuality in the elderly.

Emotional and spiritual growth in the later years

We shall now turn to an examination of some of the more positive aspects of the process of growing older, which allow at least some women to enjoy and develop themselves productively in their later years of life. As at other stages of life, these more positive aspects of the ageing process are usually to be found as a result of an individual woman's ability to distance herself from the demands and judgements of her society, and to be able to be herself and pursue her own goals as she wishes. When she is freed from the need to please employers, parents, husbands, or in-laws, she no longer has to rely so much on social standards and conventions to govern what she thinks and does: instead she can do more or less what she pleases. She can also explore in detail what it means to be herself. For example, Barbara MacDonald writes:

> I like growing old. I say it to myself with surprise. I had not thought that it could be like this. There are days of excitement when I feel almost a kind of high with the changes taking place in my body, even though I know the inevitable course my body is taking will lead to debilitation and death.... My own body is going through a process that only my body knows about. I never grew old before; never died before. I don't really know how it's done.
>
> (MacDonald, 1984:19)

Of course, not all women can be as open as this to the positive aspects of later life. For example, Simone de Beauvoir (1977) paints a pessimistic view of old age in her account of ageing, as seen not only through anthropological studies but also in literature and autobiography, describing it as being characterised by declining bodily and mental powers. Yet strangely absent from de Beauvoir's documentation are accounts of those who, despite the infirmities of old age, retain a commitment to their fellow human beings, or belief in fulfilling their own dreams, which enables them to be active participants in life rather than passively waiting for the end. Women like Dora Russell, for example, who continued all her life to support humanitarian causes, and who was actively campaigning against nuclear weapons when she died; or like Denise St Aubyn Hubbard, who in 1988, at the age of 64, became the oldest woman to sail the Atlantic Ocean single-handed. In fact, Simone de Beauvoir is also a good example herself, as she continued to initiate and support political campaigns, particularly those concerning women and the Third World, right up to her death.

Belief in spiritual or religious causes becomes central to many women at this stage of their lives. Many of the older women interviewed by Janet Ford and Ruth Sinclair (1987), for example, described how important their faiths or beliefs were to them, be they religious, humanist, or political. Faced by the loss of loved ones, many of the women in the study described the comfort that they gained either from a personal belief or from the rituals and practices of a familiar religion. Some, believing in an after-life, were comforted by the thought that they might eventually meet up with a deceased partner or parents.

The seemingly endless activity determined by years devoted to working, caring for dependants, and maintaining relationships with others may disguise for many women the need to consider their own spiritual selves, as well as allowing the postponement or delay of any true consideration of the meaning of life. Whilst no woman who has brought a child into the world, or who has suffered the death of a loved one can have escaped wondering about the meaning of life, or asking what the future will hold, nevertheless the threat of war, nuclear annihilation, or environmental catastrophe often make these thoughts too painful to be considered rationally. Encouraged to bury such thoughts under a veneer of false optimism and 'busy-ness', women who do think deeply about such issues are often perceived to be so threatening that they may be scorned or described as emotionally unstable. As a consequence, it is often only in later years that they find the courage to look at such issues again. Such opportunity for meditation and reflection can bring both peace and tranquillity, and a sense of perspective, which has been crowded out of the bustle and reponsibilities of their earlier lives.

However, having said that, for some women the increasing years and accumulated tragedies may prove to be unbearable. For example, Phyllis Rose (1978) has described how Virginia Woolf, unable to face the horror of another world war and the seemingly inevitable Nazi invasion, instead chose death at the age of 59 years. Her mother's early death, sexual abuse by her step-brothers, and the personal losses incurred through the destruction of the 1914–18 war had left her vulnerable to later disappointments. The tragic result was her death by suicide.

Facing up to the inevitability of death must represent the ultimate test of our ability to confront fears about separation and loss. As Lily Pincus (1981) has argued, facing this final loss very much depends on how previous losses have been responded to. Whereas some will continue to defend against the reality of death, others can plan and structure the way they would like to leave this world. The writer Marguerite Yourcenar, for example, who was the first woman ever to be admitted into the prestigious Academie Française, died at the age of 88 years. In her last interview, she described how she felt herself to be ready for death, and had even prepared her own memorial stone in the garden of her home, next to that of her friend and companion who had died eight years earlier. She described how she wanted to die 'with eyes open', so as not to miss this last experience (Josyane Savigneau, 1987). Probably most women would like to be able to greet their deaths in this way. Sadly, it has to be said that women of advanced years are more likely to be left unsupported and unprepared for the ending of their lives. Those who spend their final years in old people's homes or geriatric wards may only be able to survive the loss of identity ensuing from institutional care by a flight into confusion. This is obviously a tragic reflection on the way in which we as a society value, or more correctly fail to value, our old people, and essentially, ourselves.

Implications for therapy

In this last section we shall look at the implications of what we have discussed so far for those who work therapeutically with older women. There is an enormous scope for making a therapeutic contribution to people of this age group, but because they often feel marginalised, and see themselves as being less entitled to help than other, more 'valuable' members of society, older women often fail to demand or even seek therapeutic help. Instead, they may suffer in silence, considering that pain and distress are either an inevitable part of growing older, or are simply their duty. Therefore, as well as struggling against general social prejudice and injustice in the way in which society treats the elderly, a therapist who works with women in their later years often has to combat the pessimism and low self-esteem of the clients themselves. Whether they are women in their mid-lives who are depressed or anxious, middle-aged supporters of elderly people, or elderly people in need of care themselves, the first step may therefore be to convince them that they are indeed worthy of help and attention from someone else.

The contribution of individual therapy

Consistent with the general neglect of all women over the age of about 50 in psychological theorising and even in feminist writing, there is a paucity of work on the therapeutic opportunities which might be helpful to women in their mid-lives or later years. In fact, many therapists tend to prefer not to see older clients, believing them to be rigid and inaccessible to psychological insight or change. Yet despite fears originally expressed by Sigmund Freud himself, age does not have to be a drawback to a psychodynamic understanding, nor to more behaviourally oriented forms of personal change. Therapists from a number of different theoretical backgrounds *have* worked successfully with older women, and have often been extremely effective. For example, the Jungian analyst Bani Shorter (1987) has described working with an elderly woman, who felt as she approached death that she urgently needed to experience release from a long-denied wish concerning an unhappy relationship. In conducting psychotherapy with this woman, Bani Shorter emphasised and made use of the woman's potential for emotional growth and interpersonal learning, right up until death. By contrast, from a behavioural and cognitive framework, Dolores Gallagher and Larry Thompson (1982) have described the use of cognitive therapy for elderly depressed women in which they helped women to challenge many of the negative assumptions which they made about themselves and their lives, and then to reinvest themselves positively in their lives and activities.

From whatever theoretical perspective is taken, it is clear that women of all ages face transitions and changes in their lives which can generate conflicts and problems. If unresolved, these conflicts and problems can then block rather than open up the way to integration and continuing development. Despite advanced years, women *can* be helped to resolve emotional conflicts, particularly to free themselves from parental constraints and disappointments. In addition, new ways of thinking and acting can develop which challenge the negative messages which often surround women. Yet too often they are not given the opportunity. Often the most important step is the first one: affirming that it is both possible and important to make the effort.

The contribution of marital and family therapy

As at other stages of life, the origins of many of the difficulties faced by older women may be interpersonal in nature. Marital therapy may be particularly helpful if, for example, retirement has revealed strains in a previously adequately functioning relationship, or if the departure of children has meant that the couple is alone together, really for the first time, and that they are now experiencing conflicts. The role of the therapist with a couple who are facing marital problems such as these in later life may be to act as an educator or facilitator, helping both members of the couple to explore the limitations of the ways in which they have previously understood their roles in relation to one another, and to develop less traditionally rigid ways of acting and feeling (see, for example, Robert Gould, 1980). This may be especially important when the woman, after years of home-making, begins to assert her wishes to become more independent and self-directed, which may then be experienced by her husband as extremely threatening.

According to Carol Nadelson and her colleagues (1979), such conflicts are often expressed through the couple's sexual relationship. The husband may complain that his wife is becoming too demanding, or he may protest that she is starting to neglect him, and that she should conform more strictly to his expectations of what a woman should be like. Meanwhile, the wife may feel increasingly trapped by the marriage, or conversely, may feel abandoned by her husband. The therapist will need to encourage more open communication between the two, as well as helping both partners to explore their views on what the relationship means to them now. It may well be that this is a particularly important task for the husband, who, freed at last from the demands of the workplace, needs at this stage of life to integrate into his view of himself his more 'feminine' and nurturing self (see Carol Nadelson and her colleagues, 1979). But in addition, the wife may also need help in learning to become more assertive and comfortable with her own independence.

In some cases, it may be more appropriate to involve the whole family. In particular, family therapy can help when a couple or a single person is experiencing stress in having to take care of an elderly parent. Using the techniques originally developed by family therapists for working with adolescents, therapists such as Elsie Pinkston and Nathan Linsk (1984) have evolved ways of working which focus upon the whole family system, incorporating, rather than scapegoating the elderly person. An important issue is often encouraging the whole family, not just the women, to participate in the caring tasks. Another possible approach is group therapy, as described by David Cooper (1984). Here elderly people can learn about themselves in relation to other people, a task which may be harder in the later years, but no less important or rewarding.

Coming to terms with physical illness

In addition to dealing with complex interpersonal issues, psychological therapy may also be indicated when the woman is having to face physical illness or death. Even when the illness is not life-threatening, the chance to talk through and come to terms with feelings about bodily symptoms and changes could be of great benefit to women with health problems commonly seen in middle age. Whilst there are some medical doctors who are skilled at listening to their patient's emotional problems and worries, their role is not really designed to provide the time and detailed attention which is required if women are to be helped through their distress. Yet for many women, counselling as a part of routine medical care could be extremely beneficial. Such help is of course even more necessary when the illness in question is mutilating or life-threatening.

Ideally, therefore, women facing both the normal bodily changes of mid-life, and more serious illnesses such as cancer, should have access to psychotherapists or counsellors who could help them to resolve their emotional reactions to the crises threatening their previous adjustment to life. For example, psychotherapy or counselling should be available to complement unavoidable surgery, particularly in women with cancer, whose emotional reactions are now seen to affect prognosis (see Martin van Kalmthout and Marina Kuyper, 1987). It is currently becoming clear that there are great benefits to be gained from paying attention to psychological factors as a routine part of treatment for cancer: work by Jenny Ashcroft and her colleagues (1985), for example, has demonstrated that allowing women to make choices about the form of operation which they would prefer for breast cancer greatly increases the chances of the success of their treatment. In this work, counselling and support for the woman when making her choice about her preferred form of treatment is an essential part of the process of medical intervention.

Besides being of use to those who have to undergo operations, the greater availability of skilled counsellors or therapists in medical centres or hospitals could also help women to avoid unnecessary medical prescriptions or surgical complications. A number of studies (for example, Jack Hayward, 1975) have shown that the provision of information and counselling reduces the amount of medication needed by surgical patients, and significantly cuts down on the length of hospital stay required. The issues which such counselling should deal with are very varied. It may involve simply the provision of information about hospital procedures and routines. On the other hand, it may involve enabling women to confront the reality of their physical condition and to express the feelings of fear and anger which often arise. This may well help to prevent a descent into hopelessness and denial. Alternatively, specific help may be needed for women who, as we have already seen, are more likely than men to be responsible for children and other dependants. Such women are particularly likely to be anxious about how all the people who normally rely upon them will fare in their absence.

In all these cases, if women are isolated by not being able to talk about their experiences, they are also more likely to feel singled out and 'punished' by some avenging deity for previous 'faults' and omissions. The feeling of 'Why me?' and the hidden anger that this can contain, can often only be expressed in a thera-peutic context. This is because friends and close relations may be too affected by their own anxiety and grief to help a woman who is seriously ill to ventilate her own feelings. Furthermore, because women tend to be the 'emotional specialists' in partnerships, and are therefore usually the ones who are able to help their husbands or lovers to express feelings, they may well find that when they themselves are in need of a person with whom they can talk in depth, there is no-one available. In addition, for some women, the need to relinquish emotional control and responsibility can seem very threatening. It may therefore only be an outsider who is able to offer the woman the help that she needs at this time.

Coping with loss

What is common to many of the most important experiences of mid-life and old age is that they concern loss. Loss of anything which has been valued highly very often leads to depression, which is, as a consequence, widespread amongst older people. The most common medical reponse to depression in our culture is, of course, the prescription of anti-depressant medication, as if the cause of the pain of grief and loss were a physical illness. While some older women may gain at least temporary relief from this form of treatment, it, of course, fails to deal with the true cause of the distress, which is the inevitable wrenching sadness of the disappearance of something or someone precious.

Yet as Lily Pincus (1981) has argued: 'the giving up of the familiar need not be experienced merely as a loss but, through the acceptance of the new situation (can be experienced) as a challenge, with the potential for growth' (p.33). Lily Pincus refers here not merely to significant separations in personal relationships and bereavement, but also to the loss incurred as a result of serious illness, physical deterioration, a change of job, retirement, moving home ... all the potentially disruptive events which can be traumatic, but also emotionally enriching once they have been adapted to. If the loss is denied, or covered up, it is impossible to mourn what has to be given up, which makes future adjustment all the more difficult. Hence medical treatment of depression or loss is unlikely to help in the long run.

In her study of old age, Lily Pincus has argued that the need to experience loss and mourn is particularly pertinent when considering people's acceptance of death, both their own, and that of loved ones. But she has also stressed the importance of positive emotional experiences earlier on in life in seeking to explain why it is that some people achieve a happy, active, and even creative, old age, whereas others merely survive or withdraw into apathy and confusion. For both these reasons, it is especially crucial at this late stage of life that psychotherapeutic help is available, so that the losses can be understood and accepted, rather than being obliterated into chemically induced cheerfulness or numbness.

Coping with changing life styles

Obviously, not all of the changes that take place in mid-life are so difficult to cope with that they need the help of a psychotherapist. Nevertheless, the opportunity to share experiences is often of great benefit at this stage of life, especially when other social contacts are diminishing because of retirement or bereavement. Self-help groups therefore have great potential as a source of help for some of the other difficulties faced by women at this age, such as the menopause. Simply discovering that experiences are shared can make an enormous difference to a woman who is mystified and frightened by the physical and emotional changes which she is experiencing. In addition, if they have become isolated in their homes after years of childbearing, a self-help group can provide for some women the support needed to go out into the world again, and to re-establish their own independent lives. For those who are widowed, such a group can provide both a source of social contact, and practical help (see Phyllis Silverman and Adele Cooperband, 1984). In the UK, organisations such as Cruse exist both to provide immediate emotional help to newly widowed women, and to provide a structure for widows to begin to rebuild their lives around a new set of social contacts.

The demands of caring

As we have pointed out, one serious problem for many women in their mid-lives is the level of demand often placed upon them by others in need of care, especially their elderly relatives. Yet little help is provided for women carers, as caring for others is usually seen as 'women's work', and many carers may feel reluctant to ask for relief, through feelings of duty or loyalty to their elderly relative. One recent response to this has been the establishment of self-help groups for carers, in which women can meet together and share some of their feelings, as well as to find out about practical solutions to problems, such as where to obtain incontinence aids, how to claim various benefits, and so on (see, for example, Marcia Ory and colleagues, 1985). Unfortunately there is often little training available for group leaders, and, as with all forms of self-help group, there is a danger that some individuals in the group can come to dominate the group and prevent others from growing and learning from their own experiences. In addition, they may not suit everybody. Some women, like Peggy, may have issues to face which can really only be done within the privacy of an individual therapy relationship, where they can look constructively at difficult aspects of themselves and their families, including their feelings of ambivalence about their role within the family.

However, perhaps more crucial than the provision of either individual counselling or self-help groups is the need to encourage modification of current social and family structures, which depend on individual women taking the prime responsibility for caring for the elderly or handicapped, which then renders them vulnerable to all of the problems that we have highlighted. It is only when more realistic state provision is made available to help carers, and when men and boys are more prepared to take on their share of domestic and caring responsibilities, that women will be able to enjoy the later parts of their lives, rather than being yet again burdened with the demands of other people. Considering the problems for women in caring for dependants, Lynne Segal has written:

The frustrations of both parties are to a large extent due to the absence of adequate back-up assistance from the state for the needs of either the care-giver or those being cared for in the home, as well as men's failure to share in the work of caring. New social policies and provisions, and new rights for carers in the workplace, as well as change in the attitudes of men, are all necessary before we can cease to exploit the work women do caring for others.

(Segal, 1987:216)

The need for social and political change

As already noted, not all changes can be responded to therapeutically, either on an individualistic or a small-group basis. Often social and political change is needed too. As in previous chapters, whereas we have focused primarily on psychological factors, it is clear that the social context in which women grow older greatly shapes and affects their experiences. For many women, concerns about lack of income and poor housing compound fears of ill-health and isolation as they grow older. It must be noted, therefore, that the provision of adequate pensions and improvements in the housing stock are as vital for raising the quality of life for older women as are any of the improved health and psycho-therapeutic measures which we have suggested in this chapter. Indeed, it may well be that the single most important measure which most 'advanced' societies could take to improve the health and happiness of their older citizens would be to increase the level of the old-age pensions provided. Sadly, precisely because of the fact that most older people lack any significant economic strength, and are, in addition, women, such changes are given a low priority.

References

Ashcroft, J., Owens, R.G., and Leinster, S. (1985) 'Informal decision analysis and treatment choice by breast cancer patients', paper presented at the British Psychological Society Conference, Swansea, March.

Barfoot, J. (1986) *Duet for Three*, London: The Women's Press.

Barnett, R. and Baruch, G. (1979) 'Women in the middle years: conceptions and misconceptions', in J. Williams (ed.) *Psychology of Women*, London: Norton.

Broome, A. and Wallace, L. (eds) (1984) *Psychology and Gynaecological Problems*, London: Tavistock.

Cooper, C. (1982) 'Psychological stress and cancer', *Bulletin of the British Psychological Society* 35:50–9.

Cooper, D. (1984) 'Group psychotherapy with the elderly: dealing with loss and death', *American Journal of Psychotherapy* 38:203–14.

Cooper, K. (1985) 'The person you loved has gone', *New Society*, pp. 106–7, 18 October.

Cox, T. (1978) *Stress*, London: Macmillan.

Datan, N. (1980) 'Midas and other mid-life crises', in W. Norman and T. Scaramella (eds) *Midlife: developmental and clinical issues*, New York: Bruner/Mazel.

de Beauvoir, S. (1977) *Old Age*, Harmondsworth: Penguin (first published 1970).

Diamond Report (1978) *Royal Commission on Distribution of Income*, London: OPCS.

Eichenbaum, L. and Orbach, S. (1982) *Outside In. . . Inside Out*, Harmondsworth: Penguin.

Equal Opportunities Commission (1980) *The Experience of Caring for Elderly and Handicapped Dependants: Survey Report*, London: Equal Opportunities Commission.

Erikson, E. (1959, reprinted 1980) *Identity and the Life-cycle* New York: Norton.

Erskine, A. (1981) 'Retirement', in L. Pincus (ed.) *The Challenge of a Long Life*, London: Faber & Faber.

Finch, J. and Groves, D. (1985) 'Old girl, old boy: gender divisions in social work with the elderly', in E. Brook and A. Davis (eds) *Women, the Family and Social Work*, London: Tavistock.

Ford, J. and Sinclair, R. (1987) *Sixty Years On: women talk about old age*, London: The Women's Press.

Franz, C. and White, K. (1985) 'Individuation and attachment in personality development: extending Erikson's theory', *Journal of Personality* 53:224–56.

Gallagher, D. and Thompson, L.W. (1982) 'Treatment of major depressive disorder in older outpatients with brief psychotherapies', *Psychotherapy: Theory, Research and Practice* 19:482–90.

Genevay, B. (1982) 'In praise of older women', in M. Kirkpatrick, (ed.) *Women's Sexual Experience*, New York: Plenum.

Gilhooley, M. (1984) 'The impact of care giving on care givers', *British Journal of Medical Psychology* 57:35–44.

Gilleard, C.J., Watt, G., and Boyd, W. (1981) 'Problems of caring for the elderly mentally infirm at home', *Archives of Gerontological Geriatrics* 1:151–8.

Glenn, N. (1975) 'Psychological well being in the postparental stage: evidence from national surveys', *Journal of Marriage and The Family* 37:105–10.

Gould, R. (1980) 'Sexual problems: changes and choices in mid-life', in W. Norman and T. Scaramella (eds) *Midlife: Developmental and Clinical Issues*. New York: Bruner/Mazel.

Hayward, J. (1975) *Information: a prescription against pain*, London: Royal College of Nursing.

Jensen, M. (1987) 'Psychobiological factors predicting the course of breast cancer', *Journal of Personality* 55:2.

Katz, P. (1979) 'The development of female identity', *Sex Roles* 5:155–78.

Kaplan, F. (1982) 'Early retirement: fulfilment or despair?' *Changes* 1:14–15.

Kaplan, H. and Sager, C. (1971) 'Sexual patterns at different ages', *Medical Aspects of Human Sexuality* 5:10–19.

Kincey, J. and McFarlane, T. (1984) 'Psychological aspects of hysterectomy', in A. Broome and L. Wallace (eds) *Psychology and Gynaecological Problems*, London: Tavistock.

Klein, M. (1940) 'Mourning and its relation to manic-depressive states', in M. Klein (1975) *Love, Guilt and Reparation and Other Works, 1921–45*, London: The Hogarth Press.

Knapp, N.M. (1984) 'Institutionalized women: some classic types, some common problems, and some partial solutions', in G. Lesnoff-Caravaglia (ed.) *The World of the Older Woman*, New York: Human Sciences Press.

Levin, E. (1982) 'Research on Carers: supporting the informal carers', report of a day conference, London: DHSS.

Levinson, D. (1979) *Seasons of a Man's Life*, New York: Balantine Books.

Llewelyn, S. (1989) 'Caring: the costs to nurses and relatives', in A. Broome (ed.) *Health Psychology*, London: Croom Helm.

Lowenthal, M. and Chiriboga, D. (1972) 'Transition to the empty nest: crisis, challenge or relief?' *Archives of General Psychiatry*, 26:8–14.

MacDonald, B. (with C. Rich) (1984) *Look Me in the Eye: old women, ageing and ageism*, London: The Women's Press.

Nadelson, C., Polonsky, D., and Mathews, M. (1979) 'Marriage and midlife: The impact of social change', *Journal of Clinical Psychiatry* 40:15–24.

Nathanson, P. (1984) 'Legal issues affecting older women', in G. Lesnoff-Caravaglia (ed.) *The World of the Older Woman*, New York: Human Sciences Press.

Nissel, M. and Bonnerjea, L. (1982) *Family Care of the Handicapped Elderly. Who Pays?* London: Policy Studies Institute.

Nolan, J. (1986) 'Developmental concerns and the health of midlife women', *Nursing Clinics of North America* 21:151–9.

Ory, M., Williams, T., Emr, M., Lebowitz, B., Salloway, J., Sluss-Radbaugh, T., Wolff, E., and Zarit, S. (1985) 'Families, informal supports, and Alzheimer's disease', *Research on Aging* 7:623–43.

Pesznecker, B. and Zahlis, E. (1986) 'Establishing mutual-help groups for family-member care givers: a new role for community health nurses', *Public Health Nursing* 3:29–37.

Pincus, L. (1981) *The Challenge of a Long Life*, London: Faber & Faber.

Pinkston, E. and Linsk. N. (1984) *Care of the Elderly: a family approach*, New York: Pergamon.

Raphael, B. (1972) 'The crisis of hysterectomy', *Australian and New Zealand Journal of Psychiatry* 6:106–15.

Ray, C. (1977) 'Psychological implications of mastectomy', *British Journal of Social and Clinical Psychology* 16:373–7.

Reitz, R. (1985) *Menopause: A positive approach*, Hemel Hempstead: Unwin (first published 1977).

Richards, D. (1973) 'Depression after hysterectomy', *The Lancet* 2:430–3.

Rose, P. (1978) *Woman of Letters: a life of Virginia Woolf*, London: Pandora Press.

Rossiter, C. and Wicks, M. (1982) 'The future of family care', *Community Care*, 1. 19, 22 September.

Sayers, J. (1982) *Biological Feminism: feminist and anti-feminist perspectives*, London: Tavistock.

Savigneau, J. (1987) 'Marguerite Yourcenar, 1903–1987', *Le Monde*, p. 21, 1 December.

Seaman, B. and Seaman, G. (1977) *Women and the Crisis in Sex Hormones*, New York: Rawson Associates.

Segal, L. (1987) *Is the Future Female?* London: Virago.

Shorter, B. (1987) *An Image Darkly Forming: women and initiation*, London: Routledge & Kegan Paul.

Silverman, P. and Cooperband, A. (1984) 'Widow-to-widow: the elderly widow and mutual help', in G. Lesnoff-Caravaglia (ed.) *The World of the Older Woman*, New York: Human Sciences Press.

Sontag, S. (1979) 'The double standard of ageing', in J. Williams (ed.) *Psychology of Women*, London: Norton.

Spence, J. (1986) 'The Picture of Health?', *Spare Rib* 163:19–24.

Taylor, P., Abrams, D., and Hewstone, M. (1988) 'Cancer, stress and personality', *British Journal of Medical Psychology* 61:179–83.

Thompson, D. and Haran, D. (1985) 'Living with an amputation: the helper', *Social Science and Medicine* 20:319–23.

van Kalmthout, M. and Kuyper, M. (1987) 'Spontaneous regression in cancer: a search for psychological factors', in H. Dent (ed.) *Clinical Psychology: research and developments*, London: Croom Helm.

Walker, A. (1983) 'Care for elderly people: a conflict between women and the State', in J. Finch and D. Groves (eds) *A Labour of Love: women, work and caring*, London: Routledge & Kegan Paul.

Woods, R. and Britton, P. (1985) *Clinical Psychology with the Elderly*, London: Croom Helm.

Chapter ten

Resolving dilemmas
The possibility of change

In her novel *Other Women*, Lisa Alther (1984) describes the unfolding relationship between Caroline, a woman who feels desperate about her life, and Hannah, the therapist whom she decides to consult. Lisa Alther weaves together the stories of these two women's lives in a way that shows clearly both the process of therapeutic change, and the reciprocal effects each woman has on the other's life. She also describes, through the unfolding of the therapy, many psychodynamic and social influences on the course of these two women's lives. In this way, Alther's novel illustrates many of the themes which we have been presenting throughout this book. As a work of fiction, this story is available to all, unlike the private moments of therapy, so we shall use it to introduce this last chapter.

At the start of the novel, Caroline, a 35-year-old nurse in a busy accident ward and the mother of two sons, feels incompetent and suicidal. She is experiencing the break-up of an important relationship with her woman lover Diana, with whom she has lived for the past five years, and whose rejection is bringing to the surface memories of other failed relationships. Hannah, the therapist she consults, who is an older woman, and whom we later find out has herself had to come to terms with some shattering life experiences, is able to use her therapeutic skills to help Caroline focus on the way in which her relationships with others are repeating patterns laid down in childhood. For Caroline, the major theme to emerge is the way in which her life is dominated by her tendency to serve the people she loves, in a desperate attempt to gain love for herself. She finds it difficult to define what she herself wants, or indeed who she is. For instance, in describing her childhood, with parents whom she initially describes as being wonderful, Caroline realises that she was forever having to look after them, and rarely experienced being cared for herself. Both her mother and her father were inveterate 'do-gooders', endlessly giving up their time and energy to worthy causes and then collapsing at home to be looked after by their daughter. Not surprisingly, in adulthood, Caroline chose in her working life to become a nurse, in the most stressful of wards, and finds that in her personal life she is forming relationships which depend on her looking after the emotional and practical needs of her partners. It is only in therapy with Hannah that Caroline is eventually able to alter some of these patterns, developing a new and strong sense of her own identity and making decisive changes in her work and personal life.

Meanwhile, Hannah, through her sessions with Caroline, has to come to terms with her envy of the younger woman's energy and vitality, while she herself is battling with menopausal symptoms as well as facing up to the eventual conclusion of her working life. In addition, in describing Hannah's side of therapy, Lisa Alther clearly points out the stresses of being a therapist: for a start, Caroline is but one of the people who consults Hannah, and Hannah has to cope with the demands of being constantly emotionally available to all of her clients. But in addition, Alther points to the special dilemmas for women carers, often able to help others because of their own experiences of personal pain, but having continually to monitor the after-effects if they are not to interfere with current therapeutic work. For example, Hannah has to struggle with the resemblance she sees between Caroline and how she imagines her own dead daughter would have been as an adult. This identification leads Hannah to feel that Caroline is somehow special, probably contributing to the success of their therapeutic relationship, but making it harder for Hannah to let go at the end of the therapy.

Caroline and Hannah's stories are particularly clear demonstrations of the influence of the past on current relationships, and the need to recognise this influence if change is to occur in the present. In this way Lisa Alther's novel reinforces one of the major themes of this book. In previous chapters we have seen, at different stages in women's lives, the way in which the 'repetition compulsion', as psychodynamic therapists have called it, often appears to govern women's thoughts, feelings, and actions. For example, in Chapter 1, Ann continually found herself in unsatisfactory relationships where she felt entitled to only a small amount of her partners' affections, and repeatedly held back her need to be loved freely. Similarly, in Chapter 7 we saw how Margaret lapsed into a state of helplessness and withdrawal whenever life became too difficult, constructing for herself a safety valve against change in the form of the protective and collusive relationship she had with her husband. Edith, in Chapter 4, was continually being dominated by partners whose primary mode of relating to her was through physical and emotional abuse, thus unhappily repeating the experiences of her childhood. For each of these women, and others whom we have described, significant change came about by recognising the current configurations through which these patterns manifested themselves, and in tracing them back to their origins in childhood.

This emphasis on childhood, and in particular on traumatic or damaging effects of patterns of relating which may have occurred with parents, immediately raises the issue of the origins of these experiences, and the actions of those who are primarily responsible for the child's early experiences. Unlike many previous theories concerning the effects of infantile experiences on the adult personality, a woman-centred approach to psychology, such as the one we have been drawing upon in this book, does not simplistically blame mothers (nor indeed fathers) for the effects of their parenting on their children. Instead, it attempts to put into perspective the child's experiences in the light of the personal limitations and external constraints imposed upon those caring for the child. Thus it includes an appreciation of the psychology of the mothering person, and an understanding of her own residual emotions from childhood, such as those of anger, despair, longing, or guilt. These feelings unquestionably affect the adult woman's relationships, both with her partners and also with her own children, for whom these early experiences of being cared for form the building blocks of their future personalities and emotional lives.

It is also crucial when trying to understand the psychology of those who care for children to take into account the constraints upon the ways in which mothers, and their mothers before them, were expected to raise their children, and how the resources available to help them in their mothering were, and often still are, so limited. In this book we have tried to show how mothering for many women is an uphill task, often unsupported in any realistic way by the child's father, the rest of her family, or the state. Nevertheless, most women do not abandon or physically assault their children, and struggle to do the best they can, in often very difficult and restrictive circumstances. Not to recognise this devalues a woman's efforts to care for the children whom she simultaneously loves and is burdened by, as well as diminishing the effectiveness of any therapeutic exploration of her pain which may have resulted from *her* own mother's ambivalence.

The women in Lisa Alther's novel had to face a number of important decision points in their lives, similar to those which we have highlighted in this book. For as well as the phenomenon of repetition, we have throughout stressed the influence of transition points in shaping women's experiences. In Chapter 2, for example, Lucy was involved in making the leap from the relative dependence of childhood to the beginning autonomy of young adulthood; while in Chapter 3, Laura had to come to terms with a new stage in her life: that of a woman who was not part of a steady relationship. Such transitions, as we have seen, involve more than just the individual concerned. In Lucy's case, her parents had to come to terms with their daughter's decisions about how she wanted to define herself as a woman; while in Laura's case, changes also had to be made by members of Laura's circle of friends. We have tended to stress the implications of these transitions for the individual women involved, but it must never be forgotten that people do not exist in social vacuums, and that change almost always has considerable implications for those around the woman, especially for her partner, family, and friends.

Negotiation of transition points is particularly crucial during infancy and childhood, as there is at this stage a constant need to redefine relationships. Close involvement with children inevitably involves a continual set of negotiations, determined on the child's part, as we saw in Chapter 7, by the push towards separation and individuation; and on the carers' part by their own need for personal growth and space. However, neither premature demands by those caring for the child that the child should become less dependent, nor attempts to hold back the child's development towards autonomy, will be helpful for the child's emotional maturity. As we have seen, this is problematic for all who are responsible for providing care, since their own needs rarely coincide with those of the developing child.

During the course of this book we have also focused on some of the major physical transition points in women's lives, particularly those involving pregnancy, childbirth, and the ending of women's reproductive lives. Although marked by biological events, we have paid special attention to the social and psychological implications of these transitions. Often seen as crises, we have shown how women's reactions, frequently based on their past experiences of change, can affect the extent to which such potential crises can themselves become points of emotional growth. In Peggy's case in Chapter 9, for example, the physical symptoms of the menopause were relieved once she started to create some order in her personal life, and her burgeoning confidence then enabled her to maintain successfully a number of dietary and social changes which in turn gained her further relief. The family dynamic behind these changes involved both her mother and her daughter, who were engaged with Peggy in a three-way conflict. This also altered with Peggy's improved health, enabling her daughter to move away and her mother to become more tolerant of Peggy's own life and choice of partner. Negotiation of this transition point thus resulted in Peggy's emotional growth, rather than stagnation in a fixed but comparatively safe set of relationships.

As well as being concerned with describing some of the psychodynamic aspects of women's lives, we have also paid attention to the social context in which women currently live. In Chapter 8, for example, we saw how Sally's decision to live alone as an independent woman was often made difficult for her because, not being part of a couple, she did not adhere to society's expectations about how to live as an adult woman. As well as being financially penalised, in terms of higher relative costs of living and reduced access to state benefits, single women living alone cannot claim the 'protection' or security of having a permanent relationship with a man. Whilst many women living with men might point out that such protection is illusory (for example, rape within marriage is still not legally an offence, and at least one in three marriages ends in divorce), a society structured around the woman–man couple and the two-child family can be experienced as being oppressive for women who are alone. A further example of oppressive social influences on women's lives was seen in Chapter 5, where we examined through Clare's story how women's working experiences are constrained by prejudice, harassment, and discrimination, as well as by the subtler processes of self-limitation and domestic responsibility.

In each of the chapters, we included a section on the therapeutic implications of our analysis. This may have been of most relevance to practising therapists from a variety of professional backgrounds, but we also intended it to be of interest to anyone who has ever talked with a woman friend in distress. For whilst we have emphasised the possibilities offered by psychotherapy in helping women to understand more about themselves and to take positive steps towards resolving conflicts and dilemmas, we also acknowledge that for many women this is inappropriate, and for some completely unavailable. This does not, however, mean that women have to remain forever stuck in their conflicts, since many of the elements necessary to provoke insight and generate emotional healing may also be found through a wide variety of experiences and activities, ranging from friendships and self-help groups to a change in role or status, such as might occur after the birth of a child or obtaining a new job. Women have always been adept at responding to and helping each other, and we hope that this book may have suggested some additional ways in which women may become more skilled and sensitive to each other's needs, and in particular, to the dual influences of past relationships and present social structures in maintaining many women's current unhappiness.

Nevertheless, we believe that for some women, an experience of psychotherapy may be the best solution. Not all women have friends who are willing or able to support them through a lengthy and often difficult examination of emotionally painful issues, and not all women would be willing to expose themselves to such an examination without the security which can be provided by a trained therapist. For these women, psychotherapy may be the most appropriate response to current emotional pain. As Lisa Alther in her novel *Other Women* tells us of Caroline, who as a nurse is a member of a helping profession:

> She'd tried all the standard bromides: marriage and motherhood, apple pie and monogamy, bigamy and polygamy; consumerism, communism, feminism, and God; sex, work, alcohol, drugs, and true love. Each enchanted for a time, but ultimately failed to stave off the despair. The only bromide she hadn't tried was psychotherapy. Members of the helping professions were supposed to pull themselves up by their bootstraps. But she'd recently been forced to concede that she was barefoot.
>
> (Alther, 1984:18)

Having said this, women as consumers of psychotherapy need to be informed and careful about their choice of therapists. As we have shown earlier, not all psychotherapy is beneficial to women, as often it is based on very limited views of women's concerns, and hence lacks an appreciation of the many difficulties often faced by women in taking control of their lives. Psychotherapists who do not understand or pay attention to the kind of issues raised in this book may be extremely harmful to a woman who is courageous enough to embark on a period of painful self-examination, but who is unlucky enough to have as her therapist someone whose attitudes towards women are far from sympathetic.

In recent years, many women have become increasingly critical of the limitations of the standard psychiatric treatment available to the majority of women in distress, dependent as this so often is on outmoded stereotypes of women's psychology, and offering the dangerously addictive panacea of psychotropic medication (see, for example, the account of current psychiatric practice by

Susan Penfold and Gillian Walker, 1984). However, it is important to recognise that not all of the problems lie within conventional psychiatry: even amongst the more recently developed therapies from within the so-called 'human potential' movement, there are many therapists who hold reactionary views about women, and who may maintain their women clients in positions of subservience and dependence (see, for example, the accounts by Richard Rosen, 1978; Maurice Temerlin and Jane Temerlin, 1982).

Because of the existence of practices such as these, some women therapists have, in recent years, offered psychological therapy specifically for women, both within state services and in alternatively funded services, which is based on a women-centred psychology. For example, the Women's Therapy Centre in the UK, which first opened in London in 1976, offers feminist psychotherapy to women as individuals, or in groups. Therapists working in contexts such as this have developed a woman-centred approach to psychological distress, and this has often proved to be immensely effective in working with women in crisis, or with longer-term problems. Their work has also been taken up by therapists working in the state services, such that it is now possible to find women-oriented services in a number of conventional contexts, such as well-women clinics, social services departments, and departments of clinical psychology and psychiatry.

The critical issue for a woman who is concerned to change some aspects of her life is to choose as her therapist, or guide, someone who will help her to grow and develop to her full potential, rather than someone who will seek to impose upon her a view of how she 'ought' to be as a woman. In addition, the therapist must be aware of all of the diversions, prohibitions, and deceptions which stand in the way of women's autonomy. Only then will a woman in emotional distress have a chance to discover how she wishes to live her own life, less encumbered either by her past, or by the structures of the social world that she inhabits.

In this book we have outlined some of the major issues that are likely to be experienced as significant events in women's lives. Whilst all therapists or counsellors will have their own particular style of working, the issues that we have addressed are likely to be focal points of the therapy. We hope that for both those women seeking help and those providing the helping services, this book will stimulate a reconsideration of women's experiences, and will lead women to more sensitive and effective forms of help.

References

Alther, L. (1984) *Other Women*, New York: Alfred A. Knopf.

Penfold, P.S. and Walker, G.A. (1984) *Women and the Psychiatric Paradox*, Milton Keynes: Open University Press.

Temerlin, M.K. and Temerlin, J.W. (1982) 'Psychotherapy cults: an iatrogenic perversion', *Psychotherapy* 19:131–41.

Rosen, R. (1978) *Psychobabble*, London: Wildwood House.

Author index

Subject index